# THE HOUSES OF PARLIAMENT

## HISTORY ART ARCHITECTURE

# THE HOUSES OF PARLIAMENT

## HISTORY ART ARCHITECTURE

David Cannadine

Dorian Church

Henry S. Cobb

Andrea Fredericksen

Christopher Garibaldi

John Goodall

Debra N. Mancoff

Janet McLean

Steven Parissien

Benedict Read

Christine Riding

Jacqueline Riding

Sean Sawyer

Gavin Stamp

William Vaughan

Alexandra Wedgwood

**MERRELL**

First published 2000 by
Merrell Publishers Limited
42 Southwark Street
London SE1 1UN
www.merrellpublishers.com

British Library Cataloguing-in-Publication Data

The Houses of Parliament : history, art,
architecture
1.Great Britain. Parliament 2.Palace of Westminster
3.Palace of Westminster – History
I.Riding, Christine II.Riding, Jacqueline
725.1'1'0942132

ISBN 1 85894 112 1

Produced by Merrell Publishers Limited

Edited by Iain Ross

Designed by Tim Harvey

Printed and bound in Italy

FRONT JACKET: The Palace of Westminster, 2000.
Photograph by David Ward.
BACK JACKET: Sir Edward John Poynter, *St George for
England* (study for mosaic in Central Lobby; detail),
oil on ceramic blocks, 1868/69. Palace of
Westminster (WOA 1986).

TITLE PAGE: Claude-Oscar Monet, *The Houses of
Parliament at Sunset* (detail), oil on canvas, 1904.
Kunsthaus Zürich, Switzerland.

## Picture Credits

Illus. on pages 109, 110, 191, 193, 219, 220 (top) by
Permission of the British Library, London

Illus. on pages 39, 48, 69, 136 © The British
Museum, London

Illus. on page 180 © the Master and Fellows of
Corpus Christi College, Cambridge

Illus. on pages 61 (bottom left), 80, 82, 91 (top and
bottom), 186 © The Dean and Chapter of
Westminster Abbey, London

Illus. on pages 182 (right), 199 (left) by the permission of the Duke of Devonshire and the Chatsworth
Settlement Trustees

Illus. on pages 30, 34, 79, 68, 71, 185 (top), 187, 218,
240 © 2000, Her Majesty Queen Elizabeth II

Illus. on pages 56 (right), 221 © English Heritage
Photo Library

Illus. on page 242 courtesy of the Trustees of the
Firle Estate Settlement

Illus. on pages 12, 39, 61 (right), 128 (top right),
130, 168, 176, 173, 192 (top), 202, 208, 267 by kind
permission of the House of Lords Record Office,
London

Illus. on page 27 and title-page image © 2000
Kunsthaus Zürich. All rights reserved.

Illus. on page 21 © Mayfair Picture Library

Illus. on pages 10, 112, 169, 162 © Derry Moore
Photography

Illus. on pages 13, 153, 214 by courtesy of the
National Portrait Gallery, London

Illus. on page 77 (bottom) reproduced by permission of His Grace the Duke of Norfolk

Illus. on pages 100 (top), 101 (top), © Public
Record Office, London

Illus. on pages 19, 220 (bottom), 226, 235 (bottom)
© PUNCH Ltd

Illus. on pages 106 (top), 137, 139, 140 (top), 141
(top), 142 (top), 143–46 by courtesy of the
Trustees of Sir John Soane's Museum, London

Illus. on pages 33–34 courtesy of the Master and
Fellows of Trinity College, Cambridge

Illus. on page 243 © Crown copyright: UK
Government Art Collection

Illus. on pages 20, 89, 97, 95 (left), 94, 96, 142, 166,
167, 170 © Victoria and Albert Museum Picture
Library, London

Illus. on page 88 reproduced by Permission of the
Trustees of the Wallace Collection, London

# Contents

View of the River Front of the Palace of
Westminster, taken from the South Bank.

# *Preface*

It gives me great pleasure to be associated with this book on the Palace of Westminster. I have had an immense fondness for the building from the time of my election as a Member of Parliament in 1973. Since becoming the Speaker of the House of Commons in 1992 I have also been Chairman of the House of Commons Commission and custodian of The Speaker's Art Fund, and so have had the opportunity to become more directly involved with the preservation of the palace and its historic collections. A number of significant additions have been made to the fine-art collection exhibited within the building. One such purchase, of which I am particularly proud, is the group portrait of *Speaker Lenthall and his Family* (acquired 1998), which is not only an outstanding painting in its own right but which also continues the series of portraits of Speakers, past and present, begun by Speaker Addington in the 1790s. Finally, I have the great privilege of living in a part of the Palace of Westminster itself, Speaker's House, which was first occupied by Speaker Denison in 1859. Speaker's House functions today in much the same way as it did in the nineteenth century: both as a private residence and as a venue for state dinners and receptions.

All of these elements have increased my respect not only for the palace itself but for those colleagues and outside professionals and scholars who research, conserve and advise on the building. This book will contribute greatly to the dissemination of information on the Palace of Westminster and, I hope, will also serve to stimulate admiration for the artists, architects and designers who have made it what it is today – without doubt one of the most famous and magnificent buildings in the world.

The Speaker

*Betty Boothroyd*
*Speaker*

The Rt Hon. Betty Boothroyd MP
Speaker of the House of Commons

# INTRODUCTION

## *Theatre of State*

Christine Riding, Jacqueline Riding

The building that is the home of the Houses of Parliament, the Palace of Westminster, is one of the most famous in the world. But despite the familiarity of the exterior, and, to a lesser extent, the interiors, through the televising of debates and the State Opening of Parliament, the history, art and architecture of the palace remain relatively, and surprisingly, unknown to the broader public. The palace forms the shadowy backdrop to the many memoirs of politicians past and present that have been written over the four-and-a-half centuries during which it has been the permanent home of national politics. But of the building itself, little exists in print. Professor M.H. Port's scholarly survey of the architectural development of the Palace of Westminster, *The Houses of Parliament* (1976), and *The History of the King's Works*, edited by Howard Colvin, have been the main sources on the palace for the last twenty-five years. The fine-arts collection has been well served by the invaluable research of R.J.B. Walker, although his catalogue, compiled from 1959 to 1977, is only available in a small number of libraries (see bibliography). The Victoria and Albert Museum's ground-breaking exhibition and accompanying catalogue *Pugin: A Gothic Passion* in 1994, as well as the unequalled knowledge and scholarship of Lady Alexandra Wedgwood, have raised the profile both of A.W.N. Pugin and his design achievements within the building. The authors and editors of this book owe a great debt to these institutions and individuals.

Joseph Lee, *The Innuendo Session*, *c.* 1975–79. Palace of Westminster.

However, it was evident to a group of curators working at the Palace of Westminster that a new publication was required, both for the interested member of the public and the scholar. The two main aims were as follows: to draw on new as well as past research to produce an updated account of the development of the Palace of Westminster and, perhaps more ambitiously, to re-evaluate the building and its decoration within a variety of historical and cultural contexts. The resulting essays, it is hoped, will encourage the reader to view this familiar building in a new light. Not covered here are any buildings on the Parliamentary estate other than the Palace of Westminster, such as Portcullis House by Michael Hopkins and Partners; the book is firmly focused on the palace itself, and divides loosely into the following sections: context, architecture, decorative arts and fine arts. Within each essay, familiar and less familiar connections and relationships are explored. Above all, the intention is to reveal the palace as a product of its royal and Parliamentary history, as well as to explore the ceremonies and historic associations that informed its physical evolution. Since its foundation in the eleventh century, the Palace of Westminster has been the stage upon which some of the most extraordinary events in national history have been enacted, and remains to this day the focus of pageant and politics: the pre-eminent "theatre of state".

## *Acknowledgements*

Many thanks to our sponsors, Martinspeed, particularly Tony Chapman and Chris Kneale, and Zoffany, in particular Philip Cadle and Andrew Krisson, who have been extraordinarily generous and enthusiastic towards the project from its inception. Without their support, this book would never have got off the ground.

The editors wish particularly to acknowledge Lady Alexandra Wedgwood and the late Dr Clive Wainwright for their extraordinary knowledge, encouragement and assistance. Both have been instrumental in the revival of interest in Victorian architecture and design and it has been a privilege to discuss with them the greatest of all Victorian buildings. In 1974, a report produced by Dr Wainwright and John Hardy resulted in the commissioning of a complete inventory of the palace's furniture. The task of organizing and supervising the cataloguing of nine thousand pieces of furniture was undertaken by Dorian Church, now the acknowledged expert on the historic furniture and soft furnishings within the palace.

There are many people to whom the editors owe thanks. Madam Speaker, the Rt Hon. Betty Boothroyd MP; the Art Committees of the House of Lords and House of Commons; the Curator's Office at the Palace of Westminster, a small and dedicated team headed by Malcolm Hay, who remained calm and good-humoured despite our constant demands for assistance; Rupert Shepherd, Consultant Curator, has not only copy-edited the entire text and worked on the bibliography and endnotes, but has also been a constant source of support and invaluable advice from start to finish; many thanks are also due to Janet McLean for her assistance in sourcing illustrations and researching caption information, and for her assurances that, despite all appearances to the contrary, the end was in sight; within the Parliamentary Works Directorate, Graham Goode, Brian Webb, Barry Hall and John Stone; the Conservation Architect, Terry Jardine; the Archivist, Dr Mark Collins, who has given advice freely and researched information and illustrations on our behalf; and thanks to the on-site staff, who remained unfazed despite bizarre requests to move microphones, chandeliers, furniture and anything else that stood in the way of a good photograph; Nicholas Bevan and Nick Wright from the Speaker's Office; the Serjeant-at-Arms Michael Cummins, Black Rod, General Sir Edward Jones and their staff; the House of Commons and House of Lords Libraries; the House of Lords Record Office; George Garbutt, who took a majority of the internal photographs of the Palace of Westminster as well as all the images from the collection; the staff of the British Library; the Victoria and Albert Museum Picture Library; The Royal Collection; The Punch Archive; Birmingham Library Services; the Heinz Library and Archive at the National Portrait Gallery; and the following individuals: Katy Barron, Emma Baudey, Ray Biggs, Alexander Bortolot, Cécile Brunner, G.C. Cannell, Catherine Casley, Joanne Charlton, Tim Clarke, Martin Collins, Brig Davies, Peter Day, Stephen Duffy, Martin Durrant, Robert Elwall, Sue Fletcher, Melissa Gold, Jon Gray, John Hardy, Bernard Horrocks, Deborah Hunter, Adrian James, Robert Jones, James Kilvington, Gerda Kram, David Law, David MacKitterick, Phillipa Martin, Nicole Mitchell, Charles Noble, Barry Norman, Bernard Nurse, Steven Parissien, Jane Phillips, Christine Reynolds, Hugh Roberts, Zoë Rogers, Maria Rossi, Jenny Sabine, Andrew Sanders, Siân Smith, Alison Sproston, Michael Susi, Sir John Sykes, Bt, Miranda Taylor, Nicole Tetzner, Jane Theophilus, Julia Toffolo, Tony Trowles, Helen Walasek, Christopher Webster, Martin Wedgwood.

Thanks also to the team at Merrell Publishers, all the contributors and a big thank-you to the designer, Tim Harvey, who remained inexplicably calm throughout. Finally, thanks to our parents John and Patricia Riding and our friends Rachel Kennedy and Rowena Shepherd for their encouragement and support; and to Eileen Sheikh, who has literally lived with this book for over two years, particular thanks for providing the tea and sympathy when it was most needed.

# I

## *The Palace of Westminster as Palace of Varieties*

David Cannadine

Charles Barry, elevation of clock face, pen, coloured wash and pencil, n.d. British Architectural Library, RIBA, London.

View of the Royal Gallery towards the Prince's Chamber, House of Lords, Palace of Westminster. Photograph by Derry Moore.

In the company of the Great Pyramid, the Taj Mahal and the Eiffel Tower, the Palace of Westminster is one of the most famous and instantly recognizable buildings in the world. Its picturesque pinnacles and cloud capp'd towers create a Gothic Revival fantasy on London's skyline that is by turns familiar, unique and much loved; and thanks to BBC Radio 4 and the BBC World Service, the chimes of Big Ben are broadcast across the nation and around the globe. But the Palace of Westminster is more than an unchanging architectural presence and a reassuringly robust clock: it is a building inside which history is constantly being made – and re-made. For it is also the place where government and opposition confront each other; where laws are enacted by the Commons, the Lords and the Crown; where the legislature, the executive and the judiciary are mixed up together; and where important rituals of the state are regularly staged. It is, in short, the building where the British constitution is visibly displayed in its efficient and dignified forms – not written down on paper, but physically expressed in masonry and mortar, sculpture and stained glass, frescoes and furniture; and personally embodied in Members of Parliament and ministers, peers and prelates, politics and pageantry.[1]

This description of Barry and Pugin's palatial masterpiece, of the people who inhabit it and of the things they do there, has held good throughout the entire century and a half of its existence. But it has held good only in the most general – and perhaps misleading – way. For while the Palace of Westminster has remained reassuringly constant in its inimitable physical form, the British constitution and British political life have been continually evolving and developing. This in turn means that perceptions of Parliament have themselves changed and altered as a result – and so have perceptions of the building that accommodates it. In order to appreciate these varying images and protean identities, we must recognize that the history of the Palace of Westminster is as much about nation and empire, politics and ceremony as it is about architecture and the decorative arts – and it is with the history of nation and empire, politics and ceremony, and their complex, contingent and changing relationship with architecture and the decorative arts, that this chapter is concerned.[2] As such, it seeks to explore and explain the Palace of Westminster not only as a theatre of state, but also as the palace of varieties.

Thus contextualized, the history of Parliament in its Barry-and-Pugin incarnation may best be described in terms of three separate but overlapping phases. As conceived and created in the 1840s and 1850s, the Palace of Westminster projected a backward-looking, conservative and exclusive image of the British constitution, in which greater importance was attached to the monarchy and the House of Lords than to the Commons or the electorate. This vision, which was both powerful and partial, remained resonant until the late

nineteenth century, albeit diminishingly so. But from the 1880s until the Second World War, the British Parliament came to mean rather different things, as a result of the broadening of the franchise to full democracy, the expansion of imperial dominion and the raising of imperial consciousness, and the multifarious demands for Home Rule and schemes for devolution. Since then, the loss of empire, the erosion of national sovereignty and the creation of local assemblies for Scotland and Wales have once again drastically altered our sense of what 'Parliament' is and does. As a building, the Palace of Westminster would still today be instantly recognizable by the architects and artists who designed and decorated it. But the activities that go on inside it, the people who work there and the meanings it has for us would most likely leave them baffled, bewildered and dismayed.

## The new Palace of Westminster

When fire destroyed much of the old Palace of Westminster in October 1834, an event watched by a vast throng that included Turner and Constable as well as Barry and Pugin, contemporary reactions were mixed. For some shocked and grieving patriots, it seemed that the very heart of the nation had been torn out: "I felt", noted a contributor to the *Gentleman's Magazine*, "as if a link would be burst asunder in my national existence, and that the history of my native land was about to become, by the loss of this silent but existing witness, a dream of dimly shadowed actors and events."[3] For those of a more robust inclination, it opened the way for the construction of a new legislature, fit for a reformed and imperial nation at the height of its international powers. For conservatives, it was proper punishment for a craven legislature that, in passing the Great Reform Act two years earlier, had surrendered to mob violence and middle-class pressure, and had grievously wounded the aristocracy and irretrievably damaged the hitherto perfect balance of the constitution. But for those of more progressive views, the fire was timely and opportune, for it swept away the ramshackle and inefficient buildings that were the physical embodiment of the world of 'old corruption', the end of which had already been portended in the legislation passed in 1832.[4]

These divisions of contemporary opinion about the meaning and importance of events as they impinged on Parliament, and as Parliament impinged on events, continued throughout the remainder of the 1830s and on into the 1840s, the period when the new Palace of Westminster was commissioned and designed, and when its construction was begun.

From one perspective, they were the most turbulent decades of the century, as the

Sir George Hayter, *The House of Commons, 1833*, oil on canvas, 1833–1843. This scene shows the House of Commons in session after the Great Reform Act of 1832. National Portrait Gallery, London.

Henry William Pickersgill, *Sir Charles Barry*, oil on canvas, 1849. Palace of Westminster (WOA 2729).

nationwide agitation for reform, followed by the abolition of so many rotten boroughs, the granting of representation to towns such as Birmingham and Sheffield, and the near-doubling of the franchise were merely the prelude to further change and disruption: the Chartist outbursts in 1838, 1842 and 1848, the agitation of the Anti-Corn Law League, the 'Hungry Forties' in Britain and the Potato Famine in Ireland, and the 'year of revolutions' in Europe. Yet these decades also witnessed unprecedented progress and improvement, in part symbolized by the opening of the Liverpool and Manchester Railway in 1830, in part as a consequence of the glut of reforming legislation: the Municipal Corporations Act, the New Poor Law, the repeal of the Corn Laws, and the Factory Acts. Either way, these were indeed the 'iconoclastic years' in British government, politics and society, and it was against this unprecedented disrupted background that the rebuilding of the Palace of Westminster was debated and undertaken.[5]

Despite, or perhaps because of, this uncertainty, the image of the British nation, constitution and society that the new building set in stone was more concerned with stability and order than strife and dissent, and with tradition and continuity than progress and change. Like the Great Reform Act, the new Palace of Westminster was less of an abrupt break with the past than apocalyptic contemporary (or historical) accounts suggested. As with the Reform Act, those responsible for commissioning and designing the new legislature did not intend that it should be revolutionary. Far from recognizing "the triumph of representative institutions over monarchical and tyrannical authority", it was meant to re-establish and reassert those visible ties to the nation's past that the fire had temporarily sundered.[6] Hence the decision of the Commons select committee appointed in March 1835 to report on plans "for the permanent Accommodation of the Houses of Parliament" that the new building must be in the 'national' style, which was deemed, rather implausibly, to be Gothic (or Elizabethan). As such, it would articulate a hierarchical image of the social and political order, stressing venerable authority, providential subordination and true conservative principles, and it would be the very antithesis of the classical style, which had become associated in the popular patriotic mind with the rootless anarchy and national enmity of revolutionary France.[7] Hence, too, the formation of a Royal Commission to judge the competition, consisting of Charles Hanbury Tracey (later Lord Sudley), Sir Edward Cust (a courtier), the Hon. Thomas Liddell and George Vivian – all of them patrician amateurs with interests in the Gothic and the picturesque.[8]

It was this essentially conservative commission that judged Charles Barry to have carried out this essentially conservative remit with matchless ingenuity and imagination. As the competition required, and as its name ('new *Palace*') implied, he designed a building that was more a royal residence than a democratic legislature – instantly antique and self-consciously historical, richly ornamented, and full of allusions to the national past, to which it provided a powerful physical link. Like the Gothic Revival castles that had proliferated across the length and breadth of Britain since the turbulent 1790s, the new Palace of Westminster as conceived by the architect was no shrine to freedom or progress or public access: it was for the use of a tiny and privileged governing élite, and it was forbidding to outsiders, with very limited accommodation for press or people (*The Times*'s call for "amplitude of accommodation for *the public* as well as for the members themselves" had been largely disregarded).[9] In all these ways, the new palace had more in common with the buildings it replaced than is sometimes recognized, and this continuity was further reinforced by the decision to build it on the same site as the old palace, and to incorporate into it the surviving medieval structures such as Westminster Hall (hence, of course, the harmonizing attraction of the Gothic style). The result was a new/old building, proclaiming continuity rather than change: a display of 'national history' and 'national historicism'.[10]

So, one of the architect's prime concerns was to create a palace that would enhance the position and assert the prestige of the monarch vis-à-vis the Lords, the Commons and the people. Hence the two hundred exterior statues with which the building was adorned, the majority of them depicting kings and queens of England and Britain since the Saxon period, rather than politicians or peers.[11] Hence the Victoria Tower at the south-east corner, which on its completion in 1858 was the tallest secular building in the world, and beneath which was placed the magnificent Royal Entrance, which was exclusively for the use of the sovereign. Hence the succession of state apartments of unparalleled splendour to which it led: the Royal Staircase, the Robing Room, the Royal Gallery and the Prince's Chamber.[12] These were the most opulently ornamented rooms in the palace, decorated with royal images, armorial bearings and heraldic devices, and with Arthurian frescoes in the Robing Room and Tudor portraits in the Prince's Chamber. Together, these right royal apartments proclaim with overpowering visual force the idea of an ordered, rooted, hierarchical, venerable society; and they reasserted that Westminster was a royal palace, and that the monarchy was at the centre of British life and British history.[13]

These elaborate decorations and imaginative embellishments were largely the work of Augustus Welby Northmore Pugin. He was a Catholic convert and a passionate believer in precedent and scholarship, who thought the medieval world better than his own time. He delighted in aristocratic clients (such as Lord Shrewsbury, Charles Scarisbrick and Ambrose Phillipps de Lisle), and specialized in designing Gothic churches and country houses. He

John Rogers Herbert, *Augustus Welby Northmore Pugin*, oil on canvas, 1845. A friend of Pugin, Herbert was nonetheless given a meagre twenty-minute sitting in order to achieve this likeness, which perhaps explains its rather sketchy appearance. The frame was designed by Pugin. Pugin's coat of arms, bearing a martlet, can be seen both on the frame and within the painting, with the motto *en avant* repeated around the frame itself. The green textile in the background was based on an Italian fifteenth-century design. Entitled 'Gothic Tapestry', it was used as a wallpaper design in a variety of colours within the Palace of Westminster. Palace of Westminster (WOA 2586).

believed hierarchy was the proper ordering of society, and thought "stage effect" and "splendid mummery" were the appropriate ways of articulating and safeguarding it. This profoundly conservative, anti-democratic, anti-utilitarian and anti-industrial vision was partly derived from such recent writers as Sir Walter Scott, Robert Southey and Sir Kenelm Digby, and it had much in common with the 'Young England' movement that was fashionable among some Tories during the 1840s.[14] Pugin's Gothic impulses reached their zenith in the Lords Chamber, which was more a celebration of the sovereign than of the peers: "fitted up for great pageants and state ceremonials, and not for the transaction of ordinary business". It was regarded as "a scene of royal magnificence", with its stained-glass windows portraying the monarchs of England and Scotland (replaced following the Second World War); with the fabulously carved and embellished throne and sumptuous furnishings; and with frescoes depicting the religious and chivalric virtues of medieval sovereigns. By comparison, the Commons Chamber was a cramped and Spartan house: there was insufficient seating for all the Members, and it was difficult to make oneself heard.[15]

As conceived by Barry and Pugin, the Palace of Westminster was not so much a legislature as a theatre of state, a building of uniquely dramatic intensity and potential, the setting for royal ceremonials that were more impressive than the somnolent debates in the Lords or the schoolboy squabbles of the Commons.[16] Here, they were following in the footsteps of Sir John Soane, who had been concerned to provide a fitting backdrop for King George IV when he appeared in Parliament to open it in state. Now Barry and Pugin in their turn had produced an even more splendid stage, where the young Queen Victoria appeared as the centre of the annual pageant of the State Opening, which was more a celebration of royal majesty and ordered hierarchy than of political freedom or legislative autonomy. There was a carriage procession from Buckingham Palace to the Victoria Tower; the queen entered the Robing Room, where she put on her crown and robes of state; she walked through the Royal Gallery to the Lords Chamber; and there she read the speech from the throne. The result was a living historical pageant, which complemented those pictures being put on the walls of the new Palace that depicted the pageant of the nation's history. Throughout the 1850s, the queen regularly opened Parliament in full state, accompanied by Prince Albert, and when the Royal Entrance was first used in 1852, she knighted Barry.[17]

As a building and as a theatre, the new Palace of Westminster embodied in stone and ceremony a view of Britain's constitution and society that was more Tory and backward-looking than progressive and forward-looking. The monarch was the most important personage in the nation and the legislature; the House of Lords was second in prestige and importance; the House of Commons came a distinct third; and the people as a whole scarcely mattered. There was *some* truth in this view of things. Victoria was no impartial constitutional monarch, but an opinionated and interfering sovereign, determined never to be queen of a "democratic monarchy", and anxious to hand on her inherited powers, undiminished, to her successor.[18] Throughout most of the nineteenth century, the Parliamentary peerage remained the richest, most powerful, most privileged group in the land, and they continued to veto bills sent up from the lower House (with the exception of those concerning finance), including Gladstone's second Home Rule Bill in 1893. As for the Commons, in terms of kinship and clientage, they remained subordinate to the Lords; their membership was overwhelmingly landed and leisured; and they were elected on a very narrow franchise. After 1832, scarcely one in five adult males had the vote, and in 1865, the franchise was arguably one of the narrowest in Europe.[19]

Charles West Cope, *Speaker Lenthall Asserting the Privileges of the Commons against Charles I when the Attempt was Made to Seize the Five Members*, 1642, waterglass, 1866. Peers Corridor, House of Lords, Palace of Westminster (WOA 2894).

Sir Edward John Poynter, *Saint George for England*, mosaic, 1869. Central Lobby, Palace of Westminster (WOA 4257).

The Palace of Westminster was also a very *British* building – visibly embodying the sense of unitary statehood and national identity that had reached its culmination with the passing of the Act of Union with Ireland in 1801. In a palace festooned with rich ornamentation, great attention was given to all three constituent kingdoms, and some to the Welsh principality. There were coats of arms of the English, Irish and Scottish royal houses, pictures and sculptures of monarchs from all three nations, and the insignia of the three great orders of chivalry: the Garter for England, the Thistle for Scotland, and also the Order of St Patrick, the motto of which, *Quis Separabit?*, proclaimed the indissolubility of the Union with Ireland. And the patron saints of England, Ireland, Scotland and Wales were designated for the four walls of Central Lobby.[20] When early- and mid-Victorians described the Palace of Westminster as the 'imperial Parliament', they meant it in the sense that it was the 'four-kingdoms' legislature. Of course, Members of Parliament and peers spent time discussing Canada, South Africa, Australia and India; but there was no serious interest in any form of overseas representation, and apart from a single fresco depicting the embarkation of the Pilgrim Fathers for New England, there were no allusions to the colonies in the original decorative schemes that were completed.[21]

But while the Palace of Westminster embodied many truths about the Victorian constitution, politics and society, they were never more than a partial picture. Despite her strong views and imperious will, the Queen could not veto bills, and she was less proactive than her uncle, William IV. Her political power did not match her Parliamentary pomp, and even that soon fell away: for after Albert died, she opened Parliament only in 1866, 1867, 1871, 1876, 1877, 1880 and 1886. She also turned her back on those accoutrements of majesty for which Barry and Pugin had provided the backdrop: there were no trumpets, coaches or robes, she wore a widow's cap, a black dress and a long veil, and she left the reading of the speech to the Lord Chancellor. Nor were the Lords the omnipotent body suggested by Pugin's lavish decorations: they generally used their power of veto sparingly; and they gave way over the repeal of the Corn Laws and the second and third Reform Bills. The best cure for believing in the Upper House, Walter Bagehot famously remarked, was to go and look at it.[22] Most ministries were made and unmade in the Commons, and after the extension of the franchise under the Second Reform Act, which roughly doubled the size of the electorate, they possessed a popular legitimacy which the Lords could not rival. And although this was the *United* Kingdom's legislature, there were already demands, in the 1840s, that the recent Union between Britain and Ireland should be repealed.[23]

The British constitution was not, then, exactly as Barry and Pugin's palace suggested it was; and nor was Barry and Pugin's palace quite what it seemed, or what was intended. The building might be in traditional Gothic style, but its historical resonances were limited by the fact that construction continued until the 1870s – by which time both Pugin (1852) and Barry (1860) were dead, and their sons were publicly squabbling as to who had been responsible for what. Throughout this period, there was almost continual controversy – about the judges and the outcome of the original competition, about the endless delays and the ever-mounting costs, and about subsequent modifications to the original design.[24] The new Commons Chamber, first used in May 1850, was greatly disliked by Members because of its poor acoustics and limited accommodation, and during Gladstone's first ministry of 1868–74, there were demands for it to be rebuilt; but they were rejected on the grounds of expense. By then, Victorian taste in Gothic had turned against the late Perpendicular style, and the building was derided by many architectural critics as a stylistic travesty, and by Ruskin as "empty filigree".[25] As for the historical frescoes that were the responsibility of a Royal Commission of Fine Arts (Fine Arts Commission) chaired by Albert, the Prince Consort, there was disagreement over the choice of artists and materials; many of the early commissions were not completed or even begun; public access was so limited that they did not fulfil the broader educational function originally intended for them; and the whole initiative came to a standstill when Albert died in 1861.[26]

During this first phase of commission, design, construction and function, the new Palace of Westminster thus presented a far from 'settled' image – of itself, or of the British constitution. On both counts, it was arguably as much about myth and make-believe as it was about truth and reality. Nor should this come as a surprise for, as Phoebe Stanton has pointed out, Pugin was a "dreamer of dreams", who possessed a "talent for creating architectural fiction" and "majestic fantasy": romantic buildings that projected images of society

After Harry Furniss, *Essence of Parliament, Extracted From The Diary of Toby. M.P.: Mr. Punch's suggestion for the Betterment of Parliament, The House of Commons altered so as to accommodate all its members,* published in *Punch, or the London Charivari,* 22 February 1890, p. 94.

and politics as they ought to be, that were in many ways at variance with the social and political realities of the time.[27] And it is scarcely coincidence that the politician from this period who relished similar illusions was Benjamin Disraeli. Like Pugin, he embraced the medieval revivalism of the 1840s, as a member of the 'Young England' party, drawing on Bolingbroke, Digby and Scott for inspiration. Like Pugin, he disliked the Reformation, industrialism and utilitarianism, and in *Coningsby* (1844), he included portraits of two of Pugin's patrons, Lord Shrewsbury and Ambrose Phillipps de Lisle, in the figure of Eustace Lyle. Like Pugin, Disraeli possessed a powerful if idiosyncratic historical imagination, and he loved the 'aristocratic settlement', the peerage and (especially) the monarchy. Hence his flattery of Victoria later in his career as the 'faerie queene' with her magic wand, who possessed greater powers than most would allow. There was about him, as about the Palace of Westminster, an unmistakable aura of Gothic enchantment, escapism and illusion.[28]

Like Disraeli, the Palace of Westminster projected a Tory vision of the constitution. But in fact and in practice, it was increasingly the setting for a Whig narrative of history — displayed, for example, in the scenes from the Civil War and Glorious Revolution that line the Commons and Peers Corridors — a scarcely surprisingly trajectory since, for most of the period from 1835 to 1885, the Whigs and Liberals were generally in power. Perhaps this was why, once the dark days of the 1840s had passed, and once complaints about the cost and the Commons Chamber had largely died down, it became in the popular imagination more fairy-tale than foreboding — an identity that it retains in some quarters to this day. By the 1870s, it was commonplace to refer to it as a fairy palace, matching, as it were, Disraeli's 'faerie queene'.[29] And it was this image that Gilbert and Sullivan caught and cultivated in *Iolanthe*, first performed in 1882. Act II opens with New Palace Yard bathed in pale, mellow moonlight: a romance of a romance. The Fairy Queen is as much a parody of Victoria as she is a Wagnerian caricature. The peers strut and process upon the stage in splendid style, while the Commons are nowhere to be seen. Ostensibly irreverent and mocking, *Iolanthe* seems to be subverting the Houses of Parliament as theatre of state: in fact, it came much closer to replicating the real thing.[30]

## Reform and Expansion, Democracy and Empire

During the first phase of its existence, then, the new Palace of Westminster embodied and projected a more ceremonial, more complex and more conservative cluster of political assumptions and constitutional values than is generally supposed. Thereafter, these meanings began to change in ways that neither Barry nor Pugin could have foreseen — or would have appreciated. Self-evidently, their Parliamentary building remained static and immutable. But much was changing outside — which meant much was changing inside as well. In part this was because, during the last two decades of the life of the 'faerie queene', Westminster ceased to be the setting for the glittering theatre of state that had flourished during the earlier years of her reign. After Victoria's non-majestic appearances in the 1870s, she scarcely visited Parliament again, leaving the grand royal rooms silent and uninhabited. Initially, this was because of her secluded grief, subsequently on account of her incorrigible hostility to Gladstone, and lastly due to her age and infirmity, which meant the steps and the walk were beyond her. Meanwhile, the revived ceremonial of monarchy became more public and less Parliamentary, centring on the queen's two jubilees and on her funeral — popular pageants with vast crowds, for which the open streets of London, rather than the exclusive Palace of Westminster, served as the backdrop.[31]

At the same time, the balance of power between the three elements of the legislature

*"Iolanthe" at the Savoy Theatre*, half-tone print, published in *The Graphic*, 23 December 1882, n.p. *Iolanthe* by William Gilbert and Arthur Sullivan was first performed on Saturday 25 November 1882 at the Savoy Theatre. Theatre Museum Collection, London.

shifted further away from the idealized model of the constitution proclaimed by the splendour of the royal rooms, the magnificence of the Lords and the relative plainness of the Commons. From the later period of Queen Victoria's reign to that of King George VI, British monarchs were involved much less powerfully and opinionatedly in politics: generally, the most they tried to do was to bring contending sides together, as in 1885 (the Third Reform Act), 1910 (the Parliament Act) and 1931 (the formation of the National Government). But the earlier, assertive partisanship was given up; the abdication of Edward VIII showed that Parliament controlled the sovereign rather than the other way round; and most twentieth-century monarchs wisely settled for their three rights as defined by Walter Bagehot: to warn, to encourage and to be consulted.[32] The might and prestige of the Lords were also dramatically reduced: with the passing of the Parliament Act in 1911, which reduced their powers of veto to two years' delay; with the scandals over the sale and purchase of peerages; with the gradual decline of the traditional aristocracy in cohesion and confidence; and with the broadening (or dilution) of the social base of the peerage.[33]

Part cause, part consequence of the decline in the relative powers of the monarchy and the Lords was that the Commons became ever more important – thereby rendering the original Barry–Pugin vision of the constitution even more anachronistic and illusionary than it had been during the mid-Victorian period. The Third and Fourth Reform Acts brought universal adult suffrage, which meant that by 1919 the lower House was representative of the entire British population for the first time in its history – although women between the ages of twenty-one and thirty had to wait until 1928.[34] As a result, the new Palace of Westminster became a symbol of (and shrine to) universal democracy in ways its creators had neither foreseen nor intended, and by the inter-war years, the Commons was dominated by middle- and working-class legislators of whom neither Barry nor Pugin would have approved. Their building remained opulent and glittering in its rich ornamentation, projecting a view of politics and the constitution that was backward-looking and hierarchical. But it now housed a people's legislature. Appropriately enough, the chimes of Big Ben were first broadcast in 1923: Parliamentary time was now everyone's time.[35]

But this was not the only way in which Parliament's meaning changed and evolved during these years. For, during the late nineteenth century, the phrase 'imperial Parliament' increasingly came to describe the Palace of Westminster not as the British legislature, but as the cynosure of a global empire and earthly dominion on which the sun never set. One indication was the greater amount of time spent discussing imperial affairs: the establishment of the Australian confederation in 1900; the granting of self-government to the former Boer republics in 1906; the creation of the union of South Africa in 1910; the passing of the Statute of Westminster in 1931; and the lengthy debates over the Government of India Act of 1935. Another sign of the unprecedented importance of imperial business in the British Parliament was that by the inter-war years, there were three secretaries of state dealing with India, the dominions and the colonies. Of course, much of this business was concerned with advancing the dominions further towards self-government; but the idea persisted until the Second World War that in some sense the imperial legislature in Britain, albeit increasingly metaphysical, remained supreme: the 'Mother of Parliaments'. When the Lord Chancellor's Woolsack was re-stuffed in 1938, it was with a blend of wool from Britain and the sheep-producing nations of the empire.[36]

This growing belief that the British, four-nation legislature was (or should be) functioning as an imperial senate was reinforced by the increase in the number of Members and (especially) peers with first-hand experience of governing the empire: Curzon, Cromer,

Anon, *This is "The House" that Man Built*, photomechanical print, 1908–14. This design forms part of a series of humorous postcards produced in London on the subject of the Suffragette Movement. Mayfair Picture Library.

Lugard, Kitchener, Halifax, Lansdowne. Virtually all proconsuls were noblemen — many when they went out, most on their return — which meant that from the 1880s to the 1930s, the empire was better represented in the British Parliament than it had been between the 1830s and the 1870s.[37] Moreover, the unprecedented ennoblement of such colonials as Lords Strathcona, Mount Stephen, Althostan, Beaverbrook, de Villiers, Sinha, Morris, Forest and Rutherford brought into the upper House peers who could genuinely claim to represent the furthest reaches of empire. One such was Sir Gerald Strickland, a Maltese aristocrat who was also a protégé of Joseph Chamberlain, and had been governor of the Leeward Islands, Tasmania, Western Australia and New South Wales from 1903 to 1917. Between 1924 and 1927, Strickland was a member of the Maltese legislature, and he sat simultaneously in the British House of Commons as Member of Parliament for Lancaster (or, his critics complained, "for Malta"). Thereafter, he was elevated to the Lords, where he continued to represent the interests of the island until his death in 1940, and campaigned for the award of life peerages to colonial premiers.[38]

From the time Chamberlain had advocated it in the mid-1880s, there were many who urged a stronger overseas representation in what they hoped would become a fully-fledged 'imperial' Parliament. The most modest proposal was to recruit colonial premiers and Indian princes to the upper House, thereby consolidating its imperial function and personnel, and such reform schemes (to which Strickland remained abidingly loyal) were much discussed in the decades before the First World War.[39] But there were also more wide-ranging proposals, which envisaged transforming the upper House from a domestic House of Lords into an authentically imperial senate, "reconstituted so as to comprise representatives from every

The Lying-in-State of King George V, photograph reproduced in *The Illustrated London News, Record of the Lying-in-State and Funeral of His Majesty King George V and the Accession of His Majesty King Edward VIII*, CLXXXVIII, no. 5050, 27 February 1936, pp. 174–75. The accompanying text reads "The vigil by night beneath the Great Roof of Richard II. The coffin of King George with its silent guard — one more historic memory added to the long annals of Westminster Hall." The funeral procession arrived in Westminster Hall on 23 February, and the Lying-in-State lasted from 24 February to 27 February inclusive (WOA 222).

British realm and colony". All other second chambers in the empire would be abolished; domestic matters would be discussed in what had previously been the local lower house; and imperial matters would be dealt with in the single surviving upper House in London. Yet a third suggestion was to extend the colonial and imperial conferences, which met intermittently in London, into permanent session, thereby making them into a new, third chamber at Westminster.[40] Such imaginative schemes clearly envisaged a very different sort of 'imperial' Parliament from that which Barry and Pugin had accommodated and designed.

It was in this much-changed context – national and imperial, political and constitutional – that the State Opening was revived by Edward VII in February 1901, as one of the first public acts of his reign. In an increasingly democratic world, he thought it important that the sovereign should be seen with all the accoutrements of regal magnificence. And so, assisted by Lord Esher, he re-established the full dress ceremonial, complete with the horse-drawn carriages, the glittering procession through the Palace of Westminster and the reading of the speech from the throne in the Lords Chamber.[41] But this was more than the revival of a state theatre that had been moribund since 1860: for Edward was Emperor of India and ruler of the British dominions beyond the seas, an imperial monarch in full finery in his imperial Parliament. And this new-old, popular-Parliamentary spectacle was dutifully perpetuated by his successors down to the Second World War – except by Edward VIII, who, on the one occasion he participated in the State Opening, cancelled the horse-drawn procession on account of the weather.[42] At the same time, new royal 'traditions' were devised with close Parliamentary association: on their deaths, both Edward VII and George V lay in state in Westminster Hall; and on his Silver Jubilee, George V received congratulations from the Lords and Commons in the same venerable building. As royal – and Parliamentary – occasions, these were events without precedent.

While the full-scale ceremonial of the king in Parliament was thus being reasserted in a more imperial and newly democratic context, renewed efforts were made to continue the wall paintings that had largely been abandoned with the death of Prince Albert in 1861. Between 1908 and 1910, six pictures were completed in the East Corridor, devoted to the Tudor period; and from 1925 to 1927, eight panels were installed in St Stephen's Hall, originally entitled *The Story of Our Liberties*, but subsequently changed to *The Building of Britain*. Their meanings were many and varied: more even than Barry and Pugin, they projected (and perpetuated) political and historical illusions. In a new era of democracy, they gave special prominence to monarchs, and they were paid for by individual peers. In a building that was a shrine to Tory constitutionalism, they presented this history of Britain as a Whiggish saga of freedom, extending from King Alfred the Great to the Union between England and Scotland in 1707. And in what had originally been a very 'British' legislature, they gave belated attention to the imperial theme, with pictures of Henry VII giving a charter to John Cabot to find new lands, and Queen Elizabeth commissioning Sir Walter Ralegh to sail for America. Here was the nation's history resumed as an unfolding pageant with the monarch at the centre, just like the revived State Opening.[43]

At the same time that this visual narrative of Whig history was being added to the Palace of Westminster, there was a growing concern to investigate – and increasingly to praise – the unique continuity and slow, ordered evolution of the legislature itself. For this was the era of Stubbs and Maitland, with their pioneering work on the origins of medieval parliaments, and of A.F. Pollard, who insisted that "parliamentary institutions have ... been incomparably the greatest gift of the English people to the civilisation of the world". It was the era of G.M. Trevelyan, who saw the history of Parliament as the history of English liber-

Denis William Eden, *John Cabot and his Sons Receive the Charter from Henry VII to Sail in Search of New Lands*, oil on canvas, 1910. East Corridor, House of Commons, Palace of Westminster (WOA 2594).

ties, and of Lewis Namier, who venerated it as an "extraordinary club", a "marvellous microcosmos of English social and political life".[44] It was the era of Josiah Wedgwood, who sought to finance a full-scale history of Parliament, so that Members would acquire some sense of the great tradition to which they belonged, and so that the people might learn from this matchless story of liberty and self-government. And it was the era of Stalin, Franco, Mussolini and Hitler: tyrants and dictators, who snuffed out the very freedoms for which the British Parliament now seemed, uniquely in Europe, to stand.[45]

The result of these changes and developments, both inside the Palace of Westminster and outside, was that by the early decades of the twentieth century, and on into the interwar years, there had gathered around Barry and Pugin's early-Victorian Gothic extravaganza an accretion of sentiments, associations, ceremonies and histories that were significantly different from those that had pertained in their own day. Parliament was more democratic and more imperial, and these additional identities and extra layers of meaning were at their most resonant during and immediately after the Second World War. It was the House of Commons that brought down Neville Chamberlain in the spring of 1940; that was in the front line of battle and destroyed by Hitler's bombs; and that sustained and criticized Churchill and his wartime administration. Thus regarded, Britain's victory in the Second World War was a "triumph of Parliamentary democracy".[46] And it was a triumph for the

British Parliament as the imperial Parliament. This, at least, was the message conveyed by the rebuilding of the House of Commons, which was reconstructed with materials donated by the dominions and colonies: the Speaker's Chair from Australia, the Clerk's Table from Canada, the two dispatch boxes from New Zealand and the furniture for the Division Lobbies from Nigeria and Uganda.[47]

But, as in the previous period, these meanings, identities and associations were not always as they seemed. The ceremonial of the State Opening might be more splendid and imperial than ever, but it concealed as much as it revealed. The monarch had never been so grandly displayed before the Lords and the Commons, and the tableau in the Upper House was unprecedented in its magnificence (Henry Channon thought it like "a six no-trumper at bridge").[48] Yet the king was far less influential than Victoria or William IV or George IV – as Edward VIII found out to his cost – and the peerage was increasingly marginal to British political life.[49] Nor did the Palace of Westminster ever house a truly imperial Parliament. Most inhabitants of the settler colonies did not like hereditary titles; the schemes for converting the upper House into an imperial senate never materialized; and having won some measure of self-government, the dominions were unwilling to surrender it.[50] Not surprisingly, attempts to give the building an imperial facelift also met with little success. In the 1890s and 1900s, there were proposals to attach to it a grand mausoleum where the heroes of

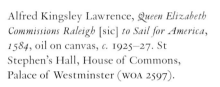

Alfred Kingsley Lawrence, *Queen Elizabeth Commissions Raleigh* [sic] *to Sail for America, 1584*, oil on canvas, *c.* 1925–27. St Stephen's Hall, House of Commons, Palace of Westminster (WOA 2597).

empire might be buried, but they were ruled out on account of their cost. And in the 1930s, Frank Brangwyn was commissioned to paint a new series of frescoes for the Lords, which were to show the fruits and products of empire. But they were deemed stylistically unsuitable, and were subsequently removed to Swansea Town Hall.[51]

Once again, then, albeit in different ways, there were elements of make-believe in the images and identities projected on to the British legislature in this post-Pugin–Barry age of imperialism and democracy. The Palace of Westminster might have been the 'Mother of Parliaments', spawning new legislatures across and around the globe. But this later British imperial style was classical rather than Gothic: Admiralty Arch, County Hall, the Treasury Building and the Mall façade of Buckingham Palace in London, as well as the legislatures and assemblies in South Africa, Australia and India, were all modelled on classical precedents (which now seemed to be Roman-imperial rather than French-subversive) rather than Gothic ones.[52] Indeed, the most resonant image of the Palace of Westminster in this period came from France: Monet's series of nineteen paintings, begun in 1899 and first exhibited in 1904. Concerned with depicting the effects of light and colour, sunshine and smoke, sky and water, and atmospheric effect, he painted the palace not as an imperial legislature, but as blurred and melancholic, constantly mutating with the weather and time of day, floating on the shimmering river and melting into thin air – sometimes as an empurpled silhouette, going up in scorching sunset flames (shades of 1834?); sometimes peeping out from a vaporous Holmes-and-Watson fog. There was no drama, no history, no politician in sight.

## Globalization and Devolution

Since the Second World War, the Palace of Westminster has continued its protean progress as the fount and focus of different meanings and myths, images and illusions, which are both projected on to it and derived from it. In the aftermath of the Second World War, Parliament's prestige was at its peak: Hitler and Hirohito had been defeated, democracy had been saved, and so it was scarcely surprising that the blitzed House of Commons was rebuilt close to the original design. For much of the ensuing twenty years, its standing remained high, in large part because it shared in the Olympian fame of its greatest member: Winston Churchill.[53] Although past the peak of his powers, his greatest speeches, both as Leader of the Opposition from 1945 to 1951, and as Prime Minister from 1951 to 1955, were unforgettable Parliamentary occasions. His eightieth birthday brought a unique tribute from both Houses in Westminster Hall, and when he made a rare late appearance in the Commons in April 1958, one journalist observed that "there is one glory of the sun and another of the moon, as we know, but there is also a glory of Parliament." When Churchill died in January 1965, his body lay in state in Westminster Hall for three days. "He was in a very real sense a child of this House and a product of it," Harold Wilson observed, "and equally, in every sense, its father."[54]

As this suggests, Westminster Hall has remained the setting for great ceremonies of state, many of which have centred on the monarchy: the Crown in Parliament. Fourteen years before Churchill, George VI had lain in state there; and Queen Elizabeth II's Silver Wedding and Silver Jubilee were both marked with loyal addresses from both Houses. But the most visible affirmation of the continued link between the sovereign and the Palace of Westminster remains the State Opening, and throughout her long reign, the present Queen has been as attentive to this task as all but one of her twentieth-century predecessors. She first opened Parliament in state in November 1952, and she has scarcely missed a year since.[55] From October 1958, the ceremony has been broadcast live on television, so that what was

Sir Frank Brangwyn, *South East Asia*, oil on canvas, from *The British Empire* panels, commissioned 1925, completed by 1930. Glynn Vivian Art Gallery Collection, Swansea.

previously a restricted group rite, confined to the members of both Houses and some special guests, has now become a public pageant. The tone and treatment of this "state occasion at its most magnificent" was established by the BBC's pre-eminent royal commentator, Richard Dimbleby, who depicted it in heightened and romanticized terms as a Puginesque tableau of hierarchy and history, with his dignified, reverential commentary, his silken descriptions of peers and judges, and his stress on the symbolism and splendour of the ceremonial.[56]

But just as the 'meaning' of the State Opening – and of the Parliament that was thus splendidly inaugurated – was different in Edward VII's day from what it had been in Victoria's, so it has become different again in the time of Elizabeth II. For this is no longer an imperial occasion in an imperial legislature: by the time the House of Commons was

Claude-Oscar Monet, *The Houses of Parliament at Sunset*, oil on canvas, 1904. Kunsthaus Zürich, Switzerland.

rebuilt as a monument to imperial consciousness and concern, the empire itself was already and rapidly on the wane. India became independent in 1947, as did most of the dependant empire in Africa during the next twenty years. There were suggestions that colonies such as Malta and Gibraltar might send their own Members to the British Parliament. But like earlier schemes, they came to nothing.[57] In Canada and Australia, the remaining vestiges of British Parliamentary sovereignty have largely been removed. The British Parliament that The Queen opens is no longer an imperial legislature appropriately inaugurated by an imperial monarch; for she opens it, not as Empress of India and ruler of dominions beyond the seas, but as a national sovereign.[58]

Yet what does national sovereignty mean in the 1990s, in terms of the monarch and her Parliament? The simple answer has to be: much less than it did even a generation ago. In part, this has been because of Britain's ever-closer ties with 'Europe'. When it joined the European Economic Community in 1972, Parliament agreed that subsequent EEC legislation "shall be recognized and available in law and be enforced, allowed and followed accordingly". Since then, Britain has adopted the Single European Act of 1985 and the Maastricht Treaty of 1992.[59] In part, too, this is because national sovereignty is being eroded worldwide: the sovereign nation state, with its laws, legislature and law-makers, is no longer seen as something permanent, unchanging and immutable, but as something contingent, provisional and temporary, which rests on the relatively uncertain foundations of myths and traditions. For in the brave new world of the global economy, electronic information and instant communication, decisions about Britain's future are as likely to be made in Tokyo and New York and Frankfurt as in London – or the Palace of Westminster.[60]

Equally, the recent creation of the Scottish parliament and of the Welsh national assembly represents the greatest transfer of power away from the British Parliament since the Irish legislation of 1919–21, and it will "radically alter the role of Westminster".[61] The recent openings of the Scottish parliament by The Queen and the Welsh assembly by Prince Charles were seen as an emphatic demonstration that the old, pan-British hegemony of the London Parliament is over. And there may be more to come – probably not in the form of an elected assembly for England, but perhaps in the form of elected mayors of the great cities. This is not to say that the break-up of Britain is nigh. But from below, no less than from above, power in Britain is being diffused: the London-based Parliament is no longer the supreme legislative body for the unitary British nation state.

The meaning of Parliament has not only changed in terms of its external resonances and relations: there have also been many changes in terms of its functioning and personnel. The Queen may continue to fulfil her ceremonial functions, but Westminster has ceased to be, in jurisdictional terms, the royal palace it has been throughout most of its history. Since 1965, the Lord Great Chamberlain has relinquished most of his rights and powers as the monarch's representative, and today it is the Speaker, on behalf of Parliament, who is the prime custodian.[62] The House of Lords has been transformed by further reductions in its powers of delay, and by the introduction of life peerages, which means that it is now less of an hereditary, aristocratic chamber, but is dominated for day-to-day business by nominated life senators, a substantial proportion of whom are now women.[63] Since the recent legislation, the status of hereditary peers has been significantly reduced. And the House of Commons has seen similar if not greater changes: the introduction of new select committees, which offer a stronger check on the executive; the live televising of debates, which enables everyone to see what goes on there; and since May 1997 the advent of an unprecedented number of women Members of Parliament. The result is that while Barry and Pugin's building may appear unaltered, this is in many ways an illusion: for the work that goes on inside it, and the people who undertake that work, have changed very significantly.

Perhaps in reaction to this, over the past half-century, veneration for the Houses of Parliament as a building and Parliament as a historic national institution has significantly increased. This shift in taste was eloquently signalled in the 1950s by Nikolaus Pevsner's uncharacteristically effusive description of the Palace of Westminster as "the most imaginatively planned and the most excellently executed major secular building of the Gothic revival anywhere in the world".[64] Since then, the paintings, drawings, sculptures and engravings in the palace have been authoritatively catalogued and a full survey of the historic furniture has been made; the *History of Parliament*, covering the House of Commons from medieval times to 1832, has been almost completed; Barry and Pugin have been recognized as the architectural and decorative geniuses that they undoubtedly were; and an extensive programme of refurbishment has been carried out, on the exterior in the 1980s and the interior in the 1990s, restoring their masterpiece to its original early-Victorian grandeur.[65] The new Palace of Westminster has never been as well cared for and admired as it is now – in 1987 it was designated a World Heritage Site – and it cannot be coincidence that this unprecedented display of consciousness and concern has taken place during a period that has also witnessed the unprecedented diminution of Parliament's powers and autonomy.

Another development – which owes much to these same circumstances and changes, but tends in a rather different direction – has been the increasing criticism of the annual pageant of the State Opening. Ever since Robin Day's 'rival' television commentary in 1958, which in contrast to Richard Dimbleby's obsequiousness was brash, brisk and irreverent, those on the Left have insisted that it is not so much a spectacle as a sham – part pantomime, part costume drama, projecting a dangerously deluded image of constitutional and national realities. For such critics, "modern political reality" is more important than this "ancient royal ceremony".[66] Of course, this is far from being a universally held view. The "timeless ritual and splendour" of the 'traditional' State Opening, and the picture of Britain it embodies and projects, retain their admirers and supporters.[67] It also bears repeating that the State Opening is the very pageant that Barry and Pugin designed their palace to accommodate.

## The Palace of Varieties

These discussions carry us a long way from the burning of the old Palace of Westminster in 1834 with which this chapter began. Of course, it is unwise and irresponsible for historians to try to predict the future. But whatever it may hold, the fact remains that our contemporary world is in many ways markedly different from the early Victorian era, when Barry and Pugin set out to create their matchless masterpiece. Put the other way, this means the new Palace of Westminster was very much a product of its time, and as such it projected a particular, powerful and partial vision of its time. Since then, the British nation and the British people, British politics and British politicians, have evolved and developed in ways that it has been possible only to sketch and summarize here. Yet the building itself has changed scarcely at all, thereby often disguising or concealing many of the variations in context and circumstance that have subsequently taken place – even as its own meaning has changed as a result of them. This is an extraordinary story about an extraordinary building – and about much more than an extraordinary building. Nor is it over yet. Its future as the theatre of state may soon be put in doubt; but for as long as British Parliamentary politics endure, the Palace of Westminster seems certain to remain the palace of varieties.

# 2

## The Staging of Ceremonies of State in the House of Lords

Henry S. Cobb

From the Middle Ages onwards, regular ceremonies have occupied a conspicuous place in the proceedings of the House of Lords. The most important of these are the royal ceremonies at which the sovereign is present, either in person or represented by commissioners authorized by the sovereign to act on his or her behalf. On such occasions, the Lords Chamber is something more than the House of Lords, being the place where the sovereign, the Lords and the Commons "in Parliament assemble". Such ceremonies are or were held for the opening of Parliament, the approval of the Speaker of the Commons, the giving of the royal assent to bills and the prorogation of Parliament.[1]

### The State Opening of Parliament in the Middle Ages

The State Opening of Parliament has always been the most elaborate of these ceremonies. In the Middle Ages, the king, unless ill or absent on campaign, was expected to be present at this and subsequent proceedings because it was his parliament.[2] By the later fourteenth century, the opening proceedings followed a well-established pattern. The Lords, and others summoned by name, assembled with the Great Officers of State in the Painted Chamber of the Palace of Westminster. The Commons gathered in Westminster Hall. Proceedings began when those peers attending were checked against the list of summons, while the Commons' names were read out from the sheriffs' election returns. The Commons were then led through to stand at the Bar of the House of Lords – in the Painted Chamber – where the king sat in state, surrounded by the Lords, who were seated in order and in their robes. An address was then given, almost invariably by the Chancellor, usually part sermon and part practical explanation of the state of the kingdom and of the reasons for the summons. Lords and Commons were told to meet separately to discuss these matters, to consider how government could be improved and to present their grievances.[3] The separate sessions of the Lords and Commons normally began on the second day, the Lords meeting in the 'White' or Parliament Chamber – their habitual place of assembly in the fourteenth century – while the Commons met in the refectory of Westminster Abbey.[4]

Responsibility for marshalling the Lords in Parliament in order of precedence lay with the Earl Marshal from at least 1376, but, after the institution of the office of Garter King of Arms in 1415, this duty was delegated to the latter.[5] Garter and the other heralds thus became responsible for marshalling and leading the procession at the State Opening.

### Tudor State Openings (1485–1603)

During the Tudor period the ceremony of the State Opening usually comprised the following elements: the assembly of peers, Great Officers of State, heralds and others at the royal

Peter Tillemans, *Queen Anne in the House of Lords*, oil on canvas, *c.* 1710. The Royal Collection.

palace in which the sovereign was then residing; the procession to Westminster Abbey, which was a popular public spectacle; the service in the abbey; the procession to the Palace of Westminster; proceedings in the House of Lords when the Lord Chancellor or Lord Keeper declared the causes for summoning Parliament and directed the Commons to choose their Speaker; and, finally, the return of the monarch to the royal place of residence.[6]

The earliest known description of the procession to and service in the abbey is to be found in a report on proceedings in the first Parliament of Henry VII, made by the members for Colchester. According to this report, the Commons assembled at nine o'clock on the day of the opening (7 November 1485) and, soon afterwards, the king, with all the Lords Spiritual and Temporal, came from the Parliament Chamber to Westminster Abbey, where the 'mass of the Holy Ghost' (the usual mass for later Parliaments) was heard. While celebration of the mass was in progress, the Lord Steward (as was customary at later openings) returned to the Palace of Westminster for a roll-call of the knights and burgesses, who then entered the Parliament Chamber. The account continues with the return of the king and the lords to the Parliament Chamber, where the Lord Chancellor delivered a "worshipful sermon" (the Parliament Roll says "of the causes of summons"). Then the Chancellor, at the king's command, ordered the Commons to assemble to elect a Speaker. The Commons, accordingly, presented their Speaker before the king, lords and judges two days later.[7]

A much more detailed account survives of the opening of Henry VIII's first Parliament

Artist unknown, *Processional Roll* (detail), Trinity Manuscript 0.3.59, vellum, 1512. Trinity College, Cambridge.

in 1510. This is the earliest known of a series of written descriptions by the heralds. On this occasion, the Lords Spiritual and Temporal assembled in the queen's great chamber, before joining the procession to Westminster Abbey, which was headed by the esquires, knights and young lords. After them came the abbots and bishops, with the heralds on either side, the dean and almoner, and Garter King of Arms. Next came the Duke of Buckingham, as Lord High Constable, bearing the Cap of Estate or Maintenance, and his eldest son bearing the Sword of State, with serjeants-at-arms and gentlemen ushers on either side, directly in front of the king. The king's train was borne by the Lord Chamberlain, assisted by the Chamberlain of the Household. All the Lords temporal followed on behind the king. The 1510 account is the first to mention that the king was met outside the abbey by the abbot and the chapter, and "took his sceptre and went under the canopy as accustomed" into the church. There the king sat in his traverse (enclosed pew) at the south end of the high altar, the temporal lords sitting in their stalls on the north side and the spiritual lords on the south side. After mass, the king processed out of the abbey under the canopy and on to the Parliament Chamber.[8] A heraldic roll depicts a similar opening procession in 1512 (omitting those preceding the abbots), with the king carrying a sceptre and walking under a canopy carried by four tonsured monks.[9]

After a fire in 1512, the Palace of Westminster ceased to be a royal residence,[10] and the opening of the 1523 and 1529 Parliaments took place in Bridewell Palace with a service in

Blackfriars Church.[11] A herald's picture of the Parliament Chamber at the 1523 opening shows one earl standing on the king's right hand, holding the Cap of Maintenance, with two earls standing on the left, one with the Sword of State and the other with the Earl Marshal's baton. The Cap and the Sword are in the same positions in which they are held today. The Lords spiritual sit in order on benches to the right of the king, and the Lords temporal to his left. The judges and serjeants-at-law occupy four woolsacks in the centre, the Clerk of the Crown and the Clerk of the Parliaments kneel behind, writing the record, and the Commons stand at the Bar of the House, the Speaker in the centre.[12]

The acquisition of York Palace (later Whitehall Palace) in 1529 gave the king a new and more convenient residence only a few hundred yards from the Palace of Westminster.[13] On the day of the 1536 opening, the king and the Lords rode from York Palace to the Palace of Westminster. There, in the Parliament Chamber, they put on their Parliament Robes before processing to the abbey for mass. On their return to the palace, Parliament was opened in the White Chamber, or House of Lords, instead of in the Painted Chamber as before. Thus began, with occasional deviations, the regular practice of opening Parliament in the upper House (or House of Lords), which continues to the present day.[14]

The procession at the opening of the 1539 Parliament was the first to go directly from the Palace of Whitehall to Westminster Abbey, the Lords temporal following the king, in order of precedence, "on horseback in their robes". The longer route for the robed procession made it much more of a spectacle for the public.[15] The procession in 1545 was notable for a permanent change in the order, with the Lords Temporal preceding the king, the barons before the bishops, and the rest following after them. This placed the monarch at the apogee of the procession.[16]

The procession to the abbey for the State Opening of Edward VI's first Parliament in 1547 was in the same order as in 1545, except that the Lord Protector Somerset went alone, directly in front of King Edward, and the Master of the Horse followed behind with "all the rest of the privy chamber". On returning to the Palace of Westminster, the king waited in his privy chamber until the Lords had taken their places. After the Lord Chancellor's oration, the king, "all noble officers" and the other noblemen withdrew to the privy chamber, and the sovereign was then escorted to the royal barge, in which he travelled to the Palace of Whitehall to wait until the Commons had chosen their Speaker.[17] Monarchs quite often went to and returned from State Openings by barge after this time.

The usual procession took place at the opening of Mary Tudor's five Parliaments. Both Queen Mary and King Philip attended the opening of the third Parliament on 12 November 1554. The king rode on horseback and the queen "in a sort of litter, open so as to expose her to the public view", a Cap of Maintenance and a Sword of State being carried before each of them. A foreign observer estimated that the participants and onlookers numbered twenty thousand.[18]

The main innovation at the opening of Queen Elizabeth's first Parliament on 25 January 1559 was that the Master of the Horse, bearing the queen's train, was followed by the "ladyes and gentillwomen according their degrees", on horseback. The Mantuan agent in London described the procession as being "neither more nor less than on the entry into London, with trumpets, kings-at-arms, heralds and macebearers".[19]

In 1571 the queen rode to the abbey, not on horseback, but in a "rich coach with a canopye very rich over her with foure pillars" and "drawne by two palfreies covered with crimson velvet, drawne out, imbossed and imbroidered very richly". On returning to the Parliament Chamber, the queen stood up and spoke a few introductory words before calling on the Lord Keeper to speak.[20]

For the 1572 opening of Parliament, the queen boarded the royal barge at Whitehall Palace and was rowed to the Queen's Bridge (the landing-stage) at Westminster. There, the coach was waiting to take her to the abbey in the usual procession. Afterwards, on entering the Parliament Chamber, the queen was preceded by noblemen carrying the royal regalia, with Garter King of Arms and "gentleman hushers goinge before to make place" as far as the throne.[21]

In 1584, the magnificent procession started from St James's Palace. The queen's sedan chair, carried by two white horses, had two small silver pillars at the back, supporting a rich covering surmounted by a crown of gold; at the front, on two pillars by the queen's feet, stood a lion and a dragon, "glistering with Gold, made with wonderfull cunning, supporting the Queenes Armes". After the abbey service there was the usual return to the Parliament Chamber, described by a German visitor, Lupold von Wedel, as:

> a separate chamber, on the platform of which was a splendid canopy of gold stuff and velvet, embroidered with gold, silver and pearls, and below it a throne, arranged with royal splendours, on which the Queen seated herself. The benches in this chamber had their seats as well as the backs covered with red silk, in the midst four woolsacks of red cloth were laid square. The walls were entirely hung with royal tapestry.[22]

Similarly elaborate processions took place in 1589, 1597 and 1601. For the last of these, it was noted that the "Westminster Streetes was hanged with Arres Tapestrye and other rich stuff, such as the inhabitants had to furnish the Streets as her Highness passed". In 1597 and 1601, the swearing-in of the Commons was bungled so that many Members were unable to enter the Parliament Chamber before the doors were shut.[23]

### Early Stuart State Openings (1603–49)

The procession from Whitehall Palace to Westminster Abbey, the service in the abbey, and the procession from the abbey to Parliament House all continued in elaborate style until 1640. In 1614, James I, on horseback, wore a crimson velvet cape, lavishly trimmed and lined with ermine, and a jewelled crown on his head. Prince Charles rode in front of the peers, who were carrying the Cap of Maintenance and Sword of State. In 1624, the king proceeded to Parliament "in great state in a chariot of crimson velvet". To hold back the crowds, the streets were railed on both sides from Whitehall to the abbey. Sometimes, as at the opening of the Long Parliament on 3 November 1640, the king proceeded to Parliament by barge, to avoid the crowds and the danger of plague. On such occasions he was met at the Parliament steps by the judges, lords and bishops, and processed with them through Westminster Hall and the Court of Requests to the abbey.[24]

During the Tudor period, it had not been the usual practice for the sovereign to speak at the State Opening proceedings in the Parliament Chamber. The speech on the cause of summons was delivered by the Lord Chancellor or Lord Keeper, phrased as though it were his speech although it was understood to reflect royal views. The situation changed with the accession of James I, who often delivered long speeches himself, sometimes entirely dispensing with the services of a spokesman. Initially, Charles I reverted to the traditional practice and generally remained silent while the speech was delivered by the Lord Chancellor or Keeper. Later in his reign, however, he intervened, and thereafter spoke with increasing frequency.[25]

## State Openings During the Commonwealth (1649–60)

The ceremony of the State Opening lapsed after the opening of the Long Parliament in 1640 and the abolition of the House of Lords in 1649. Much of the ceremonial was, however, revived for the opening of Oliver Cromwell's 'other House' on 20 January 1658.[26] Cromwell came by water from Whitehall to Westminster and thence by coach to the palace, "in great pomp". Other coaches followed, along with some magnificent horses, unmounted, "adorned with superb saddles and cloths, majestic for the gold and jewels they contained", with the usual guards on horse and foot. A large crowd assembled out of curiosity to watch the procession. When Cromwell, "His Highnes", was seated in his "Chayre of State" and the 'Lords' were in their places, Black Rod was sent to summon the Commons. After they had come to the Bar with the Speaker, Cromwell delivered a speech, followed by Nathaniel Fiennes, one of the Lords commissioners of the Great Seal. The Commons then returned to their House.[27]

For the opening of Parliament on 27 January 1659, the Protector, Richard Cromwell, the 'Lords' and some of the Commons attended a service in Westminster Abbey. When the Protector and 'Lords' had returned to the Parliament Chamber and were all in their places, Black Rod was sent to summon the Commons, but some one hundred and fifty Members refused to attend and to recognize the 'other House'. The Protector made a "very handsome speech", followed by "Lord Keeper Fiennes", and the Commons then withdrew.[28]

## Late Stuart State Openings (1660–1714)

After the restoration of the monarchy in 1660, the full State Opening ceremony was itself restored with the opening of the Cavalier Parliament on 8 May 1661. At seven in the morn-

Anon., *The Most Magnificent Riding of Charles II to the Parliament*, engraving, published in *London Prospects*, V, *c.* 1670, f. 24. Harley Collection, The Society of Antiquaries of London.

ing, the Lord High Steward administered the Oaths of Supremacy and Allegiance to members of the Commons in the Court of Requests ("a place anciently used for that purpose"). In the meantime, King Charles II, wearing the 'imperial crown', and the Lords Temporal in their robes rode to Westminster Abbey. The procession was composed of the same elements as in 1640 except for the Lords spiritual, who did not return to the upper House until November 1661. In the abbey, a "learned Sermon" was preached by the Bishop of Bristol. The procession then returned to the House of Lords, where the peers sat in their accustomed order, except that the king's brothers sat immediately to the left of the Chair of State, and Prince Rupert, as Duke of Cumberland, occupied the first place on the ducal bench. After the Commons had been summoned by Black Rod, Charles II made a "most gracious speech" which was seconded by the Lord Chancellor. The Commons were then dismissed to choose their Speaker.[29]

For his second Parliament, in 1679, Charles II was advised for safety reasons (presumably for fear of the Popish Plot) not to ride in procession to Parliament or to attend a service in the abbey. From this time, the searching of the vaults by the Yeomen of the Guard became a regular ceremony before each State Opening.[30] The Westminster Abbey service appears to have been abandoned permanently, although the procession continued in a modified form. Queen Anne is said to have travelled to a State Opening in a sedan chair. With the expansion of the peerage from the late seventeenth century onwards, the practice of all the peers participating in the procession was dropped, and only the more important Members and Great Officers of State took part. Gold-Stick-in-Waiting was introduced into the procession as being personally responsible for the safety of the sovereign.[31]

Until 1679, Charles II usually made short introductory speeches that were expanded by his spokesman. In that year, the spokesman's speech was discontinued, and thereafter the only speech delivered when the sovereign was present was his own. The exceptions were George I's speeches, which, because of his poor English, were all read for him by the Lord

Thompson after E. Pugh, *The Houses of Parliament with the Royal Procession*, engraving, published by Richard Phillip, 20 April 1804. Palace of Westminster (WOA 1333).

Chancellor, and Queen Victoria's, after the death of the Prince Consort in 1861, again read by the Lord Chancellor. Until 1660, it had been the usual practice for the speech declaring the causes of summons to be delivered only at the opening of a new Parliament and not a new session. Since 1660, however, it has been the invariable practice for every session of Parliament to be opened with a speech.[32]

### Hanoverian State Openings (1714–1837)

George I and George II were assiduous in attending the State Opening, as was George III until 1805. For the State Opening on 25 November 1762, George III rode to Parliament in his new, lavishly decorated and gilded State Coach. The crowds that assembled to see the King were greater than at his coronation. An onlooker in 1776 described "the elegant state coach, which is glazed all around and the body elegantly gilt, with a gilt crown on the top ... drawn by 8 dun horses, the finest I ever saw". There was an "amazing string of coaches" and a "vast crowd of spectators in the streets and in the windows of the houses, of ladies richly dressed, and the groupe of figures from the first gentleman to the lowest link-boy was very picturesque". All this "exhibited an idea of the grandeur and importance of a British Monarch".[33] It was while travelling in this coach for the opening of Parliament in 1795 that George III was attacked by a mob clamouring for bread and peace (see illus., p. 39).[34] There were complaints throughout the eighteenth century of the Lords Chamber being crowded with strangers at the State Opening. In 1720 it was ordered that, prior to the king's arrival, all doors leading to the Lords Chamber should be shut to the general public, and none should be admitted except peers, their eldest sons and assistants. Entry was also granted to foreign ministers and dignitaries authorized by the Lord Great Chamberlain, and certain ladies and gentlemen previously nominated by peers. The foreign dignitaries tended to crowd around the steps of the throne, and George III was said to have had difficulty in getting to it "through the multitude which surrounds it".[35]

James Gillray, *The Republican-Attack*, coloured engraving, published by H Humphrey, 1 November 1795. When the king drove to open Parliament on 2 October 1795, the state coach was attacked by a mob. Lord Lansdowne accused government ministers of provoking the disturbance for their own ends. This caricature shows the king sitting impassively in the coach whilst Britannia lies prostrate on the ground on the right. A number of political figures are also shown: William Pitt the Younger is the coachman, Charles James Fox and Richard Brinsley Sheridan run along side the coach brandishing clubs, and Lansdowne himself is shown firing a blunderbuss through the coach window (for further information see M.D. George, *Catalogue of Political and Personal Satires*, VII, no. 8681, London, photolithe edition, 1978, p. 196). Department of Prints and Drawings, The British Museum, London.

The REPUBLICAN-ATTACK.

George IV, as Regent, opened Parliament five times between 1812 and 1819.[36] It was not, however, until his accession in 1820 that he was able to demonstrate his sense of theatre and a taste for extravagant pageantry. Sir John Soane, at the king's command, carried out improvements to the old palace that included a new Royal Entrance to the House of Lords, with a staircase (the Scala Regia) leading to the Prince's Chamber and thence into the Royal Gallery, which was connected with the Painted Chamber, the King's Robing Room and the Lords Chamber (since 1801 the former Court of Requests). In March 1824, Soane announced that "The approach for His Majesty to the House of Lords is completed".[37]

In 1820, for his first State Opening as king, George IV altered the traditional processional route that ran from St James's Park to Westminster. George IV's procession started at Carlton House and proceeded down the Mall, through Cockspur Street, Charing Cross and Whitehall, so providing greater opportunities for people to line the route and enjoy the spectacle. The king, reported *The Times*, was cheered "both in going and returning". A detachment of the Coldstream Guards, with a band, was stationed by the entrance to the House of Lords. So many peers wished to attend that, an hour before the palace doors were opened, the line of their carriages reached the end of Parliament Street; and the ladies canvassed for seats in the Chamber. George IV tried to keep up the momentum of this popular enthusiasm by making the annual State Opening and prorogation of Parliament equally spectacular. In 1821 and 1822, however, he was greeted with less enthusiasm, and in the latter year "there was an unusually great display of military", including a squadron of the Blues in Pall Mall and the first regiment of Life Guards, who lined the route inside the Palace of Westminster. George IV did not open a Parliament in person after 1826.[38]

William IV was more assiduous than his brother in attending State Openings, missing only the opening of the final session of his reign on 31 January 1837. William's appearances were greeted with great enthusiasm from crowds both outside and within the palace. His arrival at the palace was heralded by the firing of a cannon, as is The Queen's today. There was a fanfare of trumpets as William entered the Lords Chamber, and the peers, peeresses and others rose and bowed or curtsied, again as happens today.[39]

A private account of the State Opening of 1833 describes the procession of five coaches leaving St James's Palace at half past two in the afternoon, the first four carrying members of the Royal Household, Gold Stick (the Commander of the Forces), the Master of the Robes and the Lord-in-Waiting. The fifth was the State Coach, "drawn by eight cream coloured

Hanoverian horses", which contained the king, the Master of the Horse and the Groom of the Stole. The liveries, horses and caparisons were "magnificent" and the route was lined by "dense multitudes". On his arrival at the Royal Entrance, the king was received by the Chancellor and other ministers, with the "Band of the Scots Fuzileer Guards playing 'the Garb of Old Gaul'". The route through the Royal and Painted Chambers to the Robing Room was lined by the "bright helmets and breast plates of the Horse Guards", which together with the "splendid drapes of the Heralds and other attendants, the clang of trumpets and the plaudits of many well dressed females" had "a most imposing effect". On entering the Robing Room, the king was robed by the Master of the Robes and received the crown from the Lord-in-Waiting. Thus arrayed, "like Solomon in all his glory", William IV entered the Lords Chamber and "read his speech with great distinctness".[40]

## Victorian State Openings (1837–1901)

At the beginning of her reign, Queen Victoria was as conscientious as her predecessor in attending the State Opening. Between 1837 and the death of Prince Albert in 1861, she missed the opening ceremony on only four occasions, each time because of pregnancy. From 1840 until 1861 the queen was regularly accompanied by Prince Albert. After a brief dispute, it was decided that Albert had the right to ride in the queen's carriage to Parliament and to sit by her side in the House of Lords on a Chair of State, especially built for him.[41]

The queen, at her first State Opening in 1837, travelled from Buckingham Palace in George III's gold State Coach, accompanied by her mother, the Duchess of Kent. They were watched by large and enthusiastic crowds. On alighting from the coach she was met by the Great Officers of State, the Prime Minister (Lord Melbourne), Black Rod and Richmond Herald deputizing for Garter King of Arms. They proceeded in the usual manner to the Robing Room and then to the House of Lords (the Painted Chamber, used as a temporary Lords Chamber between 1835 and 1847). Within the Lords Chamber, the Earl of Shaftesbury – with the Cap of Maintenance – the Lord Chancellor, the Earl Marshal and the Duke of Somerset – bearing the crown on a cushion – stood on the queen's right. On her left were Lord Melbourne, holding the Sword of State, and members of the Household. The Duchesses of Kent and Sutherland stood behind the throne, and the queen's uncles, the Dukes of Cambridge and of Sussex, at the foot.[42]

The Royal Procession from the Robing Room to the Lords Chamber followed very much the same order in the 1840s as it does today. It was led by the pursuivants and heralds, followed by the gentlemen ushers and equerries, household officers, more heralds, the Lord Privy Seal and the Lord President, the Lord Chancellor, Black Rod and Garter King of Arms (flanked by the serjeants-at-arms with their silver-gilt maces). The Earl Marshal, the Lord Great Chamberlain, the Sword of State and the Cap of Maintenance were directly in front of the queen, who was followed by the Mistress of the Robes and the Lady-in-Waiting, the Lord Steward, Gold Stick and the Master of the Horse, the Lord-in-Waiting, the Page of Honour, the Groom of the Stole and the Lord-in-Waiting to Prince Albert, the Captains of the Yeomen of the Guard and of the Corps of Gentlemen-at-Arms, the field officers of the guard on duty and the gentlemen-at-arms.[43]

Barry's Royal Approach in the new palace – the Royal Staircase, the Queen's Robing Room and Royal Gallery – was first used when Queen Victoria opened Parliament in February 1852. It was in that year also that the queen purchased, in Dublin, the Irish State Coach, which is still used at State Openings today. Thousands lined the route as the queen and Prince Albert drove in procession from Buckingham Palace along the Mall, Whitehall and

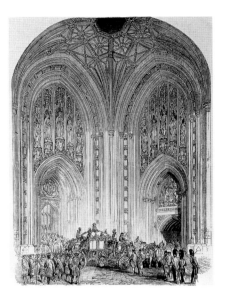

*New House of Lords. – Her Majesty's Arrival at Victoria Tower*, wood-engraving, published in *Illustrated London News*, XX, no. 544, 7 February 1852, p. 120. Palace of Westminster (WOA 2015).

*Opening of Parliament – The Royal Staircase, Victoria Tower: Her Majesty's Arrival*, wood-engraving, published in *Illustrated London News*, XX, no. 544, 7 February 1852, title page. Palace of Westminster (WOA 5012).

Parliament Street. On alighting from the coach under the Victoria Tower, she was received by the Great Officers of State, the Duke of Wellington, Garter and the Yeoman Usher of the Black Rod. The procession mounted the stairs on the north side of the tower to the Norman Porch, and then turned right into the Robing Room. Having robed, the queen processed through the Royal Gallery, with the Duke of Wellington carrying the Sword of State, the Earl of Albermarle the Cap of Maintenance and the Marquess of Normanby the crown. As today, the gentlemen-at-arms were already stationed in the Prince's Chamber before the queen passed through it into the Lords Chamber. Within the Lords Chamber, Prince Albert sat on a Chair of State to the left of the queen. The Commons having been summoned, the Lord Chancellor, as today, advanced to the throne, knelt and delivered the Royal Speech to the queen, who read it "in a clear and distinct voice".[44]

After Prince Albert's death in 1861, Queen Victoria did not open Parliament again until February 1866. She now refused to appear in state: "there were no trumpet fanfares, there was no pageantry, there were no gingerbread coaches or royal robes." Instead, the queen wore a widow's cap, a black dress and a long veil. She nodded to the Lord Chancellor, who read the speech on her behalf while "she sat expressionless as if she did not hear a sound". The Prince of Wales sat at the queen's right hand. On six subsequent occasions, the last in 1886, the precedent of 1866 was followed and the old pageantry was omitted.[45]

A conspicuous feature of State Openings in the time of Queen Victoria, as in the time of her two predecessors, was the presence of a large number of ladies seated in the Lords Chamber, the peeresses in full state robes. It was said that, early in the nineteenth century, "the number of ladies even exceeded that of peers, usually amounting to 200 or 300, stationing themselves along the side galleries and on the rows of benches on either side of the floor, excepting only the government front bench". In 1852, *The Times* remarked that "one might

*The Opening of the New Parliament by the Queen – The Royal Procession Crossing the Prince's Chamber on the Way to the House of Peers*, wood-engraving, published in *The Graphic*, 30 January 1886, pp. 116–17. Palace of Westminster (WOA 7003).

The State Carriage of King Edward VII and Queen Alexandra at the State Opening of Parliament, 14 February 1901. Benjamin Stone collection, Birmingham Library Services.

The arrival of the Royal Carriages at the State Opening of Parliament, 16 February 1909. Benjamin Stone collection, Birmingham Library Services.

suppose that a House of Peeresses had been added to the institutions of the country, and the half-hundred elderly gentlemen in robes of scarlet and ermine who occupied the front bench sat as assessors to a female Parliament". While ladies-in-waiting had been present at the State Openings of Elizabeth I and, in the eighteenth century, peeresses and other ladies had obtained orders of admission from the Lord Great Chamberlain, they did not appear in such numbers as in the nineteenth century. Pictures of the State Opening by Alexander Blaikley in 1845 (see illus., p. 183) and by Joseph Nash in the 1850s show the House almost exclusively occupied by ladies at State Openings of that time, peers having given up their customary places in the Lords Chamber to their wives, daughters and other ladies.[46]

## Twentieth-Century State Openings

The accession of Edward VII in 1901, like that of George IV, marked the revival of the traditional grand ceremonial at the State Opening of Parliament. Like George IV, the new king had a taste for pageantry. *The Times* noted that "the chamber was thronged by a vast assemblage of peers in their robes and peeresses in mourning attire", while on the processional route from Buckingham Palace "immense crowds of people had gathered, long before the hour fixed for the starting of the procession". Their majesties "were greeted with a roar of cheers … along the whole route" from "vast and orderly crowds". The only complaint was that the Lords Chamber was so crowded, because of the large number of peeresses who came, that Members of the House of Commons had great difficulty in finding room to stand where they could see or even hear the Royal Speech, and there was "an unseemly scramble" when Black Rod summoned them.[47] Such 'unseemly' scrambles of the Commons when summoned to the Lords had occurred quite often since the later Parliaments of Elizabeth I.[48]

After S. Begg, *Parliament Prorogued on the Friday and Reopened on the Monday: The Regal Ceremony at Westminster*, half-tone print, published in *Illustrated London News*, CXCII, no. 3856, 15 March 1913, pp. 334–35. Palace of Westminster (WOA 4062). The print shows George V and Queen Mary entering the Lords Chamber from the Prince's Chamber, Palace of Westminster (WOA 7044).

A joint select committee was set up in 1901 to investigate this and other problems that arose at State Openings. Evidence was taken from two Members who claimed to have been injured (one knocked to the ground) in the rush to get to the Lords, and from other Members and officials of both Houses. The joint committee recommended that room for more seating should be created on the floor of the Lords Chamber, that seats in the Strangers' Gallery and in other galleries in the Lords Chamber should be reserved for Members of the House of Commons, and that the Royal Gallery should be fitted up so as to allow peeresses who could not be accommodated in the Lords Chamber, as well as the wives of Members of the Commons, to view the Royal Procession on its way from the Robing Room.[49] Since that time, the procession of Members to the Bar of the House of Lords to hear the King or Queen's Speech has been comparatively orderly in nature.

Edward VII opened every session in person until his death in 1910, and his son and successive monarchs have since maintained the tradition almost without a break. Since Edward VII's time, the Royal Speech has again been read by the monarch in person.[50]

At present-day State Openings, The Queen, who may be accompanied by members of her immediate family, leaves Buckingham Palace in the Irish State Coach. Other coaches carrying members of the Royal Household precede the State Coach, and there is an escort of mounted Household Cavalry. The State Coach turns in under the Royal Entrance of the Victoria Tower, where The Queen is received by the Earl Marshal and the Lord Great Chamberlain, who are attended by the heralds. As The Queen moves up the steps leading to the Norman Porch, a signal is sent to the top of the Victoria Tower, where the Royal Standard is broken on the flagpole, and salutes are fired in Hyde Park and at the Tower of London. The staircase is lined by members of the Household Cavalry, and The Queen's procession is preceded by the Lord Great Chamberlain, walking backwards so that he faces The Queen, and holding his white wand. At the top of the staircase, The Queen turns to the right and enters the Robing Room. As already mentioned, the Royal Procession from the Robing Room to the Lords Chamber is in very much the same order as in the 1840s. The principal differences are that The Queen wears the crown rather than it being carried before her, four Pages of Honour follow immediately behind The Queen (there is no Groom of the Stole); next come the Captains of the Yeoman of the Guard and Gentlemen-at-Arms (the Chief and Assistant Government Whips in the House of Lords), then the Chief of the Defence Staff, the Comptroller of the Lord Chamberlain's Office, and the Field-Officer-in-Brigade-Waiting. The Lieutenant of the Yeoman of the Guard and his opposite number in the Corps of Gentlemen-at-Arms take up the rear of the procession. The Yeomen of the Guard line the processional route.

As The Queen enters the Lords Chamber, the lights of the House, which have been dimmed, are turned up in a theatrical manner. If attending, the Duke of Edinburgh sits on a throne on The Queen's left, Prince Charles on the Prince of Wales's Chair of State, and Princess Anne on the other Chair of State, both of which stand below the two central thrones. The Great Officers stand in their customary places, the Mistress of the Robes and Ladies of the Bedchamber stand behind the throne on the left, and the pages stand on the right. The Commons are summoned by Black Rod to the Bar of the House, and when they arrive, the Lord Chancellor ascends the steps of the throne, withdraws the Royal Speech from his purse and hands it to The Queen. After the Speech, the procession returns to the Robing Room in the order in which it came, and The Queen is escorted to the Irish State Coach as before.[51]

## Presenting the Speaker

The other ceremonies at which the sovereign was present or was represented by commissioners did not involve a procession on the scale of the day of the State Opening, nor any service or ceremony in Westminster Abbey. Nevertheless, the sovereign was crowned and robed, and the peers would wear their Parliament Robes on such occasions, the Great Officers of State bearing the regalia before the sovereign on entry into the House. This occurred at the Commons' presentation of the Speaker for royal approval at the Bar of the House of Lords. The Speaker, on these occasions, made a disabling speech expressing his unworthiness for the office, which was answered by the Lord Chancellor, speaking in the king's name and expressing royal approval of the Commons' choice.[52] The last occasion on which the monarch personally participated in the election of the Speaker was in 1790, since which time the direction to the Commons to elect a Speaker and the approval of their choice has been carried out by commissioners, robed and seated in front of the throne.[53]

## The Royal Assent

Another occasion on which the sovereign used to be present was at the giving of the royal assent to bills. Originally, this occurred only on the final day of the session. During the sixteenth century, royal assent was sometimes given on other occasions, and in 1542, for the first time, Henry VIII delegated the giving of the royal assent (in this case for the Bill for the Attainder of Katharine Howard) to commissioners. Since 1660 it has been the established practice for royal assent to be given at regular intervals during the session. After 1764, George III increasingly delegated this function to commissioners, and George IV, William IV and Queen Victoria each gave royal assent in person only once apart from at prorogations, the last occasion being in 1837.

At a commission, the Lord Chancellor and the other commissioners, sitting in front of the throne, order Black Rod to summon the Commons to the Bar of the House. The Speaker and a group of ministers, and members of other parties, come to the Bar. The Clerk of the Crown reads the title of each bill, and the Clerk of the Parliaments gives the royal assent in Norman French. In 1967, however, provision was made for the royal assent to bills to be notified to the two Houses, sitting separately, by their respective Speakers, and this is now the normal practice, except at prorogation.[54]

## The Prorogation of Parliament

The prorogation of Parliament on the final day of the session originally consisted of four main elements. First, the Speaker made his speech, which was chiefly concerned with the subsidy bill that he had brought up from the Commons. This was followed by a speech from the Lord Chancellor or Keeper replying to the points made by the Speaker and expressing thanks for the subsidy. The royal assent was then given to the bills passed by both Houses. Finally the Lord Chancellor, in obedience to the instructions of the sovereign, either prorogued or dissolved Parliament. The monarch was customarily present on these occasions. From the seventeenth century onwards, the sovereign usually made the speech before prorogation or dissolution.[55]

In the early nineteenth century the prorogation was still accompanied with considerable ceremony, as in 1815 when the Prince Regent rode in the State Coach with an escort of cavalry through St James's Park to the Palace of Westminster, where his arrival was announced by a salute of cannon. In the Lords Chamber, the peers were dressed in full robes, with a number of peeresses and other ladies in full dress. The Commons were summoned by Black Rod, and the usual speeches by the Speaker and the Regent, and prorogation by the Lord Chancellor, followed. The Regent then retired, disrobed and returned to Carlton House.[56] George IV and William IV often attended prorogations.

In 1837, Queen Victoria rode in her robes of state and her elegant carriage to prorogue the last Parliament of William IV, watched by large crowds. In response to the Speaker's speech she read the prorogation speech "in a clear and unfaltering tone". In the 1840s, the procession from the Royal Entrance to the Robing Room and thence to the Lords Chamber appears to have been identical in composition to that at State Openings. Victoria continued to prorogue Parliament regularly until 1854, after which she ceased to attend, allegedly because she disliked the ceremony. This was the last occasion on which the sovereign prorogued Parliament or gave the royal assent in person. It was also the last time the Speaker made a speech at prorogation.[57]

From 1855, a prorogation speech, prepared by the cabinet, was read by the Lord Chancellor, and in 1867 Disraeli introduced the custom of having the Lord Chancellor read the prorogation address in the first person, as if the queen were speaking the words herself. By the early twentieth century, the proceedings were said to be purely formal and "only participated in by a handful of legislators who have been detained reluctantly at their posts by business or official duties". In recent decades, when Parliament has met all the year round, the prorogation of one session has usually been followed by the opening of a new session of Parliament only a few days later.[58]

Elizabeth II opening Parliament, 24 November 1998. Photograph by Terry Moore. The photograph shows The Queen seated on the throne in the Lords Chamber, with Charles, Prince of Wales seated on her right.

# 3

## The Medieval Palace of Westminster

John Goodall

On the night of 16 October 1834, the banks of the Thames were lined with a great crowd watching a fire consume the old Palace of Westminster. The blaze was first noticed at about seven o'clock in the evening, and it quickly took hold, helped by the circumstance of an unusually low tide, which made it difficult for the firefighters to collect water from the Thames. "The spectacle", wrote the *Times* correspondent, "was one of surpassing though terrific splendour ... through a vista of flaming walls you beheld the Abbey frowning in melancholy pride over its defaced and shattered neighbours." By two in the morning the fire had spent much of its ferocity, but it had left the heart of the palace a gutted wreck: "nothing met the eye but an unsightly ruin, tinted with dark red glare from the smouldering embers at its feet."[1]

For those familiar with Westminster today, it is all too easy to see this great fire as the defining moment in the history of the palace, when its ancient buildings were all but swept away and the present purpose-built seat of Great Britain's modern Parliamentary state rose like a phoenix from their ashes. But the fire of 1834, destructive as it was, was simply the most recent and best-documented of a whole series of disastrous fires suffered by the palace in its long history. And the subsequent rebuilding, which re-incorporated such structures as the Great Hall of the medieval complex, is only one of a catalogue of vastly ambitious projects that have sought to recast the palace architecturally. Indeed, the modern Palace of Westminster, despite its predominantly Victorian exterior, is – in a very real sense – the product of nearly one thousand years of architectural development as a centre of government and a royal residence.

Westminster Palace stands on the north bank of the River Thames along the foreshore of Thorney Island, a low eminence in the river flood plain, defined on its landward sides by streams of the tributary Tyburn. The establishment of a major royal residence on this narrow and marshy site is bound up with the early medieval history of London, and the foundation of the great abbey church of Westminster. [2] From the late third century, the Roman city of London fell into gradual decline, and during the Anglo-Saxon period a new settlement was established outside the walls, along the river bank to the west of the city in the area of what is now the Strand. It was probably to serve this new Saxon settlement that a church, or minster, dedicated to St Peter, was first established on Thorney Island in the early eighth century. Credit for the foundation is usually given to the East Saxon king Offa, and his church became known as Westminster, to distinguish it from the city minster of St Paul to the east, now St Paul's Cathedral.

But the new Anglo-Saxon settlement of London was not to survive long. After taking London from the Danes in 887, King Alfred moved the population back into the Roman city,

Anonymous, *Seraph*, oil-based paint on panel, after 1263, originally in the ceiling of the Painted Chamber, Palace of Westminster, now in the British Museum, London. This is one of two panels, the other depicting a prophet, that recently came to light in Bristol. They were preserved only because shortly after their execution the medieval decorative bosses of the ceiling were affixed over them.

which he fortified as a burgh. The site of the former settlement then became known as the 'old city', or – in Anglo-Saxon – the old 'wyck', hence the modern name of Aldwych. Westminster stood isolated. Subsequent to the removal to London, Westminster might easily have passed into oblivion but for two circumstances. The first was its reform and reconstitution as a Benedictine abbey by St Dunstan in *c.* 960, and the second was its adoption as a royal church. It was this royal interest in the abbey – both as a burial place and a public expression of Christian kingship – that prompted the construction of a palace at Westminster, and the awkward site occupied by its buildings was dictated by the fact that the church and monastery already occupied the best land on the island.

The precise date at which a palace was first constructed at Westminster is a matter for speculation. That one twelfth-century writer described King Canute's celebrated dispute with the tide as occurring at Westminster may suggest that a royal residence existed there before his death in 1035; and the burial of King Harold I at Westminster just five years later, in 1040, might further corroborate this supposition.[3] Most modern authorities, however, agree that the palace was more probably founded by Edward the Confessor, a figure of exceptional importance in the subsequent history of Westminster. Edward, wrote an anonymous eleventh-century biographer, was drawn to favour the abbey because "it lay hard by the famous and rich town of London and also was a delightful spot, surrounded with fertile lands and green fields and near the main channel of the river, which bore abundant merchandise of wares of every kind for sale from the whole world to the town on its banks". As a special devotee of St Peter, continued the writer, Edward decided to be buried in the church, and he set about rebuilding it.[4] The new church he raised was a seminal work of architecture, by virtue both of its unprecedented size, and of its style as a Romanesque building of Norman inspiration, the first of its kind in England.[5]

Of the Confessor's palace that developed beside this splendid new church we know little. It would have taken the form of a collection of buildings, and these must have included a hall and a private chamber block for the king, both commonplaces of domestic design in the period. The latter is probably represented, alongside the new abbey church of Westminster, on the Bayeux Tapestry, although it cannot be taken for granted that the depiction is intended as a likeness or was even made by artists who had seen the palace. Although there is no evidence to prove it, it seems likely that Edward's buildings formed the core of the early medieval palace, and parts of them may even have survived unidentified and in remodelled form right into the nineteenth century. With these buildings there developed a sense of the prestige of Westminster as the principal royal residence and church of the English monarchy. That this sense was well established by Edward's death is vividly illustrated in the dramatic events surrounding the Norman Conquest of England.

Edward the Confessor died at Westminster, and his body was interred, as he had directed, in the abbey on 6 January 1066. On the same day and in the same place, despite the fact that no coronation had ever taken place there before, Harold was acclaimed and crowned king of England. Famously, William the Conqueror challenged Harold's right to the throne on the grounds that he was the promised and rightful heir of the Confessor. William's victory at Hastings won him the kingdom, and, significantly, it was again at Westminster, on Christmas Day 1066, that he was crowned. It was not an auspicious ceremony. At the acclamation, the guards outside the monastery, "hearing the great shout in a foreign tongue, took it for treachery and fired the neighbouring houses", and in the ensuing panic William sat in the sanctuary of the church, trembling violently on the throne.[6]

But as much as these events reflect the new-found political importance of Westminster, it should not be forgotten that they conspired to enhance it as well. Despite the social and governmental changes wrought by the Conquest, William thought of himself as the legitimate heir to the existing kingdom of England, not the creator of a new one. He desired to demonstrate the dynastic and political continuity to which he laid claim, and his adoption of his predecessor's palace and church at Westminster was one means of doing this. For William's successors, the burial of Edward the Confessor in the abbey was also of great significance. Edward was canonized nearly a century later, in 1161, and, as an ancestor of England's kings, with a shrine in the abbey immediately adjacent to their principal palace, he was to become the patron saint of the royal house, with remarkable and far-reaching consequences.

Although William did make alterations to the existing palace at Westminster, it seems likely that the first major post-Conquest addition to it was the construction of a new Great Hall by William Rufus between 1097 and 1099.[7] Great halls were an essential element of any nobleman's house in this period, as both a living and architectural focus to the whole. That at Westminster, built to accommodate the huge numbers that might attend major royal occasions, was a leviathan of a building, much larger than any comparable structure of the period or indeed any other hall ever built in England. Such is its length (over two hundred and forty feet) that it had to stand parallel to the river in order to fit along the narrow strip of land occupied by the palace, and, remarkably, it survives as the centrepiece of the present complex. The original architectural details of the building are now entirely obscured by later medieval alterations, but its dimensions are still apparent to the modern visitor, and its salient architectural features in the eleventh century may be reconstructed.[8]

The hall was entered through a central door in its north gable wall, an unusual arrangement dictated by the orientation of the building in relation to the river. This door was flanked on either side by a blind arch to create a three-part composition reminiscent of the main façades of large churches. Such an allusion was perhaps felt to be appropriate in a building that expressed the magnificence and power of an anointed king. Above these features was a decorative blind arcade, superimposed over a band of chequered masonry laid in contrasting blocks of Caen and Reigate stone. Internally, the building had a clerestory with a wall passage in front of it, set above high, windowless walls. There is no direct evidence for the original form of the roof, but it has been convincingly argued that, although the width of the hall is enormous by contemporary standards (sixty-eight feet), it may well have been covered, as it is today, in a single span.[9] Even to a twelfth-century generation, familiar with the vastly-conceived new cathedrals being erected all over England, the effect must have been astonishing.

William Rufus's hall gave Westminster an architectural pre-eminence over all other royal residences in England, but in practical terms the palace remained little different from any other. Since the court, its officials and all the instruments of government followed the king on an almost continuous itinerary, a particular residence was only of importance while he was staying there. But in the century following the construction of Rufus's hall, offices began to break away from the itinerant royal household and find a permanent home at Westminster. By the mid-twelfth century, in the course of Henry II's reign, the Exchequer came to be established there; and during the reign of his son John, the Treasury, which had previously settled at Winchester, followed suit. This gradual settlement of the mechanics of government at Westminster made it an increasingly important centre, even in the king's absence.[10]

There is little evidence about the development of the palace during the twelfth century. It is documented that Henry II spent lavishly on the buildings after they had fallen into ruin

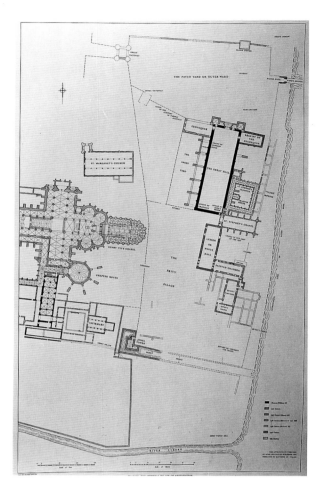

'Plan III: The Medieval Palace of Westminster', published in *The History of the King's Works: Plans*, published by HMSO in 1963. This plan shows the relationship of the abbey (left) and palace (right). The destruction of the Privy Palace after a fire in 1512 means we have little idea of how the residential buildings were arranged. Drawing Office, Ancient Monuments Branch, Ministry of Public Building and Works, London.

during the civil war of Stephen's reign, but in the absence of any physical remains the precise nature of his work is impossible to determine. It is usually supposed that he was responsible for constructing a smaller hall, entitled the White Hall, to the south of that erected by William Rufus, as well as a two-storey building – probably his chamber, which subsequently became the Painted Chamber – contiguous to this. Nineteenth-century surveys also suggest that the neighbouring Queen's Chamber stood on Romanesque foundations, so this may have belonged to Henry II's palace too. [11] Equally, however, these buildings may be earlier structures altogether that Henry remodelled. Indeed, it is perfectly possible that the White Hall was originally a building from the Confessor's palace. Whatever the case, the existence in the twelfth century of a Great and Lesser Hall, the latter presumably for everyday use, looks forward to a distinction that was to develop in the palace between its function as a residence on the one hand and as a public seat of government on the other.

This distinction between the public and residential was not really to come into its own, however, until the thirteenth century, when Westminster and its palace were transformed by the Plantagenet kings. The critical figure in bringing about this change was Henry III, who came to the throne in 1216 at the age of nine. In the course of his long reign, he undertook a series of important alterations to the palace, but these have to be understood in the context of a quite different undertaking, the reconstruction of Westminster Abbey from 1245. This task was unquestionably the single most remarkable architectural project of Henry's reign, and stands among the most lavish acts of patronage in English history. [12] It made manifest a new relationship between the palace and abbey that was to establish Westminster as the undisputed centre of royal government in England.

William Capon, *View of the Interior of the Painted Chamber, Looking East*, watercolour, 1799. Before the medieval wall paintings were exposed in 1819 the walls were hung with tapestries. Notice the wooden roof, formerly painted, and the bosses affixed to it. It was beneath two of these bosses that the surviving panels from the roof were found. The king's state bed stood at the far end of the chamber. The Society of Antiquaries of London.

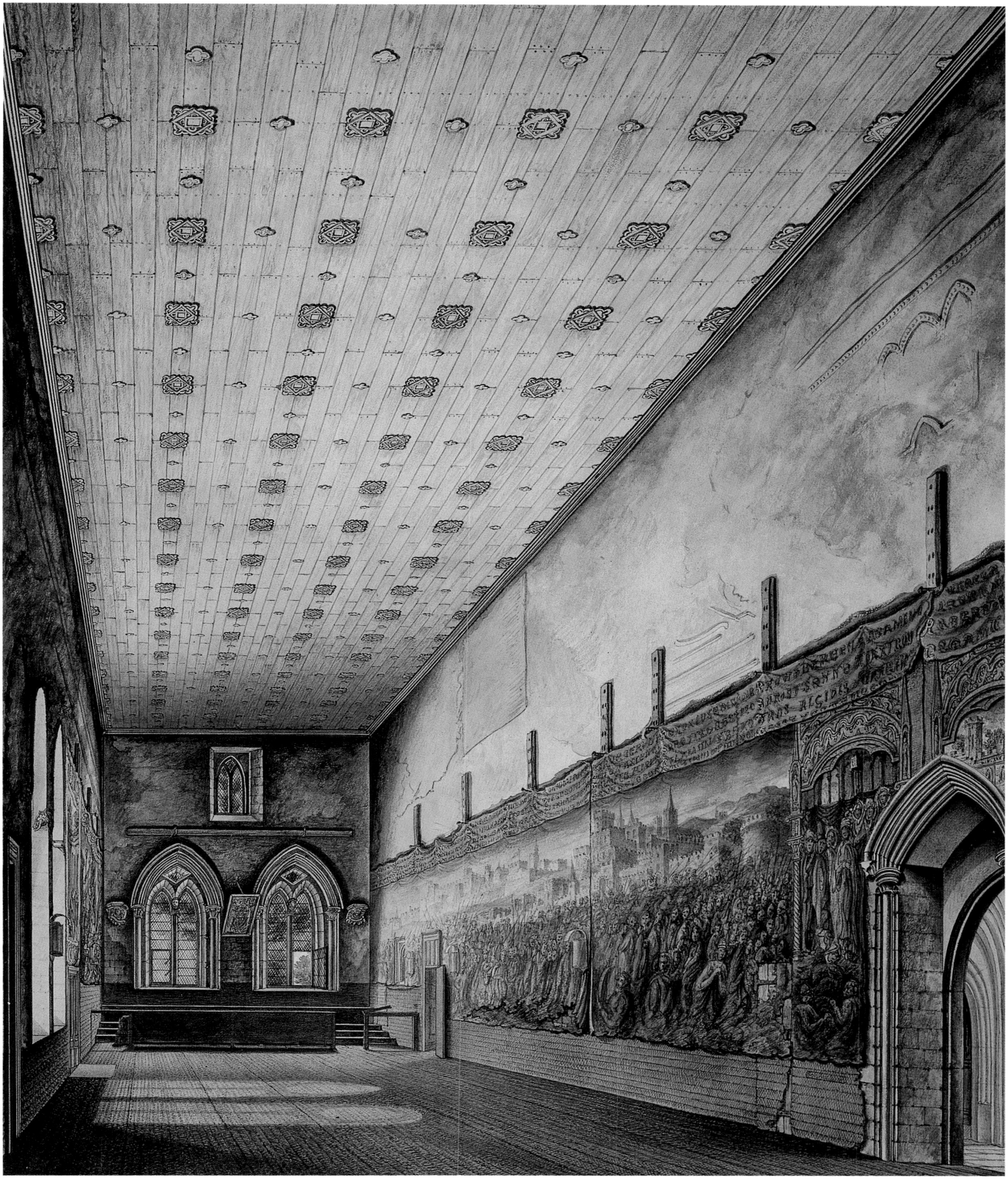

At the heart of this new relationship was the figure of St Edward the Confessor and his shrine in Westminster Abbey. Until Henry's reign, the cult of the Confessor seems to have attracted little attention, but upon his majority in 1228 the young king began to mark this saint out for particular devotion. Exactly what inspired him to do so is not clear, but as a supposed paragon of kingly virtue, and an ancestor, he was an ideal royal patron saint. Henry actively propagated the cult in order to bolster his authority, and bound it up inextricably with his own person and the exercise of his kingly office. Rebuilding Westminster Abbey and its shrine was a central element of Henry's identification with the Confessor. In undertaking it he not only honoured his forebear: he also, by extension, celebrated his own kingship, as well as the ritual that raised him to that dignity, the rite of coronation and anointing, which now customarily took place in the church.[13]

This architectural celebration of royal power also had one important side effect. Because the body of the Confessor was physically located at the coronation church of Westminster, it invested the palace there with a special significance as the principal royal residence in England. What Henry effectively created was a capital in which the temporal governance of the realm coexisted in one place with the spiritual forces that gave it legitimacy and authority. Other European monarchies in this period also associated themselves with dynastic saints and coronation churches, but in no case was the alliance of all three so ideologically or geographically coherent. Over time, it was strengthened by custom and underscored in new ways. In particular, from Henry III's reign onwards, it became the practice to bury kings in the abbey around the Confessor's shrine. Gradually, there came into existence a family tree of England's rulers, written in tombs and illustrated with the gilt effigies arranged around their ancestral saint. There exist few more immediate statements of

Charles Stothard after Master Walter of Durham?, *The Coronation of Edward the Confessor (Cest Le Coronement Seint Edeward)*, watercolour, 1819. This depiction of the Confessor's coronation, probably painted by Master Walter of Durham in 1266–67 and recorded by Stothard, was enclosed beneath the canopy of the king's state bed in the Painted Chamber. The quatrefoil to the right is the chapel squint. The Society of Antiquaries of London.

dynastic pretension and power.

Henry III's development of the palace adjacent to the abbey reflected the particular importance of Westminster to the king. None of the buildings Henry created now remain, but three of the most splendid apartments, all clustered together to the east of the lesser hall, survived into the nineteenth century and are well documented. These were the Queen's Chapel, the Queen's Chamber and the King's Chamber, a remodelling of the one attributed to Henry II. Of these, it is the last that has attracted the greatest scholarly attention. The King's Chamber, known from the fourteenth century onwards as the Painted Chamber, was a long and narrow room, which housed a state bed at one end. It served as a reception room and was chiefly remarkable for the sequence of paintings that covered its walls. Henry III first began work on the chamber in the 1220s and 1230s, but a serious fire in 1263 destroyed the original decoration, and it had to be reworked. Several later kings also made additions to its painted murals.[14]

Something of the spectacular richness of the interior of the Painted Chamber may be gleaned both from records and from a few surviving elements of its decoration. Nineteenth-century records show that the state bed stood against the wall and was guarded to one side by the painted figure of an armed sentry. Enclosed within the canopy of the bed was a depiction of the coronation of Edward the Confessor, and also a squint, which gave a view into an adjacent chapel. The ceiling of the Painted Chamber was painted, and studded with brightly coloured bosses. Two fragments from the ceiling, depicting a seraph and a prophet, have recently been rediscovered, and these testify to the quality of the other lost paintings (see illus., p. 48).[15] Depicted around the walls were a series of Old Testament stories with explanatory texts. These were executed in sequentially wider bands from the ground upwards, a feature presumably intended to facilitate their legibility. In the window splays there stood larger-than-life figures of the Virtues, trampling Vices beneath their feet.

There is considerable evidence of the increasing importance of Westminster Palace as a governmental centre during the reign of Henry III. New Exchequer buildings were erected at the north end of the Great Hall, and the Court of Common Pleas, which in 1215 Magna Carta had demanded be held at a fixed place, came to be located in the palace. In 1245, the first mention is made of a throne that stood on a dais against the south wall of the Great Hall. This throne symbolized the king's continuous presence at the ceremonial heart of the palace, and it was occupied by him and his successors on the greatest occasions of state. It probably resembled the surviving throne of Edward I at Westminster Abbey, and we know – from a documented discussion between Henry and the craftsman who made it – that it was flanked by gilt-copper sculptures of leopards (see illus., p. 186).[16]

From Henry III's reign onwards, Parliament also began to be convened regularly at the palace, although it continued to be held elsewhere in England, and even in other places in London, until the end of the Middle Ages.[17] There is a remarkable consistency in the location and form of these meetings in Westminster from the late thirteenth century. They began with a proclamation in the Great Hall, forbidding the bearing of arms and the playing of games in the palace during Parliament. From as early as 1259, Parliament itself opened in the Painted Chamber, to hear the cause of its meeting. Afterwards, the Lords proceeded to the Queen's Chamber, the seat of the House of Lords beyond the Middle Ages, for their conference. The Commons, however, who only began to be summoned to Parliament as a matter of course in the fourteenth century, had no fixed chamber. From 1376, and probably for long before that, they usually sat in the Chapter House of Westminster Abbey, and during the later fifteenth century in the monastic refectory.[18]

LEFT: G. Earp, *St Stephen's Chapel: A Conjectural Reconstruction*, watercolour, *c.* 1880. The chapel, begun in 1292, was a two-storey structure (this image shows the upper storey). The lower stone-vaulted chapel survives today as the Chapel of St Mary Undercroft or 'Crypt Chapel' (see illus., p. 132, bottom). When it was completed in 1348, the upper chapel had a clerestory; this was removed in 1692. This is a fanciful image of the chapel but gives an indication of the polychrome interior decoration. Palace of Westminster (WOA 2257).

ABOVE: The Chapter House of Westminster Abbey, completed by 1259. The Chapter House served as the Chamber for the Commons until the end of the fourteenth century. Written in the tiles is the boast: "As the rose is the flower of flowers so is this house the house of houses." English Heritage Photo Library.

As well as serving as a centre of government, Westminster Palace was also put to regular use by Henry III as a setting for public occasions. Among the most remarkable of these were royal distributions of food to the poor. It was expected of a king that he make generous gifts of alms, and Henry, inspired by the example of Edward the Confessor's charity, did not stint in this respect. To mark great feasts, huge distributions of food were made from royal palaces and castles, of which Westminster was the most regularly used. On one such occasion in 1244, for example, ten thousand poor were fed at the palace in a single day. In order to accommodate the numbers, the old and sick were fed in the Great and Lesser Hall, children in the Queen's Chamber, and the remaining poor in the Painted Chamber.[19]

The next major building project in the palace after the death of Henry III was the construction of St Stephen's Chapel, begun in 1292 by his son Edward I. Domestic chapels were an important element of any great house in the Middle Ages, and despite the presence of the abbey, Westminster is known to have possessed at least two from the late twelfth century. Edward's decision to rebuild one of these, the Chapel of St Stephen, was probably driven by a spirit of competition and emulation. King Louis IX of France had recently completed Sainte-Chapelle as part of his palace on the Isle de la Cité at Paris. With no less an

R. Dixon, *St Stephen's Chapel: Interior Elevation of the Easternmost Bay of the North Wall of the Upper Chapel*, ink and watercolour, *c.* 1800. The design of the elevation ingeniously reproduces the miniature details of the stall canopies at the base of the wall on a larger scale around the window heads. The interior was formerly richly painted, and the windows glazed with stained glass. The Society of Antiquaries of London.

object than Christ's Crown of Thorns at its heart, this French royal chapel was executed at enormous expense in the likeness of a vast and preciously-detailed reliquary.[20]

Edward began work on a response to the Sainte-Chapelle in a building designed in a very English architectural idiom. A mason, Michael of Canterbury, was responsible for the initial design of this remarkable two-storey chapel. With brilliant inventiveness, he applied the rich, miniature, architectural detailing that ornamented the portals of contemporary French churches to the internal furnishings of St Stephen's as well as to its full-scale design. The result was a building in which there was a correspondence of detail between the whole and its component parts. This simple idea was subsequently to prove enormously influential in shaping the so-called Perpendicular style of Gothic architecture, and St Stephen's is a building of central importance to the subsequent development of mainstream English architecture.[21]

Although begun in 1292, the work of constructing and decorating the chapel was very protracted, lasting into the middle of the next century, but Michael's architectural design was respected in most points throughout. Construction was first interrupted in 1297 by a financial crisis, and the following year a serious fire gutted a large portion of the palace. When Edward II came the throne in 1307, it took a year of intensive work to render the buildings habitable, and it was not until 1320 that work on the chapel recommenced. This in turn was brought to an end in 1326, and it was not until well into the reign of Edward III that work again resumed. The architectural shell of St Stephen's was completed in 1348, and in its final form it included an upper tier of windows (a clerestory), an addition to Michael of Canterbury's original design. Then Edward, enriched by his triumphs at Crécy and Calais, began to decorate the building in the most magnificent fashion with stained glass and painting, a process that took a further fifteen years to complete.[22] Meanwhile, he endowed a college of thirteen chaplains to serve the new church, and the line of their houses, from which

R. Smirke, St Stephen's Chapel, copy of the paintings on the north half of the altar-wall, tempera and gold leaf on paper, between 1800 and 1811. The upper register shows the Adoration of the Magi, and the lower Edward III and his sons being presented to the Virgin and Child by St George. The Society of Antiquaries of London.

Canon Row takes its name, was built between the river and the Great Hall.[23]

Edward III also made considerable changes to the so-called Privy Palace at Westminster, the title applied at this time to the residential elements of what was by now a large and rambling palace. He constructed a series of new buildings, including another small chapel, along the banks of the Thames at the southern extreme of the palace site. These buildings were subsequently added to and altered in the fifteenth century, but there is little evidence of what they looked like, and most were destroyed in the sixteenth century. One element of Edward III's work that does survive in this area, however, is the Jewel Tower, under construction in 1365–66. This was built on land appropriated from the abbey at the edge of the Privy Garden – a private garden adjacent to the royal apartments – and was intended to serve as a store for the king's plate and jewels. It was a small consolation to the irate Westminster monks that one of Edward's keepers of the Privy Palace subsequently choked to death on the bone of a pike caught in the moat surrounding the tower. [24]

Along with the expansion of the Privy Palace in the fourteenth century, the public part of Westminster, now entitled the Great Palace, was developing too. At exactly the same time that he erected the Jewel Tower, Edward III also built a high clock tower in the great court-yard to the north of the Great Hall, later known as New Palace Yard. This stood near its modern-day successor, which contains Big Ben, and dominated the palace in much the same way. The Great Hall remained the centre of its affairs, and from Richard II's reign onwards, the particular location of three courts that were regularly held in its gigantic interior are certainly known. Most important of these was the Court of King's Bench. It occupied an honorific position on the right of the dais at the high end of the hall, so as to take place in the notional presence of the king as represented by his throne. Occasionally, the Chief Justice of King's Bench would actually sit in the throne, so as to represent the king's person more fully. Opposite this, on the left of the dais, was the Court of Chancery, the next court

Wenceslaus Hollar, *New Palace Yard from the East, with the North Façade of Westminster Hall (Sala Regalis cum Curia Westmonasterii, vulgo Westminster haall)*, etching, 1647. This shows the outer courtyard of the medieval palace, later New Palace Yard, still intact, with the high clock tower (right), the fountain, and, beyond, the Great Gate (centre right), together with the stately façade of Westminster Hall. Palace of Westminster (WOA 701).

in importance, and at the low end of the hall was the lowest court, the Court of Common Pleas. The courts were divided by timber partitions, and from at least the 1290s onwards their proceedings would have had to compete with the noise generated by the numerous shops that also lined the interior. Their rents, along with those of hawkers, were a perquisite of the Keeper of the Palace.[25]

This bustling and cluttered interior arranged for daily business would have been swept away whenever the hall was prepared for a major ceremony or royal appearance, and it was with a view to creating an appropriate setting for such occasions that perhaps the most famous building project at Westminster was initiated. Richard II followed in the footsteps of Henry III as a particular devotee of St Edward the Confessor. So closely did he identify with that royal saint that from about 1395 he actually impaled his coat of arms – as a wife's arms are impaled by her husband's – with those of the Confessor.[26] Like Henry III, he had a high conception of his authority as an anointed king and turned to architecture as a means of expressing this. Rufus's long-serving Great Hall, the administrative and symbolic heart of his principal palace, was an obvious object for his patronage. In 1385, Richard II made some attempt to aggrandize its antiquated interior, but it was not until 1393, possibly goaded by his recent political humiliation at the hands of his enemies, that he began work to transform it completely.[27]

Under the direction of the Master Mason, Henry Yevele, the Romanesque clerestory was blocked up, and the hall refenestrated. Inserted around the interior beneath the windows was a cornice decorated with Richard's heraldic devices, including the white hart, and to the east – contrary to strict heraldic custom – the beasts turned to the left so as to face the throne. The entire lower zone of the wall was blank, a purely functional detail that facilitated the partitioning of the space when in everyday use. During celebrations, this area

The Great Hall ('Westminster Hall'), Palace of Westminster, c. 1903. Built by William Rufus and remodelled by Richard II, this vast chamber has stood at the heart of national events for over nine hundred years. The roof is one of the technical triumphs of medieval carpentry. The marble sculptures on the left were transferred to the Central Criminal Court, Old Bailey, in 1915 (see chapter 16). Farmer Collection no. 637, House of Lords Record Office, London.

of the wall would have been concealed beneath hangings. Externally, the north gable was also recast, again in close imitation of contemporary church architecture, with two towers and a central doorway surrounded by statues of the kings and queens of England. This array of royal statuary was echoed at the opposite end of the hall where the marble throne itself was flanked by the figures of six kings beneath high canopies in the manner of a church reredos.[28]

But grander by far than Yevele's work is one of the universally acknowledged masterpieces of English medieval carpentry, the roof of the Great Hall. The designer and builder of this was Hugh Herland, the King's Master Carpenter, and it is an astonishing artistic and technical achievement. It is supported on thirteen principal trusses, each of which springs from the internal cornice of the hall and is intricately detailed like a screen, to slice up the space of the roof. The principal timbers of the trusses visually describe two massive outlines: a soaring arch spanning the whole space and, within it, an inner arch, supported on either side by an inward-curving brace and hammer-beam. At the head of each hammer-beam, apparently bearing the roof on their backs, are gigantic figures of angels, bearing the arms of England. That these angels are intended to represent a celestial court gathering in counterpart to the terrestrial court in the hall beneath is suggested by one detail of the design. At either end of the hall, the trusses are separated from the wall. This not only permits the gable windows to exceed the dimensions of the roof-arch span, but also gives equal importance to each of the thirteen trusses. The use of thirteen trusses was almost certainly intended as an allusion to the number of Christ and his apostles, and was meant to suggest that the terrestrial court mirrored its celestial counterpart and met, literally, under its aegis.[29]

Within this space, familiar to the present day, every kind of royal celebration took

ABOVE: Thomas Canon, *A King*, Reigate stone, with Totterhoe stone crown, 1385, South Wall, Great Hall ('Westminster Hall'), Palace of Westminster (WOA S132). This photograph shows one of the kings on exhibition in Westminster Hall after restoration in 1995 and prior to their reinstatement on the south wall. Thomas Canon, a London marbler, was contracted to provide this figure. Each statue cost £2. 6s. 8d. The niches they stand in cost twice as much, a reflection of the relative values attached to architecture and sculpture in this period (see illus., p. 265). All six kings are made of Reigate stone, with Totterhoe stone crowns. The orbs, sceptres and swords are nineteenth-century additions.

LEFT: The exterior of the north façade of Westminster Hall from New Palace Yard (see also illus., p. 84).

RIGHT: St Stephen's Cloister, Palace of Westminster, 1526–29, photograph, c. 1903. Although heavily restored, this is a unique surviving example of an English two-storey cloister. The lower walk is vaulted throughout and the bosses are richly cut with the arms and symbols of Henry VIII and Catherine of Aragon. Farmer Collection no. 646, House of Lords Record Office, London.

ABOVE: An angel from the roof of the Great Hall ('Westminster Hall'), Palace of Westminster. The gigantic figures of angels bearing the royal arms apparently support this vast roof on their backs. This artistic conceit of an angel-borne roof subsequently became popular throughout England.

ABOVE: The interior of Henry VII's Chapel, Westminster Abbey, looking east, 1501–09. This Lady Chapel was originally built to house the body of England's latter-day royal saint, Henry VI. In fact Henry VII himself lies buried here with his queen. His tomb is visible within the screened enclosure visible behind the altar.

place. Of particular importance was the role of the Great Hall in the coronation ceremony. Not only did the king symbolically take the throne in the Great Hall on the morning of his anointing, surrounded by the peers of the realm, but the coronation feast itself was held here. So, too, were other celebrations, such as tournaments, and it is quite possible, although there is no evidence for it, that the combatants at these were mounted. Certainly, Richard II's coronation feast was patrolled by horsemen, whose duty it was to prevent violence among guests.[30]

There was no slackening in the redevelopment of Westminster Palace over the course of the fifteenth century. The core of major medieval buildings now established in the Great and Privy Palaces continued to be adapted and expanded as the need arose, but in the absence of good documentation or physical remains it is impossible to discern the details of such work.[31] Westminster Abbey also continued to attract royal burials, such as those of Richard II and Henry V. In 1501, Henry VII began work on one of the great masterpieces of late medieval architecture: the Lady Chapel at the east end of the abbey. This was originally designed as the funerary chapel of England's second royal saint, Henry VI, but in the end Henry VII was himself buried here, and it is now popularly known by his name.[32]

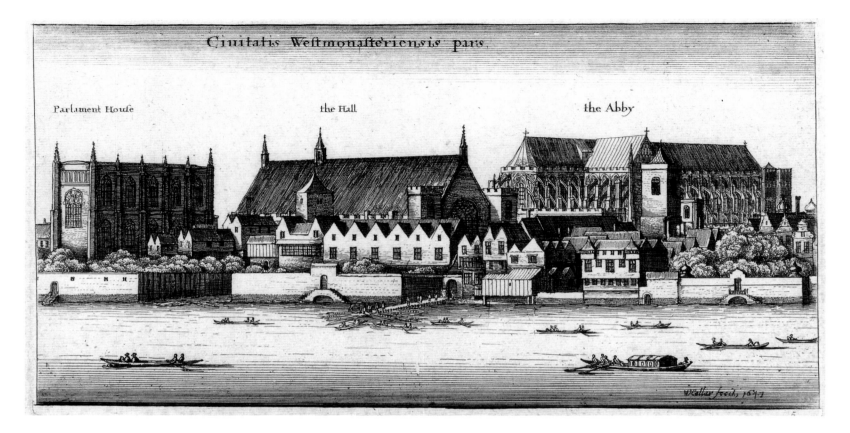

Parlament House   the Hall   the Abby

In the early sixteenth century there was also one private work of patronage in the palace that deserves to be better known. This was the rebuilding of the cloister of St Stephen's College by its dean, John Chambers, between 1526–29. The victim of both the 1834 fire and German bombing in the Second World War, the cloister is very heavily restored. Nevertheless, the richness of the original two-storey design, with a polygonal chapter house projecting from its east range, a design probably inspired by the important late fourteenth-century cloisters at St Paul's, is still readily apparent. Of particular interest are the surviving bosses of the vaulted lower cloister walk, among which are the arms and symbols of Henry VIII and his first queen, Catherine of Aragon. The quality of this architecture is not only a reminder of the vitality of the late medieval architectural tradition in England, but also of the continued prestige and wealth of this royal college of St Stephen.[33]

But even before this cloister was begun, the character of Westminster Palace had begun to change fundamentally. In 1512 a fire destroyed much of the Privy Palace. No attempt was made to repair the buildings, and in 1529 Henry VIII appropriated York Palace, the London residence of the Archbishop of York. This palace is now familiar as Whitehall, and its situation adjacent to Westminster rendered the ruined lodgings there redundant. Twenty years after the fire, therefore, most of the Privy Palace was demolished, and its materials carted away as rubble. Shortly afterwards, in 1536, the ancient Palace of Westminster was declared by Act of Parliament to be "only a member and parcel" of Whitehall.[34]

With the destruction of the residential part of the palace, the surviving buildings at Westminster were given over almost exclusively to the law and administration. Four new financial courts were established in the palace between 1536 and 1542, and in 1548, after the suppression of the college, Edward VI gave St Stephen's Chapel to the Commons as their first permanent Chamber.[35] The works accounts from this period are full of the details made for maintaining and altering the buildings. Among the more significant changes were the

ABOVE: Wenceslaus Hollar, *View of Westminster from the River* (*Civitas Westmonasteriensis pars*), etching, 1647, Palace of Westminster (WOA 845). St Stephen's Chapel is shown on the left ("Parlament House"), Westminster Hall in the centre and the abbey to the right.

RIGHT: Peter Tillemans, *The House of Commons in Session*, oil on canvas, c. 1710. Tillemans shows the Commons Chamber – formerly St Stephen's Chapel – after Wren's alterations. All evidence of the Gothic structure is concealed, but the fabric of the chapel was largely intact beneath Wren's fixtures. Palace of Westminster (WOA 2737).

construction in 1537 of the Court of Augmentations and the extension of the Court of the Exchequer in 1569–70. These two buildings formed a range to the west of the Great Hall façade, half of brick and half of stone.[36] On the other side of the hall, a long timber-frame range was erected, probably in 1517, and it was remodelled by Elizabeth I between 1599 and 1602. This may have contained the celebrated Court of Star Chamber, which in 1588–89 had had its eponymous roof renewed and affixed with "a verie large starre".[37]

For much of the seventeenth century, the palace continued to be repaired and developed in a piecemeal fashion to serve the needs of the institutions it housed. But from the 1690s the pace of alteration increased, and its distinguishing medieval features began to be lost. The first important change in this respect was the remodelling of the House of Commons – formerly St Stephen's Chapel – by Sir Christopher Wren in 1692. He dismantled the clerestory and recast the whole structure as a classical building, with internal galleries to either side. Shortly after this, in 1692, Edward III's clock tower was demolished, and then, with the aim of improving access to the palace, the two medieval gates to New Palace Yard were also pulled down, the Great Gate in 1707 and the smaller gate towards St Margaret's Lane in 1728. Proposals to construct a bridge at Westminster demanded further changes to the environs of the palace, and after 1736 the Bridge Commission began to take an active role in the gradual transformation of the medieval courtyards of the palace into Georgian thoroughfares.[38]

In the meantime, there were increasing problems with transacting the ever-increasing quantities of Parliamentary and judicial business in the ageing and inadequate palace buildings. Such was the discomfiture of the existing arrangements for the Courts of Chancery and King's Bench in the Great Hall that a grand screen in the Gothic style was designed in 1739 by William Kent to enclose them. The pressure on space, meanwhile, led to the construction of a new building in the Palladian style facing on to St Margaret's Lane. The so-called New Stone Building was erected between 1755 and 1770, and provided space for the storage of documents, as well as offices and committee rooms.[39] It was actually built lacking one wing, and this was to be supplied in another building project nearly half a century later.

Throughout the period of these changes, there were demands that an entirely new Parliament House be constructed. Wren had put forward designs for such a building as part of a new royal palace at Whitehall, and his example was followed by such figures as William Kent in the 1730s and John Soane in the 1790s.[40] Nothing came of these plans, but in 1799 the architect James Wyatt received a commission to remodel the House of Lords. He received this over the head of Soane, who had just put forward a proposal for the same project in which the Painted Chamber and St Stephen's Chapel were to be restored to their medieval appearance, and incorporated within a new set of classical buildings. Wyatt took the opportunity to effect a complete – and largely cosmetic – change to much of the exterior of the palace, covering it with crenellations and Gothic detail. To a government hard-pressed by the costs of the Napoleonic Wars, such a remodelling was a financially appealing alternative to any wholesale rebuilding, and Wyatt was helped in his project by his political connections, and in particular by the willing ear of George III.[41]

Ironically, this project to Gothicize Westminster coincided with what has become one of the most notorious acts of destruction to its medieval fabric. The Act of Union with Ireland in 1800 necessitated the creation of more seating in the House of Commons, and Wyatt set to work ripping out the existing furnishings of the Chamber. In doing so, he exposed Edward III's paintings, which were destroyed with little ceremony. At the time, few people were concerned by this act of wanton vandalism, but their loss provoked vociferous opposition

Augustus Charles Pugin and Thomas Rowlandson, *The Interior of Westminster Hall*, colour aquatint, published December 1809 in R. Ackermann's *The Microcosm of London*. This print shows the Great Hall with William Kent's screen, designed to enclose the Courts of Chancery and King's Bench. The pilasters on the walls were added to articulate the huge blank medieval walls, now stripped of shops. Palace of Westminster (WOA 3835).

John Preston Neale, *Speaker's House 1815*, view from the River Front, watercolour, 1815. James Wyatt bestowed architectural coherence on the medley of palace buildings with a veneer of Gothic detailing. He hoped to create the effect of a rambling country house (see illus., p. 197). The Speaker's House was executed in a simple, castellated Gothic style. Palace of Westminster (WOA 2448).

from the antiquary John Carter, who wrote angrily to the *Gentleman's Magazine*.[42] Having destroyed the real medieval interior of the chapel, Wyatt proceeded to remodel its exterior, inserting false tracery in the east window that Wren had so carefully classicized.

Wyatt's behaviour over St Stephen's was indefensible, but he was to acquit himself better when he subsequently restored Henry VII's Chapel, a project perceived to be of sufficient public importance to be funded by Parliamentary Grant.[43] While his work on both the palace and the chapel reflect the growing interest in Gothic architecture, as well as their conceived appropriateness in the context of this ancient palace, it shows how idiosyncratic the results of this interest could be. Wyatt's blend of attention and irreverence towards things medieval was a strong theme in the Victorian development of the palace. There is nothing slavishly antiquarian, for example, in the architecture of the palace today. For all the greater accuracy with which Barry copied Gothic detailing, the combinations of forms he used are not merely inconceivable in a medieval context, they are truly bizarre: vaulting patterns derived from St Stephen's Chapel juxtaposed with window tracery in the style of Henry Yevele and decorative motifs from Henry VII's Chapel.

There were two further important architectural contributions to the palace before the fire, both undertaken by Wyatt's rival, John Soane. The first of these was the construction of new courts, following the decision to remove King's Bench and Chancery from the Great Hall after their centuries of residence there. Soane chose the area immediately to the west of the Great Hall for the court buildings, and in 1821 he put forward a proposal that involved remodelling the New Stone Building and throwing out a second wing in neo-classical style to the north of it. Soane's designs for the new Law Courts met with opposition from Members of Parliament. It was argued that when viewed from New Palace Yard, their classical detailing would clash absurdly with the north gable of the Great Hall. This gable had only recently been cleared of houses, and the furious Soane was forced, among other changes, to create a Gothic façade on this side of the buildings (see illus., p. 66, top left).[44]

At the same time that this work was going forward, Soane was also approached to

design a new chamber for the House of Lords and remodel Old Palace Yard. The Act of Union with Ireland in 1800 had so swelled the number of peers that the House of Lords had been forced to move from its long-established location in the Queen's Chamber to the Court of Requests, formerly Henry II's White Hall. This building and its immediate environs, as transformed by Wyatt, were generally execrated, and from 1822 Soane was involved in the piecemeal reconstruction of the entire area. The work involved the demolition of all the buildings to the south of the Painted Chamber, including two important medieval structures, the former Queen's Chapel and Chamber. Happily, the medieval features of these buildings were relatively well recorded, a reflection in part of the interest and admiration generated by the exposure in 1819 of the long-concealed medieval wall paintings in the Painted Chamber.[45]

Soane's buildings of the 1820s were really the first architectural concession to the total inadequacy of the medieval palace as a centre for modern government. Even subsequent to his changes, the palace preserved something of its rambling medieval character, its buildings

ABOVE LEFT: C. Burton after S. Russell, *View of Westminster Hall, Law Courts &c from the North-West*, lithograph, published in 1835. Soane remodelled and extended the New Stone Building to create his Law Courts (right) in the 1820s. It was demanded by Members of Parliament that he truncate and Gothicize the north façade of the new building so it would not clash with the Great Hall. Palace of Westminster (WOA 1420).

ABOVE RIGHT: C. Burton after S. Russell, *View of the King's Entrance &c. From the South-West*, lithograph, published in 1835. After 1800 the Lords Chamber was in the Court of Requests, formerly Henry II's White Hall (centre). Palace of Westminster (WOA 1422).

William Capon, *The Prince's Chamber and House of Lords*, pencil, 1808. These buildings, the Queen's Chamber and Chapel of Henry III's palace, were in a very poor state of repair before their demolition in 1823 to make way for Soane's redevelopment of the House of Lords, as this view shows. Palace of Westminster (WOA 79).

sprawling along the Thames. It is in this quality of architectural coherence that the existing palace principally distinguishes itself from its predecessor. Although they incorporate much that is medieval, the new buildings are physically discrete and form a unified architectural whole. Cut off from the abbey and its environs by busy roads, as well as from casual visitors by security, the palace has never stood as isolated as it does today. Its effective removal from the public domain lends its extraordinary history an almost perfect, but deeply ironic, symmetry. A palace built by kings first opened its doors to a Parliament composed first of noblemen and then of commoners. The kings, although still nominal owners of the palace, left it in the sixteenth century; the hereditary peers are now ousted from their seats; and today it is the interloping commoners who, like cuckoos in the nest, lord it over the others.

G.F. Robson, *View of the Palace of Westminster from the River*, watercolour, 1808. Palace of Westminster (WOA 1654).

# 4

## Romancing the Past: Image and Theatre at the Coronation of George IV

Steven Parissien

J.L. Marks, *The Coronation of King Punch*, July 1821, coloured engraving, frontispiece to a verse satire, *The History of the Coronation of Punch and the Humours of his Wife Judy*, published by J.L. Marks, 1821. British Museum, London.

Sir Thomas Lawrence, *The Coronation Portrait of George IV* (detail), oil on canvas, 1821. The Royal Collection.

The coronation of George IV in 1821 was not merely a colourful episode in the history of the old Palace of Westminster. Admittedly, despite its scale, flamboyance and melodrama, the spectacle did little to enhance the reputation of the new monarch, and to some observers proved more pantomime than apotheosis. Nevertheless, the coronation was an important step in creating the concept of a national monarch, in which the actual occupant of the throne was of less importance than the position's increasingly symbolic role as a figurehead for patriotic sentiment. Aside from being merely fashionable, the coronation was a Gothic Revival pageant staged in the ancient national monuments of Westminster Abbey and Hall, underlining the appropriation of Gothic as the national style in the first half of the nineteenth century. This self-conscious 'Britishness', frequently ascribed to the post-Waterloo period, was to be enshrined in the fabric and decoration of the new Palace of Westminster.[1]

George IV's coronation can be described as the first to celebrate nation before monarch. For John Cannon and Ralph Griffiths, the reign of George IV marked the beginning of the modern monarchy, or, as they describe it, "popular monarchy": "not in the sense that the monarchy was always popular ... but [in] that it compensated increasingly for the loss of formal political power by adopting a less remote attitude, by appealing to a wider range of its subjects, and by concerning itself greatly with its public image."[2] Linda Colley has pointed out that when George IV's great-grandfather was crowned in 1727:

> Whig and Tory activists in many provincial centres organized separate and competing festivities for the occasion. By contrast, most of the local committees organizing celebrations in 1821 (George IV's coronation), 1831 (William IV's coronation) and 1837 (Queen Victoria's coronation) were ostentatiously bi-partisan and controversial emblems, mottoes or colours were banned from their arrangements.[3]

By 1837, coronations had become patriotic celebrations at which the sovereign represented the nation.

Part of the reason for this development must lie with the calibre of early nineteenth-century British monarchs. Neither George IV nor his brother William IV were figures likely to inspire much political fervour; even the most ultra-leaning Tory would be unlikely to dash to the barricades in defence of any of George III's sons. This did not mean, of course, that Britain was becoming a nation of republicans. All but the most radical fringe continued to revere the institution of monarchy – in abstract, if not in person – as the cornerstone of the nation's avowedly successful constitution, and thus as the guarantor of the nation's liberties. It was simply that the undeniably controversial personality of George IV became an increasingly embarrassing element in this constitutional equation. After the victory at Waterloo in 1815, London's newly-enriched plutocrats, in Colley's words,

> lavished money on royal banquets, bestowed their Freedom on as many members of the Royal Family as would accept it and invested in special banners to be used on all occasions of royal celebration, emblazoned with the letters SPQL. Leading citizens of the new Rome, they wanted Caesar in their midst and were prepared to fête him.[4]

Increasingly, it seems, the Caesar they sought to conjure was a representation of monarchy plucked from the rose-tinted mists of Britain's past, rather than that offered by the unedifying recent history of the House of Hanover.

To George himself, the coronation was not merely an excuse for dressing up, nor for a party, both of which would have been sufficient reason for the former Regent to spend large quantities of public money. It provided the decidedly unpopular new monarch with an opportunity to eradicate the memory of his past misdemeanours – and his more recent, disastrous attempt at divorce from his estranged wife, Caroline – by casting himself as the embodiment and inspiration of a newly confident and militarily successful nation. As David Cannadine has remarked, since George could hardly present himself – as his father, George III had done – as the incarnation of family values, he attempted to reinvent himself as 'Britannia', and thus the centrepiece of a shimmering pageant, heavily laden with allusions to the nation's glorious past.[5]

George was uniquely fitted with the vision and the props to create this theatrical extravaganza. Two of the governing passions of his life were France and dressing up, themes that became the cornerstones of his coronation. Lord Grey had observed at the outset of George's Regency that "parade and ceremony ... are, in truth, the things which most occupy him".[6] With his accession in 1820, George was finally allowed to indulge himself. Fortified by Sir Thomas Lawrence's fabulously fictitious images of the post-Waterloo Regent as a heroic patriot-prince bestriding the European stage like a colossus – and by his own perennially buoyant ego – the new king employed costume and his admiration for France to fashion a compelling image of himself as the nemesis of the only European head of state who could truly be described as heroic: Napoleon Bonaparte. To all but George IV, the image of the new king as the Gloriana of the age and the encapsulation of national virility was a risible one. That the ailing, drug-dependant monarch should, by the close of his short reign, begin to confuse fact with fiction – promoting himself, for example, to a key role at Waterloo itself – was a predictable progression from the fanciful tableaux of 1821.

In George IV's hands, his coronation was designed to emphasize the central place that hereditary monarchy occupied in the lives of Britons, juxtaposed with the recently invented and short-lived Napoleonic brand of self-made emperorship. Evoking the fabled lives and military successes of his Tudor ancestors in the coronation ceremony, George IV was both underlining the permanence and legitimacy of the British monarchy – in stark contrast with the temporary glories of the First Empire and its satellite puppet-rulers – and identifying himself with the iconic resonance of the English Renaissance and the court of Elizabeth I. In fact, George's historicist coronation aped Napoleon's in appropriating an 'ancient' national style. Napoleon, who well understood the power of visual association, took the inspiration for his lavish coronation ceremony in 1804 from Charlemagne – whose Holy Roman Empire claimed to be directly descended from that of ancient Rome. As an imperial pageant, the coronation was "a clever compromise between the traditional (in the style of ancient royalty) and the classical (the modern Caesar)".[7] The spectacular results were recorded by

Jacques-Louis David in his *Coronation of Napoleon* (1805–07, Musée du Louvre, Paris) and Jean August Dominique Ingres's *Napoleon on the Imperial Throne* (1806, Musée de l'Armée, Paris). Accordingly, as king of the most powerful country in Europe, George IV's coronation was explicitly designed to outshine Napoleon's.

As a rival to Napoleon, George IV required a suitably elevated stage. In 1821, work continued apace on the renamed Waterloo Chamber at Windsor Castle, which George had been planning since the temporary peace of 1814. Here, George and his immediate family were given pride of place among a Valhalla of heroes, kings and statesmen of the allied nations. Adding to the panegyric display was the so-called 'Waterloo Vase', recently commissioned for the chamber by George. In 1815, the Duke of Tuscany had presented the then Regent with an unfinished vase carved for Napoleon himself from a fifteen-foot-high block of marble. Four years later, George asked the sculptor, Sir Richard Westmacott, to adorn the vase with representations of Napoleon's defeat. The finished composition depicted George on his throne watching the emperor dismount from his horse – a clear case of wishful thinking on the part of the corpulent king.[8]

George's self-identification with the Allied defeat of Napoleon was similarly woven into the imagery of the coronation. Since 1812, the official beginning of his Regency, George had viewed the French emperor's sumptuous court as a challenge and a rebuke – a glittering rival to be outshone by his own generously funded confections. This manufactured rivalry is shown undisguised in the official coronation portrait of 1822 by Lawrence (see illus., p. 68).

Sir George Hayter, *The Trial of Queen Caroline*, oil on canvas, 1820. National Portrait Gallery, London.

George, resplendent, if a little unsteady under his weighty coronation regalia (and suitably slimmed down by the flattering painter), rests his right hand on the Table of the Grand Commanders, the favourite of all his recent French acquisitions. This circular neo-classical table, commissioned by Napoleon in 1806, is supported by Roman fasces and a plinth in the form of a shield, and surmounted by Sèvres porcelain plaques with gilt-bronze mounts. The latter features framed heads of great generals of antiquity, revolving round the porcelain profile of Alexander the Great. An obvious embarrassment to the restored Bourbon king, Louis XVIII, it was given to George (who had previously offered to buy it) in 1817. The table was placed at the centre of the State Dining Room at Buckingham Palace. It seems likely that it was the king's decision to give it a central place in the imagery of the coronation.[9] Lawrence's bombastic creation is one of great symbolic richness. George's pose, in relation to Napoleon's table, conveys a sense of imperious dismissiveness that – with great economy – implies the king's sincere belief in the importance of his personal role in Napoleon's defeat: George's face betrays more than a glimmer of contempt for the vanquished foe. But, more deservedly, it underlines the exquisite nature of his connoisseurship. It was an image that so entranced the king that he had numerous copies made and sent to friends, foreign embassies and European courts.[10]

The new king was understandably determined to produce something far more spectacular than George III's typically penurious coronation of 1761. In planning the event, his courtiers and officials ignored the humdrum precedents set by the king's Hanoverian forebears, and used as their bible Francis Sandford's detailed description of James II's coronation, published in 1687, underlining George's well-documented fascination with the House of Stuart, and, in particular, his identification with its Catholic branch. Preparations for the ceremony – initially planned for 1 August 1820 – began as early as 29 March.[11] But in the months that followed it increasingly appeared as if there would be no coronation at all. The new king was fifty-seven years old and in bad health.[12] His worsening condition ultimately caused the coronation to be postponed. Queen Caroline's trial in the House of Lords for adultery (see illus., p. 71) – which proved both divisive and futile – made any coronation celebration inadvisable; particularly in view of the king's growing unpopularity during the proceedings. In the end, the ceremony was held on 19 July 1821, eighteen months after George III's death, and, rather poetically, less than three months after the death of Napoleon.

The postponement did at least allow more time to be spent on the practical arrangements. To house the guests in Westminster Hall, John Soane was directed to build tiers of timber seats (which he sensibly supported on an iron frame), a raised floor and dais, side boxes for the royal family, a triumphal arch at the north entrance, and stables for the Royal Champion's horse. The style of the decorations was perhaps not to Soane's impeccably neo-classical taste. But the Gothic theme of the panelling, chairs and other finishes helped to reinforce the sense of Tudor pageantry that George and his advisers were intending to conjure up, blending Soane's temporary structures with the medieval hall. Across the road, Westminster Abbey's organ case was provided with a fake Gothic façade, and British carpets and fabrics were liberally employed.[13]

Uniquely, the coronation was a bespoke creation, in which all the main participants wore clothes made specifically for the occasion. This had not been the case before, or, indeed, since.[14] In an attempt to guarantee visual uniformity, the College of Arms issued guidance on the style of dress to be adopted by the various ranks of nobility and Officers of State, in the manner of a Hollywood designer marshalling the extras. For the official costumes, the

[B. Winkles], *Westminster Hall as Fitted up for the Banquet*, published in J. Whittaker, *The Coronation of His Most Sacred Majesty King George the Fourth*, London 1821–41, II, pl. 67, hand-coloured etching with gold-leaf border. Yale Centre for British Art Collection, Paul Mellon Collection.

Lord Chamberlain's department hired twenty-eight tailors, six gold lacemen, two sword cutlers, two goldsmiths, plus numerous other craftsmen.[15] The dress was designed to fashion the coronation into an Elizabethan pageant, in which George was cast as a male counterpart to the Faerie Queene herself; symbol of the nation's cultural richness and martial success.[16] Aileen Ribeiro notes that the "choice of Elizabethan costume behind such dress gave the processions and ceremonies the kind of visual unity that had been lacking at previous coronations".[17] Even the Privy Councillors were stuffed into "white and blue satin, with trunk hose and mantles, after the fashion of Queen Elizabeth's time".[18] To complete the pantomime effect, their white shoes were fixed with huge red rosettes.

The king's coronation costume cost a spectacular £24,704. 8s. 10d. and was so heavily weighted that George almost fainted on more than one occasion. It comprised a silver doublet and hose, a crimson surcoat and an ermine-lined, gold-embroidered mantle of crimson velvet, the last of these being so massive that it required eight peers' sons to carry it, rather than the habitual six. The robes' vivid golds and patriotic reds, whites and blues were set off by an enormous plumed hat in the manner of the Bourbon king, Henry IV, atop thick curls that today would politely be termed hair extensions.[19] George had also ordered a new crown of St Edward to be made, with considerably more jewels than had previously been thought sufficient by his predecessors. To supply this, the royal jewellers, Rundell, Bridge & Rundell, presented a conservative estimate of £100,000 (approximately £5,000,000 today).[20] For his return from the abbey to Westminster Hall, the king wore a royal-purple Cap of State, surmounted by a jewelled circlet and large, white ostrich feathers, while the pages at the ensuing banquet wore coats of scarlet trimmed with gold lace, blue sashes and white silk stockings.

Given all the preparation and expense, the coronation should have been the apogee of George's public career. This is indeed the impression given by the numerous images of the coronation executed by James Stephanoff, George Jones, Augustus Charles Pugin (father of Pugin) and others.[21] In reality, the solemnity of the proceedings was punctuated by a distinct lack of decorum and sense of occasion. On the morning of the coronation ceremony – fresh from his overnight stay in Speaker's House – the king proceeded to Westminster Hall for the traditional assembling of the procession and presentation of the regalia. From there, he tottered to the abbey beneath a gold canopy carried by the sixteen barons of the Cinque Ports, and preceded by the King's Herb Women – Miss Fellowes and her six maids – who strewed the raised platform with fragrant herbs.[22] The weather was kind: bright sunshine filtered through the abbey windows, making the vividly coloured fabrics glitter. Disaster almost struck, however, when the king – weighed down by the immense costume, restricted by his too-tightly laced corset and overheated by the sun — "appeared distressed, almost to fainting".[23] Fortunately he recovered, and thereafter showed surprising endurance during the gruelling five-hour ceremony.

A good part of the audience – both inside and outside the abbey – were not as long-suffering as the king. After the procession had entered, much of the crowd rushed away to nearby Green Park "to witness the ascent of Mr Green in a magnificent air balloon", and then on to see William Congreve's marvellous firework display in Hyde Park.[24] Similarly, when the king left temporarily for St Edward's Shrine – where he stayed a mere ten minutes – the audience simply got up and left. On 22 July 1821, *The Observer* reported with undisguised relish that "When the King returned, he had empty benches, covered with dirt and litter, on one hand, and the backs of his courtiers expediting their exits with a 'sauve-qui-peut like' rapidity, presented themselves to his view on the other." The report concluded

*General View of the Procession from Westminster Hall to Westminster Abbey,* published in J. Whittaker, *The Coronation of His Most Sacred Majesty King George the Fourth,* London 1821–41, II, pl. 69, hand-coloured aquatint with gold leaf border. Yale Centre for British Art Collection, Paul Mellon Collection.

that this decidedly "unpicturesque arrangement" had "the appearance of a want of respect to the Sovereign".[25]

Queen Caroline's attempt to gatecrash the coronation threatened to turn the day into a low comedy. The euphoria surrounding her acquittal in November 1820 had largely evaporated by the following July. While the king smirked at ladies attending the ceremony inside the abbey, outside, the queen was repeatedly refused entry by the burly guards, who, having been primed, had expected such an assault. Storming over to Westminster Hall – where she was espied by Lord Hood, who "thought she looked like a blowsy Landlady" – the queen was likewise repulsed; the doors were slammed in her face.[26] The serious violence and insurrection that the authorities feared – due to the queen's presence - did not materialize.

Inside the hall, conspicuous consumption had literally begun. The exotically dressed pages served a staggering twenty-five thousand pounds' worth of food to the guests:

> Twenty-three kitchens, supervised by Jean-Baptiste Watier, produced 160 tureens of soup, a similar amount of fish dishes, roast joints of venison, beef, mutton and veal, vegetables, and appropriate gravies etc presented in 480 sauce boats. Cold dishes, including ham, pastries, seafood and jellies number 3,271. All this was washed down with 9,840 bottles of various wines and 100 gallons of iced punch.[27]

The entrance of the King's Champion at the height of the coronation banquet – a tradition

*The King's Herbwoman, with her Six Maids* (detail), published in J. Whittaker, *The Coronation of His Most Sacred Majesty King George the Fourth*, London 1821–41, I, pl. 5, hand-coloured stipple and line engraving on vellum, with gouache and gold leaf on vellum with gold engraved letters. Yale Centre for British Art Collection, Paul Mellon Collection.

that dated back at least to the fourteenth century – was not greeted at the present occasion with the awe that it was undoubtedly meant to have inspired. The position itself was hereditary, and in the hands of the Dymoke family. Unfortunately for the king, the current hereditary 'champion', John Dymoke, was a clergyman, who asserted that the very nature of his calling prevented him from offering violence – albeit in defence of the king – by throwing down his gauntlet in public. No doubt it had occurred to Dymoke that the spectacle of an Anglican vicar offering to fight all comers was a ludicrous one. Instead, the Reverend sent his son, Henry, in his place. Alas, Henry appeared rather young for the task, was too small for the Tudor suit of armour that came with the job, and a little unsteady on the horse. Fortunately the animal was used to crowds, having been "hired from Astley's circus for the occasion".[28] Even Sir Walter Scott acknowledged that Dymoke junior had "a little too much the appearance of a maiden-knight to be the challenger of the world in the King's behalf". And, underlining his antiquarian credentials, Scott criticized the champion's shield for "being a round 'roundache', or Highland target – a defensive weapon which it would have been impossible to use on horseback".[29]

To the sound of trumpets, the King's Champion entered the north end of the hall on horseback, accompanied by the Duke of Wellington and Lord Howard of Effingham. He read his challenge and threw down his gauntlet three times as he approached the king, who was seated at the south end. After being given back his glove, he drank the king's health (he kept

[F.C. Lewis after J. Stephanoff and A.C. Pugin], *The King Seated in St Edward's Chair Crowned by the Archbishop of Canterbury*, published in J. Whittaker, *The Coronation of His Most Sacred Majesty King George the Fourth*, London 1821–41, II, pl. 62, hand-coloured aquatint with gold. Yale Centre for British Art Collection, Paul Mellon Collection.

[W. Bennett after J. Stephanoff and A.C. Pugin], *The Ceremony of the Homage in Westminster Abbey*, published in J. Whittaker, *The Coronation of His Most Sacred Majesty King George the Fourth*, London 1821–41, II, pl. 64, hand-coloured aquatint with gold leaf border. Yale Centre for British Art Collection, Paul Mellon Collection.

the gold cup, which counted as his fee) and left. After this attempted Ivanhoe-style challenge, all sense of propriety appeared to evaporate. As George left the hall, pandemonium struck as guests rushed to seize the coronation plate as if they were at the winter sales. The Lord Chamberlain succeeded in rescuing the more expensive items from the plunder, but much of value was lost.

Most spectators' impressions of the coronation appear to correspond with their existing prejudices. Those who wanted confirmation of their opinion of George IV as a reckless spendthrift and figure of fun saw exactly that. One cartoon, entitled *The Coronation of King PUNCH!!!* (see illus., p. 69), showed George obese and drunk on brandy; but then George was no stranger to the caricaturist.[30] A Westminster schoolboy thought the king "looked too large for effect, indeed he was more like an Elephant than a man".[31] Lady Cowper sympathized with the monarch, thinking him "more like the victim than the hero of the fête".[32] Those guests who hoped for a more elevated spectacle preferred to view the ceremony in a better light. Lord Denbigh told his mother that the coronation "exceeded all imagination and conception", although his subsequent comments suggest that he was more interested in the worth of the jewels worn than the significance of the ceremony itself.[33] The poet Thomas Hood declared that the occasion "brought home to the observers the full dignity of kingly office".[34] And the normally cynical artist Benjamin Haydon admitted that even at Dymoke's shaky challenge "My imagination got so intoxicated that I came out with a great contempt for the plebs".[35]

Sir Walter Scott's agenda was clearly along the same lines as the king's. What he yearned to see was the illusion of his own novels made real: a pan-Britannic celebration at which George IV would be reincarnated as the Father of the Nation, much in the manner of his recent celebration of British history, the medieval romance *Ivanhoe* (1819). He described the coronation in a similar literary style:

> the rich spectacle of the aisles crowded with waving plumage, and coronets, and caps of honour, and the sun, which brightened and saddened as if on purpose, and now darting a solitary ray, which catched [*sic*], as it passed, the glittering folds of a banner, or the edge of a group of battle-axes or partizans, and then rested full on some fair form, 'the

cynosure of neighbouring eyes', whose circlet of diamonds glistened under its influence.[36]

Compare this with a description from *Ivanhoe* of a medieval tournament:

> The lists now presented a most splendid spectacle. The sloping galleries were crowded with all that was noble, great, wealthy, and beautiful ... and the contrast of the various dresses of these dignified spectators rendered the view gay as it was rich, while the interior and lower space, filled with the substantial burgesses and yeomen of merry England, formed, in their more plain attire, a dark fringe ... around this circle of brilliant embroidery, relieving, and at the same time setting off, its splendour. [37]

George IV's throne from Westminster Hall, giltwood and composition, made by John Russell, Vallance & Evans and upholstered by Bailey & Saunders, 1820. Standing over seven feet in height, this imposing throne was used by George IV during the coronation banquet. Collection of the Grimsthorpe and Drummond Castle Trust.

What Scott sought from the coronation was both a reaffirmation of the values of kingship and a personal assurance that George IV was uniquely fitted for the role. His subsequent account of the coronation in the *Edinburgh Weekly Journal* (20 July 1821) was inevitably rather over-indulgent in its praise. Sadly for Scott, the reality seems to have been more a burlesque; the teetering, corpulent George IV – not the romantic figure of Richard I – was its focus, and Henry Dymoke served as a poor substitute for Wilfred of Ivanhoe.

George IV's coronation was the most expensive ever staged at Westminster. In 1823, the Treasury estimated that in total it had cost a colossal £238,238. 0s. 2d. Of this, £100,000 was voted by Parliament; the rest was paid out of the war reparations imposed on the French in 1815. As Valerie Cumming has observed, "The French nation therefore had, directly and indirectly, paid for the two most lavish coronations celebrated in the period 1800 to 1840."[38] This delicious irony, given his assumed affinity with Napoleon, would surely have delighted George IV.

Sir Walter Scott typically criticized those of his contemporaries "who sneer coldly at this solemn festival, and are rather disposed to dwell on the expense which attends it, than on the generous feelings which it ought to awaken".[39] Looking back seventeen years later, from the time of Victoria's coronation, Scott's biographer noted that "The coronation of George the Fourth's successor [William IV] was conducted in a vastly inferior scale and splendour and expense".[40] James Lockhart's comments were, as so often, deliberately ambiguous. Never again would a British coronation attempt the costly medieval pageant enacted by George IV.

Historians have debated the cultural impact of this coronation. David Cannadine remarks that "George IV's flirtation with grandeur was so unsuccessful that it was not repeated for the next half century".[41] However, the generation after 1821, while shrinking from the memory of the king's self-advertisement, eagerly seized upon the coronation's clever synthesis of national aspiration and invention of tradition in shaping the new Palace of Westminster. It is surely no accident that the coronation of 1821 and the 1835 competition for the design of the new palace focused on the same Gothic and Tudor eras. Indeed, what connects the coronation and the palace is this sense of fantasy. In her discussion of the coronation, Aileen Ribeiro has commented that "It was like a vast history painting which had come to life – a tableau vivant romancing the past".[42] The same could be said of the new Palace of Westminster. Alas for George IV, the principal difference between the two was that in the new palace – among those decorative schemes that were completed – he was cast not as patriot-king, the Victor of Waterloo, but demoted to a mere link in the royal chain that joined the Saxon kings to the reigning monarch, Queen Victoria.

George Jones, *The Coronation Banquet of George IV*, oil on canvas, 1821. The Royal Collection.

# 5

## "My Gorgeous Palace": Richard II, Restorations and Revivals

Jacqueline Riding

> This royal throne of kings, this sceptred isle,
> This earth of majesty, this seat of Mars,
> This other Eden – demi-paradise –
> This fortress built by nature for herself
> Against infection and the hand of war,
> This happy breed of men, this little world,
> This precious stone set in the silver sea,
> Which serves it in the office of a wall,
> Or as a moat defensive to a house
> Against the envy of less happier lands;
> This blessèd plot, this earth, this realm, this England ...[1]

These words by Shakespeare form undeniably one of the most famous passages in English literature. And yet few would know that this pre-eminent example of patriotic sentiment derives from his *King Richard the Second*. Equally, the historical Richard remains elusive to the wider public. But of the kings and queens whose images or heraldic symbols embellish the interior and exterior of the new Palace of Westminster, Richard II (reigned 1377–99) stands out for the sheer volume and variety of media in which he is celebrated.[2] At first glance it is a surprising choice, considering the canon of heroic monarchs who have maintained a powerful hold – then and now – over the popular imagination, and whose contribution to the development of the nation – and indeed Parliament – is more widely understood. The grandson and son of martial heroes, Edward III and Edward the Black Prince respectively, Richard had much to live up to. But despite early indications of 'heroic' potential – particularly his courageous personal stand against the rebels during the Peasants' Revolt[3] – Richard II is perceived as a man who combined a belief that his right to rule was divine and unquestionable with a lack of political acumen: a combination that led to his deposition in favour of Henry Bolingbroke (Henry IV) and subsequent murder.

Recent scholarship has challenged this simplistic assessment of Richard's reign, but, as Anthony Goodman observes, "that he was, with Edward II and Henry VI, one of a trinity of notably crass and unsuccessful rulers, has had a long currency".[4] Histories produced in the early nineteenth century reveal little sympathy for Richard's style of government, unsurprising perhaps in a period of Parliamentary reform. In his *History of England* (published 1819–30), John Lingard writes:

English School, *Richard II Enthroned* (detail), oil on panel, *c.* 1395. Westminster Abbey, London.

... his conduct in the twenty-first and twenty-second years of his reign betrayed such a thirst for revenge, and habit of dissimulation, such despotic notions of government, and so fixed a purpose of ruling without control, that no reader can be surprised at the catastrophe which followed. We may, indeed, abhor the wiles by which he was ensnared; may sympathize with him in his prison; and many condemn the policy which afterwards bereaved him of life; but at the same time we must acknowledge that he deserved to be abandoned by the people, on whose liberties he had trampled, and to forfeit that authority which he sought to exalt above the laws and constitution of his country.[5]

But despite the political ignominy of Richard II's reign, the nineteenth century saw a reappraisal of the king himself for two main reasons: first, an increasing antiquarian interest in the remaining examples of Richard's artistic and architectural patronage (the majority are assembled at the Palace and Abbey of Westminster);[6] and second, the humanizing of the medieval period through the romances of such popular writers as Sir Walter Scott. The former, exulting in the exquisite remainders of Richard's patronage, offered an image of the king that was distinct from the critical assessments of his character and reign. Richard, through his patronage, was adopted as a defining example of medieval magnificence, fundamental to the appropriation of the Age of Chivalry within the Victorian self-imagery of the 1830s and 1840s. The latter effectively reinvented the medieval period within the popular psyche as an age populated by human beings invested with all the sensibilities and passions of their modern counterparts. This pervading climate of engagement and identification, I suggest, encouraged a reassessment of the events leading to Richard's downfall as an essentially human tragedy: the despotic king recast as the flawed, and therefore human, tragic hero. This approach was to a large extent instigated, and in turn validated, by the accessibility of chronicles written by observers apparently intimate with the king and the events of his decline and murder: Jean Creton's *Metrical History of the Deposition of Richard II* and the anonymous *Chronique de la Traïson et mort de Richart Deux Roy Dengleterre*, both of which were translated and published for the first time in antiquarian journals in 1824 and 1846 respectively.[7] Although these were essentially partisan accounts, produced to discredit the 'usurping' Henry IV,[8] nineteenth-century scholars, if not wholly won over to Richard's cause, were beguiled by the pathos of the king's final months as described within these works.

It is not surprising, therefore, that William Shakespeare's eponymous history play, the action and pervading sense of melancholy of which derived ultimately from these chronicles, should have been 'rediscovered' in the first half of the nineteenth century, after generations of neglect. Within Shakespeare's drama, the emotive accounts of Richard's final years are intensified for dramatic effect, and the tragedy of his situation is heightened by the play's focus upon the vulnerability and frailty of the individual, when removed from the abstract mysticism of kingship. On a fundamental level, the play, with its tournaments, knights and pageantry, honour and chivalry, offered a public entranced by the warriors and distressed maidens of Scott's devising the opportunity to witness the authentic recreation and reanimation of the Middle Ages. Richard II's increased standing, both culturally and personally, within the collective consciousness, no matter how momentary, contributed to the monarch taking his rightful and prominent place within the iconography of the new Palace of Westminster. Furthermore, the old palace provided the setting for a number of significant scenes within Shakespeare's play. Perhaps the most poignant, the king's public abdication, was set within the most grandiose example of Richard's patronage: Westminster Hall. As decades of neglect were redressed by extensive restoration work, within both the

English School, *Richard II Enthroned*, oil on panel, *c.* 1395. Westminster Abbey, London.

English School, Hart, stone, *c.* 1395. East wall, Westminster Hall, Palace of Westminster.

abbey and palace at Westminster, the resulting body of scholarly publications relevant to the setting of Shakespeare's play created the potential for the staging of a Gothic extravaganza. By the mid-century, the heady mix of human tragedy, the glamour of the Middle Ages and the interest in archaeological authenticity culminated in one of the theatrical sensations of the Victorian period: Charles Kean's 1857 staging of *King Richard the Second*.

Westminster Hall, conceived by William Rufus in the eleventh century, was extensively remodelled by Richard II in the 1390s. The arms of Richard and his personal device, the white hart, are a prominent and continuous motif throughout the interior decoration. Above the extraordinary expanse of the hall is the great hammer-beam roof, a feat of medieval craftsmanship and engineering. With every detail, Richard sought to stamp his authority upon a building that represented, more than any other, the heart of English secular life. The significance of the hall within the national consciousness soared after the building's miraculous survival of the fire of 1834. As the publisher Charles Knight later recalled:

> There was a time when the destruction of Westminster Hall seemed almost inevitable. To those who mixed amongst the crowd in Palace Yard, and knew that the antiquities of a nation are amongst its best possessions, it was truly gratifying to witness the intense anxiety of all classes of people to preserve this building, associated with so many grand historical scenes. "Save the Hall!" "Save the Hall!" was the universal cry.[9]

The emotional response to the impending loss of the hall, and the jubilation at its survival, guaranteed its creator a significant place in posterity – if only by association. At the very dawn of the nineteenth century, this association had been evident, at least, to the topographer and antiquarian John Carter[10] when he wrote:

> ... no common command bid these walls arise; no, a splendid king said, this my intended palace shall surpass all the architectural works of my contemporaries; here shall be seen the world's habitable wonder! How well this royal resolution was carried into effect. ... We who are Antiquaries enjoy and feel all the raptures which this remaining memorial of kingly state can possibly inspire. We faintly speak; but our extasies [*sic*] tell it all.[11]

For almost twenty years, until his death in 1817, Carter conducted a passionate campaign through the pages of the *Gentleman's Magazine* that highlighted the woeful condition of the nation's ancient buildings, and included a vitriolic critique of the current state of Westminster Hall. Indeed, the lack of regard for the hall during the eighteenth century bordered on wilful neglect. The exterior was partially obscured by an unsightly collection of coffee houses and taverns (see illus., p. 85, top), described by Carter in 1800 as the "usurping excrescences [*sic*] of sheds, hovels, taverns, and alehouses, that blot out and disfigure the walls of old English Splendour and old English hospitality".[12] A report in 1789 produced on behalf of the House of Commons (and signed by such architectural luminaries as Robert Adam and John Soane) provides a detailed description of the motley assemblage of buildings that crowded around the hall, many of which, the authors noted prophetically, "increase the Danger of Fire and its Communication".[13] The dignity of the interior was marred by the squalor of the law courts that lined the walls, and the book and wig stalls that serviced them (see illus., p. 85, bottom). In 1805 the decision was made to improve the Courts and, as described in the *Universal Magazine*, "all the sheds which now disgrace that venerable pile are to be pulled down and the entrances to the Hall repaired and beautified".[14]

English School, *The Exterior of Westminster Hall: North Façade*, watercolour, *c*. 1810. This watercolour is a rare image of the north façade just after the coffee houses were removed and prior to the mysterious disappearance of the remaining exterior statues commissioned by Richard II, which can be seen to the left of the door and on the lower level of the right tower. Palace of Westminster (WOA 2679).

It is tempting to suggest that the greater interest in addressing the shoddy condition of the British Parliament buildings was a result of an upsurge of patriotism during the Napoleonic Wars. Certainly, the criticisms of Carter and his contemporaries appear to have shamed the authorities into action. The clearance of the north façade was the beginning of an extensive programme of restoration to the exterior of the hall that continued throughout the subsequent decades, under the supervision first of James Wyatt and then of John Soane.[15] The interior remained in an "opprobrious state of dilapidation and disfigurement", as Sydney Smirke phrased it,[16] until 1834, when his brother, Robert, commenced work. On 16 October of that year, it seemed that the effort had been for nothing.

By the time the fire had reached Westminster Hall, the Commons Chamber – housed within the medieval Chapel of St Stephen – and the Painted Chamber had been gutted. The hall was arguably the last significant element of the ancient Palace of Westminster still remaining. As *The Times* reported:

> The country will have reason, all things considered, to be thankful that Westminster Hall, the scene, the witness we had almost said the living associate, of so many of the most ancient and noble passages of English History, has escaped this deplorable visitation.[17]

This response was by no means unique, and it demonstrates that general complacency had evolved at this moment of national crisis into something infinitely more profound. The ancient buildings of the monarchs and Parliament of England and Great Britain had achieved significance beyond mere function; they were recognized as the reliquaries of collective memory:

> ... let them stand, while a particle remains, to remind us who live, that those historic evidences which we read are not romantic fictions; and that we may emulate those

Attributed to Joshua Bryant, *New Palace Yard*, c. 1804, pencil and wash on paper. Palace of Westminster (WOA 3818).

C. Moseley after H. Gravelot, *The First Day of Term*, engraving, published 6 November 1797 (first published 1738). Palace of Westminster (WOA 1403).

deeds of high renown recorded by the pens of inspired Bards, which gave prophetic harmony to the enrapturing harps of the enchanting Minstrels![18]

As Carter's prose suggests, the antiquarian impulse to define and delineate co-existed with a passionate and sentimental identification with the history the physical evidence of which he strove to record, and although his vision reached a large audience through the *Gentleman's Magazine*, this 'romantic antiquarianism' found its greatest expression and achieved phenomenal popularity through the novels of Sir Walter Scott.

In his account of the history of the Gothic Revival, published in 1872, Charles Locke Eastlake wrote:

> The time may perhaps have now arrived when the popular mind can dispense with the spell of association, and learn to admire Gothic for its intrinsic beauty. ... But fifty years ago, in the darkest period which British art has seen, we were illuminated by one solitary and flickering flame, which Scott contrived to keep alive. It was the Lamp of Memory.[19]

The friend of antiquarians such as Sir Samuel Rush Meyrick, the collector and first great historian of armour,[20] Scott suffused his novels with unprecedented archaeological detail (even if chronology and historical fact were occasionally ignored), and in his evocative descriptions of both countryside and architecture, he inspired his readership actively to identify with their ancestors and national heritage. This was at its most poignant when legend and history, interchangeable within Scott's narrative, were contextualized within topography familiar or at least accessible to the reader: a geographical continuum between ancient and post-industrial Britain. The following example comes from the opening paragraph of *Ivanhoe* (1819):

> In that pleasant district of merry England which is watered by the river Don, there extended in ancient times a large forest, covering the greater part of the beautiful hills and valleys which lie between Sheffield and the pleasant town of Doncaster. The remains of this extensive wood are still to be seen at the noble seats of Wentworth, of Wharncliffe Park, and around Rotherham. Here haunted of yore the fabulous Dragon of Wantley; here were fought many of the most desperate battles during the Civil Wars of the Roses, and here also flourished in ancient times those bands of gallant outlaws whose deeds have been rendered so popular in English song.[21]

History and fairy tale, landscape and folklore, presented to the reader in prose that is both captivating and accessible. As one reviewer of *Ivanhoe* stated:

> Kings, crusaders, knights, and outlaws, Coeur de Lion, and the Templars, and Robin Hood, and Friar Tuck, and the Forest of Sherwood, the names, and the times, and the scenes, which are entwined with the earliest and dearest recollections, but which we never hope again to meet with in serious narrative, become as familiar in our mouths as household terms.[22]

As Scott's popularity allowed 'history' to be accessed by a broader audience, extant architecture achieved significance as the monumental stages upon which this history had been acted out. As a result, his most popular novels, such as *Ivanhoe* and *Kenilworth* (1821), were cited as having been instrumental in creating the environment within which the Gothic Revival style could achieve universal appeal. To quote Eastlake once more:

OPPOSITE: Frank O. Salisbury, *The Great Roof*, oil on canvas, 1924. This theatrical image of Richard II (centre left) inspecting the work on the roof of Westminster Hall, with his master carpenter Hugh Herland to the right, was painted by Salisbury after the completion of the restoration of the roof in 1921 and prior to the removal of the scaffold. From his unique vantage point, the artist was able to sketch at close range the elements of the roof, including one of the angels. Here Richard is seen as the great patron of the arts and, as is evident from his sumptuous attire, a man who indulged his interest in displays of magnificence. However, the two figures cast in shadow to the bottom right of the composition act as a portent of the reaction against the king's extravagance and his eventual downfall. Palace of Westminster (WOA 2730).

The truth is that the service which Scott rendered to the cause of the Revival was to awaken popular interest in a style which had hitherto been associated except by the educated few, with ascetic gloom and vulgar superstition.[23]

Evidence of this can be seen within the canvases inspired by Scott, painted by Romantic artists such as Richard Parkes Bonington, Eugène Delacroix and Léon Cogniet. In his *Rebecca and Brian de Bois-Guilbert*, Cogniet vividly illustrates the description from *Ivanhoe* of the abduction of the Jewess Rebecca by the Templar de Bois-Guilbert, with the Norman castle of Torquilstone engulfed in flames providing a sublime backdrop to the action. These artists visualized not only the period detail but also the emotional intensity of Scott's novels, and thus demonstrated their dramatic potential.

Theatre provided a further dimension. Enterprising managers, keen to capitalize on the success of Scott's novels, transposed them to the stage with unseemly haste.[24] The ballet *Kenilworth* was produced at the King's Theatre in 1831, and among the scene painters and 'advisers' was none other than the precocious Gothicist, Augustus Welby Northmore

Thomas Grieve, theatre model for the production of *King Henry the Eighth* at Covent Garden, watercolour and pencil, 1831. Theatre Museum, London.

Pugin.[25] In the same year, Pugin assisted the theatrical designer and scene painter William Grieve in the Covent Garden production of Shakespeare's *King Henry the Eighth*, with Charles Kemble in the lead role. This production, above all others, is cited as having had the greatest influence on Pugin's career as both architect and designer.[26] But it was his involvement with the ballet *Kenilworth* that was used as evidence by his son that the conception of the new Palace of Westminster (*i.e.*, its Gothic authenticity) was Pugin's and not Barry's:

> ... let me first discuss the probability of the designs being made by my father. His powers at this time were very far in advance of his contemporaries. He was thoroughly competent to produce the designs. In fact, there was not another man in England who could take his place. Any one who has beheld his scenes and decorations in the Operas of Kenilworth (in London), or La Juive and Count Ory (in Paris), will have recognized a richness of conception, powers of delineation, and a knowledge of Gothic Architecture and detail perfectly wonderful.[27]

Indeed, Pugin was one of a growing number of antiquarians and architects who were encouraging and in turn responding to the trend for archaeological accuracy within theatrical productions. John Carter, a keen musician, had himself written two 'medieval' operas, *The White Rose* and *The Cell of St Oswald*, for which he had designed and painted scenery (although neither were professionally performed).[28] Plays based upon historical events, such as Shakespeare's histories, were perhaps the most susceptible to this authentic approach to costume and scenery. As the nineteenth century advanced, the expanding body of antiquarian publications provided producers with copious source material. An example was Charles Knight's *Pictorial Edition of the Works of Shakspere* [*sic*], published in the late 1830s. Knight later wrote:

> ... it became necessary for me to look carefully at the plays, to see whether the aid of art might not be called in to add both to the information and enjoyment of the reader of Shakespeare, by representing the Realities upon which the imagination of the poet must have rested. There were the localities of the various scenes, whether English or

foreign; the portraits of the real personages of the historical plays, the objects of natural history, so constantly occurring; accurate costume in all its rich variety.[29]

Clearly, Knight's purpose was to encourage a greater understanding and appreciation of Shakespeare in the general reader. His method, which can be seen as an extension of Scott's novels, was to include visual representations of the scenes and characters, while increasing the didactic quality of the publication through the inclusion of extensive explanatory text and sources. Knight had proved his antiquarian credentials in previous publications such as James Robinson Planché's *History of British Costume* (1834), produced on behalf of the Society for the Diffusion of Useful Knowledge. Significantly, Planché had been the production designer and adviser for Charles Kemble's 1823 revival of *King John* at Covent Garden, and, in the course of his research, he was introduced to Samuel Rush Meyrick and fellow antiquary Francis Douce. The success of the production was extraordinary, and, as Planché later wrote, "a complete reformation of dramatic costume became from that moment inevitable upon the English Stage".[30] In the spirit of this antiquarian 'reformation', Knight, in his *Pictorial Edition of the Works of Shakspere*, draws extensively on the sources then available. For the costumes illustrated in *King Richard the Second*, for example, Knight refers to the contemporary writings of Chaucer and Froissart, and the Westminster Abbey painting of *Richard II Enthroned* (see illus., pp. 80, 82) – then known as the Jerusalem Chamber Portrait – to name but a few. Knight acknowledged the assistance of Planché and, for the period armour, the publications of Meyrick. Within the topographical engravings, both Westminster Hall and New Palace Yard are represented. The latter, as Knight explains, was based upon the seventeenth-century etching by Wenceslaus Hollar, "but many of its earlier features are preserved, and the engraving affords a key to explain several authentic particulars as to its condition two centuries and a half earlier, of which a restoration is here attempted".[31] The imaginary interior depicted for Act I included in its decoration tapestries "the well-known cognizances of Richard II, the sun and the white hart".[32] It is an indication of the increasing knowledge of Richard II, at least among antiquarians, that Knight describes these devices as

ABOVE: After John Carter (?), *Richard II*, engraving, published in C. Knight, *The Pictorial Edition of the Works of Shakspere* [sic], 1838, *Histories*, I, p. 101.

ABOVE: W. Harvey, Frontispiece to *King Richard II*, engraving, published in C. Knight, *The Pictorial Edition of the Works of Shakspere* [sic], 1838, *Histories*, I, p. 79.

LEFT: After Wenceslas Hollar, *Exterior of Westminster Hall (New Palace Yard)*, published in C. Knight, *The Pictorial Edition of the Works of Shakspere* [sic], 1838, *Histories*, I, p. 129.

ABOVE: English School, *The White Hart*, wall painting, 14th century. Muniment Room, Westminster Abbey, London.

ABOVE: English School, Tomb effigy of Richard II (detail), gilt bronze, 1397–99, Westminster Abbey, London.

"well-known". Certainly, evidence of the white hart, the rising sun and the broomcod, all associated with Richard II, could readily be found within the abbey, the Wilton Diptych and Westminster Hall. Further examples were discovered in 1840, when the cleaning of Richard II's tomb effigy, described in an article by John Gough Nichols in 1842, revealed the pounced harts, suns and broomcods, "which had been so entirely concealed by the accumulated dirt of centuries that they were at length forgotten and unknown".[33]

As the Gothic Revival gained greater cachet, both in architecture and literature, the staging of Shakespeare's lesser-known medieval histories, *King John* and *King Richard the Second*, became a viable proposition. More importantly, in the period that spawned that ultimate medieval pantomime, the Eglinton Tournament (see chapter 15), *King Richard the Second* provided an opportunity to indulge in the escapism of the 'Age of Chivalry'. But during the eighteenth and early nineteenth centuries, *King Richard the Second* remained one of a small number of Shakespeare's plays that had received little attention. During the eighteenth century, the great actor-impresario David Garrick had re-established the Bard within the canon of popular theatre. But, as the critic William Hazlitt wrote in 1817, "Richard II is a play little known compared with Richard III which last is a play that every unfledged candidate for theatrical fame chuses [*sic*] to strut and fret his hour upon the stage in".[34] The actor-manager Richard Wroughton offered the explanation that it was "considered too heavy for representation ... [and] bordering too much on the Mono-drama".[35] It would seem that, at the turn of the century, the role of Richard lacked the virility and swagger demanded by actors and audiences alike. Any attempt to render the part 'heroic' was doomed to failure. As one commentator on Edmund Kean's 1815 performance observed:

> ... we think it was not a true portrait of the weak and melancholy Richard. This King, who disappointed all expectations, who dishonoured the bold blood from which he sprang and belied the promises of his own youth ... was not fierce nor impetuous, but weak and irritable, and in his downfall utterly prostrate in spirit. We did not recognise these qualities in the acting of Mr Kean who was almost as fiery and energetic as he used to be in Richard the Third.[36]

In Samuel Taylor Coleridge's uncompromising opinion, Richard "is weak, variable, and womanish, and possesses feelings, which, amiable in a female, are misplaced in a man, and altogether unfit for a king".[37] Despite the growing appeal of the period in which Shakespeare's play was set, and the body of source material for its authentic recreation, it is unlikely, judging from the opinions of Coleridge and his fellow critics, that the play could have achieved any success on the English stage without some fundamental transformation in the perception of the central character.

An eighteenth-century theatre manager would have received little encouragement from histories of England published at that time. Both Tobias Smollett and Hugh Clarendon judge the historical Richard in terms as dismissive and disparaging as Coleridge's later precis of the monarch's literary incarnation.[38] Although David Hume presented a more objective view, rightly questioning the credibility of Lancastrian (or pro-Henry IV) sources, he concludes that "he still appears to have been a weak prince, and unfit for government".[39]

Histories published in the first half of the nineteenth century judged the removal of Richard II as a necessary evil for the sake of the nation's political development. In Thomas Keightley's *The History of England* (published 1839), Richard's downfall is equated with the Glorious Revolution of 1688 and the enforced abdication of James II.[40] However, despite the consensus among nineteenth-century historians that the events leading to the king's deposition were justifiable for the greater good, a compassion for the man himself is more than evident, and can be seen as a departure from the earlier attitudes of Smollett, Clarendon and Hume. In his history of 1825, Sharon Turner considered Richard's accession to the throne at the age of eleven as the catalyst of his moral decline, concluding that:

> Richard's moral imperfections must be censured for the sake of society which royal vices peculiarly afflict. But it is just to consider him as in a great degree the victim of his situation and circumstances. This is neither an apology nor an atonement for his misconduct; but it is a claim on our compassionate sympathies, for, with such inducements to error, who is there but might have fallen?[41]

In Lingard's essentially critical precis of Richard's reign, quoted at the beginning of this essay, a similar sympathy is evident regarding the manner of his demise. However, both Turner and Lingard had returned, unlike earlier histories, to Creton's *Metrical History* as a source for their texts,[42] and it must therefore have heavily influenced the sympathetic and compassionate elements of their interpretation. This engagement is certainly evident in John Webb's introduction to his translation of Creton's *Metrical History* (published in *Archaeologia* in 1824):

> It is also highly interesting to the general reader; for it offers an original circumstantial account of the fall of Richard the Second, who, whatever may have been his errors, is rendered by his misfortunes an object of commiseration.[43]

For Webb, the history offered a reliable account of the beleaguered monarch's final months. Further, through the author's apparent intimacy with the events described and the king himself, "we become close observers of his injudicious and ill-fated career ... with almost as strong an impression as if ourselves had witnessed the progress of the melancholy affair".[44]

Both Creton's *Metrical History* and the anonymous *Traïson et mort* were sources for Holinshed's chronicle, the basis for Shakespeare's history play. As nineteenth-century historians had returned to these same chronicles, it is not surprising that the two Richards, the historic and the literary, should be perceived as synonymous: an axiom that to a large degree remains true today. Commenting on the painting *Richard II Enthroned* (before its restoration in 1866; see illus., p. 95, left), a writer from *The Times* observed, "It has been entirely painted over, and is now a ruin, but even the ruin shows us the fair, soft, weak face which we should expect, and it is, in all probability, a contemporary monumental picture".[45] The author's expectation almost certainly derived from Shakespeare and the writings of antiquarians. The "fair soft, weak face" evident from the king's likeness confirmed the veracity of this interpretation. As Charles Knight affirmed, "The Richard II of Shakspere [*sic*] is the Richard II of real history".[46] The belief that Shakespeare's essentially sympathetic interpretation was based upon historical fact and reliable eye-witness accounts assisted in the rehabilitation of Richard II, both in history and literature. The prevailing sentimentality of the period, coupled with an interest in and identification with the Middle Ages, completed this process. Pondering the appeal of Richard II, Charles Knight wrote:

> ... why is it that Richard II still commands our tears – even our sympathies? It is this:– His very infirmities make him creep into our affections – for they are so nearly allied to the beautiful parts of his character, that, if the little leaven had been absent, he might have been a ruler to kneel before, and a man to love. We see, then, how thin is the parti-

ABOVE: English School, Hart, stone, *c.* 1850. Staircase, south end, Westminster Hall, Palace of Westminster.

RIGHT: Designed by or after A.W.N. Pugin, manufactured by Minton, encaustic tile showing Richard II's devices of the crowned initial 'R' and the chained hart. Members' Entrance, House of Commons, Palace of Westminster.

tion between the highest and the lowliest parts of our nature – and we love Richard even for his faults, – for they are those of our common humanity.[47]

In 1775, the painting *Richard II Enthroned* was removed from the stalls in Westminster Abbey and hung in the Jerusalem Chamber within the abbey complex. Accessible to a privileged few, it was known to a limited audience through the engraving by George Vertue (1718) and the more accurate version by John Carter of 1786.[48] In 1857, it emerged from obscurity to be exhibited at the Manchester Art Treasures exhibition, where, as George Scharf Jr later wrote, it became one of the revelations of the event, "partly it may be from its size; partly the subject, and, most of all, from its Gothic quaintness".[49] In the same year, Charles Kean unveiled his supremely antiquarian production of Shakespeare's play. The timing was providential, to say the least. In the introduction to his version of Shakespeare's text, Kean observed:

> An increasing taste for recreation, wherein instruction is blended with amusement, has for some time been conspicuous in the English public. ... Repeated success justifies the conviction that I am acting in accordance with the general feeling. When plays, which formerly commanded but occasional repetition, are enabled, by no derogatory means, to attract audiences for successive months, I cannot be wrong in presuming that the

course I have adopted is supported by the irresistible force of public opinion, expressed in the suffrages of an overwhelming majority.[50]

In terms reminiscent of Charles Knight, Kean sought to educate as well as entertain his audience through "accompaniments *true* to the time which he writes – *realizing* the scenes and actions which he describes – exhibiting men as they once lived".[51] In the wake of the successes of both Kemble and, later, William Charles Macready, Kean called upon the services of a regiment of antiquarians, including George Scharf and Planché (both of whom, unsurprisingly, were involved with the Manchester exhibition), to create, as he described it, "a true portraiture of medieval history".[52] In addition, the armour and costume publications by Meyrick, F.W. Fairholt and Joseph Strutt[53] were consulted, and contemporary manuscripts trawled. Kean could announce, with some justification, that "I guarantee the truthfulness and fidelity of the entire picture", backed as it was by the expertise of antiquarians "whose conviction of the usefulness of my efforts is a gratifying encouragement to adhere to the plan of illustration I have hitherto adopted".[54] Kean was elected a fellow of the Society of Antiquaries on 18 June 1857.[55] The wealth of antiquarian detail was acknowledged by one overwhelmed reviewer in *The Times*:

> We have now enumerated the principal 'effects', decorative and histrionic, that belong to this most remarkable revival. Or rather we have started where the 'effects' occur, for the wealth of archaeological detail lavished on the scenes and the costumes is almost beyond the reach of imagination, much more that of description.[56]

But the production did not simply recreate archaeological detail for its own sake; this was a conscious attempt to bring the past to life, and the medium of theatre was uniquely placed to achieve this. In fact, what Kean produced was the precursor to the Hollywood epic. As his biographer later wrote:

> the by-gone ages of the world are called into new existence, placed before the sight, and presented to the mind of the spectator and auditor as in a living panorama.[57]

Thomas Grieve and others, preliminary designs for stage settings and costumes for Charles Kean's production of *Richard II*, Act I, Scene i, performed at the Princess's Theatre, 1857, pencil and watercolour, 1857. Theatre Museum, London.

RIGHT: *Richard II Enthroned* (as in illus., pp. 80, 82), photograph prior to restoration, *c.* 1865. Victoria and Albert Museum, London.

FAR RIGHT: Charles Kean as Richard II at the Princess's Theatre, 1857.

In his desire to present "a living panorama", Kean included a scene that is only described in the play's text; the entry of Richard and Bolingbroke into London after the former king has relinquished the crown (Act V, scene ii). Richard's abdication was to be publicly formalized in Westminster Hall, but Kean clearly hoped to increase empathy for Richard by acting out this humiliating public event before the theatre audience. In addition, the scene allowed for the creation of a theatrical spectacular with a cast of hundreds. The scenery, representing a London street, was created with the advice of George Godwin FSA. To expand upon the description within Shakespeare's play, Kean used both Creton's *Metrical History* and the *Traïson et Mort* for the general ambience of the event, as well as the specific cries from members of the assembled mob.[58] The resulting 'authenticity', both verbal and visual, assisted the illusion that an actual historical event was being replayed before the audience's very eyes:

> If a citizen of London, at 1399, could have been actually revived, and seated within the stalls of the theatre without passing through the changed external world, he would have fancied that he saw a living repetition of what he once had taken a part in.[59]

Reviewers acknowledged the success of the production as a whole, and the street scene in particular, in blurring the distinction between theatre and reality. As *The Times* correspondent wrote, "of theatrical convention there is not a trace ... It seems a real mob – nay a real people".[60] In Act I, scene i, the audience was treated to the extraordinary sight of Kean, as Richard II, in a costume derived from the 'Jerusalem' portrait:[61] a painting that the public were to view in Manchester in their tens of thousands. Through this conceit, Kean was transformed into the monarch himself:

> ... the veritable Richard stood, moved, and spoke before us ... as transferred from the pages of the histories, warmed and coloured by the imagination of the poet, and called into re-animated existence by the kindred genius of his interpreter.[62]

In addition, the accurate reconstruction of the interior of Westminster Hall for the play's denouement – that exquisite irony, as described by Kean, "the Great Hall at Westminster, rebuilt by Richard, in his pride of kingly sway, and afterwards selected as the place where unkinged Richard was constrained 'With his own hands to give away his crown'"[63] – offered the viewer the by-now hallowed national monument in a historic context. Thus, the iconic image was transformed into flesh and blood: the ancient architecture no longer the 'evidence of history' but visualized at the moment in which 'history' was actually being made. Here, surely, was Sir Walter Scott's literary vision taken to its natural conclusion: the culmination, perhaps the ultimate expression, of the Gothic Revival.

The production had its critics. Some believed that the play had been subverted for the sake of spectacle. But Kean's popular success indicates that his *King Richard the Second* had struck a chord with the public. One might go so far as to say that he had tapped into the mid-nineteenth-century *Zeitgeist*. As Walter Pater recalled at the end of the nineteenth century:

Thomas Grieve, design for stage setting of the deposition scene in Charles Kean's production of *Richard II* performed at the Princess's Theatre, 1857, watercolour, 1857. Theatre Museum, London.

A.W.N. Pugin, design for Richard II heraldic wallpaper, pencil, bodycolour and coloured washes, *c.* 1842–52. Victoria and Albert Museum, London.

Yet it is only fair to say that in the painstaking 'revival' of *King Richard the Second*, by the late Charles Kean, those who were very young thirty years ago were afforded much more than Shakspere's [*sic*] play could ever have been before – the very person of the king based on that stately old portrait in Westminster Abbey, "the earliest extant contemporary likeness of any English sovereign", the grace, the winning pathos, the sympathetic voice of the player, the tasteful archaeology confronting vulgar modern London with a scenic reproduction, for once really agreeable, of the London of Chaucer.[64]

# 6

## Parliament's Genius Loci: The Politics of Place after the 1834 Fire

Andrea Fredericksen

"Consult the Genius of the place in all." This precept determined the whole question. It became, therefore, necessary to have a place with a Genius belonging to it; and it was soon determined that in no place could there be more genius than in that of the present Houses of Parliament.[1]

A wise man may cling fondly to the associations connected with free institutions; but to hold the doctrine that there is but one spot of ground in Great Britain upon which an altar to freedom can be erected, is mere lunacy.[2]

Writing on the decision to rebuild Parliament's home upon its original site after the 1834 fire, the pamphlet-writer 'Archilochus' explained that the reasons had been determined entirely by the "genius of place". Appropriating Alexander Pope's celebrated phrase for landscape gardeners to lend further credence to the choice, the writer's comment affirmed the age-old associations tied to Westminster as Parliament's ancient home.[3] Only upon this site, in close proximity to the historic Westminster Hall and Abbey, the commentator suggested, could the new building properly convey important connections to the past.

This statement supports recent studies of the city as a landscape of 'collective memory', indicating how locations or buildings serve as 'cues for remembering', or containers of national meaning.[4] But while the inclination to rebuild at Westminster may seem a natural one today – given Parliament's long history on this ground – the choice involved a series of calculated decisions regarding location and style. These factors are telling when one considers the compelling arguments that were made for finding an alternative to the notoriously impractical site at Westminster, based upon such pressing issues as health, accommodation and convenience. The ensuing debate played an important role in defining what constituted meaningful urban design, which confirmed this "one spot of ground" as the place where politics and power ought to be directed and performed. The rebuilding of the Palace of Westminster was guided by "the invention of tradition", or the desire to imply – through a carefully staged architectural programme that both pilfered from and lent to the historical associations of the Westminster setting – a continuity with a suitable past perceived as the nation's Golden Age.[5]

### The Power of Place: Arguments for the Westminster Site

At six o'clock in the evening on 16 October 1834, fire broke out under the debating chamber of the House of Lords. By the following day, the centre of the area that at that time comprised the old palace was in ruins. The Lords Chamber was left with only the walls

J.M.W. Turner, *The Burning of the Houses of Lords and Commons, October 16, 1834*, oil on canvas, 1834 or 1835. The John Howard McFadden Collection, Philadelphia Museum of Art.

standing. Both the Painted Chamber and St Stephen's Chapel were roofless, their celebrated wall paintings damaged or destroyed. Half of the sixteenth-century cloisters were burnt out, and many of the later buildings, such as Soane's Commons Library, and much of Wyatt's work overlooking Old Palace Yard and the River Thames, had likewise been gutted.

The question of how and where to relocate the now homeless Parliament became a priority. William IV immediately offered the almost completed Buckingham Palace as a permanent replacement. But the idea was rejected by those who felt that John Nash's grandiose structure was better suited to a royal palace than a legislative seat.[6] A few officials asked whether a new building was needed at all, given that substantial areas to the north and south remained relatively untouched.[7] Robert Smirke, the only remaining architect attached to the Board of Works, was directed to patch together temporary accommodations for both Houses. These were completed by 17 February 1835. Smirke was also asked to prepare plans for rebuilding on a "moderate and suitable scale of magnitude".[8] But when rumours abounded that Smirke had designed a new building at the behest of a handful of Members, there was a general outcry from the press, who called for a new system for choosing architects, based upon an open, anonymous competition.[9] Given that recent attempts to improve the accommodation of the House of Commons had been abandoned because Members had been unwilling to see the destruction of their historic home, fate had now provided a unique opportunity to design a purpose-built structure for both Houses of Parliament, on a scale that would reflect Britain's pre-eminent position on the world stage, and act as a worthy focus for national pride. Such an opportunity, it seemed, could not be wasted.[10]

As a result, the Commons committee to consider rebuilding, set up in 1835 along with one for the Lords, was swayed by the press campaign and an influential open letter to the Prime Minister written by a former Tory Member of Parliament, Sir Edward Cust.[11] Cust argued for the appointment of commissioners who were interested in architecture to organize and judge a competition for designs for a new legislature for Parliament, and subsequently to superintend its construction. The committee accepted these proposals, except that it was decided to keep the superintendence of the building under Parliamentary control.[12] The resolutions of the Lords and Commons committees, published on 3 June 1835, announced an architectural competition to which anyone was free to submit an anonymous

William Railton, *Perspective View from the South West, Shewing the Entrances of the King, Lords and Commons in Old Palace Yard,* competition design for the new Houses of Parliament, 1835, awarded the fourth prize. Public Record Office, London.

William Taylor after R.W. Billings, *View of Interior of the House of Commons as Fitted up 1835,* engraving, February 1835, published in *The History of the Ancient Palace and Late Houses of Parliament at Westminster* by E.W. Brayley and J. Britton, London 1836, pl. xxxix, p. 433.

entry. The committees also resolved two other important issues: that the style of the new palace should be either Gothic or Elizabethan, and that it should be built upon the original site. Each entrant was provided with very basic specifications for the accommodation to be incorporated into the new building, and a copy of the resolutions of the Rebuilding Committee, together with the evidence presented to it. A lithographic plan – provided at a cost of £1 – set out the location's boundaries, forcing the entrants to work with an awkward, rectangular-shaped site that included Old Palace Yard, Westminster Hall, St Margaret's Church and Henry VII's Chapel to the west, the busy thoroughfare leading to Westminster Bridge to the north, and the River Thames – still without its embankment – to the east.

By the deadline of 1 December 1835, the Royal Commission had received ninety-seven competition entries, many the work of young and obscure architects. The catalogue of designs displayed at the National Gallery the following April revealed that the competitors had mostly adhered to stylistic requirements, as well as incorporating portions of the old palace complex (see also chapter 7).[13] At first, entrants muttered about the lack of preparation time. But when the commissioners announced Barry's Perpendicular Gothic design as the winner, they proceeded to attack not only the committee's designated style, but also the basic premises underpinning the choice of location.[14] Given the force and the validity of their arguments, the decision to proceed with a new complex in the Gothic style and upon its original location demonstrates the overriding importance of memory, association and tradition to the symbolic meaning of this national monument.

The committees' decision on location and style was, in many ways, a romantic gesture, prompted by the overwhelming response to the destruction caused by the fire, relief that Westminster Hall had survived the blaze, and nostalgia for the lost structures. On the night of this historic event, crowds of spectators had watched, either mourning the loss of national heritage or celebrating the spectacle as a bonfire that would instigate much-needed change.[15] The porter at the Royal Academy reputedly announced to the students working in the library, "Now gentlemen; now, you young architects, there's a fine chance for you; the Parliament House is all afire."[16] Numerous artists, such as J.M.W. Turner and the theatre designer William Grieve, recorded the sublime effects of the conflagration, and journalists recounted the progress of the fire as though it were a major theatrical staging.[17] Both Barry

LEFT: J.M.W. Turner, *The Burning of the Houses of Lords and Commons, October 16, 1834*, oil on canvas, 1834 or 1835. The John Howard McFadden Collection, Philadelphia Museum of Art.

BELOW LEFT: J.M.W. Turner, *The Burning of the Houses of Parliament*, watercolour, 1834. Tate Gallery, London.

RIGHT: George Scharf, *Panorama of the Ruins of the Old Palace of Westminster*, oil on paper on canvas, 1834. Scharf arrived at the Palace of Westminster the day after the fire and spent the following three weeks sketching from the roof of Westminster Hall. The finished painting was originally on two canvases, which were attached by hinges (this is the left canvas), the intention being that the canvases should be positioned at an angle to one another to achieve the full panoramic effect. The right canvas, which depicted the House of Lords round to Westminster Abbey, remains unlocated. The gutted remains of St Stephen's Chapel can be seen to the right, while St Stephen's Cloister (centre left) and the castellated Speaker's House above remain relatively unharmed. Scharf included in his painting sightseers who wander around the ruins and clamber over roofs. Within St Stephen's Cloister, figures operate a water pump, and another figure seated in the corner, who appears to be sketching, may be the artist himself. Palace of Westminster (WOA 3793).

William Grieve, *The Palace of Westminster on Fire, 16th October 1834*, watercolour, 1834. Palace of Westminster (WOA 1054).

and Pugin were among the spectators; it would seem that Barry's mind had already turned to a "conception of designs for the future".[18]

One witness in the *New Monthly Magazine*, who described the scene as "certainly the grandest thing, at one period, we have ever witnessed", asked his readers to consider the value of buildings as "memories and living records of the past".[19] While these memories would survive the loss of St Stephen's Chapel and the Painted Chamber, with the deeds of ancient kings and the words of Parliamentarians living on in the public's imagination, the article rightly proposed that the buildings made this relationship with the past more immediate, emotional and binding. The fire brought these connections to the fore. It also increased the cultural significance of Westminster Hall, which "like a giant of the Gothic age had outlived so many historical events and revolutions", and whose every stone seemed to provide irreplaceable bonds to these important events.[20] Such assertions transformed these historic places into storehouses of ideas, showing how monuments preserved important historical information, and nurtured the citizen's sense of national identity.

By fixing the Houses of Parliament to this precise location, the committees undoubtedly felt that the project would benefit from and reinforce the political and cultural meaning ascribed to the Westminster area. For some commentators, the surviving buildings would provide the spectator with an instant connection to the past. The hall and abbey, for instance, would serve as reminders of former kings and their venerated Christian tradition. Once cleaned and made more durable, "in them", the *Gentleman's Magazine* stated:

> the true interests and liberties of the subject [will] be ultimately consolidated, the splendour and vigour of the monarchy preserved, the national Church, its firm ally and

J.H. Lynch after Thomas Hopper, *New Palace Yard, Drawing for the Westminster Competition, 1835*, colour lithograph, 1840. Palace of Westminster (WOA 1658).

best pillar, protected, and Old England still continue by such means to dispense the blessings of real liberty of intellectual light, unclouded by superstition or fanaticisms, to the nations of the earth![21]

Presenting a political order that, to the writer of the *Gentleman's Magazine* article, had become "constitutional and prescriptive", the Houses of Parliament must be positioned on the grounds of this ancient royal palace, "like other courts under [the king's] authority".

Considering the political climate of the mid-1830s, when various groups battled over the progress of Parliamentary reform, the reinsertion of the two Houses into Westminster's historic assemblage suggests that Parliament had become integrated into a symbolic programme that gave primacy to ancient royal associations.[22]

Claims for the Westminster location as the only place of genius for the Houses of Parliament made the choice of architectural style a crucial one. When the committees announced that designs must be submitted in either the Gothic or Elizabethan style, competitors interpreted the requirement as a desire to harmonize the new building with the area's overriding character.[23] In his competition design, for example, Thomas Hopper replicated the Gothic façade of Westminster Hall in order to create a bizarre unity of expression between old and new.[24] Such examples supported the increasingly popular theory that by adopting architectural ornamentation modelled on surviving examples, neo-Gothic buildings would similarly stimulate ideas connected to ancient royal splendour and the traditional "interests and liberties" of the subject.[25] The architect and champion of Gothic A.W.N. Pugin saw this architectural reinvention as a means by which the historic precinct of Westminster could be wiped clean of Soane's modern additions and Wyatt's misguided castellated façades, and a purpose-built, stylistically unified monument constructed.[26]

Pugin's reaction to the destruction of Wyatt's stylistic mixtures foreshadowed a new, more serious attitude towards the Gothic. The style had come back in fashion in the late eighteenth century with the construction of such eccentric country houses as William Beckford's Fonthill Abbey, begun in 1796 by James Wyatt.[27] Primarily concerned with drama

ABOVE: George Hawkins Jr after Thomas Hopper, *Entrance to the House of Lords, Drawing for the Westminster Palace Competition of 1835*, lithograph, *c.* 1840, Palace of Westminster (WOA 009).

ABOVE: T. Higham after J. Martin, *Fonthill Abbey, View of the West & North Fronts from the End of the Clerk's Walk*, lithograph, published 2 June 1823 in *Delineations of Fonthill and its Abbey* by John Rutter, London 1823, pl. xi, p. 66.

RIGHT: H. Jones after Thomas Hopper, *Perspective Elevation of the River Front, drawing for the Westminster Palace Competition of 1835*, lithograph, 1840. Palace of Westminster (WOA 1659).

and picturesque effect, Wyatt built a cathedral-style complex that was briefly celebrated as a theatrical backdrop to Beckford's Gothic extravaganzas. The Elizabethan or Tudor style was also rediscovered by landscapists, antiquarians and novelists for its ability to evoke romantic images of the past, this time of the reign of Elizabeth I, Gloriana.[28] Both styles increasingly satisfied moves to define and assert a national identity, nurtured above all during the period of the Napoleonic Wars.[29] But as the rebuilding of the Houses of Parliament was the first occasion for a public building to be clad in either the Gothic or Elizabethan mode, entrants were not entirely clear how to utilize what they perceived as 'palatial' or ecclesiastical styles. Indeed, it was commonly held that, on the whole, the competition designs were too cathedral-like, too monastic.[30] Hopper's drawings for the House of Lords interior – a fantastical stage set occupied by moody Gothic figures – show how the Gothic style still conjured up images of an imagined past in the romantic vein of Fonthill Abbey. Pugin's call for purity and accuracy, based upon archaeological fact and empirical study, indicated, therefore, an important shift away from royal and aristocratic Gothick follies and castles to the highly moral and serious-minded Gothic Revival of the Victorians. In the words of Robert Furneaux Jordan, the "building that resulted established Gothic as the national style, took it away from the eccentrics and made it official".[31]

While the Gothic style may have been the most obvious choice, Pugin still had to convince a number of sceptics. For the decision to build in the style had not met with everyone's approval, provoking a fierce debate over what style would best suit the Houses of Parliament. Up to this point, the architectural language most often used for public buildings had been classical. Previous architects, such as William Kent, Robert and James Adam, and latterly John Soane, had envisaged a monumental, neo-classical structure as the ideal home for Parliament. Advocates of the classical style wanted a 'senate house' that would clearly express the legislative function of the buildings.[32] W.R. Hamilton felt the style would be comprehensible to all as a sign of progress, the advance of civilization and the triumph of representative institutions over feudal authority.[33] Apologists for the Gothic tried to undermine the ongoing popularity of this argument by pointing out the inherent pagan connotations of the classical style. While the Gothic may have been tied to the superstition

of popish rites, chivalrous tournaments and the fanaticism of the Middle Ages, it was better, the architect Benjamin Ferrey maintained, than conjuring up recollections of human immolations, intolerable imperial edicts and the cruel massacres of classical times.[34] Pugin questioned the propriety of using a style "in vogue about 2000 years ago, among nations whose climate, religion, government, and manners were totally dissimilar to our own".[35] This conviction formed the basis of his highly contentious and influential manifesto, *Contrasts* (August 1836, second edition 1841), in which he compared the virtue and humanity of Catholicism and its accompanying Gothic architecture with the brutality of the contemporary industrial age and its degenerate classicist architecture.[36] Building in a pure Gothic style, Pugin argued, would not only supply the visual harmony required for the spectator to comprehend the achievements of a thousand years in a single glance, but would also inspire the modern viewer to emulate the moral, religious and political associations supplied by this architectural language.[37]

### Contested Ground: Arguments Against the Westminster Site

Several Parliamentary Members, such as William Mackinnon, Lord Grosvenor and Col Davies, questioned whether any of the historical associations discussed above could be retained by place.[38] How could one suppose that the new Palace of Westminster would recall memories of the nation's past, such as the contest of liberties, or more general ideas attached to the Gothic period, when the actual witnesses of these events, the buildings themselves, had been eradicated by the fire? While Ferrey and Pugin would argue that both the style and the ground upon which the new structures were built would help recall important associations, a few outspoken critics maintained that all ties to history were severed on the night of the fire in October 1834.

In one of the many Parliamentary sittings debating the chosen site of the new complex, for instance, the Tory Member of Parliament William Mackinnon reconsidered the necessity of building upon the original site:

No one can venerate more than I do the site of recollections, endeared by deeds of days

Robert and James Adam, *Design for the Houses of Lords and Commons*, pen and ink and grey washes, *c.* 1762. Sir John Soane's Museum, London.

A.W.N. Pugin, 'The same Town in 1840, Catholic Town in 1440', published in A.W.N. Pugin, *Contrasts, or a parallel between the noble edifices of the fourteenth and fifteenth Centuries and Similar buildings of the present day, shewing the decay of taste*, 2nd edn., London 1841.

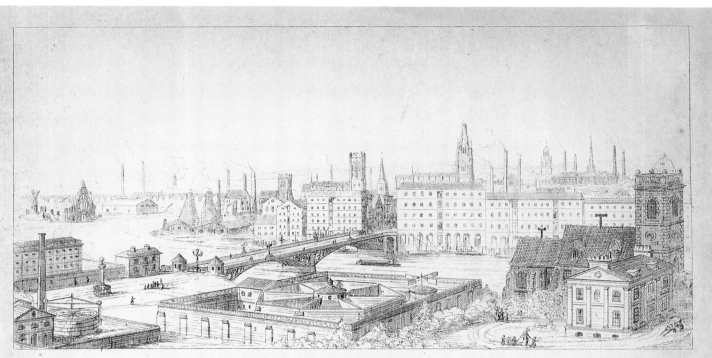

THE SAME TOWN IN 1840.

1. St Michaels Tower, rebuilt in 1750. 2. New Parsonage House & Pleasure Grounds. 3. The New Jail. 4. Gas Works. 5. Lunatic Asylum. 6. Iron Works & Ruins of St Maries Abbey. 7. Mt Evans Chapel. 8. Baptist Chapel. 9. Unitarian Chapel. 10. New Church. 11. New Town Hall & Concert Room. 12. Wesleyan Centenary Chapel. 13. New Christian Society. 14. Quakers Meeting. 15. Socialist Hall of Science.

Catholic town in 1440.

1. St Michaels on the Hill. 2. Queens Crofs. 3. St Thomas's Chapel. 4. St Maries Abbey. 5. All Saints. 6. St Johns. 7. St Peters. 8. St Alkmunds. 9. St Maries. 10. St Edmunds. 11. Grey Friars. 12. St Cuthberts. 13. Guild hall. 14. Trinity. 15. St Olaves. 16. St Botolphs.

of former years, where the liberties of our country have been raised, confirmed, cherished, and secured, and where, from the contests of parties, an interest is excited that makes history so valuable to the statesman and the patriot.[39]

But the argument for building upon the old ground would be more convincing "if the old walls really existed, but they are not to be seen; nothing remains except the foundation of St Stephen's Chapel; the charm is broken, the prestige is gone". Arguing that the historical associations of Westminster were lost when the fire destroyed the actual walls of this container of memory, Mackinnon rallied support for the reopening of the issue of location, based upon questions related to health, convenience and visibility.

The acknowledged leader of the push to relocate the Houses of Parliament was the outspoken critic of all governmental extravagance and abuse, the Radical Member Joseph Hume (1777–1855).[40] Hume's interest in the Westminster buildings had begun long before the fire had destroyed the old structures, when committees were appointed in 1831 and 1833 to consider the possibility of building a new House of Commons after years of complaints regarding cramped quarters, poor ventilation and general inconvenience.[41] Basing his ideas on Enlightenment studies of the body, which focused upon the flow of blood, respiration of lungs and the discharge of waste as crucial components of the individual's health, Hume employed an organic paradigm to define the fitness of the Westminster location.[42] Even though members "cherished a strong recollection of events that had passed in that house, and were, in consequence, very anxious that no change should take place", Hume concluded that the government would have to alter the present situation if they wanted to make the building habitable and conducive to Parliamentary work.[43] He reopened the issue of site in Parliamentary debates after the fire, and again after the competition, continually playing down the importance of tradition, and promoting an alternative plan based upon practicality.[44] By building at a new location, one that provided greater circulation of air and people, Hume predicted the increased efficiency of the Members and the whole Parliamentary system. A structure that followed the basic principles of utility would also provide, according to Hume, evidence of Parliament's more progressive purposes, as well as a visual statement of its ability to maintain the well-being of its citizens. Hume had long argued for a new – though unspecified – site, but, when pressed, suggested either St James's Park or the area behind the National Gallery as places that could guarantee Members' good health, but also inspire the individual's faith in government.[45]

Because Hume and other critics advanced their own criteria concerning an urban genius, they played down Parliament's historical ties to Westminster. In the days immediately after the fire, for instance, the *Westminster Review* published an article disputing that Parliament had an ancient home.[46] Looking to history to discount the historical value of the old buildings and site, the object of the article was "to establish how entirely unconstitutional are successive parliamentary meetings in the same locality ... and from collateral evidence to show, that even the size of the present building is directly opposed to the spirit of the institutions of wise antiquity". Comparing the original legislative system to the current modern assembly, the article provided reasons why the ancient legislation would never have endured those conditions that the opposition presented as part of a long-standing tradition. For example, the sturdy knights and barons making up this earlier assembly would have required and demanded a larger space than St Stephen's Chapel, due to fear of typhus and "an atmosphere of singular destructiveness and vapours of noxiousness in every variety". Not only would these men have found such a suggestion insulting, but Members would

William Daniell after Sydney Smirke, *The Proposed Situation in the Green Park for New Parliamentary Buildings*, April 1834, published in S. Smirke, *Suggestions for the Architectural Improvement of the Western Part of London*, London 1834, n.p. British Library, London (787.i.19).

have found any excuse to avoid attending their posts. Besides, the article continued, the legislative body never met at the same location, moving continually – to wherever the monarch was residing and to more convenient locales – until the sixteenth century. Because the importance of Parliament lay in its purpose as a legislative assembly, its symbolic significance followed it from place to place and never attached itself to a particular spot. According to this argument, the choice of location should rely upon the institution's purpose, its smooth-running efficiency as well as its representative function, and not upon unpractical and illogical theories concerning history, association or memory.

Instead, the *Westminster Review* prioritized ventilation and fitness to Parliament's purpose, listing such specific requirements as the dryness of the area, its convenience, easy access and its external effect within the wider metropolitan arena. Finding a site where the buildings could sit high and dry would safeguard Members from the noxious influences of damp, but also ensure that Parliament would not be "in the midst of the noise and bustle of a great public thoroughfare, or in a densely peopled neighbourhood".[47] The buildings should also be more convenient and accessible, since Members or those conducting business at the Law Courts had long complained about the difficulty of reaching Westminster. The same writer also emphasized that the new Houses must be visible in order to ensure their effectiveness, for "the new Houses will be regarded by the public as their own, and ought to be rendered an object of national pride". For these very reasons, Hume had earlier designated St James's Park as an ideal location, while the *Westminster Review* chose Green Park, a site

Sydney Smirke, *Plan shewing the proposed improvements of Part of London: the red tints shew the new avenues or such as are proposed to be improved* [detail], published in S. Smirke, *Suggestions for the Architectural Improvement of the Western Part of London*, London 1834, p. 1. This detail of the street plan published in Smirke's *Suggestions* shows the river Thames on the right, the Palace of Westminster and Westminster Abbey bottom right, St James's Park lower centre (with Buckingham Palace to the left). Green Park is shown on the left with the cross-shaped ground plan of the Parliamentary Buildings shown in illus., p. 109. Piccadilly, Pall Mall, Charing Cross and Leicester Square are shown at the top. British Library, London (787.i.19).

already promoted by the architect Sydney Smirke in his pre-fire scheme to build a new, classical Parliament House.[48] The area was elevated, removed from street noise and commotion, and close to the town houses of many Members of Parliament. The move would also have further symbolic implications. By rebuilding the Houses in this open spot, free from the historical associations provided by Westminster Hall and Abbey, the institution could better express its present function as the home of the recently reformed Parliament. The implication was that Parliament would thereby loosen its symbolic ties with the monarchy and invest itself with more democratic connotations.

Another critic to reconsider the merits of the Westminster location was the architectural theorist, gardener and editor John Claudius Loudon (1783–1843).[49] In his *Architectural Magazine*, a journal wherein architects commented upon every stage of the project, Loudon argued that Westminster Hall and Abbey should be restored, and the area around these surviving monuments cleared, so that their historical value as relics of the nation's history would be visible and available for future admiration.[50] But he made it clear that any new buildings could only damage such sacred ground and affront antiquarian taste. He explained that there could be "no mode of rebuilding the Houses of Parliament on the site at Westminster that will not materially injure the exterior effect, not only of Westminster Hall, but of Westminster Abbey". He also thought that any new building would be overshadowed by these established buildings, and their symbolic significance would be undermined. As an alternative to Westminster, Loudon proposed Leicester Square.[51] Here, the architect would have to clear the area north of Trafalgar Square, taking away houses and other visual obstacles between Haymarket, Gerard Street, St Martin's Lane and the new National Gallery.

Loudon also published the art dealer Alexander Rainy's plan for a complex at Charing Cross, on the site of Northumberland House, an alternative location that would have fitted the requirements of health, centrality and convenience.[52] Rainy's more expansive and unified scheme would have connected the new Houses of Parliament with the completed Regent Street project, a major metropolitan improvement commissioned by George IV that cut a grand street from Regent's Park through Oxford Circus to Waterloo Place, the site of the king's former residence at Carlton House.[53] Rainy wanted to continue the "magnificent line of communication" through to Trafalgar Square, to his proposed Parliamentary buildings, and then across the river to the south. By appropriating George IV's triumphal route, his plan would have reconfigured the city as an organized spectacle revolving around the seat of legislature.

The architect of the Covent Garden Market, Charles Fowler (1792–1867), proposed an alternative location that would have allowed for greater visibility.[54] Fowler emphasized the disadvantages of building the new Houses in close proximity to the older structures and in a manner that tried to unify their plan. He explained that the spectator would be so struck by the size, decoration and historical importance of Westminster Hall that he or she would fail to recognize the significance of the modern Parliament buildings. Instead, Fowler considered the benefits of rebuilding at a site near Westminster (Bridge Street to Richmond Terrace, between Parliament Street and the river), as a way of exploiting the associations of the Westminster location, while remaining distant enough not to be overpowered by the ancient monuments. The lone-standing senate house would thereby demand the spectator's full attention. Fowler hoped to open up the question of location, not for reasons related to ventilation, centrality or accommodation, but because he felt that the structure must be seen in its full glory in order successfully to express itself as the new 'Palace of Legislature'.

Undoubtedly, Mackinnon, Hume, Loudon and others were fighting a losing battle. However, their debates reveal that it was not a foregone conclusion that the Houses of Parliament were to be located at Westminster. Indeed, these debates show that a new questioning spirit had entered into the planning of public monuments, involving a vocal mixture of Members of Parliament, architects and interested citizens who hoped to shake up what they saw as prejudices and predilections. To 'consult the genius of place' was no longer an aesthetic decision made by one aristocratic landscape designer, but a highly contested matter opened up to public debate and political intrigue. In many ways, this push for a new location can be seen as part of the political drive of the mid-1830s that sought to redefine Parliament's representative role and increased efficiency in modern society. By resisting the seemingly grounded quality of Westminster's historical associations, critics symbolically sought to separate the Houses of Parliament from the old Palace of Westminster, and to find a new home for a recently reformed Parliament. At the same time, their arguments introduced the basic concerns of a modern metropolis, where such problems as ventilation, health, accessibility and visibility were on the minds of the city's inhabitants. Influenced by progressive theories of urban design, they tried to undermine attachment to tradition by pointing out the disadvantages of the Westminster site, its remoteness, poor ventilation and cramped quarters. According to this argument, attention to and the expression of practical suitability would generate and instil pride in Parliament's present-day abilities.

In the end, however, nostalgia for a Golden Age, rather than practicalities, won the day. The committees were unanimous that the historical associations supplied by the Westminster site and the Gothic style would best serve the Houses of Parliament. They believed that by working with and reinforcing the area's ancient character, the complex would provide a necessary connection with the past that would at once trigger the spectator's ancestral ties with Old England, and underline the continuity of the British Parliament. Ultimately revealing the ideological nature of urban design and heritage, the decision concerning the style and location of the new Palace of Westminster showed that it was tradition, as perceived in the nineteenth century, that underpinned Westminster's power of place.

# 7

## The New Palace of Westminster

Alexandra Wedgwood

On 31 January 1836 the commissioners announced that the competition had been won by Charles Barry. At this date he was a promising architect, who, after a thorough training in a surveyor's office and a long study tour that took him as far as Egypt and Syria, had set up his own London office and had become well known for his successful clubhouse, the Travellers' (1830–32), in a new and attractive Italianate or 'palazzo' style. The commissioners endorsed their decision in ringing terms. The plan:

> marked 64, with the emblem of the portcullis, bears throughout such evident marks of genius and superiority of talent, as fully to entitle it to the preference we have given it ... [and] the elevations are of an order so superior, and display so much taste and knowledge of Gothic Architecture, as to leave no doubt whatever in our minds of the Author's ability to carry out Your Majesty's Commands.[1]

The drawings for his entry, however, have been lost in somewhat mysterious circumstances.[2] His competition designs therefore have to be judged from preliminary versions or copies (see illus., pp. 114, 115), whereas the drawings of the other prize-winners still exist, making it possible to judge the schemes of Barry's closest rivals.

The second prize went to J.C. Buckler, who shared the enthusiasm of his father, John Buckler, for sketching ancient buildings, and applied his assured pencil technique to his competition drawings (see illus., p. 100, top). His design for the river front, which was symmetrical, plus an adjoining Speaker's House to the north, was divided by banks of oriel windows set one above the other, and flanked by octagonal turrets with ogee caps. Otherwise, it had repetitive details of hood moulds, tall chimneys and low battlements in a basic, Tudor, domestic style. It does indeed recall his designs in 1826 for the country house Costessy Hall in Norfolk. His plan provided for the two Chambers in the middle range, with a grand staircase tower between them, which added a point of emphasis to the river front. The importance given to staircases in the competition must have been one of the lasting influences of John Soane's impressive Scala Regia (see chapter 8), which, though it survived the fire, was to be demolished in the rebuilding. Another legacy from Soane was the caution with which competitors, including Buckler, treated the façade to New Palace Yard, adjoining Westminster Hall to the east, in large part repeating the façade to the west, which had been forced upon Soane by a select committee. By contrast, Buckler made a great show in Old Palace Yard, where he proposed to restore the former Commons Chamber as the original medieval St Stephen's Chapel, to be used as the Commons Library. The library, however, would then be isolated from the new building, adding to the awkwardness of the circulation of Buckler's plan, where committee rooms and refreshment rooms in particular are scattered about.

A view of the Lords Chamber from the Bar, looking towards the throne. Photograph by Derry Moore.

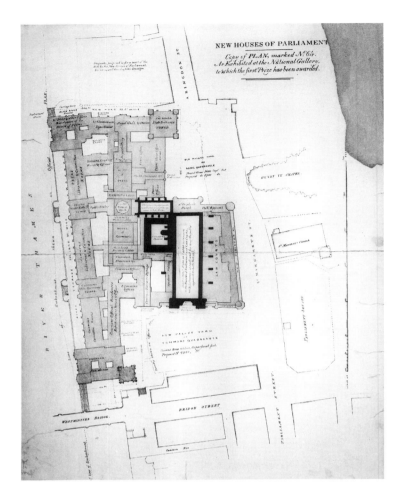

After Charles Barry, *New Houses of Parliament: Copy of Plan, marked Nr. 64. As Exhibited at the National Gallery, to which the first prize has been awarded*, engraving, 1836. This is the principal floor (i.e. first floor) plan. The heavy black at the centre indicates the medieval elements of the old palace that Barry integrated into his design. Top left, St Stephen's Chapel (used as the Commons Chamber before the fire); below, St Stephen's Cloister, and to the right, Westminster Hall. Society of Antiquaries of London.

The third-prize winner, David Hamilton, who for a long time had been Glasgow's leading architect, took a very different approach. He proposed to destroy St Stephen's Chapel and its adjoining cloister, thus obtaining a straightforward space on which to place a coherent plan. This was to have an almost symmetrical river front with large courtyards behind, separating it from a central range that contained both Chambers. The monarch and Speaker, however, were to be seated looking away from each other, and separated by passages and a low octagonal conference room in the middle of the building. As with Buckler, the ceremonial spaces were the staircases: that to the Commons at the north end, that to the Lords at south, with the monarch's entering from Old Palace Yard. The most striking aspect of Hamilton's design is, however, the style, which is based on Elizabethan and Jacobean examples, introducing Renaissance details with tall, narrow, rectangular windows, pierced balustrades, strapwork and decorated classical pilasters.

William Railton, winner of the fourth prize, was a younger man and at the start of his career. He kept all the surviving medieval buildings by using St Stephen's as an entrance hall and placing most of the plan clearly but unimaginatively around large courtyards on the southern part of the site. The Chambers, aligned in the central range, were separated by long corridors. He chose a typical, simple, early nineteenth-century castellated Gothic style, the emphasis being on a lively skyline of many battlements and turrets. Most delightful is the view of Old Palace Yard (see illus., p. 101, top). By contrast, the river front is long, low and repetitive.

In this company it is easy to agree with the commissioners that Barry's design really stood out as an important building, for the clarity and coherence of its plan, the excitement of its elevations, and the expertise shown in the handling of the Gothic details. Large early nineteenth-century Gothic buildings, such as Lowther Castle (1806–11) by Sir Robert Smirke (1780–1867), were often dull and repetitive, and it required a genius such as Barry to avoid this. The complexity of the site and the requirements of a modern legislature made an original and effective plan essential. Barry treated the medieval buildings in a particularly interesting way: the south end of Westminster Hall was opened up and, together with a rebuilt upper chapel renamed St Stephen's Hall, became a splendid entrance for the public, leading into a central hall set between the two Chambers in the heart of the building. The circulation was also worked out for the various users of the building: the king (William IV) was to enter under a great square tower at the southern end of the site, peers at the south-west and Members at the north. Each then had a grand flight of stairs leading respectively to the Robing Room, the House of Lords and the House of Commons. This, again, reflected the influence of Soane's Scala Regia. The Speaker's House, as in several other plans, was placed at the north-east corner, and the libraries and committee rooms, requiring a quiet situation, were set on the river front. Because Barry kept the original east–west alignment of St Stephen's Chapel, his western ranges at this stage were not parallel with his eastern ones. This made awkward shapes of some of the courtyards.

As important as the plan, however, was the style. Here, again, Barry triumphed by choosing the Perpendicular. It was a style with which he was familiar, and that he had already used to good effect in his recent design for the Edward VI Grammar School in Birmingham (1833–37). It was a sensible choice for a nineteenth-century public building, because it allowed for a regular façade and for several floors with reasonably sized windows that did not have too-complicated tracery. It was, moreover, a national style dating from a period that recalled England's greatness. The overwhelming reason for this choice, however, was surely the close presence of the Perpendicular Henry VII's Chapel, with its impressive panelling, bays, rectangular windows and octagonal turrets. Barry also observed and copied its decorative sculpture with its motifs. Indeed, his choice of the portcullis as his competition motto, a prominent symbol in the chapel, where it represents the Beaufort family, probably reflects the connection he wished to make between the buildings. Barry made use of carvings of the portcullis, with or without a crown, throughout the new work. It was at this period that it became the accepted symbol for Parliament. Barry's confidence in the suitability of the Perpendicular style is reflected by his use of it to replace the mixture of styles surrounding Soane's Law Courts.

Charles Barry, *Elevation for the New Houses of Parliament, West Front*, pen and ink, 1836. British Architectural Library, RIBA, London.

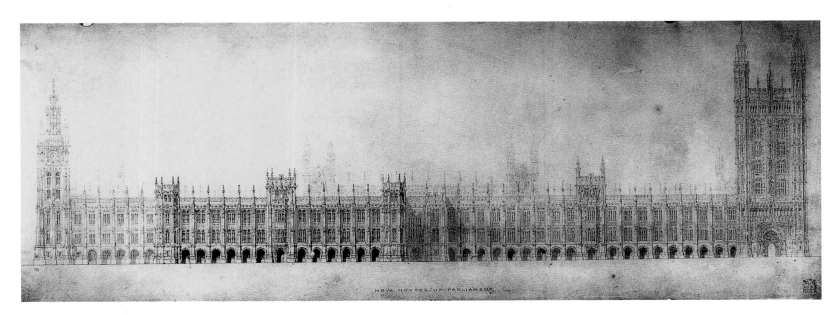

The style and the plan also worked well in three dimensions: the long, symmetrical river front was balanced by the asymmetry of the façades to the Old Palace Yard and New Palace Yard. This is further emphasized by the positions of the two towers. The larger one at the southern end, which was then called the King's Tower and corresponds to the present Victoria Tower, marked the Royal Entrance, and the shorter one at the northern end, in the position of the present taller and slimmer Clock Tower, then marked the position of the Speaker's State Dining Room.

Barry's composition could be recognized as belonging to the picturesque movement, which had developed out of Romanticism some thirty to forty years before. Its greatest exponent in architecture was probably John Nash, who adapted it to the urban scene in Regent's Park and Regent Street from 1812. The picturesque was never a precise style in any of the arts, but in architecture its aim was for the building and its setting to produce an appropriate emotional response. Its characteristics were variety, movement and asymmetry. Barry correctly calculated that at Westminster the public wanted a building that would emphasize the age and the dignity of the institution of Parliament, and reflect its national pride. It also fulfilled Barry's own architectural criteria for "grandeur of outline" and "richness of detail". The competition came at a turning point in the history of the Gothic Revival, when the more fanciful picturesque phase gave way in the early Victorian period to the more serious study of medieval buildings. The palace as it was built, with its Romantic silhouette and its accurate late fifteenth-century detail, reflects both phases.

One of the catalysts for this change was the publication in 1836 of *Contrasts: or, a parallel between the noble edifices of the fourteenth and fifteenth centuries, and similar buildings of the present day* (see illus., p. 107). It contrasted "glorious" medieval buildings with their "mean" modern counterparts, and it was written by the young Pugin, who drew Barry's competition entry. At this stage of his life, Pugin was a brilliant draughtsman with an unrivalled knowledge of medieval architecture, who was already helping Barry with the Gothic interiors of the Birmingham Grammar School. Although, as previously mentioned, these competition drawings have not survived, they were clearly most attractive, to judge from the comments made about them, and in this way Pugin certainly helped Barry win the competition.

Winning the competition was only the first step. The commissioners' report was laid before Parliament and then studied by committees of each House. They recommended the adoption of Barry's plan but had reservations about the cost, which Barry estimated, for the building alone, to be nearly three quarters of a million pounds.[3] Since January, Barry had been altering and improving his plan: he realigned both the river front and the central range, which contained the Chambers, making them parallel to each other. This meant that the rebuilt St Stephen's Chapel (now called St Stephen's Hall) joined the Central Hall (now called Central Lobby) at a slight angle, which was later masked by making the lobby octagonal. He extended the building substantially to the south, which enabled him to place the main parts of the central range further apart and make the courtyards more nearly rectangular and larger. He now included a larger and more gradual Scala Regia in the central range, replacing his former stair on a cross-axis. He altered the balance of the two towers, making the King's Tower taller and the Speaker's Tower into a slimmer Clock Tower, emphasizing the asymmetry in order to counterbalance the symmetry of the now very long river front. This design was adopted and published in May 1836.

Inevitably, considerable controversy was aroused among the unsuccessful competitors as soon as the result of the competition was known. A group of them asked for a commission of inquiry before the final choice was made,[4] and complained that Barry had not followed the

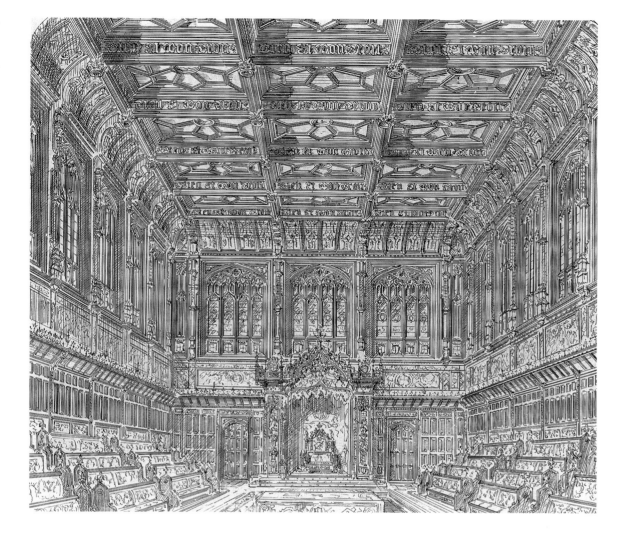

specifications accurately, in that he had included an extra eight 'minute drawings' that, as they were done by Pugin, may have unduly influenced the judges. The main result of this, however, was an exhibition of the unsuccessful designs, held in the National Gallery in April 1836, the catalogue of which contains descriptions of their own entries by the competitors. Barry, meanwhile, got on with the next part of his work, which was the preparation of drawings from which to make a "close estimate",[5] and for this he again needed Pugin's help. There is some documentation for Pugin's involvement,[6] and a number of Pugin's drawings survive, although most of them are in the form of tracings of the originals.[7] Barry called them "exquisite details",[8] and these designs show the youthful Pugin at his most inventive and exuberant. It must be emphasized, however, that, although they seem to have been much copied in Barry's office, they are not working drawings and were never used in the construction of the building. By the end of January 1837, Barry had sufficient drawings for the Government Surveyors to work out an estimate, which by April had been calculated at about £865,000. There were no further tasks for Pugin to perform on the project, and, at the same time, his career as a independent architect began with work on Scarisbrick Hall, Lancashire, and buildings for the Roman Catholic Church. He did not return to Westminster until the autumn of 1844.

The site had been greatly increased by the proposed embankment of the River Thames, and it was logical to begin the building on that side. Therefore, the first thing to be done was the construction of a coffer dam behind which the embankment could be built. This was

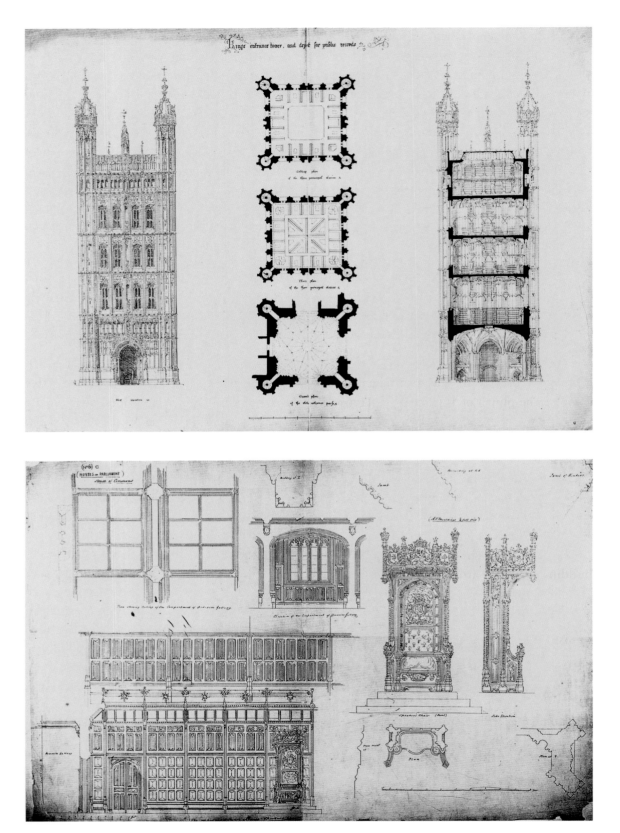

Charles Barry, *Kings entrance tower, and dept for public records*, pen and ink, 1836. The Society of Antiquaries of London.

A.W.N. Pugin, designs for the House of Commons including Speaker's Chair (estimate drawings), pen and ink, 1836. The Society of Antiquaries of London.

a huge feat of engineering, carried out under the joint direction of the civil-engineering partnership of Walker & Burges and the architect. The contract was won by Messrs John & Henry Lee of Lambeth, who were inexperienced and slow, but who were used to build the river wall and terrace, work on which began on 1 January 1839. The next important step was the choice of a good building stone. Sir Robert Peel had suggested an investigatory commission,[9] and Barry was appointed, along with Sir Henry de la Beche and William Smith, both prominent geologists, and Charles Harriott Smith, a distinguished stone carver. During the summer of 1839, they visited many old buildings and quarries, concentrating on magnesium limestone and at length choosing that of Bolsover Moor. It was, however, discovered that the stone there could only be obtained in small pieces. Therefore, Smith and Barry continued the search and this time selected Anston stone. After several trials, they decided on the Duke of Leeds's Anston quarry. Port has summed up the result:

> It was a sad irony that so much effort to select the best stone should have resulted in the choice of one characterized by joint planes running through the beds, leading inevitably in time to extensive lamination and consequent failure of the stonework. The unmarked stone was frequently not laid in its natural bed, so that decay set in rapidly.[10]

For the inside of the palace, Painswick stone was specified, but from 1843 Caen stone was extensively used. Care was also taken to secure the best bricks. The foundation stone, "the angle of the plinth of the Speaker's House nearest the bridge", was laid by Mrs Barry on 27 April 1840,[11] by which time it was obvious that Barry's deadline of six years in which to build the palace would not be met.

Construction began with the river front, and Barry, after many revisions, worked hard to perfect his design for that elevation, with his main stylistic inspiration always coming from the adjacent late Perpendicular of Henry VII's Chapel. He was concerned to balance the horizontal, which he emphasized with continuous bands of panelling, with the vertical, which he marked with the polygonal turrets that ended high above the walls. He also introduced steeply pitched roofs that emphasized the lively skyline. The third contract, for building the river front, was let to Grissell & Peto, who began work in January 1840 and

William Henry Brakespear in the office of Charles Barry, *New Palace of Westminster, south front elevation, preparatory to the first contract drawings*, pen and ink and wash over pencil, February 1840. Palace of Westminster (WOA 4563).

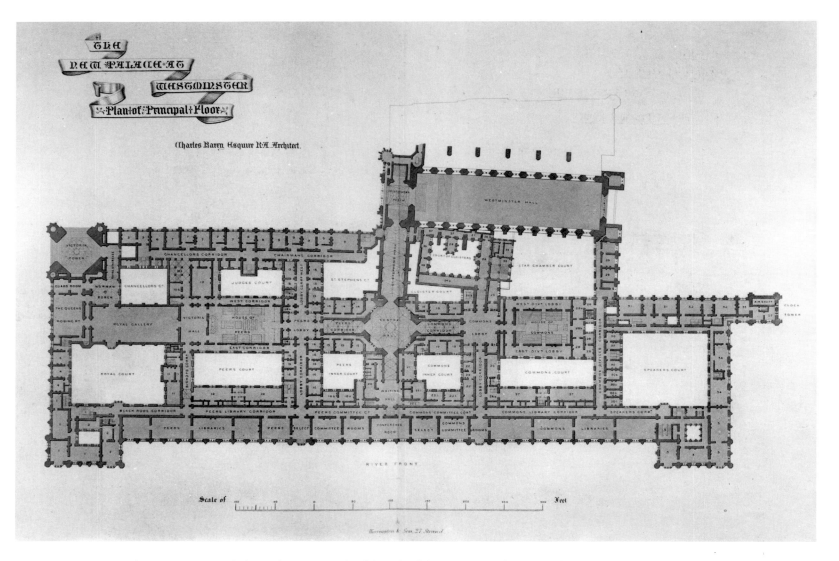

After Charles Barry, *The New Palace of Westminster*, plan of principal floor, published in Henry T. Ryde, *Illustrations of the New Palace of Westminster*, London 1849, pl. i.

were to construct the major part of the palace. Once building had begun, ventilation had to be considered, and in October 1839 Barry asked Lord Duncannon, First Commissioner of Woods and Works, to appoint a practical engineer, "to direct, superintend and be responsible for the proper execution of all the works that may be requisite in carrying out the details of the system that may be agreed upon".[12] Dr David Boswell Reid, a chemistry teacher from Edinburgh who had successfully been in charge of the ventilation of the temporary House of Commons, immediately lobbied Duncannon, who placed the ventilation of the new palace entirely in his hands from 1 April 1840 until the end of the first session after the occupation of both Houses. His remit was limited only by an instruction to defer to the architect in respect of "either the solidity or the architectural character of the building".[13] Barry was aware of Reid's ignorance of the practical side of building, and this, in Professor Port's words, "coupled with his inability to make up his mind, his megalomaniac demands and his readiness to take offence, made it impossible that he should prove a satisfactory colleague".[14] Reid also caused prolonged delays and changes to Barry's plan because his system involved building a central tower to act as a great chimney for both 'vitiated air' and smoke. This purely functional addition was welcomed by Barry as an improvement to his design, and the resulting Central Tower, in the form of an ornate spire, balanced the long river front, the slim Clock Tower and the massive Victoria Tower. Further small ventilation shafts, also in Gothic dress, were eventually added to the cluster of towers on the Westminster skyline.

Barry had to change his plan as a result of Parliamentary decisions to give residences to several Parliamentary officers, but he also made alterations on his own initiative, with the purpose, as he saw it, of improving the design. The most important of these were those affecting the Royal Approach: he replaced the gradual grand staircase in the central range with a steep one to the north of the Victoria Tower, and in its place put the Victoria Gallery (now the Royal Gallery), a great processional room of the same height as the House of Lords. The Lords, who were uncomfortable in their temporary Chamber, discovered the alteration early in 1844 and were considerably annoyed by what they saw as Barry's high-handedness. Barry was allowed to keep most of his changes, but divided the Royal Gallery to form a small lobby next to the House of Lords, to be called the Prince's Chamber, and by the end of 1844 the plan was in all major respects in its final form.

From 1843, Barry added a great deal of sculpture and decoration to his external façades. In order to carry out this work he engaged John Thomas, who had worked for him on the Gothic stonework of the King Edward VI Grammar School at Birmingham. Thomas was not officially appointed Superintendent of Stone-Carving at Westminster until 1846, but he had an arrangement with Barry that was approved by the Office of Woods on 13 May 1841.[15] The internal decoration was in part dependent on decisions of the Fine Arts Commission, which had been set up in 1841, under the chairmanship of the Prince Consort, to consider "the promotion of the fine arts in this country in connexion with the rebuilding of the Houses of Parliament".[16] It was principally concerned with commissioning the paintings and sculpture, and deciding the subjects to be represented. Barry wanted to design the interiors as a whole, but had control only of the architecture and the decorative arts. In the event, the paintings sometimes look out of place. His report in 1843 to the commission mentioned that the "plain surfaces of the walls should be covered with suitable architectonic decoration, or diapered enrichment in colour, occasionally heightened with gold and blended with armorial bearings, badges, cognizances, and other heraldic ensignia emblazoned in their proper colours". He also mentioned "groined vaults", Tudor decorations, "screens, pillars, corbels, niches", "encaustic tiles", oak framing and stained glass.[17]

It was a rich vision, and Barry intended to hold to it. Meanwhile, in May and August 1844, the Lords were pressing him: work on the House of Lords should be "advanced with all possible speed", but temporary fittings should not be used.[18] He also feared that, unless he acted decisively, he would suffer further interference from the Fine Arts Commission, who in 1843 had invited designs for decorative works for the new palace. The entries had been exhibited in 1844, and the vast majority had been mediocre and ham-fisted interpretations of Gothic forms. In these circumstances he turned to the one man with the knowledge, ability and speed to help him, Pugin. By 1844 Pugin was well known as a powerful writer in the cause of the Gothic, which, according to him, was synonymous with Christian architecture. He was also the country's leading Roman Catholic architect. It seems that he was at first unwilling to help Barry,[19] but when Barry wrote to him again on 3 September, Pugin had just suffered a personal tragedy with the death of his second wife. Barry wrote:

> I am in a regular fix respecting the working drawings for the fittings and decorations of the House of Lords, which it is of vital importance to me should now be finished with the utmost possible despatch. Although I have now made up my mind as to the principles, and, generally, as to the details of the design for them, including a new design for the throne, which is at last perfectly satisfactory to me, I am unfortunately unable to

get the general drawings into such a definite shape as is requisite for preparing the working details, owing to a lameness in one of my legs, which has laid me on my back.

He invited Pugin to stay with him in Brighton for a few days:

> for the purpose of making out the drawings in question, and of enabling me to consult you generally, and enter into some permanent arrangement that will be satisfactory to you, as to occasional assistance in the future in the completion of the great work, as well as for the discharge of my obligations to you for what you have already done.[20]

This time, Pugin was persuaded. He visited Barry from 12 to 16 September, and Barry subsequently went to Ramsgate to stay with Pugin from 7 to 10 November. He arranged for Pugin to be given an official post, with a salary of £200 a year and the title of Superintendent of Wood-Carving at the New Palace. This might sound as if Pugin was in charge of the many carpenters who were on the site, but, as he made clear in a letter to Barry that laid down his conditions for the work, "I am only responsible to you in all matters connected with the work. I act as your agent entirely and have nothing to do with any other person."[21] It was a very personal arrangement between the two men, with Barry in ultimate control. It is important to remember this nowadays, when there is so much interest in Pugin that Barry's role is almost forgotten. John Birnie Philip, the future sculptor, gave a good account of how they worked together:

> I was introduced by an eminent painter still living to the notice of Mr Pugin, who engaged me to make models for the guidance of the numerous workmen engaged in executing the wood-carvings in the workshops at Thames Bank. ... The usual course was that Mr Pugin visited the works, averaging certainly not oftener than once in a fortnight, leaving a great number of sketches executed during the few hours he was with us. Sir Charles Barry was in the habit of visiting the works two or three times in each week, or oftener. It continually happened on these visits that Sir Charles not only set aside and disapproved of Pugin's designs, but superseded them by designs made by himself.[22]

The partnership of Barry and Pugin started with the interior of the Lords Chamber, which indeed forms the climax of the building and their joint masterpiece. The shell of the Chamber in which they began would have had all the stonework in place, and also a pierced iron floor through which hot air would have been pumped. The vitiated air passed through the ceiling, which was suspended from an iron framework under the roof, into flues that led to the Central Tower. The shape of the Chamber was the classical one of a double cube, and was 90 feet long by 45 feet wide and high. The long sides, east and west, each had six, big, pointed windows, and the short sides each had three shallow, arched recesses, the same size as the windows. This was the space within which Barry and Pugin had to create a magnificent interior. Its arrangements are based on those of its immediate predecessors. It has a tripartite division lengthways, placing the throne at the southern end. The body of the Chamber is divided in the centre by the Bar from the northern end, which is used by the House of Commons at State Openings of Parliament, and above which there is a gallery used by the public and the press. The overwhelming impression is one of richness and colour, with a wealth of vivid and convincing medieval ornament. The detail is, however, always subordinate to the construction and the proportions, thus following Pugin's own 'true principles' of design. But it remained a stylistic hybrid. Pugin famously described the exterior as "Tudor details on a classic body",[23] and the same applies here.

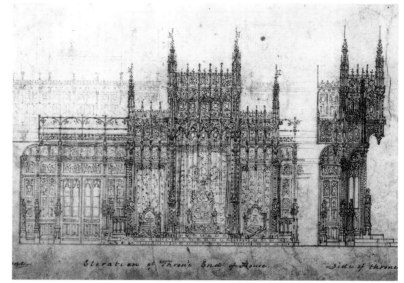

The Chamber has a ribbed and compartmented wooden ceiling with gilded carvings, pierced inscriptions and mouldings, and also painted panels. Below the window-line, dark, carved wood predominates, with panelled walls and oak bench ends, all richly carved. More colour comes from stained-glass windows and brass railings to the gallery and around the throne, as well as the cove to the gallery that is painted with the arms of the Lord Chancellors, the brass candelabra to either side of the gilded throne canopy, and the carpets. The pew-like benches emphasize the solemn atmosphere. Everything was the work of Barry and Pugin apart from the statues of the Magna Carta Barons set between the windows and the recesses, and the frescoes in the recesses. These paintings, with their realism and perspective, sound a somewhat discordant note with the surrounding medievalism and, had Barry been free to choose, would probably have been replaced by a more stylized Gothic scheme.[24]

The room is focused on the throne and its canopy: Pugin's initial ideas were decidedly ecclesiastical in feel, and not what Barry wanted for the proportions and character of his Chamber. Barry prevailed, established his outline, and then carefully revised the vibrant and exciting designs with which Pugin filled it. When Barry was satisfied, the carpenters began on the designs. As usual, Pugin wanted the carpenters to work surrounded by the best examples of the fifteenth-century style he was aiming at, and to this end he built up in the Thames Bank Workshops a remarkable collection of more than two thousand casts and a few actual medieval wooden panels.[25] The quality of the woodwork is outstanding, and the organization of the Thames Bank Workshops must have been excellent. The man in charge of the everyday work at Westminster was Richard Bayne.[26] It seems that young men were selected to be carpenters, perhaps because it was more likely that they would do as they were told.

As well as the wooden fittings in the House of Lords, Pugin designed the splendid furniture, with the throne as the principal piece. It is closely based on the early fourteenth-century Coronation Chair in Westminster Abbey. To either side of the throne were placed the Chairs of State, which, with their upholstered X-frames, were based on sixteenth- and seventeenth-century models. They and the throne were made by John Webb of Bond Street, who was both an antique dealer and a high-class cabinet-maker, a contact of Pugin's since at least 1837.[27] Webb also made the impressive Clerks' Table that stands in the centre of the Chamber. It is almost square, with four legs to each side. The symbolism of its curious design was explained in contemporary literature:

Thames Bank Workshops, carved oak panels on bench ends facing the throne, 1846–47. Lords Chamber, House of Lords, Palace of Westminster.

They [the legs] are connected to each other by a deeply moulded bar, and bars stretch across from foot to foot having sunken panels between them, so as to convey in plan the general character of a portcullis – intended to represent the ancient arms of Westminster.[28]

The furniture in the Prince's Chamber was also part of this commission for Webb, and consisted of two octagonal tables and sixteen chairs, as well as two clock cases, all in oak. Pugin had a particular love of octagonal tables and designed them throughout his life, always producing variations. The tables in the Prince's Chamber are among his most successful and important. The ogee braces to the legs show Pugin's deep understanding of timber framing, and the balance of the carved decoration is perfectly judged. The chairs, with the X placed at the side, and lion heads to either side at the back, are of equally high quality.

The Prince's Chamber itself is the same height and width as the Chamber, which it serves as a lobby, as well as forming a passage on the east–west axis that leads from the libraries on the east (or river) front, past the Lords Refreshment Room (now the Peers Dining Room), through the Prince's Chamber to the Lords Staircase and the offices on the west front. The carved oak panelling, the doors, the carved stone fireplaces, the grates and firedogs, the panelled ceiling painted with heraldic shields of the United Kingdom, and the design of the carpet were all executed at the same time as the fittings in the House of Lords, and are of similar quality and style. They also reveal very clearly the balanced harmony of Pugin's and Barry's decorative work. The only original item no longer existing is the stained glass with the badges of the United Kingdom on a diapered ground, which was destroyed during the Second World War and has been replaced by another scheme. The Fine Arts Commission chose the theme of the Tudor dynasty for this room, and Barry planned the architecture to accommodate their commissions, which, however, all took considerable time to be executed. They consisted of bronze relief panels illustrating scenes of British history, made by William Theed between 1853 and 1856, and, above these, portraits of Tudor kings, queens and other relations, executed in imitation of surviving contemporary likenesses by Richard Burchett and his pupils at the Royal School of Art, South Kensington, in the years between 1854 and 1860 (see chapter 14). The upper panels on the north and south walls, lit by the windows on the east and west walls, were to be covered with copies of the famous Netherlandish tapestries that showed the course of the defeat of the Spanish Armada, which had hung in the House of Lords and were burnt in the fire of 1834. They were never commissioned and the panels have been covered with wallpaper. The room is, however, dominated by a colossal white marble statue of Queen Victoria, seated on her throne and flanked by Justice and Clemency, sculpted by John Gibson and completed by 1856. Again, there is little stylistic harmony between these statues and the surrounding decoration.

Barry recognized the necessity for Pugin to work at Westminster, as he did on his other projects, with his close group of colleagues John Hardman, Herbert Minton and J.G. Crace, who understood his ways and, most importantly, could interpret his rapid drawings. In 1838 Pugin had persuaded John Hardman, originally a button-maker in Birmingham, to manufacture metalwork to his designs, especially for ecclesiastical purposes. The setting of the House of Lords, where the rich colour of brass was especially appropriate, gave him a whole range of new opportunities. The major items were the great pierced doors from the Peers Lobby to the Chamber, the massive candelabra by the throne (originally there were also candelabra on the Bar, at the other end of the Chamber) and the railing to the gallery. There were many difficulties in the manufacture of the brasswork, particularly the railings, largely

View of the Prince's Chamber, House of Lords, Palace of Westminster. The suite of furniture of two octagonal tables, sixteen X-frame chairs and two wall clocks was designed by A.W.N. Pugin and made by John Webb. The marble group of *Queen Victoria*, *Justice and Clemency* by John Gibson is discussed in chapter 16. The bronze reliefs and Tudor portraits are discussed in chapter 14.

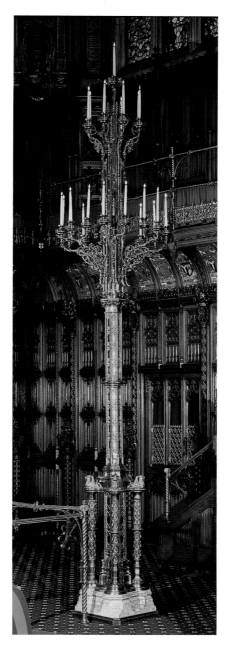

ABOVE: John Hardman after A.W.N. Pugin, one of a pair of candlebra either side of the throne canopy, brass, 1846–47. House of Lords Chamber, Palace of Westminster.

LEFT: View of the Peers Lobby, looking towards the Lords Chamber, House of Lords. The brass gates and corona (chandelier) were designed by A.W.N. Pugin and made by John Hardman. The encaustic tiles were designed by Pugin and made by Herbert Minton.

as a result of Barry's changes of mind. Most of the problems were caused by uncertainty over the means of lighting to be used. At first the railing was designed so that it could accommodate gas fittings, but these were abandoned by November 1846 for gas branches that sprang from the base of the niches on the walls above the gallery. These branches, which no longer exist, followed the recommendation made by Michael Faraday. They were not made by Hardman and probably not designed by Pugin.[29] The final decision was that, though the gallery might be illuminated by gas, the floor of the Chamber was to be lit only by candles. This necessitated adding more branches to the candelabra and, inevitably, and most unusually for Pugin, resulted in a cluttered appearance instead of clear, flowing lines. Hardman also made much ironwork, including a large number of elaborate hinges.

Pugin had been in contact with Herbert Minton, the innovative ceramics manufacturer in Stoke-on-Trent, since at least 1840. He had revived the medieval technique for making encaustic tiles, and Pugin used them extensively in both his ecclesiastical and domestic buildings. Pugin must have quickly persuaded Barry that these tiles would make the most suitable and hard-wearing surface for those main areas of the new palace that were not carpeted. Together they visited Minton's factory on 2 October 1845.[30] The first pavement that was completed with his tiles was that of the Peers Lobby. Here, Pugin's simple designs in rich, dark colours were magnificently realized by Minton's perfect technique. The final member of Pugin's team of colleagues at Westminster was J.G. Crace, the head of the well-known firm of London decorators. His appointment at the new Palace of Westminster in 1845 – where he started work in the House of Lords on all the decorative painting, the ceiling, the reveals of the windows, the heraldic cove beneath the gallery and the throne canopy – was made officially by Barry,[31] but must have been the result of Pugin's recommendation. Crace also supplied the textiles, such as the carpet for the throne, and subsequently the wallpapers, though it is not known who manufactured them.

Pugin and Barry saw stained glass as an important element in their overall scheme for the decoration of the principal interiors, and the House of Lords received the most elaborate programme. The subject was established by the Fine Arts Commission and consisted of standing figures of English and Scottish monarchs and their consorts between William I and Victoria.[32] Unfortunately, this glass was destroyed during the Second World War and has been replaced with a different scheme. Pugin always used stained glass as a major decorative feature in his churches, but he frequently had difficulties with his stained-glass manufacturers, and he tried several, who were often unable to reproduce the results he wanted. In the summer of 1846, the Fine Arts Commission gave the work to the winner of its 1843 competition, Ballantine & Allan of Edinburgh. Their fussy and weak sketch designs survive and make it obvious why Barry had no hesitation in rejecting their full-size cartoons in 1846. Barry got Pugin to redraw the cartoons and, though Ballantine & Allan were still to manufacture the glass, Barry commissioned Hardman, who had just started making stained glass for Pugin, to make the first window to serve as a model. This window was in place by April 1847. After the House of Lords, Hardman made all the stained glass in the new palace.

Apart from stained glass, Barry and Pugin succeeded by April 1847 in completing the furniture and fittings of the House of Lords, together with those of the Peers Lobby and the Prince's Chamber to either side, and it was opened by Queen Victoria. There were still many gaps among the fresco paintings and sculptures that had been commissioned by the Fine Arts Commission. The House of Lords was received with universal praise and immediately became a source of great national pride. The descriptions given in the *Illustrated London News*[33] were repeated in the first guide books, where it was called "without doubt the finest

specimen of Gothic civil architecture in Europe: its proportions, arrangement and decoration being perfect, and worthy of the great nation at whose cost it has been erected". Hardman's work was mentioned with approval,[34] and so was that of Webb, Crace and Minton,[35] but Pugin's name did not appear in any account. 1846 had been an unhappy year in both his professional and private life, and he had been very hard pressed to finish the House of Lords. His friends urged him to go to Italy, and on 26 March 1847 he set out on his longest continental tour, not returning until 14 June.

Meanwhile, as well as overseeing every aspect of the design, Barry bore the weight of the public side of the project, which was constantly under scrutiny from both Parliament and press. He had endless important visitors to the site (Tsar Nicholas I in 1844, Prince Albert in 1845, to mention only the grandest), committees and commissions to attend, as well as problems with Dr Reid to be dealt with. The libraries, refreshment rooms and committee rooms on the river front were all progressing, with rich oak carving made in the Thames Bank Workshops, stencilled ceiling panels painted by J.G. Crace, many brass fittings made by Hardman, and carpets and curtains supplied by Crace as the main parts of their decoration.

The next major interior to be tackled was, of course, the Commons Chamber, always planned to be smaller and slightly less elaborate than the Lords Chamber. It was ready to open by May 1850. Members, however, who were used to their comfortable temporary home, were immediately critical of their new Chamber, particularly of the provision of seating, the lack of space in the division lobbies and the inadequate acoustics. After much inconclusive discussion, Barry was forced to enlarge the galleries and the division lobbies, and to lower

ABOVE LEFT: Joseph Nash, *Interior View of Charles Barry's New House of Commons Looking towards Speaker Denison*, gouache on paper, 1858, Palace of Westminster (WOA 2934).

ABOVE RIGHT: Members Lobby, House of Commons, *c.* 1903. The lobby and chamber were destroyed in 1941 (see chapter 9). Farmer Collection no. 723, House of Lords Record Office.

View of Central Lobby looking towards the Commons Corridor and the Commons Chamber.

the ceiling of the Chamber, thus cutting the height of the windows by half.[36] These substantial alterations were completed in early 1852. The prevailing impression then must have been of dark, carved wood, relieved only by the stained-glass windows containing the arms of municipal boroughs,[37] and the painted ceiling panels. There was much less colour than in the House of Lords, with no frescoes or sculpture, although Barry originally proposed to decorate the cove to the gallery with the armorial bearings of the speakers.[38] This scheme seems to have been abandoned in the general mood of annoyance at the expense and the length of time that the rebuilding had taken.[39] These feelings, however, did not prevent Barry being knighted on 11 February 1852, shortly before the State Opening of Parliament, when both Houses were in use for the first time.[40] At about the same time, Pugin's final illness began, and he was prevented from further work before his death.

After Pugin's death, his designs continued to be used and adapted, particularly for metalwork, wallpaper, textiles and furniture. He had more or less completed the patterns for stained glass and tiles, including the magnificent ones for Central Lobby before he died. The 1850s were difficult times for Barry, as building slowly continued, and costs rose, seemingly out of control, to the mounting annoyance of Members. Moreover, he was fighting an ongoing battle over his fee: he wanted the traditional 5% of the outlay for the architect's remuneration, whereas in 1838 the Treasury had agreed to pay him a fixed sum of £25,000. Although by 1854 he had received £40,000 commission, Barry continued to argue, before submitting to the Treasury's final offer in July 1856.[41] The problems of heating and lighting were not solved by the dismissal of Dr Reid in 1852, and remained a major concern.[42] Barry also stood out against any interference by the various First Commissioners of the Office of Works, who changed with the

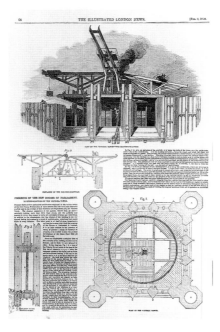

*Progress of the New Houses of Parliament. Hoisting-Scaffold of the Victoria Tower*, wood engraving, published in *Illustrated London News*, XVI, no. 411, 2 February 1850, p. 68. Palace of Westminster (WOA 5284).

*The Palace of Westminster from Old Palace Yard*, 1854, colour lithograph, published by Vacher & Son. Palace of Westminster (WOA 1639).

succeeding governments. One of these, Sir Benjamin Hall, who was First Commissioner of Works from 1855 to 1858, tried particularly hard to control Barry and get the building finished. Barry, however, was determined that there should be no compromise of his ideals for the building, and, as Port noted, "by a most masterly process of misunderstanding, bland assurance and equivocation Barry quite outplayed the Office of Works".[43]

The completion of the three towers – the Victoria Tower, the Central Tower and the Clock Tower – which are the major elements in the external design of the new Palace of Westminster and the architectural balance between them, remained one of Barry's chief preoccupations as they slowly grew during the 1850s. The Victoria Tower, originally "the largest and highest square tower in the world"[44] was designed as a royal entrance and depository for the records of Parliament. It was subsequently also used for ventilation. Because of its prominent position at the southern end of Old Palace Yard and its part in royal ceremonial, Barry designed particularly rich carving and sculpture for the exterior and the underside of the entrance arch. It was also a major example of nineteenth-century structural engineering and was built using innovative techniques, as was the scaffolding. The Central Tower was added specifically for ventilation, and Barry designed it as a spire to contrast with the other two towers, though its proportions were much revised before he found a satisfactory shape. This tower, because of its position in the centre of the building, was the first to be finished, and also required considerable engineering skill and unusually shaped scaffolding. The Clock Tower involved different problems, some connected with the clock itself and others to do with the design. It is known that Barry had great difficulty working out how to make the clock sufficiently prominent, and it is generally assumed that his solution, a projecting clock storey surmounted by steeply sloping roofs, was taken from the prototype that Pugin had designed for Scarisbrick Hall, Lancashire, in 1837 (see illus., p. 132, right).[45]

The history of the clock is long and complicated. It began in March 1844, when Barry asked B.L. Vulliamy, the royal clockmaker, who supplied many clocks for the new Palace of Westminster, about the terms on which he would supply a specification for the clock. In November 1845, E.J. Dent applied to be allowed to tender, which he did at a very cheap price. In 1848 Dent found a backer in the person of E.B. Denison (later Lord Grimthorpe), characterized by Port as "one of the rudest of Victorian controversialists",[46] who from then

on was associated with the work. Dent started to make the clock but died in 1853 before it was completed. After some delay, it was completed in 1856 by Dent's stepson, Frederick Ripon, who later took the name of Dent. For the bells, Barry had recommended a limited competition on specifications drawn up by Denison, but he advocated a new method of casting patented by Warner of the Cripplegate Foundry. In August 1856, the great bell was cast at Warner's Norton Foundry, where it acquired the nickname 'Big Ben', probably after Sir Benjamin Hall, the First Commissioner. It was brought to London, where the quarter bells were cast. Then, in October 1857, Big Ben cracked. After mutual recriminations by Warner and Denison, it was recast by Mears of Whitechapel in April 1858 and raised to the top of the Clock Tower in October 1858, from where it has successfully rung ever since.

The residences were among the last parts of the building to be completed, and the grandest of these was always intended to be the Speaker's House, which occupies a twin-towered pavilion at the north-east corner of the new palace, next to the river and to Westminster Bridge. In April 1857, when the house was ready for fitting up, John Evelyn Denison was elected Speaker. He immediately negotiated his requirements with Barry. He wanted his residence completed in a fit and appropriate way for both state and domestic purposes. In August 1858, the tender for the manufacture of the furniture submitted by Holland & Sons was accepted. The new Speaker's House, with its sumptuous interiors and furniture, was finally ready for occupation in January 1859, when Speaker Denison and his family moved in (see chapter 12).

In May 1860, Sir Charles Barry died suddenly. Although the building appeared substantially complete, there were still a surprising number of important parts to finish, and for them the new First Commissioner of Works turned to Edward Middleton Barry, Sir Charles's second son. He had been working with his father for nearly ten years. He had also worked independently and was by no means a slavish follower of his father's style. Sir Charles had

A.W.N. Pugin, Scarisbrick Hall, perspective drawing of the entrance façade (detail), pencil, 1836. British Architectural Library, RIBA, London.

View of the chapel of St Mary Undercroft, looking towards the altar, *c.* 1897. Benjamin Stone collection, Birmingham Library Services.

The baptistery of the Chapel of St Mary Undercroft. The octagonal baptistery was added by Sir Charles Barry. The font and other furnishings were designed by E.M. Barry.

long proposed the enclosure of New Palace Yard, with two ranges of offices on the north and west sides, connected by a gateway that probably would have been called the Albert Gate. When this scheme was abandoned in 1864,[47] E.M. Barry was asked to design a new layout. He provided iron railings, gates and stone piers, and he added a new covered arcade that linked the entrance to the House of Commons with a proposed public subway under Bridge Street. This was built of Portland stone, which is much whiter than Anston stone, because the latter was already causing serious problems of erosion. The effect was distinctively 'High Victorian' in style, richer and more elaborate than his father's 'Early Victorian' work.

Another of E.M. Barry's works in the 1860s was the restoration of the chapel of St Mary Undercroft, frequently, but wrongly, called the 'Crypt Chapel'. This was undertaken "rather quietly" because of the "rigid economic and anti-ecclesiastical prejudice in the House of Commons".[48] The decision to reinstate it as a chapel was much debated, and for a short period after work was finished no religious services were held there. It was slowly brought into use, the first services being baptisms. The chapel had been built in the late thirteenth century, an early example of a lierne vault with remarkable, large, carved bosses showing scenes of martyrdoms, that of St Stephen being over the altar. The stonework had been much calcined in the fire, and it was entirely renewed with great skill by Sir Charles in 1858–59, who also added the octagonal baptistery as part of his symmetrical façade to Old Palace Yard at the south end of Westminster Hall. E.M. Barry designed vigorous fittings, particularly the font and the iron railing and gates at the west end, inspired by the grill made in 1294 for the tomb of Eleanor of Castile in Westminster Abbey. He decorated every surface, including elaborate tiles and stonework: in particular there was an inlaid alabaster dado by William Field; stained glass by J.H. Powell; metalwork by John Hardman; walls, nave vault and probably the altar reredos with British saints painted by J.G. Crace; and the chancel vault painted by Clayton & Bell. The result is very High Church, with much symbolism and a text in Latin giving the story of St Stephen's martyrdom. It is also typical of its period and distinct from the rest of the palace in its colour and emphasis on strong details. It is a fascinating mixture of High Victorian art in a late thirteenth-century framework.

Among other conspicuous areas of decoration were Central Lobby and the Robing Room. For Central Lobby, Barry proposed mosaic in place of the fresco paintings, which had proved somewhat unsatisfactory. Only the vault and the figure of St George had been completed before the scheme was considered too expensive by Acton Smee Ayrton MP, who, as First Commissioner of Works from 1869 to 1873, felt it his duty to prune expenditure. Work in the Robing Room with painting and sculpture on an Arthurian theme included the parquet floor and the panelled ceiling, the stained glass by J.H. Powell, the wall panelling and the figures of 'princesses',[49] a throne canopy and a magnificent fireplace, which with its emphatic colour and bold plasticity, again shows the characteristics of the High Victorian period.

E.M. Barry was also much taken up with planning alterations, though little ever came of them. During major political controversies in the 1860s there were frequently more than five hundred Members in the Chamber, which seated only three hundred on the floor and one hundred and twenty in the gallery, and back-benchers became increasingly dissatisfied with the facilities provided for them. Between 1867 and 1868, a committee chaired by a back-bencher, Thomas Headlam, recommended as the best solution the building of a new House of Commons in the Commons Court.[50] Barry designed a plan accordingly, making the existing House of Commons into the Lobby, and filling the Commons Court with a new square

Detail of the coffered ceiling of the Robing Room, with heraldic devices, designed by E.M. Barry.

The West Wall of the Robing Room, showing the fireplace designed by E.M. Barry and the frescoes, from left to right: *Courtesy*, *Religion* and *Generosity* by William Dyce (see chapter 15).

Chamber, which would seat about five hundred and fifty Members. The fatal objection to the scheme, however, was the cost, and, in Port's words, "Gladstone effectively ditched the whole conception".[51] Barry then submitted an estimate for converting the conference room and adjoining committee rooms, situated on the principal floor (river front), into a common dining room for Lords and Commons, and forming a new conference room out of the small rooms on the east side of the Peers Inner Court. The newly appointed Acton Smee Ayrton, however, decided to have the work done by his department. He followed this up by abruptly dismissing Barry in January 1870 and demanding that he hand over to the Office of Works all the contract drawings and papers connected with the Houses of Parliament.

This high-handed treatment was part of the "process of establishing a proper system of responsibility for all public works"[52] with a government department headed by a Parliamentary minister. E.M. Barry's dismissal really marked the end of the construction and decoration of the new Houses of Parliament. The few further major alterations were connected with the removal in 1882 of the Law Courts from the western side of Westminster Hall, the demolition of Soane's buildings and their replacement by the annexe (see illus., p. 12, top), designed in a late thirteenth-century style by J.L. Pearson and built in 1886–88. This work was the subject of much critical debate from the newly founded Society for the Protection of Ancient Buildings, as was the question of how to restore the surviving six fourteenth-century flying buttresses and fragments of Romanesque masonry.[53]

The main concern during the first four decades of the twentieth century was restoration, and two major projects were undertaken. The roof of Westminster Hall needed strengthening in the 1920s, when the damage caused by death-watch beetle was discovered. It was fortified with steel reinforcements, and much timber was replaced. During the 1930s, much of the stonework, statues and carving on the exterior of the entire building was renewed. The building itself continued to function efficiently, in spite of increasing pressure from its users, in particular since both Members and ministers required far more office space and better dining and library facilities. These trends became overwhelming after the Second World War, but little was done, apart from the infilling of courtyards and building on roofs, until the 1990s.

The Gothic Revival changed direction during the course of the nineteenth century, and, after the construction of the new Law Courts in the Strand in the 1880s, was infrequently used for public buildings. Even at times when the Gothic was deeply unfashionable, such as throughout much of the twentieth century, the new Palace of Westminster has retained the affection of its users and its visitors, and its interiors have been remarkably little altered, apart from widespread lightening of the oak panelling. The building has thus survived as the pre-eminent monument of its period and is extravagantly admired today.

# 8

## Sir John Soane and the Late Georgian Origins of the Royal Entrance

Sean Sawyer

In 1851, the artist George Scharf indulged his enthusiasm for construction sites by making a view of the new Palace of Westminster.[1] Taken from the south side of Old Palace Yard, this showed the immense Victoria Tower of Barry and Pugin's new Royal Entrance soaring alongside the minuscule, but functionally identical, *porte-cochère* of John Soane's existing Royal Entrance. In September of the same year, Soane's structure was demolished, and the following February, the Victoria Tower received the queen's coach for the first time.[2] As Scharf's drawing so strikingly depicts, the Victorian Royal Entrance did not spring unheralded from Westminster's Gothic soil, but rather constituted an aggrandizement of Soane's late Georgian work. The aim of this essay is to summarize the history of the Royal Entrance, with particular reference to contemporary developments in royal ceremonial, specifically the State Opening of Parliament.

The construction of Barry and Pugin's palace was not only the fulfilment of long-stand-

RIGHT: George Scharf, *Palace of Westminster under Construction with the Remains of Soane's Royal Entrance on the Left*, pencil, 1851, reproduced in *Peter Jackson, George Scharf's London: Sketches and Watercolours of a Changing City, 1820–50*, III, London 1987, p. 30, no. 678. The British Museum, London.

LEFT: Office of Sir John Soane, *View of the Royal Gallery*, drawn by Joseph Michael Gandy, pen and watercolour, 1824. Sir John Soane's Museum, London (folio vi, LXI, p. 37).

ing architectural aspirations for the nation's seat of law and government, but also the product of a period of intense debate over the relationship between architecture and national identity at Westminster. Both the ceremonial programme and Gothic style of the Victorian palace were determined during the formative period in British national culture, from the 1790s to the 1830s, when prolonged war with France and domestic social and political unrest tested and clarified the bonds between the citizen and the state. On the one hand, Parliament and the monarchy emerged as the unifying forces in British society, distinguishing the nation from 'dictatorial' and 'regicidal' France; on the other, Gothic became the national style that identified British architecture as a thing apart from continental neo-classicism.[3]

The aesthetic splendour and historic associations of Westminster's medieval monuments were instrumental in casting Gothic as the national style. Yet, even as Parliament's status as the definitive forum for national politics and protest was confirmed, the ancient Palace of Westminster languished in a near-derelict state. From the 1790s, this physical decrepitude combined with the growth in Parliamentary business and a renewed concern for the ceremonial circumstances of the monarchy to motivate a programme of urban renewal and historic preservation that aimed at creating a safe, efficient and even magnificent civic complex at Westminster.

John Soane and James Wyatt were the architects involved in this tortuous process, and they vigorously contested the image of the palace. Beginning with his commissioned design for a new House of Lords in 1794, Soane advocated a cosmopolitan, neo-classical vision, akin to the civic architecture of Sir William Chambers. Wyatt had greater influence with George III, however, and became Surveyor-General of the King's Works upon Chambers's death in 1796. Asserting his prerogative, he displaced Soane at Westminster in 1799, and reconstructed portions of the palace in the castellated Gothic style that he was then utilizing for the king's new palace at Kew. Although widely condemned in the capital, Wyatt's lath and plaster façades represented the ascendant taste, and were underpinned by veneration for Westminster's medieval heritage. Soane had to confront this shift in taste when Wyatt's death gave him a second chance to realize his vision for the Palace, as Attached Architect in the reorganized Office of Works from 1815 to 1832.

The reawakening of concern for the urban and architectural context of royal ceremonial was a principal factor in the late Georgian renovation of the palace.[4] In particular, the State Opening and Closing, or prorogation, of Parliament were the most significant events in the monarch's limited ceremonial calendar, and signified both his real political authority and the constitutional integrity of the nation: Lords and Commons convened and dissolved at the king's will, just as his tenure on the throne was sustained with their acquiescence. Moreover, his procession through the capital *en route* to and from the House of Lords made Londoners party to this constitutional enactment, and transformed the quotidian urban fabric into a theatre of state. During the last three decades of George III's reign, however, both the violence of radical protest and the king's mental instability, which prevented him from attending Parliament in person during the last sixteen years of his reign, threatened the viability of the State Opening and Closing. Most notably, during the State Opening of 29 October 1795, the king's coach was attacked by an anti-war mob as it approached the House of Lords, and the window was shattered by what was either a bullet or stone. Such incidents, along with the desire to improve the general flow of traffic, resulted in the clearance and widening of the approaches to the palace by the Westminster Improvements Commission during the war years.[5] George IV's accession in 1820 transformed this largely reactive

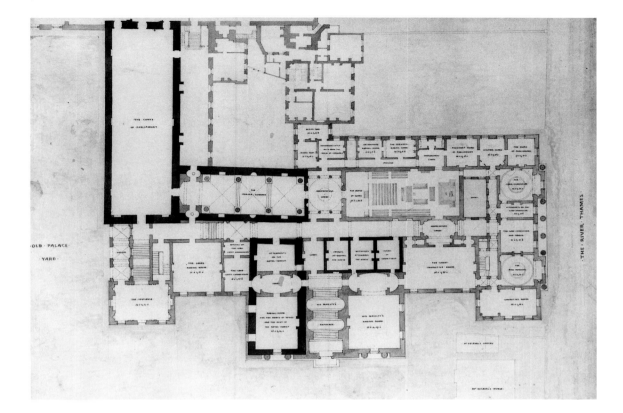

Office of Sir John Soane, *Plan of Design for a New House of Lords*, pencil, pen and coloured washes, December 1794. Sir John Soane's Museum, London (36/4/40).

Office of Sir John Soane, *Perspective of Design for Scala Regia*, pencil, pen and coloured washes, varnished, 1794. Sir John Soane's Museum, London (71/1/1).

approach into an architectural imperative to reconstruct the Royal Entrance itself, as the immensely unpopular Regent attempted to reinvent himself in the image of a king. He appealed to the transformative power of pageantry, most famously with his extravagant coronation of 1821, but more effectively, perhaps, in the annual State Opening and Closing of Parliament.[6]

Throughout the Georgian era, the Royal Entrance to the House of Lords had been altogether unceremonious in character: a modest, pedimented, Doric colonnade, denoted by a pair of small obelisks.[7] This fronted the steep stairway to the thirteenth-century Prince's Chamber that served as the king's robing room, and from which he passed to the throne at the south end of the adjacent Lords Chamber, via a small lobby. Once the State Coach arrived in Old Palace Yard, the king's progress became more like that of an actor scurrying to prepare for the curtain than that of a monarch proceeding in state to assert his legislative prerogative.

A monumental Royal Entrance formed the central feature of Soane's designs of 1794 "to render the House of Lords and the rooms and offices appertaining thereto more commodious".[8] His plan extended a new Lords Chamber toward the Thames from the medieval Painted Chamber, which was to be renovated as a cross-vaulted, Doric entrance gallery and conference room, along with the adjacent Court of Requests. While office and committee room suites surrounded the House to the north and east, the post-medieval structures on Old Palace Yard, as well as the Prince's Chamber, were to be demolished to create a monumental south elevation, with the new Royal Entrance at its centre. Its principal feature was a barrel-vaulted, three-staged stair that Soane called the Scala Regia, at once a reference to Bernini's staircase at the Vatican and to the host of English royalty – headed by Alfred the Great as the icon of enlightened kingship – that was to line it. The synchronization of the strongly articulated walls and vault with the cascading stair, together with the abstracted neo-classical ornamentation, created a space for dynamic yet stately ascent.

The drama faded, however, when the king turned right at the top landing to enter his robing suite, whence he passed directly to the throne in the Lords Chamber.

This perspective was evidently among the drawings that Soane presented to George III at Windsor on 26 October 1794. He later reported that "His Majesty was very much pleased ... with the idea of the Great Scala Regia, to be decorated with Statues of our Kings".[9] Despite the king's approval, the deepening crises of war and associated domestic unrest prohibited Pitt's government from proceeding with the project, and in February 1795 Soane was notified of its deferment. The next year, Wyatt assumed the Surveyorship, and in May 1799, when the impending Union with Ireland necessitated significant renovations at the palace, it was he to whom the king and his ministers consigned the work.

Informed of Wyatt's charge only by reading of it in the *Morning Herald* on 11 July, Soane was incensed, and campaigned to regain the commission over the next year. Along with exhibiting two exterior views for his project at the Royal Academy in 1800, he substantially revised his designs for the interiors, to compete with Wyatt's more decorative approach, with the help of his assistant, Joseph Michael Gandy (1771–1843), who had been a pupil of Wyatt's.[10] Gandy made a watercolour view of the new design for the Scala Regia, in which dramatic lighting effects and distortions of scale create an aura of Romantic grandeur. Yet the architecture itself is almost reactionary in comparison with the earlier design. The basic form of a staged, barrel-vaulted stair, lined with statues of monarchs, persists, but the forms are more traditionally composed, and enriched with archaeologically correct ornament: principally a giant Corinthian order with a full entablature. This, along with the broadening of the space, diffuses the almost intestinal sense of propulsion of the original design. Yet the addition of side aisles where spectators might gather, and the revision of the plan of the king's robing suite to create a 'Recess for Spectators', demonstrate that Soane's ceremonial impulse continued to strengthen.[11] Nevertheless, he had sacrificed the integrity of his reductive neo-classical style for the fashionable appeal of decorative enrichment.

Soane's revisions were futile, however, since Wyatt not only had a firm hold on work at the palace until his death, but also proposed to rebuild in the Gothic style. First, however, Wyatt provided for the influx of Irish Parliamentarians by relocating the House of Lords to the Court of Requests and literally carving seats for the new Members from the walls of St Stephen's Chapel, eradicating sections of its splendid fourteenth-century murals. Already labelled 'the Destroyer' for his alterations at the cathedrals of Salisbury, Hereford and Durham, Wyatt's desecration of St Stephen's deepened the enmity between him and antiquarians, principally John Carter, who was spearheading the effort to make Gothic the national style.[12] In the influential pages of the *Gentleman's Magazine*, Carter derided the castellated façades Wyatt subsequently erected, and in 1808 the House of Commons debated a motion to demolish them, during which they were compared to those of a prison and even a gentlemen's lavatory.[13]

This controversy, combined with Wyatt's gross mismanagement of the Office of Works, served to stymie his greater project for the palace, which included a new Gothic Royal Entrance. This is shown in a plan for his reconstruction of the House of Lords precinct, preserved at Sir John Soane's Museum, London.[14] The open arcade that fronted his new offices along Old Palace Yard is outlined and terminates on the right with a larger, slightly projecting, arched opening. This was the king's entrance portal and led into the square pavilion that masked the old stairs to the Prince's Chamber. His intention was to replace these stairs with a staged, quadripartite, vaulted staircase that would have led directly to the Painted Chamber, and thence into the king's new Robing Room that he had erected at the

Office of Sir John Soane, *Perspective of Design for the Scala Regia*, drawn by Joseph Michael Gandy, watercolour, August 1800. Sir John Soane's Museum, London (P283).

Levens, *Old Palace Yard*, line engraving, 1810. View showing Wyatt's reconstructions. Palace of Westminster (WOA 25a).

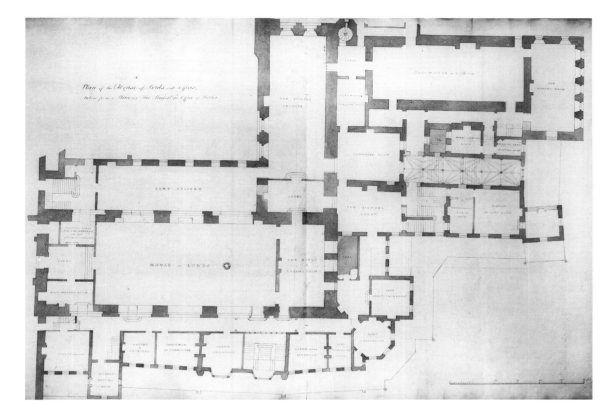

Office of James Wyatt, *Plan of Design for the House of Lords and Offices*, pencil, pen and coloured washes, *c.* 1808. Sir John Soane's Museum, London (51/1/1A).

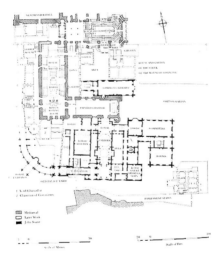

Plan of Sir John Soane's works at the Houses of Parliament (detail), 1822–32, published in H.M. Colvin (ed.), *The History of the King's Works*, VI, HMSO, 1973, p. 522, fig. 21.

south end of the Court of Requests. This was not completed, and Soane inherited the Royal Entrance in disarray when appointed the palace's architect in 1815.[15]

In his first annual survey report for the Office of Works in March 1816, Soane emphasized the unceremonious character of the Royal Entrance and identified its reconstruction as a priority.[16] The political and economic resources to do so did not exist in the desperate times after the Battle of Waterloo (1815), but George IV ordered alterations in his accommodations at the House of Lords immediately following his accession in January 1820. Moreover, for his first State Opening of Parliament as monarch, on 27 April 1820, he redirected his procession from its usual route across St James's Park to one through Whitehall and Parliament Street. His choice of this markedly more urban route clearly demonstrated his intention to utilize the State Opening and Closing to reform his public image. It paid immediate dividends, since *The Times* reported that "the assemblage, both within the walls of the House and in the streets, was the most numerous that we have ever seen [and] the King was cheered, both in going and returning".[17]

George IV's campaign to raise the profile of the monarch in the annual rituals of governance culminated in his commissioning of a new Royal Entrance in February 1822. By this time the economy was booming, and Lord Liverpool's government had already commissioned Soane to reconstruct the Law Courts at the palace. When the king approved the designs for the Courts on 28 February, he also "complained of his entrance into the House of Lords from the Street" and directed Soane to make a plan for improving it.[18] Ultimately, he succeeded in reconstructing the entire Royal Entrance in two phases: the entrance 'cloister' and Scala Regia of 1822–23, and the Ante-Room and Royal Gallery of 1823–24. In plan, Soane's Royal Entrance was extremely conservative. He retained Wyatt's entrance portal and vestibule, and demolished the old staircase and medieval chambers beyond, only to replicate their sequence and configuration. In its decoration and spatial effects, however, it presented a sophisticated synthesis of neo-classical design and picturesque aesthetics, in the service of renewed royal ritual.[19]

In the light of George IV's promotion of royal ceremonial, my first concern here is to understand how Soane's designs responded to the processional nature of the commission by producing graceful, fluent, sequential movement. Outside, he extended the existing arcade in an arc and projected a *porte-cochère* to receive the king's coach, so that it could roll to a stop without any inelegant manoeuvres.[20] In the design of the interiors he employed formal, structural and lighting effects to mark and modulate the spatial transitions and create discreet yet continuous spaces that sound and reverberate the processional rhythm.

To represent this symphony of form and function is the unmistakable intent of the sequence of exquisite drawings executed by Gandy at the completion of the project (see illus., pp. 143–46).[21] Although sequential, the views are episodic: they effect persistent forward movement, yet provide glimpses backwards and across the spaces, in a remarkable conjunction of Gandy's pictorial vision with Soane's scenographic architecture. In the first view, the lobby's great portal opens on to the virtual landscape of the Scala Regia, where a shaft of orange light from the oculus of the central vault floods the gentle slope of the staircase, and the bands of horizontal rustication and the trabeated screen pulls the viewer forward. The large windows and lunettes of the central bay were filled with dark glass that must have produced a church-like aura, appropriate to the sense of mystery and ritual that was increasingly cultivated in royal ceremonial. While there is a tendency to over-compensate for Gandy's pictorial exaggerations, this truly was a grand space: the stairway measured a generous, if not monumental, nine feet, nine inches in width, and the oculus rose twenty-five feet over the central landing. The next view looks backwards from the bottom of the

Office of Sir John Soane, *View of the Porte Cochère with the Royal Carriage*, pencil and watercolour, *c.* 1824. Sir John Soane's Museum, London (71/2/77).

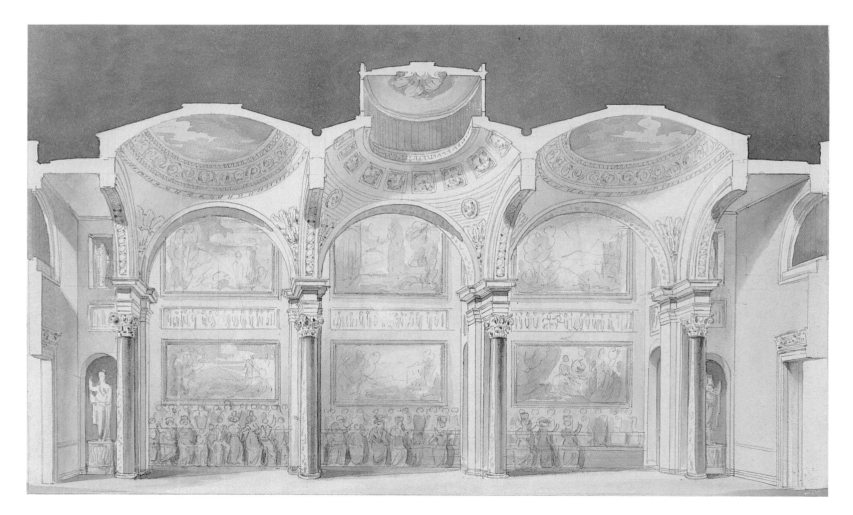

ABOVE LEFT: Office of Sir John Soane, *View of the Scala Regia*, drawn by Joseph Michael Gandy, pencil and watercolour, 1823. Sir John Soane's Museum, London (folio vi, LXI, p. 29).

ABOVE RIGHT: Office of Sir John Soane, *View from the Vestibule to the Cloister* pencil, pen and watercolour, *c.* 1823. Sir John Soane's Museum, London (folio vi, LXI, p. 28).

OPPOSITE: Office of Sir John Soane, *Sectional Perspective of a Design for the Royal Gallery of the Palace of Westminster with Spectators*, pencil, pen and ink wash, 1822. Victoria and Albert Museum, London (Richardson Collection, 3306.105).

stairs to the Gothic 'cloister', which emphasizes the passage from Wyatt's Gothic 'gloom' into Soane's more magnificent neo-classical realm. A group of three views then moves across the top landing of the Scala Regia and pauses in the intimacy of the sumptuously textured ovoid alcoves that flank it, before passing into the square Ante-Room. Here, four pairs of pink scagliola columns that frame the bi-axial openings offer a moment of stasis, before the ceiling pattern and doubled columns on the left redirect the procession towards the Royal Gallery. Gandy now turned to present two views: a detail of one of the immense torchères in the openings between the Ante-Room and the alcoves (not shown); and a deep perspective back down the Scala Regia that summarizes the itinerary to this point. He represented the Royal Gallery with two contrasting images: an asymmetrical view back toward the Ante-Room that emphasizes the continuity of the two spaces; and a broader, axial view that both expands upwards to the radiant, templed cupola and drives onwards to the dimmer sanctity of the Painted Chamber.

Throughout Gandy's images, a varied cast of soldiers, robed peers and fashionable ladies animates these processional spaces and conveys their spectacular nature. Here, one both saw and was seen – more usually as a privileged visitor to the inactive spaces, but more spectacularly as an invited guest at the State Opening and Closing, which were the pivotal experiences around which Soane crafted the architecture. Any doubt as to the self-conscious-

ness of this process is dispelled by the sectional perspective of an early design for the Royal Gallery, in which ranks of spectators await the king's passage and, with it, the enactment of the drama of constitutional legitimacy in this, the first theatre of the modern British monarchy (see illus., p. 142).[22]

As this drawing represents, Soane intended from the outset that the interiors of his new Royal Entrance would be neo-classical. This was in keeping with both his persistent conception of civic magnificence, and the king's long-standing, classicizing, Francophile tastes.[23] Yet he had to ensure both that its iconography was demonstratively British, and that it incorporated Wyatt's Gothic elements. He effected this transition by enclosing the last bay of the arcade beyond Wyatt's existing portal as a kind of architectural airlock, wherein Gothic and neo-classical forms and effects were combined in order to signify the passage from one stylistic zone to the other.[24] The portal itself was given a tracery-enriched pediment on its outer face, and an antique frame with an anthemion and feather cornice (perhaps a reference to the Prince of Wales's badge) on the interior. The spaces over the lobby's lateral doorways were filled with elaborate double-console pediments. Yet an explicitly Gothic note was struck by the series of diminutive, fan-shaped pendants suspended around the ceiling's edge, which seem to mimic the pendant vaults of Henry VII's Chapel and suggest a notional fan-vaulted space in their configuration.[25] In the principal spaces

ABOVE LEFT: Office of Sir John Soane, *View into the Anteroom from the Top Landing of the Scala Regia*, drawn by Joseph Michael Gandy, pencil and watercolour, c. 1823. Sir John Soane's Museum, London (folio vi, LXI, p. 31).

ABOVE RIGHT: Office of Sir John Soane, *View down the Scala Regia*, drawn by Joseph Michael Gandy, watercolour, 1824. Sir John Soane's Museum, London (folio vi, LXI, p. 30).

ABOVE LEFT: Office of Sir John Soane, *View in the Alcoves at the Top of the Scala Regia*, drawn by Joseph Michael Gandy, pencil and watercolour, 1824. Sir John Soane's Museum, London (folio vi, LXI, p. 36).

ABOVE RIGHT: Office of Sir John Soane, *View of the Anteroom Looking toward the Royal Gallery*, drawn by Joseph Michael Gandy, pencil and watercolour, 1824. Sir John Soane's Museum, London (folio vi, LXI, p. 33).

beyond, he maintained a more rigorously neo-classical vocabulary, and cultivated a character of antique magnificence. This produced a stylistic treatment that was at once more formally conservative and texturally enriched than his typical interiors, such as those at the Bank of England or the Dulwich Picture Gallery, and, as John Harris has suggested, it was clearly cognizant of the work of Charles Percier and Pierre Fontaine in the Tuileries and the Louvre in Paris, but also that of Michelangelo Simonetti at the Vatican Palace.[26]

The iconography was explicitly monarchical and imperial, but emphatically classicizing: the royal coat of arms appeared over the doorway into the Scala Regia and atop the architrave between the Ante-Room and Royal Gallery; roundels at the bottom of the Scala Regia allegorized the 'Rise and Fall of Rome'.[27] Yet there is no evidence that the statues of medieval kings intended for the stair's niches were executed.[28] The pendentives of the Scala Regia's central canopy were decorated with compositions that symbolized the colonial, mercantile and agricultural benefits of royal government. These consisted of a globe, the caduceus of Mercury, and two cornucopias of fruit and flowers that also contained George IV's coronation medals. The caduceus reappeared in the vaults over the lateral bays of the Royal Gallery, but this space was primarily to be decorated with sculpture and painting, as its name implied. These were to be triumphal in nature, principally showing large paintings of the battles of Waterloo and Trafalgar. But commissions for these were not forthcoming.[29]

Although the fire of 1834 consumed the central portion of the old Palace of Westminster, it spared Soane's Royal Entrance. His suite of rooms continued to serve the House of Lords until 1851, and was where the young Victoria learned the rituals of the constitutional monarchy.[30] Although Prince Albert's death in 1861 initiated a quarter of a century that has been called "the nadir of royal grandeur and ceremonial presence" – during which the queen opened Parliament only six times – George IV and Soane had established the ceremonial and architectural infrastructure of the monarchy's presence at Westminster.[31]

Indeed, Barry's plan for the Royal Entrance, in his winning entry in the competition of 1835 for the new palace, closely paralleled Soane's. It consisted of the same elements almost identically configured: a *porte-cochère* leading to a staged stair, and a square ante-room that redirected the line of procession into a tripartite gallery. However, unlike Soane, Barry had the luxury of disregarding the existing structures, in order to provide direct access to the Robing Room from his gallery. Of the four prize-winning designs, Barry's not only provided the most direct route to the throne, but also the most distinctive and legible exterior expression of the Royal Entrance, in the tower that anchored the south end of his composition. The grandeur of this tower, along with Pugin's exquisite Gothic detailing, was cited as a principal factor in Barry's victory.[32] In 1836 he isolated the stairway as the central element of the design and placed it on an axis with the Lords Chamber, creating what would have been a grand, if exhausting, route. Around 1840, he reinstated the gallery as the centrepiece and

ABOVE LEFT: Office of Sir John Soane, *View at the Juncture of the Anteroom and Royal Gallery toward the Scala Regia*, drawn by Joseph Michael Gandy, pencil and watercolour, 1824. Sir John Soane's Musuem, London (folio vi, LXI, p. 32).

ABOVE RIGHT: Office of Sir John Soane, *View from the Royal Gallery*, drawn by Joseph Michael Gandy, pencil and watercolour, 1824. Sir John Soane's Museum, London (folio vi, LXI, p. 35).

George Baxter, *State Opening of Parliament 1837*, mezzotint, published by Dixon & Rose, 1869. Palace of Westminster (WOA 1850).

condensed the stairway into the space behind the north-east pier of the tower. While this complicated and chastened the initial stage of the royal progress, it also aggrandized the royal accommodations by providing space for a large Robing Room on the south façade, and the immense Royal Gallery, half as long again as the Lords Chamber itself.[33] Barry, his son later related, "conceived the notion of the Royal Gallery, as a hall for the use of the House of Lords, for the viewing of the royal procession, and for the display of architectural effect, unrestrained by the encumbrances which business renders necessary in the Houses of Lords and Commons".[34] This had been exactly Soane's conception two decades earlier, and, as a spectacular, processional space, Barry's Royal Gallery is the direct descendant of Soane's.

Yet the Gothic magnificence of the ornamentation, along with the elaborate iconography of the decorative programme – as conceived and sponsored by the Fine Arts Commission under Prince Albert – imparted an altogether distinct character to the Victorian Royal Entrance. Rather than the drama of spatial and structural effects, and the symbolism of the Roman imperial past, it utilizes sheer scale and ornamental opulence, together with a more nativist iconography of Arthurian legend and British history, to convey its message of monarchical legitimacy and sovereignty. Moreover, the dazzling cloth of Gothic ornament is punctuated with symbols of national unity throughout: from the patron saints in the archway of the Victoria Tower to the shields and emblems of the kingdoms that decorate the canopy over the throne in the Robing Room, and the doorway into the Royal Gallery. This symbolism, along with the thematic decoration of the Robing Room and Prince's Chamber, with bas-reliefs and paintings of Arthurian and Tudor subjects respectively, represents a more self-conscious conception of the Royal Entrance as a didactic space in which to forge national political and cultural identity than that which operated in Soane's conception of the Royal Entrance. However, both the statues of Norman kings originally proposed by the Fine Arts Commission for the porch at the top of the Royal Staircase, and the designation of the Royal Gallery as a space in which to illustrate "the military history and glory of the country", parallel Soane's concern for representing Britain's heritage of crown and conquest in his equivalent spaces, down to the paintings of the battles of Waterloo and Trafalgar that line the walls of the extant Royal Gallery.[35]

With a remarkable degree of specificity, therefore, the form and function of the Victorian Royal Entrance derived from developments in the ceremonies of the State Opening and Closing of Parliament, and their architectural setting, put in place during the late Georgian era. Barry began by repeating the configuration of Soane's existing entrance almost verbatim, but eventually he contorted it in order to aggrandize the Royal Gallery, while Pugin gave the entire Palace a glorious Gothic form that finally succeeded in giving resonance to the assertion that Gothic was the 'national style'. As the Faustian saga of the British monarchy has progressed over the last century and a half, and ceremonial has become its principal expression of authority, the stature of the Royal Entrance has grown. Yet the recent decentralization of Parliamentary power and the reformation of the House of Lords will surely challenge its role as the crucible of royal and national identity.

# 9

## "We Shape Our Buildings and Afterwards Our Buildings Shape Us": Sir Giles Gilbert Scott and the Rebuilding of the House of Commons

Gavin Stamp

Damage caused by the bomb on 26 September 1940. House of Commons Library.

Winston Churchill and Brendan Bracken in the ruined House of Commons, May 1941. Popper Photo.

During the night of 10 to 11 May 1941, the House of Commons and Westminster Hall were set on fire by German incendiary bombs. The fire brigade concentrated on saving the medieval hall, so that by the following morning, all that was left of the debating chamber was a smoking void within the surrounding buildings of Charles Barry and Augustus Pugin's new Palace of Westminster. A few days later, Harold Nicholson recorded how:

> suddenly, when I turned the corridor, there was the open air and a sort of Tintern Abbey gaping before me. The little Ministers' rooms to the right and left of the Speaker's Lobby were still intact, but from there onwards there was absolutely nothing. No sign of anything but *murs calcinés* and twisted girders.[1]

Although he recognized that to rebuild the House of Commons was inappropriate while the nation was fighting a world war, the Prime Minister, Winston Churchill, wanted to ensure that a plan was approved so that work could begin as soon as possible. He foresaw that politics might be "very fierce and violent" following a General Election when the war was over, and felt that "we must have a good, well-tried and convenient place in which to do our work. The House owes it to itself, it owes it to the nation, to make sure that there is no gap, no awkward, injurious hiatus in the continuity of our Parliamentary life."[2] The Director of Works, T.P. Bennett, therefore prepared a scheme for reconstructing the Chamber while incorporating necessary improvements. And on 28 October 1943 the House of Commons debated the proposal, moved by the Prime Minister, that "a Select Committee be appointed to consider and report upon plans for the rebuilding of the House of Commons and upon such alterations as may be considered desirable while preserving all its essential features".

Churchill introduced the debate and, in a magnificent speech, enunciated that great truth, so often quoted, that "we shape our buildings and afterwards our buildings shape us".[3] He insisted that the rectangular shape of the old Chamber – planned by Barry to maintain the shape of St Stephen's Chapel – was responsible for the development of the two-party system that he saw as the essence of British Parliamentary democracy. Churchill therefore wanted to see the Commons "restored in all essentials to its old form, convenience and dignity", and this required the recreation of the two characteristics that, he knew, would "sound odd to foreign ears". The first was "that its shape should be oblong and not semicircular". The second was:

> that it should not be big enough to contain all its Members at once without overcrowding and that there should be no question of every Member having a separate seat

reserved for him. ... We attach immense importance to the survival of Parliamentary democracy. In this country it is one of our war aims. We wish to see our Parliament a strong, easy, flexible instrument of free Debate. For this purpose a small Chamber and a sense of intimacy are indispensable.[4]

In the debate that followed, there was remarkable unanimity among the Members of Parliament present about the desirability of building a new Chamber on the general lines of the old. Nobody spoke in favour of building a semicircular Chamber; it was even suggested that this form had been "the death warrant of parliamentary democracy on the Continent", and that if the French parliament had enjoyed the boon of a rectangular Chamber, "the effect on democracy in France might have been far different".[5] Nancy Astor, however, complained that "the Prime Minister has always looked backwards, more or less", and that it was time to look forward. Tacitly recognizing the truth of the observation made by her old adversary about the effect of buildings on human behaviour, the first woman Member to take her seat recommended a circular Chamber, as:

> I have often felt that it might be better if Ministers and ex-Ministers did not have to sit and look at each other, almost like dogs on a leash, and that controversy would not be so violent. I do not think there is any merit in violent controversies, and I do not believe that the fights in the House of Commons helped democracy.[6]

No one agreed with her.

The only truly dissentient voice was that of James Maxton, the leader of the Independent Labour Party. While claiming great fondness for the destroyed Chamber, Maxton complained that the select committee had far too narrow a mandate and that all options should be considered – including leaving the ruins of the Commons Chamber as a historic monument (shades of William Morris's *News from Nowhere*) and building a new Chamber elsewhere. "I think we should think of growing into a new type of world after this war, and I think we should think in terms of starting in different surroundings to make plans and preparations for the new world." Curiously, Maxton was worried about future conflicts and felt that the select committee "should consider housing Parliament in premises where there would be greater protection for the House of Commons and the Noble Lords when they are carrying on their labours". His solution was to erect "the finest building that British architecture can devise" some twenty miles outside London, "in good English park-land", but complete with a railway station, a fine car park and an aerodrome, all on "the finest and biggest scale".[7] This naïve vision of garden-city modernism was aptly dismissed by the Member for Penryn and Falmouth as "a sort of Potters Bar Canberra".[8]

There was general agreement that the ventilation, heating and lighting of the new Chamber must be better than that in the old, and that it was essential that the size of the visitors' and press galleries be greatly increased to make the work of the Commons more visible to the nation and the empire. Several Members complained about the poor accommodation and the absence of places to interview visiting constituents, the Member for Glasgow, Gorbals, comparing the old Commons tea room to "an apology for a bad butcher's shop" to which one could not take a lady.[9] A few disagreed with the Prime Minister about the size of the old Chamber. Sir Alfred Beit asked that the words "preserving the essential features" be omitted from the motion, so that the select committee might consider enlarging the Chamber, particularly if there was to be a future redistribution of seats. The debate was taking place in Barry and Pugin's Lords Chamber, and one Member observed that he had noticed:

John Piper, *Council Chamber of the House of Commons*, oil on board, 1941. Palace of Westminster (WOA 496).

a distinct change in the nature of this House of Commons since we have come into this actual place. I have noticed more difficulty in controlling the Government, as it were, a lack of intimacy, a falling off in the quality of Members' speeches, owing to the great size of this Chamber.[10]

There was surprisingly little debate about the *style* of the proposed new Commons. Beit expressed the conventional view of the time about the Gothic Revival when he described the old Chamber as being a product of "an extremely unhappy period in British architecture", and another Member insisted that "we do not want quite a replica of some of the rather tawdry, Victorian Tudor-Gothic which was rather carried to excess in the Old Chamber", while yet recognizing that:

> we do not want to disfigure the extraordinary success of this surprisingly successful façade by building an entirely new type in the middle of it. We have to make a compromise between the old and the new, which is, after all, a fitting thing to do.[11]

The Member for Farnham, Godfrey Nicholson, however, was prepared to defend the Gothic of Barry and Pugin, arguing that "it is dignified and in the true English tradition and that is peculiarly suited to Parliamentary democracy. It is not a pompous but a dignified and good style".[12]

Mr Hannah, the Member for Bilston, while advocating the partial retention of the calcined stone lobby of the Commons, advocated a classical Chamber, with Ionic pilasters below and a Corinthian order above, carrying a coffered roof, which "might give us a better effect than anything Gothic", but his was a lone voice.[13] Maxton, however, was not the only Member who envisaged something "built by modern people with modern ideas", if without having any clear sense of what this might mean. Another Glasgow Member, Mr Buchanan, hoped that the new Commons Chamber would be "designed by some of those who are now in the Forces. It would be the best testimonial to the men – something done by themselves and not by outworn past". But there was no serious opposition to Churchill's motion, which implied that the new Chamber would somehow repeat the style as well as the shape of the old, and it was carried by 127 'Ayes' to 3 'Noes'.

The select committee was appointed in December 1943, with Earl Winterton as chairman. Its report was issued in October 1944 and debated by the Commons on 25 January 1945, when Churchill pleaded – successfully – for the retention of the fire-damaged arch into the old Chamber in the Members Lobby, "as a monument to the ordeal which Westminster has passed through".[14] The report was accepted without a division, and the clearance of the site and preliminary work for the new Chamber were begun in June 1945. The foundation stone was formally laid on 26 May 1948. On that occasion, the Prime Minister, Clement Attlee, echoed his predecessor's words in stating that "the new Chamber which is now arising will, by the wise decision of the wartime parliament, reproduce the features of its predecessor; for its form has had no small effect on the development of our parliamentary system". And Churchill, now Leader of the Opposition, was glad to associate himself with what Attlee had said, and felt that "we owe him a debt – and his colleagues a debt – for having adhered, in spite of some temptation to the contrary, to the form of the Chamber which we agreed to in the wartime government"[15] – which suggested that, as Churchill had feared, the Labour majority elected in 1945 had been rather more sympathetic to the idea of a modern Chamber.

The select committee, constrained by the resolution of the Commons, had been:

> unanimous in their opinion that the sense of intimacy and almost conversational form of debate encouraged by the dimensions of the Old Chamber should be maintained. They believe that the present intimate and traditional style of discussion is firmly established in the customs and affections of the nation.[16]

Perhaps the committee's most important task was to choose an architect, and, having decided that a competition was unsatisfactory, as it could only have been held within

'The Churchill Arch', Members Lobby, House of Commons, Palace of Westminster.

Laying of the foundation stone of the new Commons Chamber on 26 May 1948. House of Commons Library.

Reginald Grenville Eves, *Sir Giles Gilbert Scott*, oil on canvas, 1935. National Portrait Gallery, London.

restricted limits, it recommended Sir Giles Gilbert Scott, OM, RA. The committee also asked the engineer Dr Oscar Faber to submit a scheme for heating and ventilating the new Chamber, under the supervision of the architect, and, in the event, he was responsible for the structural steelwork of the new building. Possibly mindful of the experience of Sir Charles Barry a century before, the report noted that:

> Sir Giles has worked in the closest amity with Your Committee since his appointment and has ever been ready to consider any suggestion. ... There has been a complete absence of that unhappy disagreement which has sometimes in the past characterized the relationship of Select Committees and the experts advising them.[17]

As the select committee had had to find the architect "best qualified to provide plans in keeping with the Gothic style of the Palace", the appointment of Scott seems almost inevitable. Born in 1880, he had won the competition to design the new Anglican Cathedral in Liverpool at the age of only twenty-two. The style was almost in his blood, as he belonged to the third generation of a dynasty of architects who had dominated the Gothic Revival in England. In fact, Scott had little sympathy for the work of his grandfather, Sir George Gilbert Scott, architect of the Albert Memorial, the Midland Grand Hotel at St Pancras and countless churches up and down the land, and was more influenced by the work of his father, George Gilbert Scott Jr, whose masterpiece, St Agnes' Church in Kennington, South London, also fell victim to enemy incendiary bombs in 1941. At Liverpool Cathedral, whose great central tower had just been completed, and his several churches, Giles Scott had demonstrated that he could handle Gothic with both accomplishment and originality, responding to the fluid conditions and more austere tastes of the twentieth century.

But Scott had other qualifications to recommend him to the select committee. Unlike, say, the older Ninian Comper, he was not exclusively a church architect. After the First World War his practice had expanded to embrace collegiate and institutional commissions, and at both the new Cambridge University Library and the New Bodleian Library in Oxford he had shown that he could handle highly complex technical briefs to produce 'modernistic' buildings that responded to the changing and uncertain tastes of his generation. Scott had designed the standard GPO telephone kiosk, and had even risen to the challenge of designing the exterior of an electric power station – at Battersea – that had become the most prominent visible symbol of modernity in London. At a time when new ideas from the Continent had undermined the certainties of the architectural profession and were capturing the hearts of a younger generation, Scott had been an ideal choice as President of the Royal Institute of British Architects, and in his Presidential Address in 1933 he said that:

> I hold no brief either for the extreme diehard Traditionalist or the extreme Modernist and it seems to me idle to compare styles and to say that one is better than the other; the old fight of my grandfather's time between Gothic and Classic and the present fight between Traditionalism and Modernism seem to me issues not worth spilling ink over. ... I should feel happier about the future of architecture had the best ideas of Modernism been grafted upon the best traditions of the past, in other words, if Modernism had come by evolution rather than by revolution.[18]

Scott's ability to achieve a creative compromise, to satisfy most parties in response to difficult and complex conditions, must surely have recommended him to the select committee.

In designing the new House of Commons, Scott was assisted by his younger brother, Adrian Gilbert Scott (1883–1962), architect of Cairo Cathedral, whose work was very simi-

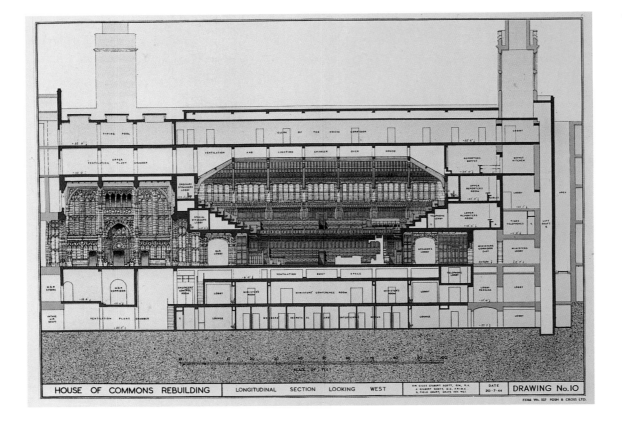

Office of Sir Giles Gilbert Scott, *House of Commons Rebuilding. Longitudinal Drawing Looking West*, Drawing 10, 20 October 1944. House of Commons Library.

lar in style. Their plans for the new Chamber and the associated accommodation were published with the select committee's report. Much of the work was technically demanding and highly ingenious, as a great deal more accommodation had to be crammed into a confined space defined by the old foundations and building lines. Neither Commons Court nor Star Chamber Court, on either side of the Commons division lobbies, could be reduced in size, nor could Cloister Court. Small courts next to St Stephen's Chapel were filled in, but the only way to satisfy the new and more demanding requirements of the House of Commons was to go downwards. Thanks to Oscar Faber's steelwork, two floors of conference rooms and other facilities were constructed below the ventilation space beneath the new Chamber, and an additional floor containing the Clerk of the House's offices was placed on top.

While preserving the general dimensions and arrangements of the old Chamber and its associated lobbies and corridors, Scott and Faber contrived to introduce modern heating, lighting and ventilation, improve circulation, provide many new rooms and improve the Whips' and staff offices. In the Commons Chamber itself, the number of seats for the press was increased from 93 to 161, and the number of other strangers' seats from 259 to 326. All this was achieved at gallery level by slightly widening the Chamber, from forty-six and a half feet to forty-eight feet, and by considerably lengthening it, from eighty-four feet to one hundred and three feet. Yet, below, the floor of the Commons Chamber was exactly the same size as before – forty-five and a half feet by sixty-eight feet – so maintaining that feeling of intimacy that was deemed so important. Scott described this as the most complex building he had ever had to deal with, as "to fit in all the arrangements was a most intricate business, and still more intricate to tuck them out of sight", and he compared the interior to that of a battleship.[19] This was an apt analogy, and an interesting one, as, during the wartime debate, Churchill had justified his anxiety to rebuild by the fact that "we are building warships that will not be finished for many years ahead, and … I rank the House of Commons – the most powerful Assembly in the whole world – at least as important as a fortification or a battleship, even in time of war".[20]

But it would be a Gothic battleship, not a Modern Movement one:

> Feeling as we do that modernist architecture in its present state is quite unsuitable for the rebuilding of the House of Commons and bearing in mind that the Chamber forms only a small portion of an existing large building, we are strongly of the opinion that the style adopted should be in sympathy with the rest of the structure, even if it has to differ in some degree in order to achieve a better quality of design …

Scott reported. That, after all, was why he had been appointed. But while Scott was in favour of Gothic in this commission, he exhibited a rather conventional prejudice against Barry and Pugin. "No attempt has been made to follow the design of the old woodwork or stonework. … The Gothic detail of the old Chamber was lifeless and uninteresting", he insisted, "and the richness was spread evenly over the whole area without relief or contrasts. It has been our endeavour to remedy this, with the result that, though still Gothic in style, the effect will be entirely different from what existed before."[21]

In his report, Scott took pains to justify his use of Gothic. "The question of style has received very careful consideration; it is always a difficult decision to make when the problem is to add to or rebuild a portion of an existing building." The difficulty, however, was, as he saw it, that:

> we have had no live traditional style for the last hundred years, and to appreciate the position it is necessary to understand what is meant by a live traditional style and what our present situation is. Throughout the ages the arts have owed their fine quality to the fact that nations, and even continents, worked in a style that was common to all their members, and this style was the result of the accumulated knowledge and experience of preceding generations and evolved slowly and gradually as the centuries passed … there was no need for the artist to consider in what style he should express himself – there was the style of his time and country ready to hand.[22]

In fact, Scott concurred with the advocates of the Modern Movement in regarding the situation of the architect in the twentieth century as peculiar and problematic; like them, he thought that genuine traditions died out after the early nineteenth century owing to the succeeding "period of individualism and the revival of past styles". The consequence was that "at present we have no traditional style that is characteristic of our times". But his conclusion was different to theirs. "Modernism", he thought:

> looks as if it might develop into such a style but at present it has no tradition behind it, being the product of a revolution rather than evolution; it throws out everything and starts again from nothing. It is at present primarily negative and lacks depth and quality, which indeed it has not had time to acquire. Its vocabulary is very limited, and in it the more subtle qualities of artistic expression are impossible. It is also at present too mechanistic, being frankly based upon the beauties of the machine rather than nature, which has always been, and surely must always be, the basis of all art. Whether it will develop a quality in, say, fifty or a hundred years time, time alone will show.[23]

The new House of Commons was opened on 26 October 1950. It looked almost exactly as Scott had proposed it should look six years earlier. The new Chamber was illustrated in the

Commons Chamber facing the Speaker's Chair, House of Commons, Palace of Westminster. The four large hanging lights were added in the 1980s.

technical press, but usually without any critical comment.[24] Indeed, it seems as if no one knew quite what to say about it. Compromise is not glamorous, and, after all, the decision to rebuild on the lines of the old had been taken by the wartime Parliament. Furthermore, Scott's work was not an exemplar of the new architecture, such as was then rising on the opposite bank of the Thames for the Festival of Britain planned for the following year. But neither was it in that abstracted, tasteful, modern, neo-Georgian manner that more traditional architects favoured. Gothic was certainly not fashionable in 1950 – neither Giles Scott's Gothic nor, for that matter, the earlier work of Barry and Pugin. Some felt that Scott should have attempted an accurate restoration – or recreation – of the destroyed buildings, but this was never a serious possibility as they had clearly needed modernization. Besides, the old Chamber had itself been a compromise: the sloping sides and ends of the ceiling – which contributed to the sense of enclosure, and which Scott faithfully reproduced – had been an alteration made, against Barry's wishes, to improve the acoustics.

The *Architectural Review* dealt with the problem by first explaining the history of the Palace of Westminster and the evolution of the Commons Chamber from the shape of St Stephen's Chapel, before concluding that "the best approach to the new Chamber is to regard it as a chimera – a fascinating monstrosity, but one which has a *raison d'être*", and then

Set of doors leading to the Commons Chamber, House of Commons, Palace of Westminster.

allowing the 'client', in the shape of Tom Driberg, to give an opinion. "Pure 'modernism' would, no doubt, have looked uncouth in the middle of the Barry building – like a single ivory tooth in a denture of gold", admitted the Member for Maldon, who confessed that:

> the moment I set foot in the new Chamber, still cluttered as it was with workmen's paraphernalia, I was greatly pleased and impressed. Even then, it had a serenity, a robustness, and a certain homeliness – all, in combination, peculiarly English, peculiarly Parliamentary, true to the nature of the Commons Chamber and of the debates therein.[25]

The most critical review, however, was published in (of all places) *Country Life*, where Robert Lutyens insisted that the new Commons Chamber was "without distinction ... a rather ugly galleried box" and that, despite the constraints imposed on the select committee, it should have been reconstructed on "at least approximately contemporary lines ... without the Gothicism which renders its appearance so ridiculous". The problem, he thought, went beyond the choice of style:

> We are a sentimental people, and thus deficient in aesthetic judgement. Whether a decision to go Gothic once again was inescapable or not, the fact remains that it is fairly deplorable from any except a sentimental point of view. ... The Gothic Revivalists at least had conviction. Their productions were often the product of firmly-founded spiritual and aesthetic belief. We have no such conviction, now that the mists of the Victorian past have dissolved into the noonday of industrial revolt. ... The new House of Commons must be regarded at least as an acknowledgement of the perplexing ambivalence of our age. Sir Giles will design Waterloo Bridge and accept a commission for a Tudor House of Commons without turning a hair.[26]

A few weeks earlier, Lutyens had written to *The Times* that "it is bad enough to be saddled with a fake new House of Commons", in discussing the style of the proposed rebuilding of Coventry Cathedral. This provoked a response from Sir Giles:

> Mr Lutyens's shocked outburst against the use of Gothic architecture has quite an old-fashioned ring about it – the battle of the styles revived. He is not the first to attach great importance to the architectural style adopted in our modern buildings, as if this affected the artistic quality of a building.

Scott then reiterated the argument he had used in his report to the select committee about the slow and gradual evolution of historical architectural styles, unlike the modern style, which was too young so that "the more subtle expressions are beyond it". The Renaissance, he pointed out, was also a revival of a past style:

> what Mr Lutyens would call a fake, a line of thought which would accuse his distinguished father, Sir Edwin Lutyens, of faking a fake, as he accuses me, in the new House of Commons, of faking Barry's fake! These battles of style create fanaticism that warps and distorts our judgement of artistic values.[27]

Unlike his grandfather, who was committed to the 'Gothic Renaissance', but like his father, Giles Scott was not partisan about style. "Architectural style", he insisted,

> implies a school of thought and is, of course, only a means to an end and not a quality in itself at all: it is, in fact, a language in which the artist expresses himself. The impor-

tant element is what he had to say and how he expresses himself, and not the language he uses.

But this gentlemanly use of the old linguistic analogy could make no headway against those who fervently believed that every age should have but one style, one inevitable expression of social, economic and spiritual life. That was certainly true of Pugin a century earlier, and it was now true of the younger architects committed to the ideals of the Modern Movement. "In any great period architecture evolves out of contemporary thought and methods of building", countered four young architects at the Architectural Association, who found it ridiculous that it was still "perfectly possible to design power-house chimneys in the manner of Greek temple columns, telephone boxes with the fenestration of eighteenth century villas, and a new Parliament building as a Tudor manor house".[28]

Giles Scott's Gothic was not, therefore, likely to convince Nikolaus Pevsner, who could not understand why the decision of a democratically elected Parliament should be allowed to overrule the *Zeitgeist*, the spirit of the age. For him, in 1957, the new Chamber was:

a lamentable anti-climax. ... The decision of the Select Committee was regrettable, coming as it did in the middle of a century which had created and widely developed a style of its own, independent of the past and expressive of the present. But Sir Giles Gilbert Scott's handling of the style selected is even more regrettable. ... Nothing could show up more poignantly the inferiority of the C20 in comparison with the early C19 Gothicists. To Pugin the Gothic style was a style, a unity of structure and ornamental enrichment. Scott thought he could keep one without the other. Had he been fully alive to the implications of a split between principles and forms, he would have built in the C20 style, a style in its principles of skeletal construction closer in spirit to the Gothic style than any since the C15. But he thought he could keep the Gothic ornament. The result could only be, aesthetically speaking, a neuter.[29]

ABOVE: Fireplace with grate in the 'Ayes' Division Lobby, House of Commons, Palace of Westminster.

LEFT: Furniture in the 'Ayes' Division Lobby, House of Commons. Shown are a writing table, armchairs, desk lamp, stationery rack and waste bin.

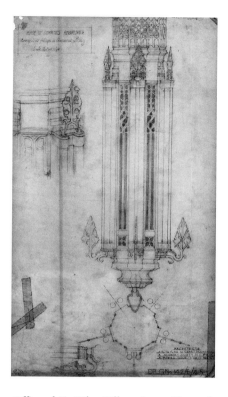

Office of Sir Giles Gilbert Scott, *House of Commons Rebuilding. Bronze Light Fittings in Commons Lobby*, pencil on tracing paper, *c.* 1950. British Architectural Library, RIBA, London.

Sir Giles Gilbert Scott, Speaker's Chair, black bean wood, brass, leather and embroidered textile, 1950. Palace of Westminster (POW 9703).

Now that it is half-a-century old, however, Scott's achievement may look rather more positive. His Gothic has weathered well; his English oak has darkened; and the Commons Chamber has a familiar, reassuring rightness within the restored new Palace of Westminster that commands respect. More to the point, it can now be seen that although the two designers were dissimilar in outlook and convictions, Scott's Gothic is not so very different in nature and intention from Pugin's. Both adopted the style because of the ideas and associations it conveys in this setting. Scott's Gothic may be applied over a modern structure of steel and reinforced concrete, but Pugin had been working within a building of cast iron as well as masonry – and the falling carved boss that might have killed the late Lord Shinwell, had he been sitting in his seat in the Lords Chamber, turned out to have been glued to a ceiling that was fixed to an iron structure. So much for Pugin's 'true principles' – but that does not undermine the quality and vitality of his decorative work any more than such considerations do Scott's.

Scott, in fact, was doing just what Pugin had done a century before. Working for Barry, Pugin applied his facility at Gothic ornament to objects that had no medieval precedent – gas lights, ventilation grilles and desk calendars – as well as to all the furniture and fittings required in what was then the most complex and technologically advanced public building in the world. Scott had to adapt his own version of the Gothic to an even more elaborately serviced structure – his inventive pendant lights in the Commons Lobby incorporated fluorescent tubes that allowed Members to coin the apt and not necessarily pejorative term 'neon-Gothic'. Throughout, Scott showed an attention to detail and a concern for craftsmanship that were quite as consistent as Pugin's, whether in designing the Speaker's Chair, wall

ABOVE: Prime Minister's Conference Room, House of Commons, Palace of Westminster.

RIGHT: Sir Giles Gilbert Scott, pen and ink stand, silver gilt, 1950, Prime Minister's Conference Room, House of Commons . Inscription reads: "The gift of St. Lucia". Palace of Westminster (POW 8074).

ABOVE: Giles Gilbert Scott, dispatch box, purruri and brass, 1947. The brass plate on the lid reads: "The gift of New Zealand". Palace of Westminster (POW 8066).

panelling, tables and chairs for committee and meeting rooms, or much smaller objects like dispatch boxes, stationery racks, inkstands and the (very numerous) ashtrays.

Nor is Scott's Gothic derivative; indeed, it is arguably more original and inventive, less dependant upon literal precedent, than Pugin's. Over the years, particularly in working on the Anglican Cathedral in Liverpool, Scott had evolved a personal Gothic style that was sometimes angular, sometimes curvaceous, but always distinctively modern in feeling — almost streamlined, in fact. In the House of Commons, he gave something of this flavour to the conventional Tudor detail demanded by arch spandrels and panelling friezes. But Scott had to rise to a further challenge. The Gothic of Pugin and Barry had an ecclesiastical character that was intrinsic to the style, as well as symbolizing the origins of the House of Commons in a converted royal chapel. But times had changed, so that, as James Pope-Hennessy put it in 1953:

> this was a note Scott has not cared to echo. His well-lit, well-warmed Commons Chamber, with its cigar-coloured woods and *eau-de-nil* leather upholstery, is discreet and impersonal, but it has more in common with some comfortable suburban hotel, or the saloon of some great transatlantic passenger liner than with the dim neo-Gothic debating room of Charles Barry.[30]

Scott succeeded in making his Gothic look secular and modern, thereby reflecting the more democratic nature of the contemporary Parliament. And his modern Gothic had to be spread much further, for use on all the various items of furniture that were given by the many nations of the Commonwealth, who associated the style with the 'Mother of Parliaments'.

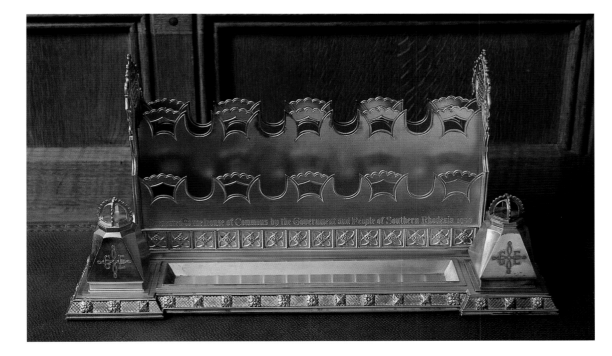

Scott therefore had to create a consistent style that was at once modern and traditional, employing a craft-based system of enrichment of the best materials but avoiding monarchical symbols like the Tudor rose, as if to emphasize democracy and to underplay the connection between the House of Commons and the medieval royal palace. If Pugin was an inspired and passionate decorative designer who rose to the challenge of architecture, Giles Scott was a great architect whose sense of scale, both large and small, enabled him to design excellent furniture in what still was, in fact, a living tradition.

The new House of Commons is a brilliant, resourceful essay in a historical style that was and is clearly of its own time and could belong to no other age. The *Zeitgeist*, after all, can be multilingual. At Westminster, as at Liverpool and elsewhere, Scott succeeded in creating an authentic modern Gothic, permitting the use of ornament and symbol so necessary in such a setting. The early Modern Movement had rejected ornament, so however fine a debating chamber a member of the MARS Group might have created at Westminster in 1944–50, it could have looked only raw and alien when surrounded by nineteenth-century symbolic and decorative splendour. This Scott understood. He was not hostile to modern architecture, but thought it would take fifty or a hundred years to mature. Fifty years on – with a richly finished and resonant new building for Parliament by Sir Michael Hopkins having risen opposite New Palace Yard – Scott's evolutionary view of architectural development may seem rather less blinkered than the certainties and shrill denunciations of his modernist critics.

Sir Giles Gilbert Scott absorbed the historical spirit of Westminster. He engaged with the problems faced by Barry and Pugin, entered into the concerns of the House of Commons and produced – by demand and by necessity – a compromise. But it was a compromise of peculiar appropriateness and real integrity that demonstrated that the Gothic Revival was not dead, and that a historical style could still perform a vital role in the life of the nation. Indeed, it had to. Whether for better or for worse, Scott played a crucial role in maintaining the continuity of the tradition of British Parliamentary democracy that had evolved in the nineteenth century. And he did it with style and conviction. He had promised that his Gothic would be "entirely different from what existed before". It is, and it is good.

Spandrel decorated with crowned portcullis in the 'Ayes' Division Lobby, House of Commons, Palace of Westminster.

# IO

## "New Furniture of a Suitable and Proper Character": The Working Interiors 1849–60

Dorian Church

I n April 1847, Queen Victoria officially opened the new Lords Chamber, the first of the two Chambers to be made ready for occupation and use in the new Palace of Westminster. Charles Barry's attentions were now directed towards bringing the House of Commons Chamber, and the ancillary spaces required for the everyday functioning of Parliament, into service. The magnitude of this task was outlined in the same month by *The Times*, which described Barry's building, when complete, as housing:

> fourteen halls, galleries, vestibules, and other apartments of great capacity and noble proportion ... it comprises eight official residences, each first-rate mansions; twenty corridors and lobbies are required to serve as the great road-ways through this aggregation of edifices; two-and-thirty noble apartments facing the river will be used as Committee-Rooms; Libraries, Waiting-Rooms, Dining-Rooms, and Clerks' Offices.[1]

### Clubland at Westminster

As the new building was going up, the business of Parliament continued in makeshift circumstances around the temporary Chambers. Buildings that had not been destroyed by the fire were fitted up for use as committee rooms, libraries, offices and residences. Additional space was hired in nearby buildings,[2] and in 1845 Barry put up temporary structures for more committee rooms in New Palace Yard.[3] Rooms were found for the Speaker's chaplain, and in 1835, a cloakroom for Members was requested as an immediate need.[4] The Speaker's residence was relocated to Eaton Square, and the Lords Librarian to Abingdon Street. Furniture for these interim facilities was supplied from the stores of the Office of Woods and Works, while Holland & Sons, a prominent furnishing firm and regular contractor for various government offices, set up and maintained the temporary interiors.[5] Some functional furniture had been salvaged from the old palace during the fire and must also have been pressed into use.[6]

The decision to build afresh at Westminster had in part been influenced by the patchwork nature of the original buildings, which, despite the best efforts of the Board of Works, had remained "confined and incommodious".[7] Beyond the ceremonial core – as represented by the royal approach and the two Chambers – the new building was to contain facilities that the committees of the two Houses had specified, in accordance with modern expectations of comfort and convenience. Their ambition was to build a new structure that from the exterior would form a resonant symbol of nationhood, and in its interior workings "should be as perfect in all its arrangements and details as possible".[8]

Barry's plans for the new building also supplied greater security for Members, Peers and

The Salisbury Room, House of Lords. Formerly the drawing room of the official residence of the Librarian, House of Lords. Photograph by Derry Moore.

official residents by separating their points of access, facilities and areas of exclusive business from the public (see illus., p. 119). The most important of these new facilities for Members and Peers lay on the principal floor, with libraries and refreshment rooms on the river-side of the new building, located away from the street and the public entrance through Westminster Hall, and adjacent to the Chambers, the heart of Parliamentary life. The increased number of committee rooms, needed for the ever-expanding volume of Parliamentary business, were located primarily on the first and second floors and accessed by a specific route shared with attending members of the public. Official offices were to fill the spaces between the Chambers, the less important extending on to other floors, and official residences were sited on the outermost perimeters of the building, furthest from the centres of most activity and general points of access. The ground, first and second floors also provided ancillary facilities and offices for support staff, as well as a smoking room, apartments for lesser functionaries, and the private areas and servants' rooms for the residences.

Barry's first plans demonstrated that he understood the complex hierarchies represented by the primary functions of the building. However, the fitting-out and furnishing of the non-ceremonial areas needed a more particularized and detailed appreciation of the various roles, statuses and needs of its diverse users and service providers. Under Barry's guidance, Pugin provided a basic range of furniture types in his unique interpretation of the Gothic style, which fulfilled the multi-purpose requirements of offices, facilities and residences. The domestic requirements of the residences necessitated an expansion of the basic range of furniture types, but much of the fitting-up of these areas was completed after Pugin's death. There was one further and comparatively new ingredient in the social mix of Parliamentary life for which Barry and Pugin had to provide designated furniture: these were the facilities, chiefly the libraries and dining areas, specified in the accommodation brief by Members and Peers.

Although the tradition of residences for officials was centuries-old, it was not until 1818 that the House of Commons established a library for the use of Members. Over the following decade, John Soane built and furnished library spaces for both Houses. In the 1770s, John Bellamy, the deputy housekeeper, had begun to provide refreshments within the building in two improvised spaces near the old Commons Chamber.[9] A smoking room was first fitted up at the behest of the Members in the decade preceding the fire. Members and Peers, brought together at Westminster, were engaged in the increasingly lengthy and time-consuming business of government. Their expectations seem to have been modelled on those facilities provided for the new gentlemen's clubs that appeared in burgeoning numbers in the 1820s, particularly situated across St James's Park from the Palace of Westminster, along Pall Mall.

Barry himself had been the architect of one of these clubs, the Travellers', built between 1829 and 1832, with the interior decoration executed in 1843. While engaged at Westminster, he undertook the design of the Manchester Athenaeum (1837–39) and the ambitious Reform Club, also in Pall Mall (1837–41).[10] The latter was innovative in its introduction of a top floor of 'lodging rooms' for members; its well-equipped and technologically marvellous kitchens were famed; and Holland & Sons provided some of the Grecian-style furniture to Barry's designs. The Grecian style was employed for the interiors and furniture of most clubs built during the middle decades of the century; it was cosmopolitan in character and marked the final flowering of neo-classicism. It represented a confluence of ideas, attitudes and assumptions that bound the refined education of the clubs' gentlemen members to the high-minded pursuits and social activities for which they were formed. The grand interiors of the Reform Club, with their modern conveniences – including dining and smoking areas, a library, meeting room, drawing room and reception rooms – were described by a contemporary writer in 1841 as giving "evidence of that combination of wealth with utility, the refinement of which is to be expressed only by a word at once original and intensely national, – COMFORT".[11]

During this period, a shift in aesthetic and cultural values was defined by greater concern for and identification with national history, rather than the 'culture of connoisseurship' associated with the aristocratic classicism of the eighteenth century. The anonymous writer above identified the values of nationalism and comfort, symbols of a revolutionary popular culture emanating from a commercially prosperous society.[12] The decision to build the new Parliamentary building in the Gothic or Elizabethan style was in part a victory for this new 'cultural nation'. Initially, the building's facilities had been directed by the expectations of the old élite of a 'polite' lifestyle and cosmopolitan grandeur. Over the following two decades, as individual assumptions of 'comfort' became more associated with standards of gentility and refinement among the middle classes,[13] the facilities became more 'domestic' in nature, associated with comfortable houses of English character rather than the classical magnificence of an eighteenth-century urban palace. The official guide to the new Palace of Westminster later described the peers' new library rooms (now the Lords Library) in this context:

> This magnificent suite of rooms has been arranged with the utmost attention to the comforts and convenience of its occupants, every portion is complete and harmonious, and even every article of furniture in the rooms has been designed and manufactured in strict accordance with the architecture, indeed, we could quite fancy ourselves in one of those artistic and lordly apartments of olden time, once to be found in the old mansions of Henry's and Elizabeth's time ...[14]

During the twenty-five years that Barry worked on raising and furnishing the new palace,

BELOW LEFT: C.T. Dolby after G.S. Clarke, *The Peer's* [sic] *Library*, lithograph, published in H.T. Ryde, *Illustrations of the New Palace of Westminster*, London 1849. The library is now called the Lords Library.

BELOW RIGHT: A. Newman after G.S. Clarke, *The Peers' Refreshment Rooms*, coloured lithograph, published in H.T. Ryde, *Illustrations of the New Palace of Westminster*, London 1849. The refreshment rooms are now collectively called the Peers Dining Room.

these new cultural values began significantly to alter the expectations of its occupants. Barry was to find this an increasing problem in retaining his vision for the building. Indeed, by 1902, the building and its comprehensive facilities, its furnishings and "the elaborate machinery which is now in operation to minister to the creature needs of the members"[15] were considered to make it "the best club in London".[16]

## Furnishing the Palace: Competition and Compromise

As previously indicated, most of the furniture for the new facilities, residences and office areas was made and supplied in the years following Pugin's death in September 1852.[17] Designs that Pugin provided between 1847 and 1851 for furniture, wallpapers, carpets and furnishing textiles – specifically for the functional interiors – enabled Barry to complete the main facilities required by the Lords and to carry forward the fitting-out of the Commons interiors to these same standards. In 1849, Henry T. Ryde's *Illustrations of the New Palace of Westminster* was published, with interior views of the Lords Library and Peers Dining Room (referred to as Peers Refreshment Rooms) as furnished by that date.[18] The rich polychromatic decoration of both rooms was complete, carried out by J.G. Crace to designs by Pugin. The library curtains, of crimson Utrecht velvet, had been installed, and both rooms were fitted with Brussels weave carpets and accompanying hearthrugs. The stamped pattern of the curtains and that of the carpets were also designs of Pugin's.[19] The small amount of furniture types depicted – the library tables, the dining tables and chairs – were made by John Webb, as were library desks, the Peers Dining-Room sideboard and other furniture in place by 1851, when tendering for furniture contracts began. Some of this early furniture may also have been supplied by Crace.[20]

As overall co-ordinator of the works, Barry's greatest difficulties in fitting out the rest of the building in the grand, richly detailed unity of Gothic design that he and Pugin had envisaged, were the measures being suggested to expedite the building works while remaining within the strictures of the reduced budget and annual allocations from the Treasury. As, during the 1850s, the cumulative costs of the new building soared beyond the original estimates, and Treasury funding slowed, Barry began to lose control of the furnishing of the new interiors to his masters, the commissioners of the Office of Works. In 1848 a royal commission was appointed at the behest of the Commons and the Prime Minister, Lord John Russell, to urge towards completion work that had already been approved. This was primarily aimed at longstanding problems such as the ventilation, but it also included the decorations, fittings and furnishings of the new Houses of Commons and Lords facilities.[21]

Despite the detail in which the building and the specifications of the interior fittings had been prepared in the 1830s, Barry had never been required to produce separate, detailed estimates for new furniture.[22] Furniture for the House of Lords, and the comparatively small amount of furniture designed by Pugin and in place by 1851, seems to have been included for approval as part of larger contracts for fitting out and decorating a specific area.[23] As he did with other building problems, Barry stalled when officially addressed. Pugin was aware that the interiors could easily be compromised, and he said in a letter to Crace in 1850, "We must have some very simple chairs that will not come very expensive or the board of works will be putting in modern things."[24]

Early in 1851, just a year before the official opening of the new Palace of Westminster, Barry presented the royal commission with two detailed inventories for fitting out the Commons. One addressed the complete furnishing of all facilities, services and offices spread over the ground, principal and first floors. Covering sixty-eight areas and almost one

ABOVE: Design by A.W.N. Pugin for pattern of Utrecht velvet curtains for the Lords Library. Department of Prints and Drawings, Victoria and Albert Museum, London (D.819-1908).

hundred rooms, it comprehensively outlined the furniture, window blinds, curtains (where appropriate), floor carpets (of different grades and types) and fire furniture required by Members, officials, clerks of varying rank, functionaries and servants. The commissioners suggested that Office of Works furniture could be repaired for continued use. But Barry, citing the special character of the building and its interiors, urged that chairs could be contracted out, with the remainder of the new furniture being made in the Thames Bank Workshops.[25] This, presumably, would have been done under the supervision of himself and Pugin.

Pre-empting instructions to put the whole of the furniture out to tender, Barry wrote to the commissioners on 8 May, offering a specification for this purpose. He also recommended cabinet-making and upholstery firms who could be invited to tender, which, unsurprisingly, included Webb and Crace. The others were long-established firms, suppliers to the top end of the market, and included Holland & Sons and Gillows.[26] The invited firms were instructed to view twenty furniture 'specimens', or prototypes – on which the contract was to be based – in the Lords Library, a committee room and office locations at the palace. This list included new types not recorded by Ryde, such as desks of varying elaboration, but the numbers required of each type were surprisingly modest. The conditions of the tender,

The Dining Room, House of Lords, *c.* 1903. Farmer Collection no. 731, House of Lords Record Office, London.

which Barry drew up and which the royal commission approved, gave him control of all details. The work was to be done "to the entire satisfaction of the Architect of the New Palace", and would include approval of the quality of the materials, the decorative carving and the surface finishes. The furniture mounts of tinned iron were to be made by the successful firm, to supplied designs.[27] Barry was trying to circumvent official intervention, but also to ensure that the winner of the contract could meet his and Pugin's exacting standards. Gillows submitted the lowest tender and won the contract.[28]

Although Crace & Son's contract for decorative painting was renewed on Barry's recommendation, the firm was obliged to compete against Gillows in November 1851 for the supply of furnishing fabrics and carpets for the interiors.[29] The tender documents comprised two different ranges of fashionable upholstery materials and traditional floor-coverings. Samples from each firm were submitted, which included newly fashionable Utrecht velvets, wool damasks, brocatelles and mixed silk and wool damasks, all of different qualities and varying numbers of colours. Crace, however, had the wider range, with appropriate patterns, such as the 'Gothic damask', the 'rose pattern Gothic' and 'fleur-de-lys', which Pugin had designed. The pattern of the Utrecht velvet for the Lords Library curtains, and some carpet patterns, had been designed specifically for Westminster.[30] The commissioners chose Crace's range. Monitoring of quantities ordered was to be the main method of official control; Barry was asked at this time to draw up an estimate for the Treasury's approval of carpet needed, according to the contract prices, for areas to be occupied before the commencement of the next sitting. Crace also supplied wallpaper from Pugin's designs for the new Commons interiors. The surviving pattern-book of papers produced for the Palace of Westminster begins in December 1851 (see illus., p. 170).[31] Committee rooms and the Members dining room were originally intended to be decorated

View of the Lords Library.
Photograph by Derry Moore.

with fresco, but, as this would delay their completion, the idea was abandoned in favour of wallpaper.[32]

Prior to his fatal illness, Pugin undoubtedly assisted Barry with the supervision of the first orders. As drawn up by Barry, Gillows's contract enabled him to re-order and ask for new furniture types; the prices were to be based on similar items in the first tendered order.[33] This was how Barry extended the modest requirements of the initial Gillows contract to the furnishing – under his supervision – of most functional parts of the Commons. A Gillows account book and two estimate sketchbooks describe and illustrate some of the furniture that was made at the firm's Lancaster branch for the new Palace of Westminster between 1852 and 1854, when their major commission came to an end.[34] This included wardrobes, chests of drawers, dressing tables, washstands, dressing glasses, towel horses and pot cupboards for the bedrooms of the official residences of the Serjeant-at-Arms and the Assistant Housekeeper, Clerk of the House and the Commons Librarian. The same furniture types and forms were also provided for Commons offices, for the comfort and convenience of high-ranking officials or in shared facilities for support staff. Tables and desks, following the form of those already in place, were made, to complete the lavish furnishing of the libraries of both Houses. Seat furniture, including the House of Lords and House of Commons pattern chairs, was provided for all areas.

The first Gillows order of May 1851 had been drawn from prototypes designed and produced before Pugin's death. The successive orders, some supplied by the Lancaster branch of the firm up to 1854, included new ranges of furniture for bedrooms and offices that Pugin may also have designed, but for which no specific drawings are known.[35] It is possible that after the onset of Pugin's illness, Gillows's draughtsmen adapted extant designs. The drawings in the Lancaster estimate sketchbooks show how Pugin's simpler table types, in place by 1851, were later made with drawers, and modified for use as either writing tables (with leather tops) or dressing tables. The undated design for a State Bed by Gillows, from the collection of papers in Barry's office, shows how carefully Gillows' draughtsmen deferred to Pugin's original designs.[36] That they made many drawings for palace furniture can be inferred from a letter of March 1855 from Gillows to the Chief Commissioner of Works: "We are now familiar with the peculiar style requisite for the private buildings and public apartments and have been at considerable expense and trouble in preparing drawings, patterns etc."[37]

However, some furniture made by Gillows for official residences emulated more conventional domestic fashions than the original range of oak furniture forms of Pugin's unique Gothic idiom. A chair designed by Pugin, with upholstered seat and oak back rail, formed part of the first Gillows order in 1851. It was supplied for public seating in committee rooms, and for office use. By 1853, the chair was being made on a smaller scale, with carved decoration on the back rail and cane seating for bedrooms and servants' rooms, and, later, in walnut and satinwood for drawing rooms. Two forms of walnut tables, made by Gillows's London business for the Clerk of the House and Librarian's residences, were a more delicate variation on Pugin prototypes.[38] This was in marked contrast to the virtually exclusive use of oak for furniture in the functional and ceremonial interiors.[39] Although Pugin did create designs for walnut furniture for J.G. Crace, in particular for marquetry table tops, he generally promoted the use of 'English' oak. Barry himself had declared that the palace interiors would be of oak, but, without the direct influence of Pugin's reforming zeal, seems to have been influenced by new fashions for the domestic interiors occupied by officials' families.[40]

In 1854, a correspondence began between the Office of Works and Barry, which led to the demise of the Gillows contract. Accounts submitted by Barry for furniture supplied to residences in Speaker's Court – including the Clerk of the House and the Commons Librarian – were returned to his office and their contents queried.[41] The Board believed that it was not their responsibility to supply the range of items (which included an expensive fitting-out of the Serjeant-at-Arms's kitchen) to official residents. The question was raised of how these orders related to the contracts of 1851 (sanctioned by the now defunct royal commission), and Barry's authority to make subsequent orders was questioned. Underlying antagonisms pervade the drafts of letters sent to Barry, and his terse replies. By March 1855, all previous arrangements had been suspended: orders for the supply of furniture and other elements of interior decoration were no longer to be directly commissioned by the architect, but would now originate in the Office of Works or pass through it. The contract for furniture

Page from the sample book of wallpaper made by Crace, after designs by A.W.N. Pugin, and supplied to the Palace of Westminster 1851–59 (detail). Department of Prints and Drawings, Victoria and Albert Museum, London (E.137-1939).

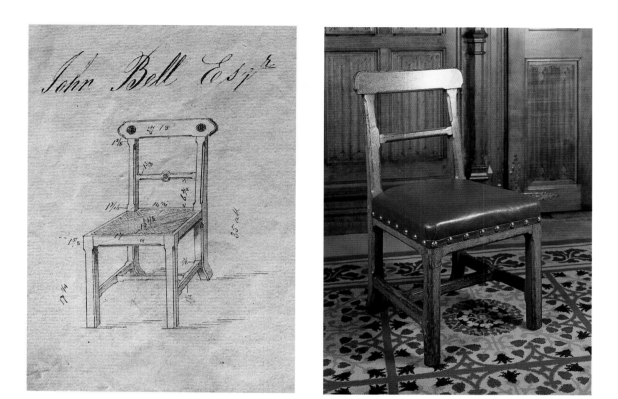

ABOVE: Design for an oak dressing table, Gillows Archive, Estimate Sketch Book 344/105, 1849–55, p. 5821. Westminster Archive Centre.

FAR RIGHT: design for an oak chair frame, Gillows Archive, Estimate Sketch Book 344/137 (1835–83), p. 345. Many of the Palace of Westminster designs were made for other clients, including John Bell Esq. Westminster Archive Centre.

RIGHT: Designed by A.W.N. Pugin, stamped 'Crace', oak chair, c. 1850. Palace of Westminster (POW 1732).

of 1851 was described by Gillows as being "really for the whole furniture of the Palace which up to this date we have supplied".[42] Pleas to reinstate this arrangement, however, were ignored.

From 1855 to 1860, as the unfinished Lords offices and official residences were finally furnished under the direct supervision of the Office of Works, individual tenders were usually won by Holland & Sons. Gillows still tendered, as did other firms that were more recently established and generally served a larger, more commercial market. Beyond the palace walls, the Gothic style of furniture, as championed by Pugin, who drew on historical

Private room of Arthur Balfour, House of Commons, 1897. Formerly part of the official residence of the Clerk of the House; the walnut table by Gillows and seat furniture covered in Utrecht velvet were probably original to the area. Benjamin Stone collection, Birmingham Library Services.

prototypes as his authority, had been subsumed by commercial developments in the furniture trade. The Gothic was 'demeaned' as it became a fashionable medium for a wide range of stylish, middle-class interiors, with their earnest, modern concerns for comfortable domesticity. This, in turn, modified the use of the Gothic style in the unfinished residences, where powerful occupants were allowed to bring their personal tastes to bear.

Although Barry had attempted to maintain control over the standard of furniture that he had evolved with the assistance of Pugin, the latter's death signalled an initial lessening of the overall concept intended for the whole of the building. When Barry finally lost command, and the Office of Works took the lead on furnishing the outstanding residences and Lords offices, the character of the final entity was unreservedly altered. An example of the struggle between quality and cost was provided in November 1856 by the Office of Works's estimate of £70 for an additional pair of Utrecht velvet *portière* curtains, required because of alterations in the Lords Library. Barry, when asked to comment, wryly responded, "I do not see any objection, to a compliance with the requisition in question; providing the new work required is executed, in accordance with the style & quality of the old work in connection with it, for the cost of which Mr. Cox's estimate does not appear to provide." [43]

The Lords facilities had been among the first interiors furnished, but by late 1856 the office apartments of high-ranking Lords officials, located on the west front, overlooking Old Palace Yard, were still incomplete. This work formed the basis of a new tender, co-ordinated entirely by the Office of Works. The specification – in marked contrast to that prepared by Barry in 1851 – stated that the work was to be done "to the satisfaction of the Commissioners of Her Majesty's Works". The tender comprised various quantities of thirty-five different types of furniture, accompanied by drawings. [44] Holland & Sons submitted the cheapest tender, beating Gillows by only £180. [45] The furniture for these rooms forms the main body of furniture made by Holland & Sons for the functional areas, to designs by and after Pugin.

The anticipated opulence of these rooms, for use by the highest-ranking Lords officials, was conveyed by fittings that were made by Holland & Sons. These included "polished and part gilt frames" for the richly carved overmantle mirrors. The window curtains, of double-sided, rich "Superfine Crimson Cloth" with matching silk trimmings, were of a plain, fashionable fabric with no Pugin-designed pattern, and were also supplied as part of the contract. (Previously, it would seem that when Gillows supplied furniture, Crace supplied such upholstery arrangements from their Pugin-designed range of textiles.) Crace did, however, supply the wallpapers, which added richness and contrast. A yellow, single-flock pattern with Tudor roses was hung in the Lord Chancellor's suite of rooms, and the same pattern in red in the Earl Marshal's office. [46]

The Commons offices, the first residences in Commons Court, and the main facilities of both Houses – as fitted out by Gillows – had been furnished with many of the same furniture types, the functional or hierarchical differences being expressed in the use of colour, upholstery or the amount of decorative carving. By the end of the 1850s, when Barry had little or nothing to do with the furniture for the Speaker's residence and the House of Lords, the furniture supplied had more in common with the upper end of the commercial market, where 'novelty' and 'variety' were the most desirable commodities, next to comfort and luxury. As most of the residences have been converted into offices during the twentieth century, much of this conventional furniture has disappeared from the palace. The surviving collections mostly characterize the essential nature of the interiors anticipated by Barry and Pugin.

## Barry and Pugin's Spectacle:
## A Unity of Function, Hierarchical Splendour and Gothic Symbolism

The propriety of Pugin's designs for the furniture and fittings of the facilities, offices and chambers of the two Houses was primarily differentiated by the ancient traditions of the old palace. Heraldry provided a primary and historically authentic source of decorative motifs for the ceilings, oak panelling, stone walls, tiled floors and stained-glass windows of the interiors. It linked the decorative unity of both houses, and, like the use of colour, also differentiated them. It further imbued Barry's new building with a sense of historic continuity by invoking the decorative spirit of the old palace. The *VR* monogram – *Victoria Regina* – carved on the royal throne and oak fittings of the Lords Chamber and painted on its ceiling, was coupled with the Tudor rose, the symbol of England and the royal dynasty associated with the Perpendicular Gothic style of the new building. This decorative and associative statement affirmed a continuum between past and present monarchs. The two motifs were used together, carved, as the main decoration of many pieces of the functional furniture made during the 1850s.[47] The crowned portcullis, another royal emblem of the old palace, was applied, together with the Tudor rose, to the Commons Chamber ceiling. On the new furniture, it was stamped, in gilt, on the upholstered back of the pattern chairs of the two Houses.[48] Chairs in the residences and the Lords offices furnished by Holland & Sons in 1857 were stamped with the *VR* monogram.[49] All three motifs were incorporated into Pugin's designs for wallpaper, together with stylized pomegranates, fleurs-de-lys or other medieval motifs.[50] Other wallpapers and carpets designed by Pugin used simpler Gothic ornaments, such as flat quatrefoil, trefoil and diaper patterns. The use of heraldic emblems accorded with the location of items and the status of their users: the grand sideboard for the Peers Dining Room was carved with the foliate and flower forms of the Tudor rose, thistle and

Committee Room 15, House of Commons, *c.* 1903. The pattern of the original wallpaper can be seen under paint, the worn carpet in a Pugin-designed pattern has had a drugget laid over the walkway and the original Hardman gasolier has been replaced by a new electrical light fitting. Farmer Collection no. 679, House of Lords Record Office, London.

Designed by A.W.N. Pugin, made by John Webb, metal mounts by John Hardman, oak sideboard, *c.* 1850. Peers Dining Room, House of Lords, Palace of Westminster (POW 9701).

shamrock, referring to the three kingdoms governed from Westminster. Humble wash-stands, towel-rails and pot cupboards for offices and residence bedrooms, as made by Gillows from 1852, were embellished by simple Tudor roses and *VR* monograms. During the final decoration of the Robing Room by E.M. Barry in 1866, proposals for heraldic devices in panels were overturned by the First Commissioner of Works, who declared that the interior of the palace already showed too much heraldry.[51]

In more modern times, during the refurnishing and redecorating process that has reani-mated the original style of the new palace interiors over the last twenty-five years, the traditional colour coding of the two Houses has been considered to be a touchstone of its historical appearance. Red, the attested colour of the House of Lords, and historically associ-ated with royalty, was revived for seat upholstery in both the new Lords Chamber and its ante-room, the Prince's Chamber. Green, which was historically identified with the House of Commons, was used for the benches of the new Commons Chamber, and seat upholstery throughout the House's functional areas.[52] This colour protocol was extended to seat uphol-stery, curtains and carpets in most areas of the two Houses. Victorian furnishing conventions that are not understood now, however, tempered this approach – such as the use of red for dining rooms – and guided the choice of red wallpaper and curtains in Commons residences and Members' dining rooms. For the latter, these were contrasted with green seat upholstery and 'green pattern' Brussels carpet and blinds, for which Pugin had provided the designs.

Conversely, curtains and seat upholstery in the reception rooms of the residences of both Houses were usually of varying shades of red textile, richly blended with green wallpa-per or wall-hangings, carpets and blinds. Examples of this are described in the residences of the Serjeant-at-Arms and the Speaker in the Commons; and in the Librarian's and Black Rod's residences in the Lords.[53] The many Commons committee rooms had green seat upholstery and blinds, but were otherwise treated somewhat differently again. The range of wallpapers used in committee rooms incorporated contrasting blends of 'electric' blue, ochre, red and green, or tonal contrasts of one of these colours. Red Utrecht velvet curtains were even hung on twelve windows in the Commons chamber. However, the statement of identifying colours for the two houses was expressed most clearly along the Commons and Lords Corridors, where the prevailing red of the Lords Library gave way to the green of the Commons library rooms, with their green Utrecht velvet curtains, green-bordered Wilton carpet and seat upholstery. This distinction was also apparent in the office rooms of both Houses.

A similar ambiguity surrounds the original dispersal and use of the pattern chair of each house, both of which had been designed by Pugin. The oak chair now associated with the House of Lords (as seen in Ryde's illustration of the Lords Library in 1851) was used throughout the functional areas of the House, in libraries, the dining room and offices. The House of Commons chair, with its simpler chamfering, was originally designed by Pugin in response to Barry's request for a chair to be used in lobbies and corridors.[54] Its use in Commons facilities and offices may have been adopted as a distinguishing attribute. Again, the official residences displayed a different hierarchical use of these chairs. The dining room and study of the Serjeant-at-Arms, as supplied by Gillows, were furnished with oak chairs of the Commons type, but covered with red morocco with the *VR* monogram on the back. The finer Lords chairs, with their octangular legs, were made in both oak and walnut, and in different sizes and for different rooms, for the residences of both Houses.

## Erosion and Decline

The Gothic style of the new Palace of Westminster, as expressed through the decoration and furnishing of its interiors, was originally intended for every functional and residential area. The new interiors were to be a rich showcase for Barry's architectural talents and perfectionism; and for the uncompromising Gothicist, Pugin, it was the most prestigious of secular forums in which to promote his complex but rich vision of the Gothic style as moral and aesthetic exemplar. Cultural values and national identity were expressed in a unity of historical style and symbolism. The complexity and richness of these ideals, however, were gradually eroded: first by the death of Pugin, and then by the replacement of Barry with the undistinguished talent of representatives of the Office of Works.[55] Finally, the personal tastes of officials, arbitrated by changing fashions and prevailing cultural concerns for 'comfort', as well as declining funds, all contributed to the dilution of the original concept.

The stylistic unity of the basic range of furniture for facilities and offices was essentially retained until Barry's death in 1860. Over the subsequent decades, demands for extended levels of provision for increasingly busy Members led to alterations to Barry's building plan. In 1867, E.M. Barry provided plans for new dining areas in the centre portion of the principal-floor River Front, with improved height, space, light and 'cheerfulness'.[56] Initially, only rooms for Members were built; two dining rooms and an additional smoking room extended these facilities to 'strangers' (non-Members). The old dining area was converted into a tea room and newspaper room. As Pugin had feared, for the most part modern furniture was installed: bentwood chairs and round-backed club chairs in the smoking rooms, and large, fully upholstered armchairs in the libraries, where once Pugin had suggested richly detailed X-frame armchairs.[57] Similar furniture was being brought into the

The Prime Minister's Office, House of Commons, *c.* 1903. Formerly the drawing room of the official residence of the Clerk of the House, its wallhangings and carpets remain, but it has been fitted out with office furniture. Farmer Collection no.706, House of Lords Record Office, London.

elegant clubs. The increasing levels of use, the expectations of convenience that the palace interiors sustained and the Board of Works' inability to replace like for like all contributed to the inevitable decay. The mass consumerism of the second half of the nineteenth century diminished inherent cultural assumptions about luxury being analogous with comfort.[58] On a broader level, the nation no longer needed or could afford a 'public memory' palace for the benefit of a small élite, albeit one engaged in service on their behalf. What was required of 'clubs' was something approaching the modern conception of convenience – 'service', as described by a commentator in 1897:

> As a rule a new member is not many hours in the Palace of Westminster before he has secured a locker, to which each member is entitled, for books and papers; smoked a pipe or cigar in the smoking-room, reclining in the armchair which was Mr Gladstone's favourite seat when at Downing Street; had dinner in one or other of the dining-rooms; read the newspapers in the reading-room, or made himself acquainted with the contents of its extensive book-shelves; strolled on the Terrace; had tea in the tea-room

RIGHT: Distemper printing for double-flock wallpaper for Committee Room 14, House of Commons, being produced at John Perry (Wallpapers) Ltd, 1999, in original colours: green distemper ground with green double flocks.

FAR RIGHT: Flocking for double-flock wallpaper for Committee Room 14, House of Commons, being produced by John Perry (Wallpapers) Ltd, 1999, in original colours: green distemper ground with green double flocks.

Piece of original wallpaper, blue distemper ground with crimson red double flocks, found behind panelling in Committee Room 10, House of Commons, in 1999.

at the table of the old House of Commons; and dispatched numbers of letters from the House to his relatives and friends giving his impressions of the great Palace of Westminster.[59]

After the Board of Works dismissed E.M. Barry and took over the development and upkeep of the palace interiors, their richness disappeared. American cloth was sometimes used as upholstery material, utilitarian carpets replaced Pugin's patterns, faded wallpaper was painted over and damage to furniture – such as the broken brattishing (ornamentation consisting of foliage and small crenellations) of clocks – was not repaired. Residences were converted to personal offices, and although domestic upholstery was retained, it was gradually subsumed by the new, simplified house style. Electric lighting was introduced by the end of the nineteenth century, which made many of Hardman's gas fittings redundant. Detail was eroded, such as the replacement of the 'matted' screws, in door furniture and furniture mounts with modern screws, and the painting black of their worn tinning. Much of the residential furniture was sold off or went into store, particularly when Victorian style entered a long period of disfavour following the First World War. Furniture and panelling were stripped to lighten the interiors, in accordance with contemporary fashions. In the 1920s, for example, one of the few residential areas to survive was remodelled for the Lord Chancellor, with the genteel 'good taste' of Georgian furniture. In the 1950s, John Gloag summed up the prevailing prejudice in *Georgian Grace*. Having quoted H.G. Wells's description of a Victorian domestic interior – summarized as "a room to eat muffins in" – Gloag mocked, "Precisely. Muffins, crumpets, Pugin, Ruskin, dark red velvet, and Gothic knobs on everything."[60]

Since the 1970s, this dismal picture has greatly receded, due to a revival of interest in and appreciation of Victorian interior design. Programmes of conservation and restoration within the Palace of Westminster, including the reproduction of wallpapers and carpets, and research into the style and furniture of the original interiors, have facilitated a greater understanding of Barry and Pugin's vision, and rehabilitated the building's validity as a cultural expression of a shared history.

# II

## The Aura of Sacred Mystery: Thrones in the New Palace of Westminster

Christine Riding

Moreover the king made a great throne of ivory, and overlaid it with pure gold. And there were six steps to the throne with a footstool of gold, which were fastened to the throne, and stays on each side of the sitting place, and two lions standing by the stays: and twelve lions stood there on the one side and the other upon the six steps. There was not the like made in any kingdom.[1]

The Old Testament description of King Solomon's throne was of profound significance to medieval symbolism and the biblical origins of kingship. Although not all components were faithfully reproduced, the description nonetheless informed the creation of thrones and their setting as symbols of supreme authority.[2]

The provision for thrones in the new Palace of Westminster – more specifically the House of Lords, "the *locus classicus* of thrones"[3] – was guided by conventions established under political circumstances very different than those of the mid-nineteenth century. In *The English Constitution* (1867), Walter Bagehot divided the constitution into two parts: "first, those which excite and preserve the reverence of the population, – the *dignified* parts"; and second, "the *efficient* parts, – those by which it, in fact, works and rules."[4] In the medieval period and later, Bagehot opines, both parts were united in the monarch. But by the reign of Queen Victoria a fundamental shift had occurred, whereby the monarchy's primary function (and its survival) lay not in the day-to-day governing of the country, which was now largely the province of the House of Commons, but in its 'dignified' capacity: its ability to capture the imagination of the populace, to maintain "an aura of sacred mystery",[5] to be a moral force and head of society, and to "act as a *disguise*", enabling "our real rulers to change without heedless people knowing it".[6] Bagehot concluded, "When there is a select committee on the Queen, the charm of royalty will be gone. Its mystery is its life. We must not let in daylight upon magic".[7] There were those, not least Victoria herself, who would have disputed Bagehot's theory that her usefulness "was no longer mainly in the realm of business but in the realm of theatre".[8] However, "The monarchy must be seen to be splendid, but above all, it must be *seen*"[9] was an axiom ignored by royalty – from the Middle Ages onwards – at its peril. And it is as adjuncts to this basic requirement that the thrones for the new palace are discussed here.

From earliest times, the king in Parliament would have been provided with a throne, the basic characteristics of which, as with all medieval 'seats of authority', were those that physically elevated the sitter above everyone assembled: a footstool (separate or attached as a foot board); a cushion on the seat; a step or steps leading up to the seat itself; and finally a dais placed before and/or beneath the seat.[10] What designated 'a throne' over and above these

Throne, Chairs of State and canopy in the Lords Chamber, 1847, Palace of Westminster: centre, the throne (POW 8031); left, the Prince of Wales's Chair of State; right, Prince Albert's Chair of State (POW 3609). The X-frame Chairs of State were designed by Pugin. The Prince of Wales's chair is placed in the Chamber only for State Openings of Parliament.

elements was the nature and quality of the decoration and dressings that accompanied it. For example, the inclusion of carpeted steps for thrones was established early on, as the carpet was in itself an indication of high estate.[11] At what point the canopy or 'cloth of estate' (the terms appear to have been interchangeable) became an integral component is not clear, although in the context of the monarch in Parliament the tradition is thought to have dated from at least the fourteenth century.[12] Evidence for the previous century exists in the *Calender of Liberate Rolls*, which records that in 1252 "a canopy (*tabernaculum*) above the king's seat in the hall with a royal chair" was ordered for Henry III in his palace at Woodstock.[13]

The combination of throne and canopy for Parliamentary sessions was indispensable by the time of the Tudor dynasty. Elizabeth I's legendary exploitation of state ceremonial naturally extended to the use of appropriate accoutrements in Parliament. A German tourist, Lupold von Wedel, described the Chamber during a session of 1584 as "a separate chamber, on the platform of which was a splendid canopy of gold stuff and velvet, embroidered with gold, silver and pearls, and below it a throne, arranged with royal splendours, on which the Queen seated herself".[14] The canopied throne was not, however, simply "gold stuff and velvet" but (with the canopied bed or state bed) was of the highest symbolic importance, commanding the same respect as that due to the monarch in person.[15] As such, it became a focus for royal ceremonial and protocol. During the evening celebrations following William and Mary's acceptance of the crowns of England and Ireland (13 February 1689), for example, Princess (later Queen) Anne "displayed her knowledge of the minute laws of royal etiquette. The attendants had placed her tabouret [stool] too near the royal chairs, so that it

ABOVE LEFT: *Apocalypse and Coronation Order*, parchment, *c.* 1330–39 (?), This scene of a coronation shows a king seated on a throne that bears stylistic similarities to the Coronation Chair in Westminster Abbey. Corpus Christi College, Cambridge (MS20).

ABOVE RIGHT: Master FVB (fl. *c.* 1475–1500), *Judgement of Solomon*, engraving, *c.* 1500. The Ashmolean Museum, Oxford.

was partly overshadowed by the canopy of state. The Princess Anne would not seat herself under it, until it was removed to a correct distance from the state-chair of the Queen her sister".[16]

The guiding principal of the reign of George III (1760–1820) was that the monarch must be both "splendid and ordinary". A devoted family man, the king understood that "the warmth of the domestic hearth must, for best public effect, be balanced by the chill of regal splendour".[17] Preparations for the coronation of 1761 occurred simultaneously with the refurbishment of the House of Lords. The suite of thrones, for use in the abbey and palace, were all executed in the then-fashionable 'French' Rococo style. The thrones destined for the Lords Chamber and the Robing Room remained in use for the duration of the reign.[18] While both the throne and canopy were sufficiently grand to cut a royal dash in the Lords Chamber, surprisingly – given their symbolic importance – all had deteriorated by the king's death. The *Mirror of Literature, Amusement, and Instruction* of 15 November 1834 reported that "The old canopy of state, under which the throne was placed, was a piece of quaint device; and, at the Union [of 1800], its tarnished and decayed condition was rendered more conspicuous by the arms of the united kingdoms being inserted ... the whole sadly lacked the *splendor loci* – the regal glitter – fitting for its appropriation".[19] As much of the Palace of

John Singleton Copley, *The Collapse of the Earl of Chatham in the House of Lords, 7th July 1778*, oil on canvas, 1779–80. The canopy installed in 1761 can be seen at the back of the Lords Chamber. Tate Gallery, London.

Westminster was in a decrepit state – in 1811 a French tourist observed, "The upper house is rather the shabbiest of the two"[20] – the condition of the throne and canopy is at least explainable. But as adjuncts to the dignity of the Crown, they were failing miserably. Even in 1776, Thomas Hutchinson was clearly underwhelmed by the British monarchy's brand of "regal glitter". During the State Opening of 31 October, he wrote:

> when a stranger, whose expectation hath formed an idea of the grandeur of an apartment for so august a body of senators, enters it [the Lords Chamber], his ideas sink at the approach of such inelegance; but it is a general observation, that even the Palace of the greatest Monarch is derogatory to the dignity of a petty prince: and the remark is too general, that the horse stables of the French Monarque [*sic*] are more elegant than the Palace of a British King.

He concluded, "I can assign no other principle for it but the national enthusiastick [*sic*] fondness for Liberty, which ever aims to reduce all to a level, and which overpowers the national principle of pride."[21]

George IV had no such egalitarian principles. But, as he had "neither the stamina nor probably the interest for long political battles", he restricted his "fitful concern for the powers of the crown"[22] primarily to outward display. Periods of national crisis, as repre-

ABOVE LEFT: Throne and foot stool from the Lords Chamber, Palace of Westminster, giltwood and upholstered in red velvet, made by Katherine Naish and upholstered by Vile & Cobb, 1761. The throne was made *en suite* with two 'High Stools', one of which is in the Grimsthorpe and Drummond Castle Collection. Collection of the Grimsthorpe and Drummond Castle Trust.

ABOVE RIGHT: Throne and footstool from the Lords Chamber, giltwood and composition, made by John Russell, Vallance & Evans and upholstered by Elliott & Francis, 1820. The throne was used subsequently by Queen Adelaide at the Coronation of William IV in 1831. Devonshire Collection, Chatsworth.

sented by the Napoleonic Wars and previously the unsuccessful conflict in America, had helped in any case to recast the monarch, in the words of Linda Colley, as "a focus for patriotic celebration", and thus instigated a wider concern than George's for regal splendour.[23]

Under the supervision of John Soane, George IV's reign opened in 1820 as the previous one had done, with the refurbishment of the House of Lords and a new suite of thrones. The imperial ensemble for the Lords Chamber was characteristically extravagant, in keeping with the king's ambitions to outdo all previous attempts at royal pageantry: a large, gilded, oval-backed armchair and footstool, positioned under "an immense canopy of crimson velvet, surmounted by an imperial crown, and supported by columns richly gilt, and decorated with oak leaves and acorns; whilst tridents, olive branches, and other emblematic figures of British glory, ornamented the pedestals". Judged "more elaborate than beautiful", they nonetheless set the pace for the new palace.[24]

By the time Barry and Pugin were engaged in the creation of a new House of Lords, therefore, a basic set of conventions (and expectations) had been established for the monarch's throne. However, the 'rules' that had previously governed seating on either side of the throne seem to have been more fluid, and thus were to prove more contentious.

At some point in 1840, the newly married Queen Victoria and Prince Albert were provided with matching thrones for use in the temporary Lords Chamber. In the history of the furnishings of the House of Lords, thrones flanked by additional seating were common practice.[25] The provision for Albert was, however, made during a dispute before and after the wedding ceremony of 10 February 1840 over his legal rank and precedence, "a problem of little concern to the people in the streets, but of great moment to the rank-ridden classes that still ruled".[26]

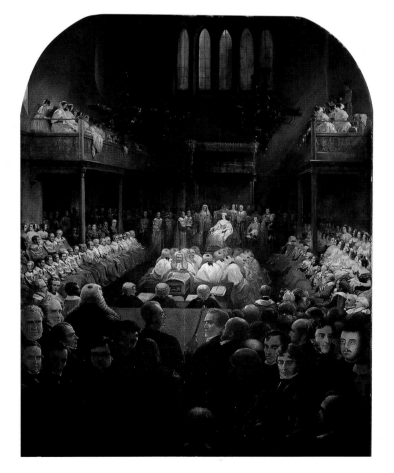

Alexander Blaikley, *Queen Victoria Opening Parliament, 4 February 1845*, oil on canvas, 1845. The three thrones, now part of the Collection of the Grimsthorpe and Drummond Castle Trust, can be seen at the back of the Lords Chamber with Queen Victoria seated in the middle and Prince Albert seated on the right. Palace of Westminster (WOA 2942).

It was also of great importance to Albert. A man of intelligence and high morality, with a strong sense of duty, the prince had been brought up in the autocratically governed principality of Saxe-Coburg, and naturally had an elevated view of the role of the British Crown. He was also keenly aware that "in large part the monarchy gained the loyal affection of its subjects by its apt representation of their exaggerated self-esteem". In this context, "the full panoply of monarchic pomp was not only suitable but indispensable".[27]

A male consort was a rare commodity. In 1840, Albert was the first in England since the opening decade of the eighteenth century, and only the second since the death of Queen Mary in 1558. Unlike his female counterpart, who by law became queen on marriage, Albert's only legal status in Britain was as a German princeling, albeit one who had married the British queen. Victoria had higher ambitions for him. With the title of King Consort in mind, Victoria demanded that her husband be granted rank — and thus precedence — above all but herself, including the existing princes of the Blood Royal, and, in theory, Victoria and Albert's own sons. For this she needed an Act of Parliament, and by inference the consent of her uncles, the Dukes of Sussex and Cambridge and the King of Hanover (formerly the Duke of Cumberland). Parliament had very different ideas. Suspicious of yet another imported monarch or consort, especially an impoverished Coburg prince, both Houses were determined that Albert should have no role in politics, no English peerage and no rank in the armed forces.[28] Victoria was furious. The matter was settled in the short term via a pamphlet by Charles Greville, then Clerk of the Privy Council, that stated that the queen could bestow rank and precedence on Albert in whatever way she chose — except in Parliament and at the Privy Council — by exercising the royal prerogative.[29] But the problem was not to be resolved until seventeen years later, when Victoria officially gave Albert the title of 'Prince Consort'.

This dispute had ramifications for state occasions in Parliament, where orders of rank and precedence were publicly displayed. Would Albert accompany the queen to Westminster and sit beside her in the Lords Chamber? The then Prime Minister, Lord Melbourne, discovered a precedent for a female monarch's consort in Queen Anne's husband George, who had accompanied her to Parliament prior to his death in 1708 (the comparison was somewhat flawed as George had been created Duke of Cumberland on 20 March 1689, giving him a seat in the House of Lords by right, and he was naturalized in 1689).[30] Although Victoria took advantage of this timely — if not wholly relevant — discovery, she nevertheless objected to any further comparison between Albert and Anne's "stupid and insignificant husband".[31] Prior to the closure of the Parliamentary session in August 1840, Albert wrote triumphantly to his brother, "In spite of Lehzen [the queen's former governess and confidante] and the Master of the Horse, I shall drive *with* Victoria in a carriage to the House of Lords, and sit beside her, on a throne especially built for me."[32]

In a letter to Lord Palmerston dated 5 June 1856, Victoria complained that while the law bestowed on the wife of a king the highest rank and honours, the husband of a queen was ignored. "No doubt", she concluded, "as is the case *now* — the Queen can give her husband the highest *place* by *placing* him *always near her person*."[33] Thus, Victoria's rejoinder to Parliament's continual resistance to her wishes was to position Albert by her side in full view of the assembled Lords and Commons. This may seem a trivial victory. However, Greville understood its significance. He wrote, "He is as much King as She can make him."[34]

The royal couple's first son — the heir to the throne and soon-to-be Prince of Wales — was born on 9 November 1841. The following January, the then Deputy Black Rod, J. Pulman, wrote to the Lord Great Chamberlain to make a case for the provision of a seat for the new prince, based on precedent from the Tudor period through to the Hanoverians.

Sir Thomas Wriothesley, *Edward I in Parliament* from *The Wriothesley Garter Book*, vellum, *c.* 1524. The Royal Library, Windsor.

Referring to an Act of the thirty-first year of the reign of Henry VIII, 'For Placing the Lords', Pulman quotes, "it is enacted that no Person, excepting only The King's Children, shall sit or have place at any side of the Cloth of Estate in the Parliament Chamber neither of the one hand of the King's Highness nor of the other".[35]

The place assigned to the heir had achieved a symbolic resonance during the reign of Elizabeth I, when "[the] two Seats on the right and left hand of the Chair of Estate were void in respect that the first was anciently for the King of Scots when he used to come to Our Parliaments: And the other, on the left hand, is for the Prince, the immediate Heir to the Crown".[36]

The text suggests that the provision "anciently for the King of Scots" was an established tradition by the reign of Elizabeth I. In the Garter Book (*c.* 1524) is an illustration of Edward I presiding over a Parliamentary session, *c.* 1278. On his right is seated Alexander III, King of Scotland (1249–1286), and on his left, Llywelyn, Prince of Wales (1246–1282). The scene is problematic as an historical account, as it is doubtful that both Alexander and Llywelyn attended the same Parliament. The former did pay homage to Edward in the autumn Parliament of 1278, although only in respect of the lands he held in England, not for the kingdom of Scotland.[37] Executed several centuries after the event, the illustration is symbolic of Edward I's demands to be acknowledged as suzerain (feudal lord) over Scotland and Wales, a claim actively resisted by both men. Edward's successful conquest of Llywleyn's principality in 1283 resulted the following year in the statute of Wales, and the allocation of the royal lands to Edward's son and heir, the first 'English' Prince of Wales, in 1301.[38] The beginning of the fourteenth century is thus the earliest date that the heir to the throne could have attended sessions of Parliament as Prince of Wales.

Whether the provision for the Scottish king was consistently observed is unclear. It had in any case become redundant by the early seventeenth century, when James I (VI of

Three thrones and *en suite* footstools, gilt-wood and upholstered in red velvet, made possibly in 1814. Prince Albert's (right) and Queen Victoria's (centre) were altered *c.* 1840 and used in the Lords Chamber until 1847. The throne and footstool for the use of the Prince of Wales (left) altered in 1842 and were *in situ* until 1847 (for the possible origins and subsequent history of these thrones, see Roberts 1989, pp. 72–73). Collection of the Grimsthorpe and Drummond Castle Trust.

Scotland) united the titles as king of both Scotland (from 1567) and England (from 1603). As a result, using Pulman's evidence once more, Charles II's brothers, the Duke of York and the Duke of Gloucester, were given permission to be seated on his right, where "the King of Scots anciently sat now seeing that Title is involved in His Majesty".[39] Pulman's research certainly did the trick. The infant prince was provided with a throne in 1842, which matched those already in use.[40] This arrangement was to be adopted in the new Chamber.

The throne and canopy for the new Palace of Westminster were the single most important feature of the whole building (see illus., p. 178). Their design went through several stages (some significant to the present essay) and was the product of close collaboration between Barry and Pugin (see chapter 7). It also illustrated their respective stylistic standpoints, eloquently described by John L. Wolfe in 1867 as follows:

> Barry, it is well-known, belonged to the classical school, Pugin to the school now in the ascendant, the romantic; and if both had been great poets instead of architects, Barry, perhaps, might have composed a 'Paradise Lost,' but Pugin 'Canterbury Tales.'[41]

In 1844, a select committee resolved that both Prince Albert and the Prince of Wales would be provided with a chair either side of the monarch's throne. On 3 September 1844, Barry wrote to Pugin concerning "the fittings and decorations of the House of Lords", stating that he had "a new design for the throne, which is at last perfectly satisfactory to me".[42] It has been suggested by Alexandra Wedgwood that the new design (not shown) was in general terms comparable to that executed for the new Chamber; a rectilinear, tripartite canopy, each section housing a throne.[43] Pugin, ever sensitive to propriety and hierarchy, disliked the fact that all three thrones were identical,[44] and substituted two X-frame chairs either side of the throne, which Barry accepted.[45] Thus, unlike the suite of near-identical thrones then being employed in the temporary Lords Chamber, the hierarchy of the Barry/Pugin suite established visually the monarch's precedence over the Prince of Wales and Prince Albert.

In general terms, the basic conventions established from the medieval period onwards were observed: canopy, throne with cushioned seat, footstool and carpeted dais. However, one element of the executed design did not feature in earlier designs: not one element of the canopy was executed in textile; the 'cloth of estate', replete with coats of arms, heraldic devices, national and chivalric symbols, was now from top to bottom a solid structure of intricately carved and decorated wood.[46] The result is breathtaking. The writer of the palace guidebook of 1848 enthused, "As every portion of her Majesty's Throne, and the Chairs for the Princes, is gilded, some idea may be formed of their splendid appearance; and standing under a canopy of the richest design, glowing with gold and colours, they produce a magnificent effect."[47] Although firmly anchored in the Gothic Revival period, the throne and canopy nevertheless exude a historical legitimacy that transcends mere 'medievalism'. This has much to do with Pugin's exquisite detailing, based on his extensive knowledge of medieval carving and decoration. But Pugin was not just a talented Gothicist. He was a crusader who abhorred the industrial age and longed for the Christian – and hierarchical – values of the Middle Ages. Not surprisingly, his designs showed, to quote J.R. Herbert, an ability "to enshrine Royalty".[48]

Looking to the past for appropriate examples – and avoiding pure Gothic fantasy – extended to the selection of two chair forms that had become identified with high estate in the medieval period. Due to the paucity of medieval prototypes, Pugin responded directly to sixteenth- and seventeenth-century examples for the Chairs of State. Nevertheless, the X-frame chair (or stool) had been associated with 'lordship' in the eleventh and twelfth

The Coronation Chair (St Edward's Chair), oak with traces of gilded decoration, *c.* 1300. The Coronation Chair was refurbished for coronations (see illus., opposite). Westminster Abbey, London.

Sir George Hayter, *The Coronation of Queen Victoria, 28 June 1838*, oil on canvas, 1838. Queen Victoria is shown seated on the Coronation Chair. As with previous coronations, the chair appears to have been refurbished for the occasion. The Royal Collection.

centuries, an ancient lineage well understood by Pugin.[49] As executed, the Chairs of State (occasionally referred to as Consorts' Chairs) ranked high in the pecking order of furniture established throughout the new palace. The chairs themselves differed only in details relating specifically to the sitter: that for the Prince of Wales sported a carved *PW* monogram, and embroidered ostrich feathers with the motto *Ich Dien*, while that for Prince Albert had a *PA* monogram, and embroidered Saxe-Coburg arms (now replaced). Such details were also incorporated into the relevant sections of the canopy. In 1848 it was noted that the chairs "in design command unqualified praise, ornament and appropriateness being so happily blended"; a gratifying judgement to the author of *True Principles*.[50]

The post and boarded form used for the monarch's throne had achieved a greater resonance than the X-frame,[51] its impeccable royal pedigree underlined by numerous medieval coronation (and religious) paintings and illuminations, such as *Richard II Enthroned* (*c.* 1395; see illus., pp. 80, 82). Neither Barry nor Pugin had to rely on illustrations, however, as a unique model existed in Westminster Abbey. St Edward's Chair – more popularly known as the Coronation Chair – was first used by Edward II in 1308, and by all subsequent monarchs. Queen Victoria had been seated on the throne – anointed "as Solomon was anointed King" – only years before, in 1838. Battered, broken and all but stripped of its decoration, it remains the earliest example of an English royal throne, and the only one to have survived from the medieval period.[52]

The source for the new palace's throne was evident to contemporaries. In the 1848

guidebook, the writer observed, "In general outline it is similar to the chair in which the Sovereigns of England have been wont to sit at their coronations, but in detail it differs widely from its plain prototype".[53] The elaborate palace throne was much closer in spirit to its ancient relative than suggested by the guidebook. In his account of the Coronation Chair published in 1863, William Burges concluded that "it must have been an artistic piece of furniture".[54] In addition to the quatrefoil carving and 'pinnacles' surmounted by royal beasts, pioneering antiquarians such as John Carter, and later Burges, established that the Coronation Chair had been elaborately decorated with glass mosaic and gilding.[55] In parallel to this, the palace guidebook noted that "The addition of crystals as enrichments to the Throne is a peculiarly happy idea, as the effect, the sparkling brilliancy they impart, is most charming".[56] And to quote Burges once more, "the great ornament of the [Coronation] chair was the gilding".[57] The same is true of the palace throne.

In 1834, the *Mirror of Literature* dismissed George III's throne as an "elevated arm-chair", and complained that George IV's "fell short of the nursery idea of a King upon his throne".[58] There is something in these charges. Bar a few decorative details, the first would not have looked amiss in an aristocratic house, and the second, immense and generously stuffed, was perhaps too similar to George IV's own person to epitomize more abstract notions of monarchy. Both show greater concern for wealth, comfort and above all fashion than with historic resonance and symbolism. In contrast, the new throne was based upon a medieval precedent, itself an allusion to Solomon's throne and symbolic of the consecration of kings. The palace throne thus not only signalled the longevity of the British monarchy, but epitomized the ineffable otherness of kingship itself.

W.A. Menzies after Jean-Joseph-Benjamin Constant, *Queen Victoria*, oil on canvas, 1924. On 4 May 1901, *The Times* described the original portrait by Constant, dated 1900, as a "generalisation of the idea of sovereignty, a vision of the head of a great Empire crowned with age and authority, and placed in the throne of State the Gothic form of which seems to connote an immemorial antiquity" (as quoted in Walker 1988, I, p. 344). Palace of Westminster (WOA 3156).

With the new Robing Room to the south of the Royal Gallery still unfinished, the Prince's Chamber (then called the Victoria Lobby) was furnished for state occasions. In 1849 the *Illustrated London News* reported that "The Robing Room is fitted up with a Chair of State for the Queen, under a canopy are chairs for the Prince of Wales and Prince Albert elevated on a platform corresponding to that of the Throne in the House of Lords". As John Gibson's massive sculpture of Queen Victoria, completed in 1856, had yet to be installed, there was adequate space for a suite of thrones in the area back to back with the Lords Chamber canopy, although the *Illustrated London News* noted "its fittings in the apartment are merely temporary being removed after the ceremony".[59] What these chairs were like, and what happened to them subsequently, has yet to be established. However, Clive Wainwright suggested that two gilded X-frame chairs, one of which is shown in on page 188, may have been those used by the princes.[60]

In the event, neither Barry nor Pugin had a hand in the design of the throne and canopy permanently installed in the official Robing Room. They were in fact the work of Barry's son, Edward Middleton Barry.[61] Dated 1866, the throne design does hark back to Pugin's round-backed Chairs of State in the Lords Chamber, but is a stylistic departure within the context of the Gothic Revival. Indeed, Clive Wainwright suggested that the overall form was Empire rather than Gothic, the inspiration having come from one of Napoleon's thrones, designed by Percier and Fontaine for the Tuileries in Paris (the palace was not destroyed until 1870).[62] The design was included in the *Receuil des Décorations Intérieures* published in Paris in 1801, which may have been known to E.M. Barry.[63] Napoleon's penchant for similar round-backed thrones can be gleaned from several of his most grandiose portraits.[64]

If the general shape is Imperial, the parcel-gilt, carved details, such as the bulky cluster-column 'supports', tracery and crocketing, are reminiscent of Pugin's earlier Gothic furniture for Windsor Castle, *c.* 1827. In later life Pugin was to reject such furniture as a travesty; no doubt he would have been equally scornful of E.M. Barry's efforts.[65] More stage prop than masterpiece, on close inspection the throne is not of the finest quality or execution, unlike its elder cousins in the Lords Chamber. However, the overall effect – of throne and en suite footstool, shallow-curved canopy (lifted from the Lords Chamber canopy), with upholstered and embroidered velvet backcloth and full-length side curtains, raised on a red-carpeted dais – is sufficiently majestic and theatrical to hold its own amongst the Dyce frescoes and profuse Gothic detailing that cover the ceiling and walls.

A departure from the layout in previous reigns, or even the temporary facilities in the Prince's Chamber, is that the Robing Room throne stands alone. Perhaps the answer lies with the death of Prince Albert in 1861, which was to have a profound effect on the State Opening and royal ceremonial as a whole. Devastated by her loss, the queen could not be persuaded to open Parliament in person.[66] Ironically, this rejection of her basic duties would have shocked and appalled her husband. In 1864, *The Times* warned, "It is impossible for a recluse to occupy the British throne without a gradual weakening of the authority which the sovereign has been accustomed to exert".[67] In other words, above all other considerations, the monarch must be seen.

Victoria remained intractable until 1866, the year E.M. Barry designed the throne. Clearly bitter and disbelieving at the continual requests for her to attend Parliament, which she compared to an execution, the queen remonstrated with the then Prime Minister, Lord Russell:

> That the public wish to see her she fully understands ... but why this wish should be of so unreasonable and unfeeling a nature, as to long to witness the spectacle of a poor, broken-hearted widow, nervous and shrinking, dragged in deep mourning, *alone in State as a Show*, where she used to go supported by her husband, to be gazed at, without delicacy of feeling, is a thing she cannot understand, and she never could wish her bitterest foe to be exposed to![68]

She attended the ceremony of 6 February 1866, but not in her Parliamentary robes. These were draped, "like cast-off skin",[69] over the back of the Lords Chamber throne.

Describing the State Opening, Victoria wrote privately:

> When I entered the House, which was very full, I felt as if I should faint. All was silent and all eyes fixed upon me, and there I sat *alone*. I was greatly relieved when all was over, and I stepped down from the throne.[70]

A robed throne – with the crown positioned precariously on top – was to feature in an engraving published in *The Tomahawk* in June 1867 entitled *Where is Britannia?*;[71] a powerful reminder that thrones are adjuncts of monarchy, not monarchy itself.

Victoria's "entirely unconstitutional view" that Albert was "the next most important

*Where is Britannia?*, lithograph, published in *Tomahawk, a Saturday Journal of Satire*, London, 8 June 1867, p. 55. British Library (2261.g.13).

personage in the realm to herself" resulted, as we have seen, in her attempts to make legal the precedence *she* had given him above the Prince of Wales.[72] Now that Albert was dead, Victoria took the stance that he was irreplaceable. Already convinced that her eldest son was irresponsible and wayward, the queen decided that to bestow on him any of the duties previously undertaken by her husband was in effect to replace Albert, and this she could not stomach.[73] In her own mind Victoria was, henceforward, "alone in State". How poignant then that her situation – largely self-imposed – should be symbolized within the State Apartments by a solitary throne.

The lacklustre nature of state ceremonial at the palace came to an end with the accession of Edward VII in 1901. With a taste for pageantry reminiscent of his great-uncle, George IV, Edward was "determined that the custom should now be resumed in the full panoply of state – a resolve that was evidence of his intention to renew all outward and visible signs of his central place in the Constitution".[74] Indeed, the rejuvenation of state ceremonial led to suggestions that Westminster Hall would better accommodate the numerous Members intent on hearing the speech from the throne. The king, however, insisted that the ceremony take place in the Lords Chamber in time-honoured fashion. But he did make one significant change to the seating arrangements under the canopy. Instead of using the former Prince Consort's Chair of State (perhaps perceived more significantly as Albert's chair) Queen Alexandra was provided with a copy of the monarch's throne, to be positioned 'cheek by jowl' to the right of the original, under the central section of the canopy. The new configuration thus upset, perhaps unnecessarily, the balance so carefully orchestrated by Barry and Pugin. A guidebook, dated *c.* 1902, noted: "The Chair for the Queen is exactly the same in all particulars, excepting that it is one inch lower, and the quatrefoiled ornament on the back has in the centre a rose instead of a monogram".[75]

What considerations guided the creation of the seat of authority in the Commons Chamber, the Speaker's Chair? The pre-fire chair was described in 1834 as "lofty and capacious ... well carved in oak" and having "an imposing appearance".[76] The need for a seat with sufficient gravitas – thus assisting the Speaker as 'referee' during rowdy debates – was highlighted in 1739 by a commentator under the title of 'Common Sense'. He opined that the Speaker's chair "ought to be placed upon a little Eminence, that it may appear to maintain a certain Superiority over the other Seats", fearing that "if some bulky, puft-up Member should over-top the Speaker, it may look as if he dictated to the Chair, – an indecent and shocking Sight". Pointedly he added, "I hope the new Chair will be strong, plain, and beautiful, without Gilding, or any other tawdry Decoration, which may make it look like a Court Piece of Furniture [the Lords throne?]", an opinion that smacks of the 'Court and Country' political divide of Charles I's reign.[77] Indeed, his assertion that the chair should be made of "right *English Oak*, if possible, of true *Heart* of *Oak*, that it may always preserve its strength" suggests that, for this writer at least, the Speaker's Chair was a symbol of the *English* nation, perhaps juxtaposed with the inherent foreignness of the Hanoverian dynasty and George II's circle.[78]

Pictorial evidence suggests that the Speaker's Chair remained stylistically the same from the early eighteenth century up to 1834: a raised armchair, upholstered in green velvet or leather, positioned in front of a tall, rectangular 'cloth of estate' with two Corinthian columns, painted white with gilded details, and surmounted by the royal arms in polychrome, the latter indicating that the Speaker's authority was derived ultimately from the Crown.[79] In total the Speaker's Chair, like the Lords Chamber throne, establishes the occupant's precedence over the whole assembly.

Throne in the Lords Chamber (left) with the copy (right) made in 1901 by Holland & Son, 1905. Today the copy throne (POW 9407) is placed in the Chamber only for State Openings. Farmer Collection no. 652, House of Lords Record Office, London.

Speaker's Chair in the Commons Chamber, June 1897. Benjamin Stone collection, Birmingham Library Services.

Design for a state chair by A.W.N. Pugin, April 1835, published in A.W.N. Pugin, *Gothic Furniture in the Style of the Fifteenth Century*, London 1835, n.p. British Library, London (2261.g.13).

The new Speaker's Chair, designed by Pugin and completed *c.* 1849, adhered to the basic conventions and, as before, was made of oak, an indigenous wood resonant with national sentiment. Based on a medieval bishop's chair, the formula of a solid, natural-wood seat, highly carved with a canopy, had been used previously by Pugin at King Edward VI's Grammar School, and figured in his 1835 competition drawings for J. Gillespie Graham (private collection). It also appeared as a design for a state chair published in *Gothic Furniture* (1835).[80] Although the Speaker's Chair undoubtedly dominated the Chamber (as does its replacement of 1950), its appearance was distinguished but subdued, above all in comparison with the monarchical pomp that dominated the other Chamber.

Explaining the relative plainness of the Pugin/Barry Commons Chamber, historians point to its being considered second in importance to the Lords – as it had been in the old palace. Because the House of Commons itself was of lesser political significance, the argument suggests, the Chamber was destined to be much less rich and flamboyant in decoration.[81] While this might have crudely represented the balance of power in the 1830s or even the 1840s, in 1867 Walter Bagehot put an entirely different spin on political power and its relationship with outward display by stating that the House of Commons's "use resides not in its appearance, but in its reality. Its office is not to win power by *awing* mankind, but to *use* power in governing mankind".[82] In this context, as the century progressed, the relative simplicity of the Chamber and the Speaker's Chair became a metaphor for the appropriation by the Commons of the day-to-day *business* of conducting power. With the rebuilding of the Chamber after the Second World War in a Gothic style even more restrained than its predecessor, the exaggerated simplicity of the Commons, in dramatic contrast to the Lords Chamber, acts as an unequivocal statement that political power is now firmly directed by the Commons. Quite simply, the Speaker's Chair is used every day when the House is in session, the throne but once a year.

As power was in the grasp of the elected – and thus transitional – House of Commons, Bagehot argued that the hereditary monarchy, with its ancient origins, associations and traditions, represented the antithesis of change, and, as previously discussed, acts as a disguise.[83] This theory could apply to the thrones in the new Palace of Westminster. Based on an ancient symbol of royal authority and ceremony, the Lords Chamber throne appropriated the stylistic and thus the historical and religious resonance of the medieval coronation chair. Its constant presence in the palace – albeit aloof – has all the appearance of intransience; its message is that nothing has changed. And yet in reality, the policies set out in the speech from the throne make it clear that the constitution, as well as the role of Parliament at Westminster, is constantly evolving.

Irrespective of shifts in political power, the throne retains its significance as a symbol of the monarch's position as head of state, and as such is the focus of the annual State Opening, the only occasion at which the three elements of the constitution are assembled in Parliament. And it is on this day that the true 'theatre' of the palace is realized:

> Were all the doors between the two legislative chambers opened, the monarch enthroned in the Lords and the Speaker on the Speaker's Chair in the Commons would confront one another down the gothic perspective of the spine, each legitimating the other's constitutional presence.[84]

# 12

## *The Speaker's House*

Christine Riding, Dorian Church, Christopher Garibaldi

### *The Origins and Function of the Speaker's House*

He lives in a Royal Palace. He has his own court, his own civil list, his own public household. He is approached and addressed with a ceremony and deference such as is shown to royalty ... He represents in his proper self the rights and privileges of all his subjects. In his own sphere his word is law, and, should that law be broken, he keeps his own officer to convey offenders to his own prison. His functions, multifarious as those of sovereignty itself, include many of a stately or ceremonial kind. He wears his own proper robes, which it is not lawful for other men to don. His sceptre is borne before him – the Mace of the most honourable House over which he rules; upon his head reposes his peculiar crown, the Speaker's wig, and just where the throne stands in the House of Lords we find in the House of Commons the Speaker's Chair.[1]

The Speaker's House within the new Palace of Westminster consolidated a number of significant developments in relation to the position of Speaker itself. Long gone were the days when a reluctant Speaker was dragged to the Chair or indeed suffered the indignity of being held down in it.[2] After the Glorious Revolution (1688), the pre-eminence of the Speaker in the Commons was, by Act of Parliament, unequivocal. As 'First Commoner of the Realm' the occupant "ranked next to the peers of Great Britain both in and out of Parliament".[3] Of course, the rise in the authority and prestige of the Speakership was synonymous with that of the House of Commons (see chapter 1). But within the House of Commons itself, the Speaker's position was unique. As the presiding officer of the House and the regulator of debates in the Chamber, the Speaker's authority was absolute and recognized by all Members. Thus the Speaker was expected to be completely impartial, the occupant having effectively 'retired' from party politics on accepting the position.[4] This otherness, underlined by the prominence of the Speaker's Chair and the designation of a permanent residence on site, may explain the extravagant language used in descriptions of the Speaker during the nineteenth century and later. For example, in 1897 Michael MacDonagh could claim that "Every Speaker ... comes in time to be regarded as a heaven-born Speaker. This, of course, is entirely as it should be."[5]

The increasingly complex and time-consuming business conducted by Parliament from the late seventeenth century appears to have resulted in the provision for accommodation for high-ranking officials *within* the Parliamentary estate. For example, the Clerk of the House petitioned the Treasury for an official house, on account of his being "obliged in the execution of his office to a very constant personal attendance at or near the House of Commons".[6] The position of Speaker seems to have put immense strain on the occupant, an extreme

View of the State Bed in the State Bedroom, Speaker's House, previously the drawing room of the Serjeant-at-Arms's residence. The picture shows some of the furniture made to furnish the State Bedroom and State Dressing-Room when both were located on the first floor of the residence: the State Bed (POW 9700), prie-dieus on the left and right (POW 66, 67), a pot cupboard on the right of the bed (POW 65) and screen, right (POW 64). Other original furnishings that survive in the Palace of Westminster collection are a fire screen (POW 10), a dressing table (POW 53) and a wardrobe (POW 68).

example being that of John Cust, whose Speakership in the 1760s covered a particularly stormy period in British politics. He died in 1770 – according to his funerary monument in Belton Church, Lincolnshire – as a result of the "unusual fatigues of his office" brought on by "the extraordinary increase of national business".[7]

By the latter part of the eighteenth century, the Speaker was provided with some form of accommodation in the various areas of the old palace around the Commons Chamber (St Stephen's Chapel). The Speaker had at his disposal a small 'withdrawing room' near the Chamber itself, and four chambers in St Stephen's Court, which may on occasion have been used for private dining, perhaps for entertaining, or, indeed, for sleeping. Even with the introduction of a Speaker's House in 1794, these rooms continued to be used until the fire of 1834.[8]

Prior to 1794, Speakers had tended to reside in and around London, at their own expense. William Lenthall (Speaker 1640–47, 1647–53, 1654–55) had lived in King Street, Covent Garden, and then moved to Goring House, the site of the future Buckingham Palace. Arthur Onslow (Speaker 1728–61) lived in a modest house in Leicester Street, Soho. In 1752 – as a sign of his increasing status – he moved to nearby 20 Soho Square, "the grandest and finest house in the square and one well suited to Speaker's levees".[9] When the Auditor of the Exchequer, the Duke of Newcastle, died in 1794, the vacated property became the Speaker's House. The following year, Henry Addington (Speaker 1789–1801) moved in, and the history of the Speaker in residence had begun.[10]

James Parker after Sir William Beechey, *The Rt Hon. Henry Addington, Viscount Sidmouth*, engraving, published in 1803. Palace of Westminster (WOA 4187).

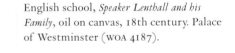

English school, *Speaker Lenthall and his Family*, oil on canvas, 18th century. Palace of Westminster (WOA 4187).

ABOVE: Sir Thomas Lawrence, *Charles Abbot, 1st Baron Colchester*, oil on canvas, 1824. Palace of Westminster (WOA 2715).

RIGHT: *The Speaker's House. From West*[minste]*r Bridge*, engraving, published 12 November 1810. View of the Speaker's House from the River Front, showing St Stephen's Chapel on the left. Palace of Westminster (WOA 1916).

Published by A. Beugo, Printseller, No 38 Maiden Lane, Covent Garden, Nov. 12, 1810.

Speaker's State Coach and Members of the House of Commons at the door of Westminster Hall on 23 June 1897 (Queen Victoria's Diamond Jubilee). Benjamin Stone collection, Birmingham Library Services.

By 1808 the Speaker's House had experienced a substantial overhaul. Charles Abbot (Speaker 1802–17) instigated a remodelling programme of considerable expense, executed by James Wyatt in a simple, castellated Gothic style. In 1805 *The Times* opined, "This will add extremely to the effect of the Speaker's House, and give it entirely the air of a grand old dwelling, of which the House of Commons will appear to be the chapel."[11] That the remodelling of Speaker's House had received such a large expenditure, elevating it to the status of a substantial Georgian town house, was, according to Mordaunt Crook and Port, "due largely to the energy and ambition of Speaker Abbot".[12] It may have been the ambition of his predecessor, Henry Addington, that established the Speaker in residence in the first place. Addington initiated, and Abbot continued, the formation of a series of portraits representing Speakers past and present (see illus., p. 205). On a practical level, these portraits served to furnish the house. But they also visualized the longevity of the Speaker's office and thus the integral part that the occupants had played – and were playing – in the history of Parliament.[13] Such was the rise in prestige of the Speakership that by the second half of the eighteenth century, the occupant was in possession of a state coach previously owned by the monarch.[14]

Inevitably, it would seem, the Speakership developed a dual role as "the head of the social as well as the political system of the House of Commons".[15] The origin of the Speaker's official social role – in the form of state receptions (called levees or levées from the French *levé*) and dinners – remains a matter of conjecture. In the history of the Palace of Westminster, functions hosted by the Speaker could not have occurred on site to any great extent before the establishment of the official residence, with its State Dining Room and levee rooms. Prior to this, the venues would have been the various town houses occupied by Speakers, as previously indicated. In this context, official entertaining may have begun from

FAR LEFT: *The Speaker's Levee: Arrivals*, wood-engraving, published in *Illustrated London News*, LX, no. 1702, 20 April 1872, p. 373. Palace of Westminster (WOA 3933).

LEFT: *The Speaker's Levee in the Morning Room of his Residence at the New Palace of Westminster*, wood-engraving, published in *Illustrated London News*, XXXIV, no. 970, 23 April 1859, p. 393. Palace of Westminster (WOA 5298).

the late seventeenth century, and the order of both the dinners and the receptions were, in all probability, established and closely adhered to by the time of Addington's Speakership.[16]

Within the newly designated Speaker's House, the east section of the under chapel of St Stephen's Chapel (now referred to as the chapel of St Mary Undercroft or the Crypt Chapel) was used as the State Dining Room. Charles Abbot (Speaker 1802–17) described one lavish dinner held by Speaker Addington in February 1796 as comprising twenty guests in full dress, who were served on plate bearing the monarch's arms.[17] "The rule," Abbot reported, "is for the Speaker to give his first Saturday's dinner to the Ministers and their friends in office, who are Members of the House of Commons. His first Sunday is for the Opposition, and afterwards his parties are promiscuous [meaning 'mixed' or 'casual'] – chiefly his private friends and those who visit his levee on Sunday evenings."[18] In 1800 the dinners were conducted on a weekly basis, habitually on Saturday or occasionally on Sunday, beginning at 5.30 pm. Addington's guests included William Pitt the Younger, Charles James Fox, Richard Brinsley Sheridan, William Wilberforce and Lord Castlereagh.[19]

The majority of the Speaker's House remained operable after the 1834 fire. In 1839, the Speaker was relocated to 71 Eaton Square, Belgravia, in preparation for the construction of the new palace. Official entertaining was by now such a feature of the Speaker's Parliamentary life that the neo-classical house required the addition of a wing for a State Dining Room, so that the Speaker could continue to host state dinners and levees in appropriate style and comfort.[20]

Throughout the nineteenth century, the dinners and levees were conducted with a high degree of formality. The guests were expected to attend wearing uniform or court dress (ordinary evening dress being strictly forbidden). The Speaker himself wore a black velvet court suit, a lace collar and cuffs, and a sword. And the dining table and sideboards were "spread with magnificent old plate".[21] In 1872, the *Illustrated London News* observed that "[the Speaker's] levées ... are attended with as much solemnity and strictness of etiquette as those held by Royalty at St James's Palace."[22] Indeed, an invitation by the Speaker "was regarded – in theory but not always in practice – as having the same force as a Command from the Sovereign."[23] This persisted into the twentieth century. According to his correspondence, Ralph Verney, the Secretary to the Speaker (1921–55), spent much time and energy rounding up the invitees. In a letter dated 24 February 1922, he wrote:

Our Dinner and Levée was a great success last night, but three Members of the Labour Party failed to turn up for the Dinner. Griffiths missed a train, but I have not had a word from the other two, Hodge and Adamson. More than 200 turned up for the Levée, so my little talk with the Whips of the parties had good effect.[24]

## The Origins of the Speaker's State Bed

Perhaps the most extraordinary indication of the prestige of the Speakership in the nineteenth century was the creation of the State Bed, which was installed in the State Bedroom in the Speaker's House in the late 1850s. In order to put this piece of furniture in context with the rest of the furnishings of the new residence, it is important to give an outline of the history of state beds.

In the medieval period, the bed was the principal item of furniture. Emphasis was placed on sumptuous textiles, sometimes embroidered in gold and silver thread, to dress the basic wooden frame.[25] The employment of such precious materials gave the bed equal rank to silver and gold plate, vestments and jewelry. And as some of the most valuable items of personal estate, beds were detailed in inventories and wills, and offered as gifts by royalty.[26] As a result, in households where social hierarchy was strictly observed through visual display, the bed became one of the most effective indicators of power and prestige.

By the early fourteenth century, the canopy, which denoted high estate, was an established feature of a seigneurial bed. Indeed, the canopy itself remained an integral part of the state bed until the nineteenth century.[27] (See chapter 11 for further discusson of canopies.) As Penelope Eames has observed, "Through its form, type of cloth and decoration, the hung

BELOW LEFT: State Bed in the State Bedroom, Chatsworth. Owned by George II and after the king's death given to the 4th Duke of Devonshire as a perquisite due to his office of Lord Chamberlain.

BELOW RIGHT: The State Bed, Speaker's House (POW 9700). The bed was sold at some point at the beginning of the twentieth century. In January 1979, *The Daily Telegraph* published an article after a lecture given by the furniture historian, Clive Wainwright. The subsequent publicity resulted in the discovery of the bed in a Welsh woollen mill. It was eventually acquired in 1981. Restoration was completed by 1984. The geranium and gold silk brocatelle hangings were produced after a design by A.W.N Pugin.

bed symbolised the ideas of lordship which were inherent in the medieval feudal system, and so eloquently did it perform this function that succeeding ages felt unable to create a sense of grandeur in bedrooms without it."[28]

The earliest documented state bed (1242–47) in England was that made for Henry III's Chamber (later called the 'Painted Chamber') at the Palace of Westminster, which functioned both as the king's principal bedroom and as his audience chamber. In a brief description, dated 1244, the bed was described as having a wooden canopy, supported by bedposts, which were decorated with gold stars on a green ground – the king's favourite form of ornament.[29] The spectacular programme of wall paintings in the Painted Chamber has already been described (see chapter 3). But as an indication of its status within the layout of the room, the bed was positioned so that the area of the wall acting as the king's 'headboard' was filled with a representation of the Coronation of Edward the Confessor – the pictorial centrepiece of the whole decorative scheme (see illus., p. 54).

Increasingly, the state bed *per se* became a focus of court ceremonial and preferment.[30] For example, records from the reigns of Henry VII and Henry VIII show that an elaborate ritual had developed during which the king's bedding was brought to his Chamber every evening.[31] As a result, a convention developed whereby such a bed – invested with honour and surrounded by ritual – became more a symbol than a utility, commanding the respect that was due to the lord of the household, and at the highest level, the veneration for the monarch. In France, during the seventeenth century, for example, the bed situated in the State Bedchamber (*Chambre de Parade*) of a royal palace was saluted by everyone who entered the room, including members of the royal family.[32] And it is interesting to note that during royal sessions of the Parlement, the French king reclined on five cushions collectively called the *lit de justice* (Bed of Justice), an ensemble which has something in common with the Lord Chancellor's 'seat of authority' in the Lords Chamber, the Woolsack.[33]

But state beds were not only made for monarchs and installed into royal palaces as part of court ceremonial. They were also ordered by members of the nobility in order to receive the monarch as their guest.[34] Indeed, it is often stated that the Speaker's State Bed itself was created for the express purpose – in accordance with the ancient tradition – of hosting the monarch at the Palace of Westminster the night before the coronation.[35] As the Speaker's House is of relatively recent origin (1794), the tradition cited must relate to the palace when it was a royal residence.

In 1820, the year before the Coronation of George IV, T.C. Banks published "a curious old manuscript" entitled 'The Ancient Form of the Coronation of the Kings and Queens of England'. This stated "Imprimus.– The king to be newly crowned, the day before his coronation, shall be brought forth in royal robes, and shall ride from the Tower of London to his Palace of Westminster with his head uncovered, being accompanied on horseback by his temporal lords, his nobles, the commons of London, and other his servants."[36] According to Alfred John Kempe's research, the procession from Tower to palace was conducted with considerable aplomb at the coronation of Richard II (1377). Having arrived in Westminster Hall, the king "then departed with his nobles and his household into his chamber and having supped in state, and undergone the accustomed formality of bathing, he retired to rest."[37]

Of course, from the Norman period to the reign of Henry VII (1485–1509), the Palace of Westminster was the principal royal residence. However, even after Henry VIII transferred his court to nearby York House (the future palace of Whitehall) in 1529, and Edward VI formally handed over to Parliament the use of St Stephen's Chapel as their debating chamber, the palace retained its royal status. For example, Elizabeth I stayed at the palace

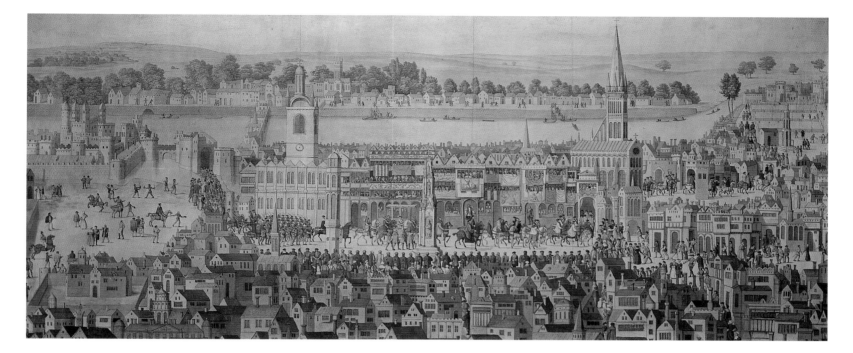

Samuel Hieronymous Grimm, *The Coronation Procession of Edward VI, 1547*, after a 16th-century mural, watercolour, 1785. The Society of Antiquaries of London.

the night before her coronation in 1559.[38] Thus the buildings continued to play a significant role in the ceremonial life of the monarch, above all during the coronation, when the Hall was used for the assembling of the procession to the abbey and for the banquet that traditionally followed the service. But by the coronation of Charles II (1660), one element had disappeared from the itinerary: the palace no longer hosted the monarch the previous night. Charles left the Tower – the last monarch to do so – and processed through the streets of London to Whitehall Palace. The following morning, St George's Day (23 April):

> about half an hour after seven in the morning, the king entered his rich barge, took water from the privy-stairs at White-hall, and landed at the parliament stairs; from whence he proceeded up to the room behind the lords house, called the prince lodgings, where after he reposed himself for a while, he was arrayed in his royal robes of crimson velvet, furred with ermine.[39]

In 1727, J. Roberts stated that on the day of the coronation, the monarch now came through St James's Park to Whitehall, with a retinue reduced to "several Noblemen and Officers", and from there took the royal barge to the Palace of Westminster.[40] And prior to the coronation of George III and Queen Charlotte (1761), the royal couple travelled from St James's Palace to Westminster Abbey in sedan chairs "like ordinary citizens going to the theatre". They returned, after the ceremony and banquet, to St James's, "as unobstrusively as they had set out".[41]

Clearly the tradition was moribund by the nineteenth century. But it was to be revived, albeit briefly, by George IV in 1820. In his account of the coronation (published 1821), Robert Huish reports that "His Majesty having expressed his intention to sleep in the mansion of the Speaker of the House of Commons, on the night previous to the Coronation, preparations were accordingly made for his reception."[42] The arrangement may have been one of expediency and convenience, rather than representing a sincere desire to reintroduce this ancient ritual to state ceremonial. After all, George was not in the best of health at the time of the coronation and was perennially nervous of the mob (see chapter 4). The Speaker's House was conveniently placed for the assembling of the procession in Westminster Hall, and was sufficiently grand to host such an important guest for one night only.

Irrespective of what was intended by George IV, this 'revival' was not followed by subsequent monarchs. William IV, "whose tastes were as simple as his predecessor's had been luxurious", slept in his "usual Bedroom" in St James's Palace.[43] Queen Victoria, whose reign admittedly began in 1837, when the Palace of Westminster was a building site, was in fact the first monarch to leave from Buckingham Palace, conveniently situated across St James's Park from the abbey. Buckingham Palace had been reinvented – by George IV and (reluctantly) William IV – from one of many royal residences into a state palace. And yet, despite the fact that the tradition had lapsed yet again, and despite the fact that the Speaker had hosted the monarch prior to the coronation only once, the new Speaker's House was supplied with a State Bed. The reason is not as yet clear. Perhaps the answer lies in the perceived romance of the palace (shades of Sir Walter Scott?) and its ancient royal associations. The State Bed remained in the Speaker's House until the early part of the twentieth century, when presumably it was thought sufficiently redundant to be sold off. Fortunately, it was returned to the Speaker's House in 1986 after a restoration project overseen by the Victoria and Albert Museum, and is displayed in the 'Speaker's State Bedroom', formerly the Serjeant-at-Arms's drawing room.

The Speaker's State Bed, c. 1903. By this time the bed had been refurbished in a much less ornate fashion than the original design, using window curtains, presumably from the residence. Farmer collection no. 665, House of Lords Record Office, London.

## The Speaker's House

The status of the Speaker was confirmed by the pre-eminence given to his official accommodation in Charles Barry's new building. For example, unlike the Speaker's House, some official residences – like that of the Serjeant-at-Arms – were not part of the original specification. During the re-allocation and adjustment of accommodation in the face of official demands, Barry continued to revise his original plans until 1841. The Speaker's House had been a notable feature of his prize-winning design. It was situated within the pavilion that terminated the north end of the River Front, nearest to Westminster Bridge. An expansive State Dining Room was located in the adjoining tower that was to rise from New Palace Yard.[44] Barry's final plan, which accommodated all prescribed residences for officials of the House of Commons, enlarged the north end of the building and placed these residences round the same courtyard. In addition to the Speaker, these included the Serjeant-at-Arms and Assistant Serjeant-at-Arms, the Commons Librarian and the Clerk of the House. Although all spaces for ceremonial and domestic life were contained within the one pavilion, the Speaker had nonetheless the largest official residence of the nine established within the new palace, which contained twenty rooms or more.

The Speaker's House had the grandest entrance porch in Speaker's Court. Flanked by panels carved with the Mace (the Speaker's emblem) and national emblems in stained glass, it opened into an entrance hall at the base of a ceremonial staircase, leading up to the official reception rooms. With its obvious reference to the Royal Entrance at the base of Victoria Tower, where the Royal Staircase leads through to a ceremonial apartment, the Speaker's House represented a palace within the palace. Barry had always understood the inherent brief for the Speaker's House, asking Pugin in 1836 to make the chimneypieces for its interiors more elaborate than those for other residences. And in 1843 he described the House as "being designed for state purposes".[45] This was realized not only by the sheer scale of the new residence, but also by the degree of opulence and the heraldic decoration planned and executed both for the interiors of the official reception rooms and the State Bedroom.

Although the structure of the Speaker's House had been in place since 1844, Barry's priorities had been to complete the two Chambers and the offices and facilities for Peers and Members. In April 1857, John Evelyn Denison (Speaker 1857–72) was elected Speaker. His wish to move his family immediately into the official accommodation in the new palace prompted action.[46] In December 1857 Barry provided the Office of Works with estimates for the interior decorations and fittings required. Basic work for bricklayers, masons, carpenters and painters was outlined, as well as the decorative painting and wallpapers from Crace. Estimates were provided for a glazier to fit stained glass, and for the fitting of grates, brass and iron door furniture, the brass balustrade for the staircase, and light fittings, all of which were to be supplied by Hardman.[47]

According to a contemporary description, the interiors were "emblazoned with ornaments after the manner of the House of Peers".[48] Although the position of Speaker had previously held by no means as much political authority within Parliament as in the nineteenth century, the profuse use of heraldry throughout the ceremonial interiors (in direct contrast with most areas of the House of Commons) ennobled the historic dignity of the Speakership. This romantic self-consciousness of the significance of the Speaker in Parliamentary history had been first evoked by the aforementioned portrait collection of Speakers Addington and Abbot. The collection, which had survived the fire, was now installed in the new residence. In the State Dining Room, a number of the portraits of former Speakers were set into fitted frames in 1859. The heraldry throughout, from the entrance-hall ceiling to the painted shields laid on the cornice of the stairwell and in the dado panelling of the state drawing room, to the stained glass that was originally fitted into the central cloister (now removed), displayed the arms and armorial bearings of past Speakers. The royal coat of arms, underlining the relationship between the monarch and the Speaker, was also clearly displayed on the first landing of the staircase.

Entrance doorway to Speaker's Residence, July 1897. Benjamin Stone collection, Birmingham Library Services.

Speaker Denison wanted certain alterations to be made to the plan and fitting-out of the interiors, for the convenience of his family. Barry had to take account of these, as well as the official requirements of the reception rooms. The proposed library on the principal floor was furnished instead as a second drawing room, for use as a family morning room, which was pressed into use for levees and other receptions, and led into the second, formal drawing room. A smaller, private dining room opened into the State Dining Room itself. Both rooms were furnished in the same manner so that the interconnecting doors could be opened to enlarge the space for ceremonial dining, if required.

This interwoven unity of state ceremonial and domestic privacy was extended to the first floor of the house, with its 'Best Bed Room', six family bedrooms, three dressing rooms, two bathrooms and the 'State Bed Room', and attendant dressing room. The upper two floors contained twelve bedrooms for the servants. The head butler had a room on the ground floor next to the entrance; the basement, the central service point for the whole of the household (the size of a major town house), was fitted with a housekeeper and under-butler's room, as well as a servants' hall and kitchen.

In 1843 Barry had declared that "the style of its finishings, fittings and decorations will be in accordance with the best examples of the Tudor period".[49] However, the Office of Works allowed Barry no part in the supply of the furniture. In April 1858 they sought authorization from the Treasury to employ a draughtsman[50] to prepare the furniture designs for the tender documents. Their choice was John Braund, one of many professional draughts-men who made a living by the production of drawings and engravings of furniture 'showpieces', for publication in pattern books or periodicals of interior design.[51] The surviving drawings of furniture to be supplied for the Speaker's official reception rooms show little original talent for design.[52]

*The New Houses of Parliament. — The State Dining-Room in the Speaker's Residence*, wood-engraving, published in *Illustrated London News*, XXXIV, no. 5, 12 February 1859, with a supplement, p. 145. The accompanying text states: "Around the room, in frames set in the wall, are placed a fine collection of a number of the former Speakers". Palace of Westminster (WOA 7010).

Mrs Gully's drawing room in the Speaker's House, Palace of Westminster, July 1897. William Court Gully (later 1st Viscount Selby) was Speaker from 1895 to 1905. Benjamin Stone collection, Birmingham Library Services.

Pugin's basic forms were reinterpreted by Braund with the application of lavish Gothic ornament to walnut that was then parcel gilt. *The Cabinet-Maker's Assistant*, published by the firm of Blackie & Son in 1853, describes fashionable ideas on furniture for contemporary drawing rooms:

> Beauty and elegance of expression being the main features to be studied in this apartment, there is not the same necessity for subordinating the ornamental to the useful, as in furniture intended for the dining-room or library; ornament may, consequently, be more freely introduced, richer materials employed, and greater license taken, both in the forms and in the colours adopted.[53]

In August 1858 the tender from Holland & Sons was accepted, and the major part of the furnishings was supplied by January 1859. Speaker Denison and his family took up residence in February of the same year. The Office of Works's specification[54] had stipulated fashionable forms — daybeds, ottomans, chiffonniers, dwarf bookcases and whatnots — as part of the repertoire of furniture types introduced for the drawing rooms. The Gothic style in oak had become most popular and conventional for dining rooms or libraries, as described by Blackie's and other contemporary pattern-books, and had been so used for all other residences within the new palace. For the Speaker's State Dining Room and family dining room (which was also used for state functions) the symbolically high-ranking X-frame chair, designed by A.W.N. Pugin and made specifically for the Prince's Chamber in 1846–47, was copied with the addition of castors for easier movement to and from the table.[55] By the end of the century, these chairs, highly inappropriate for the purpose of dining, were no longer in use in the State Dining Room.

A similar status of Barry and Pugin's established designs and precept for the palace

Drawing Room (looking north), Speaker's House, Palace of Westminster, July 1897. Benjamin Stone collection, Birmingham Library Services.

interiors that diminished the final character with the products of contemporary taste and fashion was accentuated by textiles and wallpapers chosen for the Speaker's House. The particular status of its occupant seems to have determined the overwhelming use of reds throughout, rather than the mixture of green and red found in other Commons residences (see chapter 10). Red Utrecht velvet and red wallpaper was specified for the dining rooms, geranium-red silk brocatelle for the wall-hangings, upholstery and curtains, with primrose-yellow lining for the large drawing room. The pattern of the brocatelle was stipulated as being "from design exhibited",[56] and, as turn-of-the-century photographs show, it was a pattern designed by Pugin and formerly supplied to the palace by Crace. The furniture supplied to this room and the family drawing room adjacent was covered in the same fabric, although the latter room was to have wall-hangings in green, again of a specified pattern.[57]

Unlike the range of Pugin-related oak furniture supplied by Gillows for bedrooms in other residences, the specification for the secondary, family bedrooms of the Speaker's House stipulated Spanish mahogany, at this time an orthodox choice. The descriptions in the specification create a picture of furniture that could be provided from the standard range, or from suppliers of the tendering firms. Gillows had made carved oak bedsteads based on a Pugin design for House of Commons residences with textile canopies, creating what were described as "French Bedsteads". But more conventional brass bedsteads, with mahogany canopies, were used for all the family bedrooms in the Speaker's House. The most elaborate, with silk hangings, was supplied to the Speaker's 'Best Bed Room'.[58] Dressing rooms and lesser bedrooms were furnished with what was described as "Watsons chintz", and an addition to the original estimate included a "Tudor rose chintz printed to special order of Lady D." for "loose cases", for which pattern blocks had to be specially cut.[59] Barry had also been provided with wallpapers by Crace, from the range made up after Pugin's designs. Lady

Denison subsequently had a non-Pugin paper hung in her private rooms, and other original textile and paper selections were also replaced.[60]

The State Bed (see illus., p. 199), an eloquent anachronism of past royal practice, also provided a vehicle for heraldic display. The royal coat of arms was carved on its footboard, and the lambrequin panels of its valence were embroidered on each side with the emblems of the three kingdoms: the Thistle, the Tudor Rose and the Shamrock. Pugin was interested in the tradition of the state bed and had produced at least two specified designs, one of which was published.[61] Both these designs drew on Pugin's authoritative knowledge of historic precedent in their form and use of carved decoration – a tester supported by a headboard, and endposts flanking a footboard. Although Pugin's designs may again have been a starting point (the semicircular panel raised above the line of the footboard for a coat of arms being a common feature), John Braund's design for the State Bed was conceived as "A Walnut wood and gilt Arabian Bedstead".[62] An 'Arabian' bed was by the middle of the nineteenth century a generic term for a particular form of bed – a half or full tester with no supporting endposts – dressed in a variety of historical styles. Braund's Gothic model has taken the basic form, given it a scale of some grandeur and added decorative features drawn from Gothic architecture – the brattishing and pinnacles of the tester, the finials of the footboard. The curtains of the bed, as in the case of those made for the windows of the reception rooms and the best bed, were of silk damask, while the valances were of shaped lambrequins, a popular attribute of curtains and portieres in the whole gamut of native historical styles since the 1830s. The upholstered headboard was a concession to modern ideas of comfort.

In response to current social and economic conditions, the Speaker's offical residence was much reduced in scale and grandeur during the Second World War. The State Apartments were retained on the principal floor and the Speaker's daily life was confined solely to a flat on the first and second floors. This arrangement has continued, although in recent years the original style of the State Apartments has been restored. When the State Bedroom was dismantled, the State Bed was probably sold off. It was recovered two decades ago and after being purchased by the National Heritage Memorial Fund, was carefully restored under the supervision of the Victoria and Albert Museum. Since the State Bedroom on the first floor of the apartments has been converted into a private drawing room, the bed and other pieces originally made to accompany it were placed in the drawing room of the Serjeant-at-Arms's residence, adjoining the Speaker's State Dining Room. The effect of the original State Bedroom was also carefully recreated.[63]

## The Speaker's State Silver

Given the existence of A.W.N. Pugin's designs for letter-racks and desk calendars – later produced by John Hardman of Birmingham for other areas of the Palace of Westminster – it is perhaps surprising that a more appropriately Gothic silver service was not commissioned for the new Speaker's State Dining Room. However, by the time the Speaker's House was being fitted up for Speaker Denison in 1857, the Treasury was keeping such a tight control over expenditure that budgetary constraints and governmental pressure may have precluded replacing the service acquired more than twenty years earlier. It seems unlikely – in view of contemporary attitudes to old plate – that any particular reverence would have been felt for what must have appeared by the late 1850s to be an incongruously outdated and unfashionable service.

The majority of the official plate of the Speaker of the House of Commons bears the London date letter for 1835/36 and was supplied by R. & S. Garrard, who had been appointed

'Crown Goldsmiths' on the accession of William IV in 1830 (they finally won the coveted title of 'Crown Jewellers in Ordinary' from Queen Victoria in 1843, following the dissolution of Rundell, Bridge & Rundell).[64] Changing fashions in dining and the need to acquire tea equipage for more informal entertaining resulted in modest additions to the service in subsequent decades.[65] But, in general, it is a remarkably complete and homogeneous early nineteenth-century dinner service, reflecting the primary requirement of the Speaker – by virtue of his constitutional position – to dine in state.

As originally supplied, the service consists of circular dinner plates, soup plates, small waiters and larger salvers, each with fairly plain shaped and moulded rims, engraved at the edge with a crowned royal crest and garter. There are similarly decorated circular vegetable dishes with domed covers, and various sizes of oval meat plates, also supplied with domes. Among the more striking pieces are a set of large, oval, soup tureens, with covers surmounted by cast-anthemion finials. The urn-shaped body on a spreading foot has two bifurcated vine-stock handles, terminating in fruiting vine mounts: a feature also shared by a series of wine coolers. The service was also supplied with a number of oval breadbaskets, rectangular entrée dishes, plain circular trencher salts with reeded rims, mustard pots, grape scissors, coffee pots, tea pots, cream jugs, sugar bowls and rectangular trays. The larger of these items were supplied with armorial panels cast in the form of the royal coat of arms and bolted to what must otherwise have been fairly standard stock items. This was no special commission.

Traditionally, silver for the Speaker that bore the royal coat of arms, supporters and crest (sometimes accompanied by the monarch's initials) was issued on behalf of the Crown by the Jewel Office, in a similar manner to that supplied to ambassadors, who represented the sovereign's honour at foreign courts.[66] In 1762, for example, the Duke of Bedford was provided with 5893 oz of 'white plate' and 1066 oz of silver gilt for his embassy to France, this "being the usual allowance on such like occasions".[67] It was finally discharged to Bedford, "in consideration of the good and acceptable services of the said Duke".[68]

Speaker's House, State Dining Room set for dinner, c. 1905. Farmer Collection no. 718, House of Lords Record Office, London.

Oval soup tureen with cover flanked by wine coolers, silver, supplied by R. & S. Garrard, date mark 1835/36, part of the Speaker's State Silver. Palace of Westminster (tureen POW 3042, wine coolers POW 3048, 3049).

Originally, this practice was regarded as a way of rewarding good service, and a form of compensating the unsalaried ambassador or Officer of State (certain other positions such as Treasurer of the Household enjoyed the same privilege) for official expenses or as a form of pension. This practice quickly developed into a perquisite or customary right claimed by all. In a similar way, the tradition arose whereby successive Speakers retained on their retirement the silverware furnished to them by the Crown, along with other items of furniture from their official residence. The most spectacular example is that of the large wine cistern known as the 'Belton Wine Cooler'. Weighing 1450 oz, with handles surmounted by cast figures of the royal supporters (the crowned lion on one side and the unicorn on the other), the wine cistern was made by Thomas Heming, Principal Goldsmith to George III, for Sir John Cust on his retirement in 1770.[69] He also retained an extensive dinner service of around two hundred pieces that bore the royal arms, having been issued with plate by the Jewel Office in 1761 and 1768.[70]

The fact that the Speaker's silver issued by the Jewel Office bore the royal coat of arms (rather than the portcullis of Parliament) and was regarded as a perquisite of office is important for a number of reasons. First, it explains why so little early silver survives in the collections of the Palace of Westminster. Secondly, and perhaps more importantly from a constitutional point of view, it raises the interesting question of the status of the Speaker in relation to that of the sovereign. Was the Jewel Office grant of silver to the Speaker, like that issued to an ambassador, intended in some way to indicate an almost 'viceregal' quality to the office? While underlining the dignity of the position, was it also intended to suggest that the Speaker in some sense represented the monarch in Parliament? Constitutionally this would appear to sit rather uncomfortably with Speaker Lenthall's celebrated assertion to Charles I that he could only act "as the House is pleased to direct me, whose servant I am here". However, perhaps the royal grant of silver simply represented the ancient status of the Speaker as one of the great Offices of State, and the continued presence of the royal coat of arms on the service, acquired on the recommendation in 1833 of a select committee that it "be permanently appropriated to the office of Speaker",[71] simply reflected this custom. Nevertheless, it might also have been intended to underline the fact that however independent Parliament regarded itself, its rights and privileges were ultimately derived from the monarch. It is interesting to note that on a Speaker's Dinner menu of 1898 it is the royal coat of arms that sits in gold-embossed glory at the top of the page, while the Parliamentary

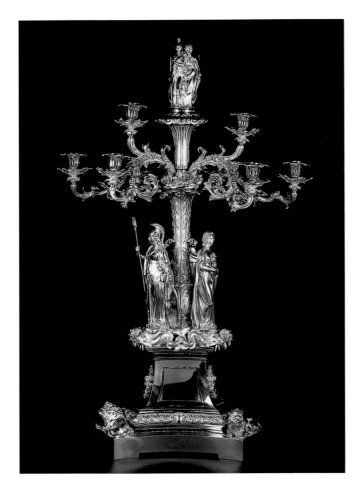

Three-branch (nine-light) candelabrum, silver, supplied by R. & S. Garrard, hallmarked by Paul Storr in London 1836/37, part of the Speaker's State Silver. Palace of Westminster (POW 3073).

portcullis is reduced to the same status as the printed border of national emblems.[72]

Whatever the constitutional subtleties expressed by the grants of plate to the Speaker, the extravagant practice of issuing plate considered to be perquisites of office generally constituted a considerable drain on resources. Frequently accused of corruption, and under the continual scrutiny of government auditors, the Jewel Office, by the end of the eighteenth century a minor department of the Royal Household compared with its central role in the Tudor and Stuart Court, came to be regarded as something of an anachronism, and, together with a number of other archaic institutions, was finally suppressed in 1782.

In the 1790s, Speaker Addington became the first Speaker to receive a salary, which at that time was £6000 per annum. In 1836 a similar sum was spent on acquiring the new silver service recommended by the select committee, which was to remain in perpetuity as a permanent fixture of the office.[73] Although, as we have seen, the body of the service was made of standard stock items, the most spectacular elements were the set of candelabra, comprising two smaller pairs and one large central candelabrum, all hallmarked by Paul Storr in London 1836/37. These were possibly subcontracted by Garrard to Storr, who had previously worked for Rundells but who was at this time in partnership with John Mortimer in New Bond Street; the candelabra are all stamped *Storr & Mortimer*. Although extremely well executed, the set is not particularly innovative: it was made to a standard neo-classical design of the period, with transitional neo-Rococo elements.[74] Storr had enjoyed an illustrious and extremely prolific career since first registering his own mark in 1793. Some of his best work had been completed during his collaboration with Rundells between 1811 and 1819, and had often involved working with some of the best neo-classical designers of the

Speaker's State Silver – detail of the candelabrum, showing Britannia (centre), Hibernia (left) and Scotia (right).

day, such as John Flaxman. This can be seen, for example, in the famous Theocritus Cups, executed during this period by Storr to Flaxman's designs, based on the description of a pottery cup in the First Idyll of the Alexandrian poet Theocritus.

However, by the time he was putting his mark on the candelabra for the Speaker, he was at the end of his career, and seems at the age of sixty-four to have been very much past his prime; he would retire just two years later. There is little that is innovative about the candelabra's design, and many of the individual elements are derivative versions of much earlier work.[75] Nevertheless, certain elements of the large three-branch (nine-light) centrepiece were regarded as significant enough in their conception to be effectively copyrighted as a design, and, to be fair, it is this piece that shows the most striking and individual elements of the whole service. On the back of the pair of classical female figures (the helmeted Marshal or Fortitude carrying a spear, the shield of Achilles at her feet, supported by Justice with a sword) that surmount the central column – almost lost in the folds of drapery – is engraved, in elegant copperplate script (as seen in many contemporary engravings):

> *N.60 Published as the Act directs by Storr & Mortimer*
> *156 New Bond Street London Feby.15.1837*

This is also found on each of the three finely executed figures that surround the base of the main stem: Britannia, with shield and trident, is accompanied by Hibernia, carrying an Irish harp, her hair dressed with shamrock, and Scotia, carrying a posy of thistles. Directly below them is a collar of dolphins (presumably an allusion to British maritime power and dominance). The incurvated, triangular, pedestal base features panels with national emblems and the royal coat of arms, and a lion sits at each corner. The whole piece is a neo-classical conceit and would have been entirely appropriate for the newly built, stuccoed splendour of 71 Eaton Square in Belgravia, which the government had rented from Thomas Cubitt as temporary accommodation for the Speaker during the construction of the new Palace of Westminster. Nevertheless, except for its similarly uncompromising confidence of scale, the piece, as in the case of the whole of the Speaker's service, constitutes a spectacular contrast to the Puginesque Gothic of the Speaker's House.

# 13

## Prince Albert and the Fine Arts Commission

Janet McLean

We see by daily experience how the statesman adorns his cabinet, the nobleman his library, the lawyer or the scholar his study; the merchant his counting-house, with some busts or portraits of those he esteems, while the works of fancy he reserves for his gallery or rooms of pleasure and recreation. Good taste and good sense tell him that the affairs and realities of life ill assort with creations of fancy. Can it be believed that this principle true in private shall be held false in public life? Shall we make the parliament the sole exception, employed as it is in the weightiest affairs of state and the last resort of justice?[1]

From the 1830s the British government came under growing censure for failing to recognize how the fine and decorative arts could be supported and used to the benefit of commerce, education and public morality. Following the findings of the Select Committee on Arts and Manufacturers chaired by William Ewart in 1835, further committees were set up to consider how an industrialized Britain might assert its artistic identity against such European rivals as Germany and France. Edward Edwards, one of the founders of the Art Union of London in 1836, addressed the dual issue of state responsibility for art education, and education through art, in *The Administrative Economy of the Fine Arts in England* (1840). Edwards related how governmental patronage of the arts would be of broad rather than local benefit to commerce. He proposed that state patronage should be implemented through the commission of history paintings and monumental sculpture for public buildings, as well as national art competitions and regular purchases from public exhibitions. Although acknowledging the necessity of private art patronage, Edwards argued that it left all artistic efforts in the promotion of a "Religion-Civilization-Social" order to "desertion and neglect".[2] He suggested that a "Minister of Public Instruction" be appointed to encourage the interrelation of art and education. Edwards concluded that the new Palace of Westminster was an ideal opportunity by which Britain's artistic reputation might be redeemed:

> The appropriate decoration of the Houses of Parliament now in the course of erection would afford a noble opportunity for the employment of the genius of our best artists on historical and national subjects. When we observe what has recently been done in this department in France, and still more strikingly, in the magnificent capital of the small kingdom of Bavaria, we may well blush for Britain, if this opportunity, like so many preceding ones, should be altogether neglected.[3]

In September 1841, Sir Robert Peel acknowledged this call to arms by proposing that a committee be established to consider how the new Palace of Westminster might be used for

After Franz Xavier Winterhalter, *Francis Charles Augustus Emanuel Albert, Prince Consort of Queen Victoria* (detail), oil on canvas, c. 1859. Palace of Westminster (WOA 3155).

KEY TO THE PICTURE OF
**THE MEETING OF THE FINE ARTS COMMISSION. 1846.**

the encouragement of a national style and standard of art, thereby becoming a monument as well as a working building. Within two months, a body of twenty-two peers, Members of Parliament and professional gentlemen had formed the Fine Arts Commission, under the chairmanship of Prince Albert. The inclusion of Albert signalled an alliance between government and monarchy. After some hesitation, Sir Charles Eastlake undertook the role of Secretary at the personal request of the prince.[4]

The mission of the Fine Arts Commission was to ensure that "advantage should be taken of the rebuilding of the Houses of Parliament for the purpose of promoting and encouraging the fine arts in the United Kingdom".[5] The most significant way this aim was to be achieved was through a series of four fine-art competitions with corresponding exhibitions held in Westminster Hall in 1843, 1844, 1845 and 1847. The device of competition played on current ideals of free enterprise, but any notion of artistic self-help was regulated by the Fine Arts Commission's gentlemanly paternalism. Apart from these anonymously entered competitions, specific commissions were made for the decoration of particular areas of the new palace.[6] The values informing the strategy of the Fine Arts Commission were closely related to the aims of the Art Union of London. This organization, based on the German models known as *Kunstvereine*, aimed at diffusing art among the 'masses'. One of its methods was the dissemination of engravings to its membership. Later, in 1874, its engraving of Daniel Maclise's *The Meeting of Wellington and Blücher after the Battle of Waterloo*, painted in the Royal Gallery of the Palace of Westminster in 1861, ran to twenty thousand copies. The Art Union made annual awards to artists for historical paintings, sculpture and engraving. Its original council included Lord Lansdowne, a prominent member of the Fine Arts Commission.

John Partridge's group portrait of *The Fine Arts Commissioners, 1846* shows the commissioners, alongside Charles Barry and Eastlake, assembled for a meeting in Gwyder House, Whitehall. The room is adorned with works of art that hint at the commission's aspiration to re-establish a 'high-art' tradition in Britain through the cultivation of history painting, heroic sculpture and portraiture, as opposed to genre and landscape.[7] Prince Albert extended his involvement as chairman into devising the public image of the commission itself. He gave a preliminary sketch for the portrait to Partridge, perhaps influenced by Johann Zoffany's group portrait of eighteenth-century dilettantism, *The Tribuna of the Uffizi* (1772–77), which had been painted for Queen Charlotte and was still in the Royal Collection.[8] The self-definition of the Fine Arts Commission as a cultivated group of historians, scholars, politicians and 'noblemen' invited debate about the qualifications of its panel. The delegation of non-artists to determine such a major artistic project engendered concern over their seemingly contradictory roles as connoisseurs and public servants. The press consistently debated whether the purported possession of such an ethereal quality as aesthetic sensibility qualified commissioners to deal with the practicalities of devising large-scale decorative schemes. The *Athenaeum* argued that the fine arts should not be viewed as a leisure activity or approached with less professionalism than undertakings in architecture:

> There is something anomalous in the appointment of a committee of noblemen and gentleman to direct and regulate the painting and decoration of the Houses of Parliament. Why should not there be a commission to direct the architect as well as to supervise the artists? Why should not the locality of the statues, their character, &c., the height of finials, width of buttresses, and other architectural details, be arranged by commissioners for the architect, if the principle of directing analogous details be recognized towards the painters? It might, perhaps, be a little more difficult so to dictate for architecture without betraying incapacity: and the toleration of this state of things, as respects painting may possibly be owing, in some measure, to the current assumption, which permits everyone to profess himself a critic of painting, though he may be ignorant of the simplest fundamental principles of art.[9]

Unlike pictures acquired for personal pleasure or domestic decoration, those commissioned for the new Palace of Westminster were intended to promote a greater good through the elevation of public taste and morality. The language used in the reports of the Fine Arts Commission pre-empts artistic debates of the 1860s on the perceived amorality and immorality of aesthetic art, as opposed to the healthy materialism of genre painting. Tensions between the issues of morality and beauty emerged through the commission's discussions of the suitability of historical or poetical subject matter for public art, and in the technical deliberations over the use of fresco or oils for its execution. Aesthetic appeal and moral message were to be reconciled through the commissioning of both historical and literary scenes. The private collections of individual members of the Fine Arts Commission were largely at variance with the type of art they promoted as a public body. With the exception of Prince Albert, few other commissioners were extensively involved in the collection of modern British art. For example, Sir Robert Peel – who initiated the commission – collected only Dutch genre painting. In her *Companion to the Most Celebrated Private Galleries of Art in*

*London* (1844), Mrs Anna Jameson described the art collections of several of the most prominent commissioners. They included those of the Marquis of Lansdowne at Bowood and Lansdowne House, the Duke of Sutherland at the Bridgewater Gallery, Sir Robert Peel, Samuel Rogers and Queen Victoria (whose collection, of course, Prince Albert was instrumental in shaping).[10] Jameson keenly favoured 'high art' in the form of religious and historical subjects, as opposed to "tableaux-de-genre and things painted for art-unions and annuals".[11] In her appraisal of the collections of the connoisseurs at the core of the commission, she made much of their cultured sensibilities. Although the collections of the Earl of Ellesmere and the Duke of Sutherland were open to the public, such democratizing impulses did not meet with Jameson's approval. Neither did she find favour with current philanthropic moves to make art accessible to a wider audience:

> I cannot help thinking that if we diffuse, by means of national galleries, cheap prints, art-unions, and so forth, the mere liking for pictures, as such, without diffusing at the same time that refined and elevated standard of taste which is the result of cultivation and discernment, and education, we are like to be deluged with mediocrity; every man, woman, and child will turn critic, and art and artists together will be essentially vulgarized.[12]

Despite the élitism implied by their status as connoisseurs, several of the commissioners were personally involved in art charities and efforts to increase public awareness of fine art. Devonshire, Sutherland, Lansdowne, Lyndhurst and Denison were among the vice-presidents of the Artists' General Benevolent Institution for the Relief of Decayed Artists, their Widows and Orphans. Stewards of this organization included William Dyce and Daniel Maclise, two of the most active artists in the decoration of the new Palace of Westminster. Finder's *Royal Gallery of British Art* had the support of Sir Robert Peel, who, among others, allowed pictures from his private collection to be engraved and publicly disseminated. Several commissioners were willing to lend objects from their private collections to public exhibitions. The British Institution Exhibition of 1839 included loans from Lansdowne, Egerton and Rogers. However, the majority of these loans were paintings by foreign Old Masters, causing the *Art-Union* to comment:

> A time is come when the Institution will be expected to show that its object is to be worked at by aiding and assisting, to give fame and prosperity to the moderns.[13]

This sentiment was more generally echoed by critics who believed that significant progress had to be made in terms of art patronage before British artists would be able to prove their true worth. The *Art-Union* consistently reproached British patrons for their half-hearted interest in supporting contemporary British art. When it was first hinted that the Palace of Westminster be used as a vehicle for promoting British art, it made the following appeal:

> To the rich, and well-disposed towards art, we say, if you really take pleasure in such objects, spare for them what may be, and often is, expended less worthily and less usefully, and remember that Raphael, Titian, Paolo Veronese, Parmegiano [*sic*], Correggio, Rubens and most of the highest luminaries in art, were panel and ceiling painters![14]

Criticism was directed at British art collectors on two levels. First, for their purchasing Old Master works, regardless of quality; and secondly, for their failure to support native talent by the commission of grand decorative schemes, as past patrons of Old Masters had done.

After Franz Xavier Winterhalter, *Francis Charles Augustus Emanuel Albert, Prince Consort of Queen Victoria*, oil on canvas, c. 1859. Palace of Westminster (WOA 3155).

Complaints against Britain's myopic approach to patronage were not new. Exactly a century previously, William Hogarth had lamented the fact that foreign dealers made a profitable trade in:

> importing ship-loads of dead Christs, Holy Families, Madonnas, and other dismal dark subjects, neither entertaining nor ornamental, on which they scrawl the terrible cramp names of some Italian masters, and fix on us poor Englishmen the character of universal dupes.[15]

As soon as the names of members of the commission were made public, it came under criticism because it was composed of so many members, not one of whom was an artist. Eastlake, the only professional artist involved with the commission, could act only in an advisory capacity as secretary. One of the more significant voices against the formation of the commission was Henry Cole, a prominent figure in the promotion of art education in the early Victorian period. He later became director of the South Kensington Museum (afterwards the Victoria and Albert Museum) and, with Prince Albert, acted as chief organizer of the Great Exhibition in 1851. In a lengthy article in the *Westminster Review* in 1842, Cole expressed doubt that any of the commissioners would be capable of copying a cartoon, with the exception of Prince Albert and Lord Lyndhurst (who "probably learnt drawing under his father Copley").[16] He stated that even if artists had been included on the panel, their opinions would have been overlooked on account of social hierarchies:

> It would be a stretch of the imagination far too visionary to suppose that, in case of any differences of opinion, the views of the artists would be suffered to outweigh those of a prince, a prime minister, and a duke.[17]

Accordingly it was not the artists but the commissioners themselves who came under censure for an anaemic approach to the pictorial themes prescribed for competition:

> When twenty of the most distinguished men in the state, either for their rank or their acquirements, generally considered to be men of taste, and who are constituted the Government Judges of Art, make no better selection of subjects, how dare we expect the artists, bound down to the fatigue of earning their daily bread to discover appropriate subjects for the cartoons, and fresco, and other competitions.[18]

Cole argued that all the most significant artistic projects undertaken in Europe had been executed under a single director, such as Leo X in Rome or Ludwig I in Bavaria. He was not alone in perceiving Prince Albert as the obvious candidate for such a prominent role, saying that "rank, judgement, knowledge of art, freedom from 'ear-wiggery', all united to point him out as the finest choice".[19] In April 1840, just two months after his marriage to Queen Victoria, the *Art-Union* remarked upon Prince Albert's interest in the advancement of British art:

> It is cheering to note that his Royal Highness takes especial interest in the Fine Arts of his adopted country; and that he has already encouraged the hope of their receiving patronage from the highest station – the fountain of honour as well as the source of success.[20]

Despite the appeal of the new Prince Consort, he became embroiled in what was undoubtedly the most contentious issue surrounding the Fine Arts Commission, namely the rumour that German artists were to be commissioned to direct and execute frescoes in the new

Palace of Westminster. From the early 1830s, British journals had been dedicating large amounts of column space to reviewing and commending German art and initiatives in state patronage. By 1842 *Fraser's Magazine* noted that:

> All travelled gentlemen and ladies who have idle time and money enough in their hands to convey them to Munich return to this country with glowing accounts of the frescoes there, and talk of the German artists as better Raphaels and Michelangelo.[21]

The artists causing such a sensation were the group known as the Nazarenes, who had been commissioned by Ludwig I to decorate his spectacular state apartments and public buildings in Munich with scenes from German history and mythology.[22] The group included Peter Cornelius (1783–1867), Johann Friedrich Overbeck (1789–1869) and Julius Schnorr von Carolsfeld (1783–1867). British admiration for the artistic advancements in Munich became tinged with competitive nationalism when Prince Albert was reputed to have suggested the active involvement of German artists in a scheme intended to resurrect British history painting. The German prince had just completed a grand tour in Italy, based mainly in Florence, where he became an admirer of the work of the Nazarenes in the residence of the Prussian Consul General Jacob Bartholdi, and in the Casino Massimo. As early as November 1841, Cornelius was invited to inspect the site and plans of the new Palace of Westminster, and formally to present his recommendations on its decoration to the Fine Arts Commission at the prince's initiative.[23] Any intimation that Cornelius might become director of the Palace of Westminster decorations was retracted when, as one art critic correctly predicted:

> The whole of Great Britain, from the Lands End in Cornwall, to the Stones of Stennis, will cry shame, and indignantly refuse to allow a foreign artist to be their Cornelius or Schnorr, and embody the great events of their history.[24]

Both to press and public it seemed contradictory that a commission established to foster Britain's artistic identity could consider engaging foreign artists. British artists, however, were for the most part willing to learn from the technical and stylistic achievements of the Nazarenes. Even Benjamin Robert Haydon, one of the most vocally nationalistic artists to enter the Westminster competitions, acknowledged:

> If the plan of Munich or Rome be not adopted, nothing will be the result, but a plan without consistency, vain struggles without results, and disjointed and futile efforts ... it is our duty to adopt the plan of foreign nations, to prevent the necessity of calling their personal aid, which must be the case if we do not.[25]

Initially the rules of the Fine Arts Competitions stipulated that foreigners could not enter designs, though this came to be modified in 1844 to allow the participation of foreign artists who had lived in Britain for at least ten years. Instead of turning directly to German artists, Albert became more involved in developing close working relationships with British artists. For the next twenty years the *Art-Union* gave regular reports of Prince Albert's visits to studios and private galleries, and his purchases and commissions of British art.[26] However, his interest in German advancements in art were never far from mind. In 1847 he presented a cartoon of Overbeck's *Der Triumph der Religion in den Kunsten* (The Triumph of Religion in the Arts) to Queen Victoria as a Christmas gift; this undoubtedly came to influence the design of Dyce's frescoes in the Robing Room. Charles West Cope said that while working on his designs for the Lords Chamber:

Johann Frederich Overbeck, *Cartoon for Der Triumph der Religion in den Kunsten*, pencil and chalk on paper, 1830–40, The Royal Collection.

L. Gruner, *Perspective View of the Pompeian Room*, engraving, published in *The Decorations of the Garden-Pavilion in the Grounds of Buckingham Palace, Engraved under the Supervision of L. Gruner. With an Introduction by Mrs Jameson.* London 1845, pl. xi. British Library, London (1267.k.7).

The Prince Consort caused a pamphlet to be translated from the German a copy of which was sent to each of the *frescanti*, describing the waterglass method, a new method of painting in Germany which was considered indestructible.[27]

Fascinated by the technical achievements of his compatriots, the prince had a small garden pavilion built on the grounds of Buckingham Palace in 1842. The sole purpose of this four-roomed folly was to allow a select group of artists the opportunity to experiment privately in fresco before the public schemes in Westminster were initiated. The Dresden artist

L. Gruner after William Dyce, *Comus V 968–975*, engraving, published in *The Decorations of the Garden-Pavilion in the Grounds of Buckingham Palace, Engraved under the Supervision of L. Gruner. With an Introduction by Mrs Jameson*. London 1845, pl. x. British Library, London (1267.k.7).

Professor Ludwig Grüner, who acted as artistic adviser to the Royal Household, selected the artists to be commissioned, and later wrote a foreword for and illustrated a guide to the pavilion written by Anna Jameson. The pavilion was intended to harmonize visual solemnity and sentiment through the juxtaposition of lyrical and historical subjects. According to Mrs Jameson, "Within a small compass, three different styles of decoration, the Cinque-Cento, the Antique, and the Romantic, have been placed in proximity".[28] In its 'Octagon Room', Clarkson Stanfield, Thomas Uwins, Charles Leslie, Sir William Ross, Edwin Landseer, Daniel Maclise, William Dyce and Sir Charles Eastlake painted lunettes based on Milton's *Comus*. In the central room, E.W. Dallas, H.J. Townsend, C. Stonehouse, James Severn and Richard Doyle painted landscapes and subjects from the poetry and prose of Sir Walter Scott. S.B. Stephens undertook *stucchi* and bas-reliefs on pilasters. Mrs Jameson praised the scheme and its inspired patronage, saying:

> In this country, till lately, Artists have rarely been employed in combinations in the Pictorial decoration of Architecture ... Even the most sanguine must feel that in what has been so auspiciously commenced under the immediate direction of Her Majesty and His Royal Highness Prince Albert, a new and important field of study and employment has been opened to the English Artist.[29]

Others were less enamoured with the project, as, despite being painted by British artists, it was orchestrated by a foreign artist, Grüner. Stylistically and technically the scheme was indebted to Nazarene influence. The restrained linearity and stage-like composition of Dyce's design for *Comus V, 968–75* echoes the work of Cornelius and Overbeck. An anonymous critic for the *Athenaeum* related the garden pavilion to the projects proposed at Westminster. Having seen the results of Grüner's artistic directorship, the critic said:

> We hope the next piece of royal patronage will be intrusted [*sic*] absolutely to some one of our own artists. These, we think may fairly ask for a chance. We could find half a dozen mere pupils of the School of Design, in whose decorative tact we should have more confidence than in the motley caprices of Mr. Gruner.[30]

Although Prince Albert's artistic loyalties were continually under public scrutiny, he threw himself vigorously into his self-appointed role as Britain's answer to Ludwig I. His overwhelming interest in contemporary art was often caricatured in *Punch*, which portrayed him

Cartoon of Prince Albert, *Punch's Pencillings. – N°.XXI. Cupid out of Place, From a Sketch Made in 'The Palmerston Gallery'*, published in *Punch, or the London Charivari*, I, 1841, p. 247.

as ineffectual in matters of state but forceful in the more effete world of art. The prince engaged in close working relationships with artists working in the Palace of Westminster, especially William Dyce and Daniel Maclise, whom he supported through private as well as public commissions. Albert purchased Dyce's *Madonna and Child* when it was exhibited at the Royal Academy Exhibition of 1846, and in the following year invited him to paint the Nazarene-inspired fresco *Neptune Resigning the Empire of the Sea to Britannia* at Osborne House, the royal family's retreat on the Isle of Wight. The prince's support of Maclise's scheme for the Royal Gallery extended to collaboration: he contributed costume details in Maclise's sketchbook for *The Meeting of Wellington and Blücher after the Battle of Waterloo* (see illus., p. 222). Before his untimely death in 1861, Prince Albert had won the admiration and respect of the British art world. Eastlake remarked that while discussing fine-art issues with Prince Albert "two or three times I quite forgot who he was – he talked so naturally and argued so fairly".[31] In practical terms, the artists themselves often found that they were hindered rather than helped by the prince's enthusiasm. While working at Osborne House, William Dyce wrote to Charles West Cope, warning him of what he might have to endure as he painted in the Lords Chamber:

So you begin to work in the Peers' House on Monday. Much success to you. Only when you are about to paint a sky seventeen feet long by some four or five broad, I don't

William Dyce, *Neptune Resigning the Empire of the Sea to Britannia*, fresco, 1847. Osborne House, Isle of Wight.

advise you to have a Prince looking in upon you every ten minutes or so – or when you are going to trace an outline, to obtain the assistance of the said Prince and an Archduke Constantine to hold up your tracing to the wall, as I have had; it is very polite, condescending, and so forth, but rather embarrassing for the artist.[32]

As has often been said, the death of the Prince Consort in 1861 – following that of Charles Barry in 1860 – accelerated the demise of the Fine Arts Commission, ending a systematic approach to the decoration of the new Palace of Westminster. Although the Westminster Hall competitions had been successful, for the most part the dealings of the Fine Arts Commission had been viewed cynically by the press and public. By the 1850s many of the winning artists had lost heart in the projects they had undertaken, finding themselves working in dismal physical conditions out of a sense of honour rather than for fair financial reward. The new high-art tradition that the commission hoped to establish did not take immediate effect in the public realm. George Frederick Watts, a prize-winner in the competitions of 1843 and 1847, was to struggle until the late 1860s to stimulate public interest in his high-art style, as opposed to his portraits. The idea that the Fine Arts Commission would give impetus to public-spirited decorative schemes was misplaced. Watts's offer to decorate Euston Station for the cost of materials and scaffolding alone was rejected by the London and North Western Railway Company, whereas private patrons such as the Marquess of Lansdowne were keen to have him paint frescoes in their country houses. Despite having the royal seal of approval, the stylistic links of Nazarene art with Catholic Italian art of the quattrocento and cinquecento contributed to an underlying resistance to its being embraced wholeheartedly in Britain. The decoration of public buildings held definite Catholic associations, with which many British public institutions were reluctant to align themselves. By the 1860s there were more art patrons and professional artists in Britain than ever before, but this can be related to the growth of a middle-class economy rather than initiatives in Westminster. The Fine Arts Commission failed to democratize fine art outside the Palace of Westminster to any noticeable extent. Indeed, private benefactors were relied upon to see

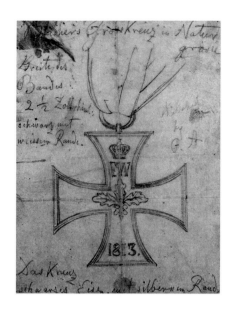

Prince Albert, *Sketch of Blucher's Gold Cross*, from Daniel Maclise and Prince Albert, *Sketchbook for The Meeting of Wellington and Blücher after the Battle of Waterloo*, pencil, 1858–61. Palace of Westminster (WOA 4496).

BELOW LEFT: Prince Albert, *Sketch of Military Uniform*, from Daniel Maclise and Prince Albert, *Sketchbook for The Meeting of Wellington and Blücher after the Battle of Waterloo*, 1858–61. Palace of Westminster (WOA 4496).

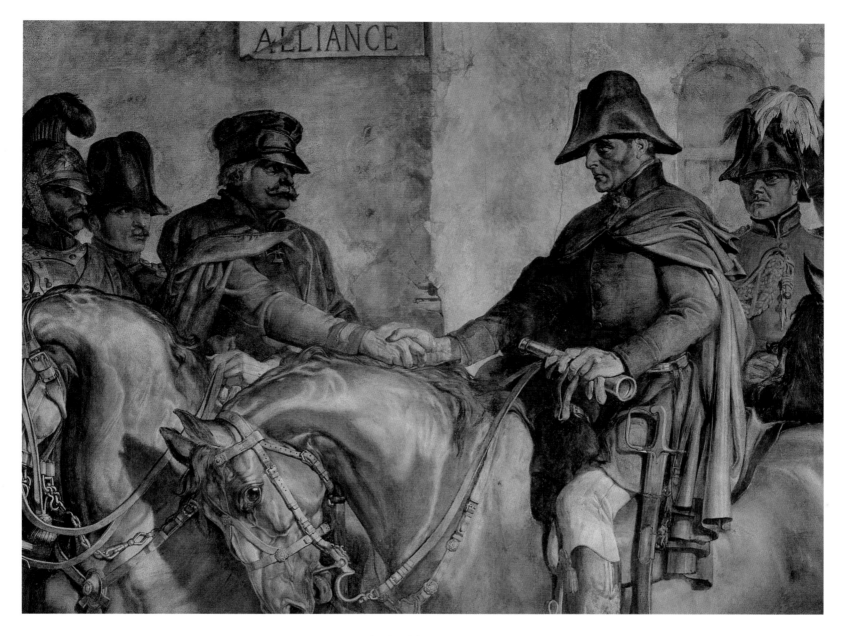

Daniel Maclise, *The Meeting of Wellington and Blücher after the Battle of Waterloo* (detail), waterglass, 1861. When comparing the fresco with the sketches, it is evident that the figure of Blücher was after Prince Albert. Royal Gallery, House of Lords, Palace of Westminster (WOA 3246).

OPPOSITE, RIGHT: Prince Albert, *Sketch of Military Uniform* from Daniel Maclise and Prince Albert, *Sketchbook for The Meeting of Wellington and Blücher after the Battle of Waterloo*, 1858–61. Palace of Westminster (WOA 4496). See above.

the decoration of the building complete. When the East Corridor and St Stephen's Hall came to be decorated, the paintings were funded not by the state but by individual benefactors. Charles West Cope predicted this dissipation of government art patronage with the loss of Prince Albert's guidance:

> The lamented death of the Prince Consort put an end to the Royal Commission of Fine Art, and the paltry sum of £4,000 per annum was considered too large for the British nation to expend on works of national art, and was withdrawn ... if the niggardly parsimony of the Government continues, may not private liberality step forward in its place, and do what it has done in other directions from a sense of noble patriotism? The loss to the nation by the death of the Prince Consort, in all matters of fine art (as well as in other directions), is irreparable, endowed as he was with bright intelligence, refined taste and enthusiastic interest.[33]

# 14

## "God Help the Minister who Meddles in Art": History Painting in the New Palace of Westminster

William Vaughan

The large paintings of historical scenes on the walls of the Palace of Westminster do not immediately stand out from the rich decorations that surround them.[1] However, they are worthy of consideration in their own right. They are, on the whole, fine examples of history painting, and provide an overview of this art as it developed in the Victorian period and in the early twentieth century. The subjects that they depict – ranging through British history from the Dark Ages to the Battle of Waterloo – were selected by a succession of government commissions. They can tell us much about the image of Britain and of its democratic processes that Parliament, through the agency of its Commissioners, wished to project at the height of the country's political and economic ascendancy.

These paintings also bear witness to a succession of attempts to provide public support for monumental history painting in Britain. During the period in which they were made, it was still believed that the noblest undertaking for a painter was the creation of heroic history paintings: the celebration of great men at great moments in a grand and idealized style, in the manner of Italian Renaissance artists such as Raphael and Michelangelo. Britain's failure to produce such art was regarded as something of a national disgrace – particularly as the French had been so successful in the field, with major practitioners such as Jacques-Louis David, Jean August Dominique Ingres and Eugène Delacroix dominating the international scene from the late eighteenth century into the nineteenth.

The situation was made all the more poignant by the fact that a large commercial market had developed for painting, in which its 'lesser' forms – in particular portraiture, landscape and genre – flourished. Art in Britain was commercial, not ideal. Only state support and intervention could turn the tide in favour of the higher forms of painting.

The new Palace of Westminster offered an opportunity, it seemed, to set this state of affairs to rights. Its vast walls were surely the perfect site for the government to commission patriotic history paintings on an unprecedented scale. But not all agreed. "God help the minister who meddles in art" was the Whig leader Lord Melbourne's response, when lobbied on the matter by the history painter Benjamin Robert Haydon.[2] There were political objections to state intervention. Larger-scale didactic historical painting smacked of absolutism. It conjured up images of Louis XIV at Versailles and of Catholic propaganda in Italian churches. Such an art, it seemed to some, was at odds with the Protestant and democratic spirit of Britain.

Such arguments might have prevailed at this time, as they had done in the past, had it not been for growing concerns about the need for state intervention to ameliorate economic and social problems. On the economic side, there was the fear that British manufacture was

Sir Edward John Poynter, *St George for England* (study for mosaic in Central Lobby; detail), oil on ceramic blocks, 1868/69. Palace of Westminster (WOA 1986).

falling behind that of its competitors, primarily because of inferior design. The technological revolution had enabled products to be made cheaply and in vast quantity. But mechanization had destroyed traditional craft practices and apprenticeship. After a select committee had explored the problem in 1836, the government took the unprecedented step of setting up state-funded schools of design throughout the country.[3] Such initiatives found their greatest expression later in the century with the Great Exhibition of 1851 and the creation of the South Kensington Museums.

It might seem something of a leap from training designers to commissioning large history paintings for the walls of the new palace. But concern about the growing social problems in Britain promoted the idea of art as a social healer. One of the arguments for setting up the National Gallery in a grand, new, purpose-built public building, for example, was that it would enable the poorer classes to receive the beneficial effects of aesthetic experience. In 1832, when this issue was being debated in Parliament, Sir Robert Peel envisaged that it would lead to "the cementing of bonds of union between the richer and poorer orders of state".[4]

In 1841, despite the opposition of Charles Barry, Parliament decided to fund the decoration of its new home with murals, both to stimulate high art and for the benefit of the public.[5] A Royal Commission of Fine Arts was set up to direct the process. It was chaired by Prince Albert, recently arrived from Germany, where there was a strong tradition of state funding of public art for moral purposes. As there was some concern whether British artists actually possessed the necessary skills to produce such work, it was decided to hold an open competition. This was for 'cartoons' (that is, designs for pictures) on subjects from British history. The results of the first competition were exhibited in Westminster Hall in 1843, and were followed by subsequent competitions and exhibitions (again publicly displayed in the hall).[6] The exhibitions aroused great public interest, but there were, of course, critical voices. In *Punch*, the cartoonist John Leech suggested that providing art for the starving to contemplate was hardly the best way to solve their problems. However, official enthusiasm was by now running high, and, after the various competitions, a group of artists was given commissions to begin painting murals in the House of Lords and adjacent spaces.

In choosing subjects, the Fine Arts Commission took great care to attend to the functions of the rooms for which the works were destined. The secretary and guiding spirit of the commission was Sir Charles Eastlake, a painter of great scholarship and earnestness who was eventually to become both President of the Royal Academy and Director of the National Gallery. Eastlake emphasized that each part of the palace was to express "some specific idea", and that, in choosing these ideas, "the especial destination of each portion of the building should be attended to".[7]

The decoration of the tall arched recesses on the north and south walls of the Lords Chamber was the first part of the scheme to be implemented. Of the four artists who worked there, two – William Dyce and Daniel Maclise – had established reputations as history painters. Their work was severe and archaic in style – reflecting the influence of the German revivalist painters, the Nazarenes, who then enjoyed an international reputation for their high-minded murals. Indeed, this 'German Manner', as it became known, was associated with the palace in general, and to some extent undermined the reputation of the work created there.[8] Yet, in fact, neither Dyce nor Maclise were direct imitators of these artists. Dyce made an extended tour of Italy before painting his work *The Baptism of King Ethelbert*, and sought to base his art directly upon the examples of mural painters of the fifteenth and sixteenth centuries.

The pictures were painted in fresco – a technique insisted on by the commission, both

John Leech, *Substance and Shadow*, published in *Punch, or the London Charivari*, v, 13 July 1843, p. 23.

for its association with the grand and idealized art of the Renaissance, and, on a more practical level, so that, according to Barry, the "paintings should be wholly free from gloss on the surface, so that they may be perfectly seen and fully understood from all points of view".[9] The commission also felt that the style and medium associated with the Renaissance was appropriate for the new building, as:

> The Tudor Style of Gothic (the style of the Palace of Westminster) is coeval with the highest developments of art in Italy; and the buildings erected in the time of Henry VII or Henry VIII might have been decorated by the hand of Raphael, had he accepted the invitation of the last-named monarch to visit England.[10]

The subjects were chosen to represent the three constituencies of the Lords: 'Chivalry' for the Lords temporal, 'Religion' for the Lords spiritual and 'Justice' for the Law Lords. Each subject was depicted both allegorically and as a historical instance. Thus, for example, the *Spirit of Justice* by Daniel Maclise was matched by *Prince Henry Acknowledging the Authority of Chief Justice Gascoyne* by Charles West Cope. The allegories were painted on the wall facing the monarch's throne and the historical events were painted on the wall behind the throne, facing the assembled Lords themselves.[11]

It is significant that the earliest subject here, Dyce's *Baptism of King Ethelbert*, should have been taken from Saxon times, for modern Britain was seen as having its origins in the

BELOW LEFT: Charles West Cope, *Edward III Conferring the Order of the Garter on the Black Prince*, fresco, 1848. South Gallery, Lords Chamber, House of Lords, Palace of Westminster (WOA 2965).

BELOW RIGHT: William Dyce, *The Baptism of King Ethelbert*, fresco, 1846. South Gallery, Lords Chamber, House of Lords, Palace of Westminster (WOA 2964).

nature and political organizations of the Saxons. The only instance of subjects from an earlier period are the Arthurian subjects that were painted by Dyce in the Robing Room between 1852 and his death in 1864. Set at the south end of the palace, this chamber, in which the monarch robes, before proceeding to the Lords Chamber on such occasions as the State Opening of Parliament, can be seen as the beginning of a progression through the building, from the royal domain to the aristocratic and finally to that of the Commons. King Arthur, being semi-mythical in nature, seemed appropriate for the representation of abstract values – particularly since the Arthurian legend was largely known through such courtly medieval narratives as that of Sir Thomas Malory.[12] They also accorded with the essentially symbolic role that the monarchy by that time performed in British government, a role that Victoria and Albert were endeavouring to endow with a new moral authority. Each scene represented a virtue. Thus, the central painting facing the royal throne, *The Vision of Sir Galahad and his Company*, stood for 'Religion' (see illus., p. 248, top). As appropriate to this mystical theme, the treatment of the work is severe, hierarchical and symmetrical, like an altarpiece. The other pictures demonstrated the values of 'Courtesy', 'Mercy', 'Generosity' and 'Hospitality' (see chapter 15).

The Royal Gallery is a large ceremonial space through which the monarch processes towards the Lords Chamber. In line with its public nature, it was seen as a space in which great events could be celebrated. The Fine Arts Commission, in their Seventh Report of

ABOVE LEFT: Daniel Maclise, *The Spirit of Justice*, fresco, 1849. North Gallery, Lords Chamber, House of Lords, Palace of Westminster (WOA 2967).

ABOVE RIGHT: Charles West Cope, *Prince Henry Acknowledging the Authority of Chief Justice Gascoyne*, fresco, 1849. South Gallery, Lords Chamber, House of Lords, Palace of Westminster (WOA 2966).

Daniel Maclise, *The Death of Nelson*, waterglass, 1865. Royal Gallery, House of Lords, Palace of Westminster (WOA 3247).

Charles West Cope, *Maclise under Difficulties, H[ouse] of Lords*, pencil. Palace of Westminster (WOA 918).

1847, designated it as a site for subjects relating "to the military history and glory of the country".[13] At the suggestion of Barry, the huge wall space in this room was divided up into eighteen compartments, and subjects were selected ranging from Roman Britain (*Boadicea Inciting Her Army*) to the Napoleonic Wars (*The Meeting of Wellington and Blücher after the Battle of Waterloo*).[14] In the event, only two of these, the facing central murals of *Waterloo* and *The Death of Nelson at the Battle of Trafalgar*, were completed. Commissioned in 1857, they were not finished until 1865, by which time the artist, Daniel Maclise, was old and sick. The rest of the commission was cancelled.

These murals were the only ones in the palace that received universal praise. Painted in waterglass – a technique Maclise turned to because of the difficulties he found in working in fresco – they have the powerful design and severe drawing style that was expected of great history painting. Above all, the artist demonstrated a formidable skill in organizing large numbers of figures – a necessary skill for a painter of battles. The whole scheme was a direct descendant of Soane's Royal Gallery, which was also to have had a military theme, featuring scenes of Waterloo and Trafalgar.[15] In a wider context, it was undoubtedly intended to rival the grand history paintings of the French. It may even have been conceived as a British

rejoinder to the vast Gallery of Battles at Versailles (constructed in 1833), which contains thirty-four paintings of French military triumphs, including five from the Napoleonic Wars. It was natural enough for the Victorians to see Britain's finest hour as the defeat of Napoleon, marked by the two key battles of Trafalgar (1805) and Waterloo (1815). By the time Maclise was at work commemorating these battles, British military confidence was somewhat shaken by the uncertain outcome of the Crimean War (1854) and by the shock of the 'Indian Mutiny' (1857). All the more need, therefore, to remember former triumphs with a display of heroic and muscular manliness.

The Prince's Chamber, decorated between 1852 and 1855, brought into focus a different aspect of state support of the arts, for here there was a strong emphasis on the decorative arts. The last stage of the Royal Procession towards the Lords Chamber, its theme is the House of Tudor, the dynasty that restored the fortunes of England after the Wars of the Roses and that was the last to enjoy supreme monarchical power. Strictly speaking, historical painting is not present in this room. However, historical subject matter abounds in the vigorously rendered bas-reliefs by the sculptor William Theed, which depict scenes from the Tudor period.[16] Above these are a range of images of the Tudor monarchs and their immedi-

Daniel Maclise, *The Meeting of Wellington and Blücher after the Battle of Waterloo*, waterglass, 1861. Royal Gallery, House of Lords, Palace of Westminster (WOA 3246).

ate relatives, accompanied by their numerous consorts, which were based as far as possible on contemporary portraits.[17] They were carried out by Richard Burchett and his pupils from the Royal College of Art, one of the government schools of design, and evoke the style of the Tudor period by incorporating such archaic features as gold backgrounds that imitate embossed leather. It is because they were seen as essentially decorative pieces that they were able to flout the naturalistic conventions that still dominated fine art in the Victorian period.

In the corridors that lead from the Peers Lobby to Central Lobby (Peers Corridor) and from Central Lobby to Members Lobby (Commons Corridor) a very different ethos predominates. This is the route to the committee rooms and the House of Commons, where the day-to-day business of government is enacted. The sumptuousness of the state apartment is replaced by sober, symbolic and decorative history pictures in a more naturalistic style. This was designated the appropriate place to display scenes from the seventeenth century, a critical period in British history that encompassed the Civil War, the Interregnum and the Glorious Revolution of 1688, during which monarchical power was challenged and eventually made subject to a constitution.[18]

The mood of this part of the scheme is altogether more relaxed and vernacular than in

Richard Burchett, with the assistance of students from the Royal School of Art, *Henry VIII*, oil on panel, 1854–60. Prince's Chamber, House of Lords, Palace of Westminster (WOA 3190).

William Theed, *Raleigh* [sic] *Spreading his Coat as a Carpet for Queen Elizabeth I*, bronze bas-relief, 1855. Prince's Chamber, House of Lords, Palace of Westminster (WOA S100).

Charles West Cope, *Charles I Raising his Standard at Nottingham, 1642*, fresco, 1861. Peers Corridor, House of Lords, Palace of Westminster (WOA 2898).

the parts of the palace that engage with regal power. The painters for the two corridors – Charles West Cope for the Peers Corridor leading out of the Lords and Edward Matthew Ward for the Commons Corridor leading into the Commons – practised a more popular brand of history painting than that of the severe and high-minded Dyce and Maclise. Their work had a 'historicist' tendency. It aimed to give a vivid and anecdotal treatment of the past, strongly influenced by the historical novels of Sir Walter Scott and the popular history paintings of their French contemporary, Paul Delaroche. Their paintings were the costume dramas of their age.

However, the intentions behind these pictures were by no means casual. The choice of subjects had been guided by the great historian Thomas Babington Macaulay, then Member for Edinburgh and on the point of writing his celebrated *History of England* (the first two volumes were published in 1848), in which the so-called 'Whig interpretation of history' received its classic formulation. For Macaulay, the triumph of the Glorious Revolution was the key to Britain's success, marking the moment when Parliament finally managed to curtail the power of the monarchy, paving the way for bourgeois ascendancy and providing a model for all other nations. As Macaulay's fellow commissioner Hallam put it, "No unbiased observer, who derives pleasure from the welfare of his species, can fail to consider the long and uninterruptedly increasing prosperity of England as the most beautiful phenomenon in the history of mankind."[19]

But while this narrative tells the story of the struggle for power in the seventeenth century, the scenes represented were intended to show that the conflict had been conducted by those involved with true British decency. The commission's deliberations over subject matter were therefore based "on the principle of parallelism, and that an attempt has been made to do justice to the heroic virtues which were displayed on both sides".[20] Thus, Cope's

*Charles I Raising his Standard at Nottingham, 1642* shows the ill-fated king conducting himself with heroic dignity. With similar circumspection, the commission chose to have Cope depict *The Burial of Charles I at Windsor*, rather than the king's execution.

Edward Matthew Ward's series in the Commons Corridor continues the story with events surrounding the Glorious Revolution. A friend of Macaulay's, he shared the historian's view that the everyday events of the past were as significant as major public occurrences. Scenes such as *The Last Sleep of Argyll* – showing an honourable man condemned to death and sleeping soundly and guilt-free just hours before his execution – exemplify this more intimate approach.

These corridors were the last part of the integrated scheme, as laid down by the commissioners of 1847, to be carried out. The other corridors and Central Lobby had to wait for later generations to complete them, invariably not in accordance with the original scheme.

Other parts of the original scheme were, however, completed in the committee-room area of the palace. The Upper Waiting Hall, or 'Poets' Hall', was decorated with scenes from the works of the British poets – Chaucer, Spenser, Shakespeare, Milton, Dryden, Pope, Scott and Byron – by the younger, untried winners of the Westminster Hall competitions. One was John Tenniel – who soon became famous for producing a very different kind of political 'cartoon', as the principle illustrator for *Punch*. Another was the great monumental and symbolic painter George Frederick Watts. His winning entry for the 1846 oil-painting competition, *Alfred Inciting the Saxons to Prevent the Landing of the Danes*, is also preserved in

Edward Matthew Ward, *The Last Sleep of Argyll*, fresco, 1858. Commons Corridor, House of Commons, Palace of Westminster (WOA 2605).

the palace. Its tone was sufficiently heroic for it to become a butt of *Punch's* relentless campaign to send up the Westminster 'cartoons', as its illustration, with accompanying text by William Makepeace Thackeray, reveals:

> I was very much surprised to find that this figure was supposed to represent KING ALFRED standing on a plank, and inciting his subjects to go to sea, and meet the Danes. … They talk of air in pictures; there is, I must say, more *wind* in this than any work of art I ever beheld. It is blowing everywhere, and from every quarter! It is blowing the sail one way, the royal petticoat another, and it is almost blowing the royal hair off his Majesty's head. No wonder the poor English wanted a deal of encouraging before they could be brought to face such a tempest as that.[21]

In view of his status, it is surprising that Watts did not receive a commission in the palace, apart from his single scene in the Poets' Hall (now the Upper Waiting Hall), *The Red Cross Knight Overcoming the Dragon*, from Spenser's *Faerie Queen*. On the other hand, it is equally striking that none of the other major practitioners of idealist art were employed there, either. There are no paintings by Pre-Raphaelites, aesthetes or even 'Olympian' classicists such as Leighton to be found in the palace. Perhaps this was simply a matter of bad timing, the commission having run out of steam after the death of Prince Albert in 1861 – precisely the moment when most of these idealist artists were beginning to establish their reputations. On the other hand, it may have been that such romantic – and usually anti-modern – dreamers had little appeal to those who espoused the Whig interpretation of history, with its emphasis on fact and solid bourgeois progress.

Only in Central Lobby is there a passing glimpse of the dreamers. This occurs in the

John Rogers Herbert, *Shakespeare, 'King Lear Disinheriting Cordelia', King Lear, Act 1, Scene 1*, fresco, 1850. Upper Waiting Hall ('Poets Hall'), House of Commons, Palace of Westminster (WOA 2884).

OPPOSITE: George Frederic Watts, *Alfred Inciting the Saxons to Prevent the Landing of the Danes*, oil on canvas, 1846. Palace of Westminster (WOA 2958).

Caricature of George Frederic Watts, *Alfred Inciting the Saxons to Prevent the Landing of the Danes*, published in *Punch, or the London Charivari*, XII, 10 July 1847, p. 8.

mosaics of *St George for England* (see illus., p. 18) and *St David for Wales*, designed by Edward Poynter, one of the Victorian 'Olympians'. The scheme for these had been laid down by the commissioners in 1847, and shows a typical desire for conciliatory even-handedness. "Bearing in mind that the Hall [Central Lobby] is the central point of the whole building", the commissioners considered it appropriate that the "nationality of the Component parts of the United Kingdom should be the idea here illustrated and would be appropriately expressed by representations of the four Patron Saints".[22] Here, right in the centre of the building, as at the extreme southern end in the Robing Room, myth reappears. The use of mosaics reflects a development encouraged by both the government schools of design and the new aesthetic standards of Pre-Raphaelitism. For painting had been replaced by a craft. Mosaic was becoming increasingly fashionable for wall decoration at this time. It had early-Christian associations pleasing to the period, and was more durable than the problematic fresco technique. It can certainly be argued that it fits appropriately with the lavish decoration of the Central Lobby. The mosaic for both the patron saints and the lobby's ceiling was carried out by the Venetian firm of Salviati, who had achieved recent fame in London for the mosaic work they had executed on the Albert Memorial. Much later on, in the 1920s, the scheme was completed with mosaics after designs by Robert Anning Bell.[23]

The commissioners of 1847 had conceived major schemes for both St Stephen's Hall, which functions as part of the public entrance leading through to Central Lobby, and for the East Corridor, positioned between Central Lobby and the Lower Waiting Hall, the public access to the first-floor Committee Corridor. The hall was intended to depict "the greatest epochs in our constitutional, social, and ecclesiastical history", from the Anglo-Saxon

ABOVE LEFT: Sir Edward John
Poynter, *St David for Wales*, mosaic, 1869.
Central Lobby, House of Commons,
Palace of Westminster (WOA 4255).

ABOVE RIGHT: Robert Anning Bell,
*St Andrew for Scotland*, mosaic, 1923.
Central Lobby, House of Commons,
Palace of Westminster (WOA 4256).

conversion to Christianity to the accession of the House of Stuart.[24] The intention for the East Corridor was to illustrate on one side the period prior to the introduction of Christianity, when "Britain appears sunk in ignorance, heathen superstition, and slavery", balanced on the opposite side by events occurring after the Glorious Revolution (depicted in the Commons Corridor), wherein a now politically enlightened and socially civilized, Christian Britain is shown offering paternal guidance to the 'ignorant' and 'uncivilized' world.[25] In retrospect, it is probably as well that the original scheme was not carried out, since it was based on that aspect of the Whig interpretation of history least acceptable today: the justification of colonial expansion.

Instead, the East Corridor and St Stephen's Hall were decorated by two separate initiatives. The first, decided on by a Lords select committee in 1906, depicts scenes from the time of the Tudors, beginning with the Wars of the Roses and leading up to the time of Mary I,[26] under the supervision of the distinguished American-born decorative artist and history painter Edward Austin Abbey. There is a strong emphasis on colour and decorative design in these works, and most of the artists involved – such as Henry A. Payne and John Byam Shaw – were strongly influenced by the later Pre-Raphaelites and the Arts and Crafts Movement. The sequence celebrating the Tudors was completed by the commissioning of Solomon J. Solomon's highly theatrical *The Commons Petitioning Queen Elizabeth to Marry*, which was sited at the top of the Committee Staircase.[27] These works, indeed, are among the most elegant, vibrant and appealing in the palace. They contribute to the rich sense of ornamentation – whereby the nation's history is portrayed as a decorative pageant – that runs throughout the building, keeping didactic intent to a minimum.

Something of the same mood prevails in the last scheme to be completed, although it is on a grander scale. A plan to decorate St Stephen's Hall and the East Corridor had been devised in 1907. However, little progress was made, and a new scheme was drawn up in 1925 by a committee under the chairmanship of Sir Henry Newbolt, the celebrated writer of patriotic and nautical verse, best remembered for his poem *Drake's Drum*.[28] The overall theme of the project was 'The Building of Britain'[29] – a poignant one in the mid-1920s, when attempts were being made to restore the nation after the shattering effects of war and industrial strife. It was also a time when the colonial view of British achievement still pertained. So the series covered not only the emergence during the Middle Ages of a Britain independent of foreign influence, starting with Colin Gill's *King Alfred's Longships Defeat the Danes*, but went on to celebrate the establishment of British influence both in America, with Alfred K. Lawrence's *Queen Elizabeth Commissions Raleigh* [sic] *to Sail for America*, and in the East with Sir William Rothenstein's *Sir Thomas Roe at the Court of Ajmir, 1614*, depicting an incident that the Prime Minister, Stanley Baldwin, described as "the first impact of English influence in the East" when he unveiled the paintings on 28 June 1927.[30] As Newbolt later wrote, the intention of the series was "to awake us to the

Henry A. Payne, *Plucking the White and Red Roses in Old Temple Gardens*, oil on canvas, 1910. East Corridor, House of Commons, Palace of Westminster (WOA 2593).

greatness and wonder of our growth as a nation, our evolution from a group of tribal states to a world-wide Commonwealth".[31]

While seeking to rebuild confidence in Britain's achievement, this series also set out to rebuild the fortunes of painting. One of the members of the committee that drew up the scheme was the Earl of Crawford and Balcarres, who was chairman of the Fine Arts Commission that had been set up in 1924. Like its Victorian predecessor, this body sought to stimulate a new era of heroic public mural painting in the country. While this might seem to have been a very old-fashioned concept in the 1920s, it was, in a sense, highly relevant. For this was a period when vast new public mural schemes were being commissioned in America, Mexico and Soviet Russia. In the age of the common man, there was a new role for public didactic art. The fact that St Stephen's Hall was part of the route by which the public came in to watch the debates in the Commons Chamber – and therefore the part of the palace most visited – must have strengthened the resolve to adorn it with images that were powerful and instructive. Newbolt's committee stipulated that the designs must have a homogenous char-

Solomon Joseph Solomon, *The Commons Petitioning Queen Elizabeth to Marry*, oil on canvas, 1911. Committee Staircase, House of Commons, Palace of Westminster (WOA 2928).

ABOVE LEFT: Glyn Warren Philpot, *Richard I Leaving England for the Crusades, 1189*, oil on canvas, 1925–27. St Stephen's Hall, House of Commons, Palace of Westminster (WOA 2601).

ABOVE RIGHT: Sir George Clausen, *The English People Reading Wycliffe's Bible*, oil on canvas, 1925–27. St Stephen's Hall, House of Commons, Palace of Westminster (WOA 2603).

acter, and therefore "must be the work of a single artist or of a team working together in the closest understanding and fellowship".[32] In the event, the latter course was chosen, and eight artists received commissions, working under the general directorship of Sir David Young Cameron, RA. The artists ranged from the veteran Sir George Clausen (born 1852) to Walter T. Monnington, fifty years his junior. Although the style of each is distinct, there is a general leaning towards colourful and decorative effect, which gave them more general appeal than many of the murals in the palace. Some – notably Glyn Philpot's *Richard I Leaving England for the Crusades* – have a truly heraldic splendour. Clausen's harmonious and tranquil *The English People Reading Wycliffe's Bible* was, apparently, a particular favourite with the public of the period – perhaps because it represented what one review described as the "quiet poetry of the English countryside".[33] In general, the scheme presents British history as cheerful and colourful – like the illustrations in children's history books of the period.

These were the last murals to be installed in the Palace of Westminster. But it was not meant to be so. Emboldened by the relative success of The Building of Britain, the commission decided to complete the unfinished scheme of the Royal Gallery, where Maclise's great Napoleonic battle scenes were displayed. The internationally renowned Frank Brangwyn, a veteran of mural painting, was chosen. In continuation of the spirit of The Building of Britain, the theme was to be a celebration of the products of empire. Brangwyn approached the theme with characteristic brilliance and ebullience – an ebullience that proved too much for the Royal Commission, which rejected the first of the works when they went on display in 1930. Brangwyn went on to complete the series, which was shown at the *Daily Mail Ideal Home Exhibition* in 1933, and was subsequently installed in the Assembly Hall of the city of Swansea's new Guildhall in 1934 (illus., p. 26). "As so often happens," remarked Dennis Farr in his account of the fiasco, "the panjandrums of official taste played for safety."[34]

The history-based mural schemes initiated in the new Palace of Westminster between the 1840s and 1920s reveal more about the cultivation of national self-imagery over almost a century than they do about the historic events or moments depicted. Through these images, we learn less about the past itself than we do about artistic and political interpretations of the past. In the end, the eagerness of the Royal Fine Arts Commission of 1841 to stimulate a national style of monumental painting, to vie with that of the continent, had little influence beyond the walls of the new palace itself. Nevertheless, the schemes that came to be painted undoubtedly fulfil the more local, but also important aim of articulating the function of the Palace of Westminster as a rich and ceremonial building, a true theatre of state.

# 15

## Myth and Monarchy: Chivalric Legends for the Victorian Age

Debra N. Mancoff

To prepare for the annual State Opening of Parliament, the monarch enters the Robing Room, and, in that simple act of passage, travels from the realm of history into that of mythology. In this private chamber – the royal inner sanctum – decorated with frescoes of the heroes of Arthurian legend, a metamorphosis takes place. Donning ceremonial robes, the temporal ruler is transformed from the monarch to 'monarchy'. Surrounded by his or her retinue, the monarch then processes to the Lords Chamber, where, in sight of frescoes extolling the virtues of Religion, Chivalry and Justice, the members of the House of Lords are assembled. Crowned and robed in ermine and velvet, the king or queen is enthroned. This ritual serves to denote the relationship of the monarch, as Head of State, with Parliament. The decorative scheme that sets the stage for this annual ceremony serves as a statement of national idealism, based on an iconography forged during the reign of Queen Victoria.

From a modern perspective, the visual programme – with its wealth of armed warriors and courtly knights – seems burnished with a romantic nostalgia. But the iconography, conceived for Queen Victoria, encodes an ideal of contemporary identity. In the early nineteenth century, the nation's strength was attributed to its enduring social structure of paternity and hierarchy, situated in the traditional bases of power: class and gender. But those bases were changing. Wealth was shifting from patrimony to industry. The Reform Bill of 1832 brought expanded enfranchisement, and, through this, new voices were heard throughout Parliament.[1] And, more significantly, the new sovereign was a young woman. The scheme chosen to decorate the chambers in which she would incarnate monarchy reveals how masculine icons of an older era were redefined to provide a symbolic rationale for a female monarch ruling over a modern state.

The primary formulation of that rationale can be seen in the selection of subjects for the six frescoes planned for the Lords Chamber. In the summer of 1844, the Fine Arts Commission proposed a scheme of paired allegories and narratives, stating that:

> ... six arched compartments in the House of Lords shall be DECORATED with FRESCO PAINTINGS; that the subjects of such Fresco-paintings shall be ... personifications or abstract representations of Religion, Justice, and the Spirit of Chivalry, and that the three remaining subjects corresponding with such representations and expressing the relationship of the Sovereign to the Church, to the Law, and as the fountain of honour, to the State, shall be, The Baptism of Ethelbert; Prince Henry, afterwards Henry V, acknowledging the authority of Chief Justice Gascoigne [sic]; and Edward the Black Prince receiving the Order of the Garter from Edward III.[2]

Sir Edwin Landseer, *Queen Victoria and Prince Albert at the Bal Costumé of 12 May 1842* (detail), oil on canvas, 1842. The Royal Collection.

Six artists – John Callcott Horsley, William Cave Thomas, Daniel Maclise, Charles West Cope, Richard Redgrave, and William Dyce – were requested, without promise of commissions, to prepare designs for the assigned subjects. The competition was then opened to outside submissions, and in July 1845 a public exhibition, including 116 entries by thirty-nine artists, was held in Westminster Hall. Of the three allegories, *The Spirit of Justice* saw the most submissions, with a total of twelve; the narrative pendant, *Prince Henry Acknowledging the Authority of Justice Gascoyne*, had six. *The Spirit of Religion* drew eleven submissions, with the corresponding subject *The Baptism of Ethelbert* attracting six. Curiously, only five artists undertook interpretations of *The Spirit of Chivalry*, with only one artist – Cope, who had been assigned the subject – addressing the narrative *Edward III Conferring the Order of the Garter on the Black Prince*.[3]

Given the general enthusiasm for medievalism at this time, the subject selection among the competitors raises questions about attitudes toward chivalry in the early Victorian era. During the 1830s, the generation schooled in the romanticism of Sir Walter Scott's novels and Kenelm Henry Digby's *Broadstone of Honour* (1822) had come of age.[4] The equation of the medieval knight with the modern gentleman was popular among the upper classes. Some men chose to explore their chivalric identity through pretence and re-enactment, such as the ill-fated Eglinton Tournament of 1839, when a group of aristocratic men discovered that medieval martial arts required prowess beyond that possessed by the modern sportsman.[5] This fascination was extended throughout society, even to the monarchy. For example, on 12 May 1842, Queen Victoria and Prince Albert appeared at a costume ball held at Buckingham Palace dressed as the most renowned chivalric couple, Edward III and Queen Philippa (see illus., p. 240).[6] The sumptuous medieval costumes were designed by the queen herself. And in 1844, Victoria commissioned Robert Thorburn to paint a highly romanticized miniature of Albert in armour (still in the Royal Collection).

But chivalry and knighthood were also tied to a political movement. In the 1830s, the Tory party splintered in opposition to Sir Robert Peel's concessions towards the industrial class. The new or 'Radical' Tories advocated a protective position based on traditional obligations, a form of 'neo-feudalism' that aspired to a revived *noblesse oblige* and a return to the paternalistic order that demanded a humane altruism from the aristocratic élite. By 1841, neo-feudalism had a spokesman in Lord John Manners, a party in 'Young England' and an emblem in the chivalric knight. The party was short-lived; it split over the Corn Laws dispute in 1846.

When the members of the Fine Arts Commission selected an allegory of chivalry for the Lords Chamber, they confronted a loaded symbol. The class connotation, the ideological bias and the political affiliation gave specific resonance to any pictorial representation featuring a knight. But, by selecting chivalry as part of the iconography of the Lords Chamber, the commission diffused its partisan subtext while at the same time preserving its traditional aristocratic associations. It is possible to speculate as to why the commissioners included chivalry in the programme dealing with the relationship between Parliament and the monarchy. However, it is not possible to ascertain what they sought in terms of the actual allegorical representation. The minutes of their debates offer nothing beyond the phrase "the fountain of honour" as the bond between sovereign and state. The modest – and limited – response to the subject by the competition artists is proof of this uncertainty. Even after the exhibition, Charles Dickens wrote, "We should have liked to have seen the Commissioner's notion of the Spirit of Chivalry stated by themselves, in the first instance, on a sheet of foolscap, as the ground-plan of a model cartoon."[7]

In this light, the invitation extended by the commission to Maclise to submit a design

Daniel Maclise, *The Chivalric Vow of the Ladies of the Peacock*, oil on canvas, 1835. UK Government Art Collection.

for *The Spirit of Chivalry* reveals a calculated strategy. Maclise was the only prominent artist of the day with a recognized reputation in chivalric (as opposed to generically medieval) subjects. In 1830, three years after his arrival in London from Cork, he was hired as a staff artist for William Maginn's *Fraser's Magazine*, a journal with strong 'neo-feudalist' leanings. During his six-year tenure with the magazine, Maclise gained fame first as a painter of large-scale history paintings celebrating chivalric sentiment, such as *The Chivalric Vow of the Ladies of the Peacock*, and secondly for portraits of aristocratic sitters in armour, a supreme example being the family group for Sir Francis Sykes, a Tory baronet introduced to Maclise by Benjamin Disraeli. But it was his austere and heroic depiction *The Knight*, submitted as a Westminster competition cartoon in 1844, that brought him to the attention of the commissioners.[8]

Maclise's early ideas for *The Spirit of Chivalry* are recorded in two versions, one in oil and one in watercolour (Palace of Westminster collection), both completed in 1845. In the oil painting, Chivalry is personified by a demure woman wearing a Saxon cloak and laurel crown. In her left hand she holds a lily to her heart, as her right hand rests on an altar behind her. To her right stand stalwart knights, devoted veterans of her order. To her left are representatives of the clergy and the government, beneficiaries of her service. Surrounding the steps to her altar are those who immortalize her: the historian, the troubadour, the poet, the bard, the sculptor and the painter. A novice kneels at her feet, petitioning acceptance to her order. Ivy and the passion flower twine around the columns of the arcade in the background, a reminder of the forces that fuel chivalry's cause: fidelity and love.

The positive reception of the design confirmed the commission's selection. The *Athenaeum* described it as "the favourite design with the many", while the *Art-Union* saw in it "a strain of purest poetry", exclaiming, "Maclise's cartoon is unquestionably one of the most remarkable efforts of genius that has been produced in our time."[9] Charles Dickens, the most enthusiastic of all, wrote:

> Is it the Love of Woman, in its true and deep devotion that inspires you? See it here! Is it glory that the world has learned to call the pomp and circumstance of arms? Behold it at the summit of its exaltation, with its mailed hand resting on the altar where the Spirit ministers. The Poet's laurel-crown, which they who sit on thrones can neither twine nor wither – is that the aim of thy ambition? It is there.[10]

As Dickens's response reveals, Maclise intended the female personification of Chivalry in his allegory to be read as a muse. She is the passive inspiration of knightly quests. She holds court as an object of veneration. In the context of pervasive early-Victorian notions of gender and power, this image aptly conveyed the relationship of a *female* monarch with her exclusively male Parliament. Maclise mediated between the historical idea of chivalry and a resonant contemporary message, and in doing so universalized the image of the knight, stripping it of its partisan implications.

The first fresco executed in the Lords Chamber was Dyce's *Baptism of Ethelbert* (1846). The commissioners then instructed the artists to use Dyce's work – with its classicized detail and evocation of early Renaissance composition – as a model for style and quality. To this end, Maclise modified some details in his final execution. He replaced Chivalry's Saxon garments with a draped classical gown. He reduced the number of figures to lend clarity and unity to his grouping, making the visual entry to the centre of the composition – via the altar steps – more accessible. He made the background arcade lower and wider, with Corinthian columns replacing the Gothic, foliate design in his original conception. He also

Daniel Maclise, *Portrait of Sir Francis Sykes and his Family*, watercolour, 1839. Private collection.

Daniel Maclise, *The Spirit of Chivalry*, fresco, 1847. North Gallery, Lords Chamber, House of Lords, Palace of Westminster (WOA 2969).

Daniel Maclise, *The Spirit of Chivalry*, oil on canvas, 1845. Sheffield Art Galleries and Museums Trust.

added a motto to the veteran knight's sword belt: it reads "*A Dieu et aux Dames*", corresponding to the repeated inscription of the motto from the royal arms, "*Dieu et mon droit*", that Pugin used in the pierced frieze on the ceiling.

In 1849, the Lords Chamber ensemble was completed. When seated on the throne – located under a canopy with carved knights representing the five Orders of Chivalry – the monarch faced the three allegories: Horsley's *Spirit of Religion*, flanked by Maclise's *Spirit of*

*Chivalry* and *Spirit of Religion*. The assembled peers viewed the historical pendants painted above the monarch: Dyce's *Baptism of Ethelbert*, flanked by Cope's *Edward III Conferring the Order of the Garter on the Black Prince* and *Prince Henry Acknowledging the Authority of Chief Justice Gascoyne* (see chapter 14). While the queen aspired to the female spirits, the peers aspired to the history-based actions of men. Thus, taking her place on the throne as part of the allegorical scheme, Queen Victoria symbolized monarchy itself, a living counterpart to the female spirits on the walls before her.

Different strategies shaped the iconographic programme of the Robing Room, but with the same symbolic end. As early as 1844, the commissioners discussed the nature of the project, with Sir Charles Eastlake commenting, "In the Robing Room, the artist might endeavour to define the power and privileges, the virtues and duties, with which the throne is invested."[11] But no subject was selected. Four years later, on 5 September 1848, the commission informed the queen that William Dyce's service had been secured to design and execute an ensemble of frescoes based on the legends of King Arthur. There was no debate and no competition. The suggestion had come directly from Prince Albert, who had been a private patron of Dyce. But the subject selection was curious.

Sir Thomas Malory's *Le Morte d'Arthur*, written in 1469–70, had been among the many lost literary works recovered during the height of the Gothic Revival. Out of print since 1634, it remained an uncommon text until the years 1816 and 1817, when three new editions appeared.[12] In 1842, Alfred Tennyson published his first major Arthurian poems, including the epic *Morte d'Arthur*. This featured an epilogue that described the king's return to the modern world:

> There came a bark that blowing forward, bore
> King Arthur, like a modern gentleman

William Dyce, *Piety: The Departure of the Knights of the Round Table on the Quest for the Holy Grail*, watercolour, 1849. National Gallery of Scotland, Edinburgh.

William Dyce, *Religion: The Vision of Sir Galahad and his Company*, fresco, 1851. Robing Room, House of Lords, Palace of Westminster (WOA 3149).

Of stateliest port; and all the people cried,
"Arthur is come again: he cannot die."[13]

As this text suggests, the Arthurian legend evolved in relation to the ideals and aspirations of the various societies that adopted it. By identifying the mythical king as a "modern gentleman", Tennyson appropriated Arthur for the Victorian age. Equally, Dyce would find his greatest challenge in translating contemporary ethics into Arthurian-based pictorial allegory.

While the Arthurian writer of the 1840s could choose from a wide range of sources, the Arthurian artist faced an iconography almost without precedent. The legend had rarely been addressed by artists since the Middle Ages. Dyce was thus charged with a tall order. Just as Tennyson was to recast the legend for the general public in a vivid new form in his *Idylls of the King*, written in 1859–82, Dyce needed to bring the legend to life visually in a manner that reflected the specific needs and values of *his* audience. In the case of the queen's private chamber, it was a highly-select audience of one.

Prince Albert's suggestion for the scheme can be traced to a conversation with Dyce when he was working at Osborne House on the fresco *Neptune Resigning the Power of the Seas to Britannia* in 1847 (see illus., p. 221). Both men were deeply passionate about history painting and longed to see British artists in the field rival their continental counterparts. Dyce ventured that noble subjects inspired noble interpretations, and he speculated that the legends of Arthur and the Round Table, with "their great interest, their antiquity, and national chivalrous character, would surpass those of the 'Nibelungenlied', of which so much has been made by the Germans".[14] Within a week, the prince proposed to the commissioners that the Arthurian legend would provide the subjects for the Robing Room, and that Dyce be fully entrusted with the programme. This choice surprised Dyce, for he believed that

William Dyce, *Generosity: King Arthur Unhorsed by Sir Bors and Spared by Sir Launcelot*, fresco, 1852. Robing Room, House of Lords, Palace of Westminster (WOA 3150).

Maclise was better suited to the challenge.[15] But, after his initial hesitancy, the painter immersed himself in the project. From July 1848 to February 1849, he read extensively, supplementing Malory's canonical text with historical and archaeological studies, beginning his search with a desire to discover the 'real' Arthur. He wrote: "At one time I had some hopes that the researches of those who conceived that Arthur was not a real, but a mythical personage might be turned to account in determining the general plan of the series of pictures – but in this expectation I was disappointed."[16]

After months of reflection, as well as negotiation and debate with the commissioners, Dyce produced his plan. Rather than illustrate or narrate the legend, Dyce proposed to design seven frescoes in which "the Companions of the Round Table [appear] as personifications of certain moral qualities ... which make up an ancient idea of Chivalric greatness".[17] As in the Lords Chamber, chivalry was seen to be the supporting strength of monarchy. But the iconography also made an explicit contribution to the room's ritual purpose. When Queen Victoria entered, she shed her individual identity, as wife, mother and even queen regnant. For Parliament, she *became* monarchy, and the Robing Room's images of the mythic king – in symbolic terms her ideal consort – set the stage for the transformation.

In the late spring of 1849, Dyce submitted five designs to the commissioners, one of which was rejected.[18] The rejected design, *Piety: The Knights of the Round Table Departing on the*

BELOW LEFT: William Dyce, *Courtesy: Sir Tristram Harping to La Beale Isoud*, fresco, 1852. Robing Room, House of Lords, Palace of Westminster (WOA 3151).

BELOW RIGHT: William Dyce, *Mercy: Sir Gawain Swears to be Merciful and "Never to be against Ladies"*, fresco, 1854. Robing Room, House of Lords, Palace of Westminster (WOA 3152).

William Dyce, completed by
Charles West Cope, *Hospitality: The
Admission of Sir Tristram to the Fellowship of
the Round Table*, fresco, 1864–66. Robing
Room, House of Lords, Palace of
Westminster (WOA 3153).

*Quest for the Holy Grail*, preserved as a highly finished watercolour sketch, reveals the inter-pretative difficulties Dyce faced in turning a medieval literary epic into a set of modern icons of virtue. His research revealed that the Grail Quest was a troubling subject. In a letter to Eastlake, he described it as corrupt, "strongly tinctured with the monastic ideas of the 13th century, and seemingly, to some extent, intended to throw discredit on Chivalric greatness".[19] But the age and authenticity associated with the mystical saga convinced Dyce to include it. His solution was to suppress the religious element. In a long, stage-like compo-sition, he portrayed a scene described in Malory's *Morte d'Arthur* (XIII.vii), wherein the king and his court assemble to bid farewell and Godspeed to the knights departing on the quest. There is no vision of the Grail, no Grail Maiden, no angels as heavenly agents to guide and inspire the knights. Instead, at the far right, Arthur clasps his hand to his heart and seems to speak Malory's words of lamentation: "Ye have set me in great sorrow, for I have doubt that my true fellowship shall never meet again." It has often been suggested that the passionate presence of Sir Launcelot on his knees before Queen Guenevere led to the commissioners' decision to reject it. But given the incident portrayed – the knights defying the wishes of their sovereign – the image undermined, rather than reinforced, kingship. Little wonder it was rejected.

In its complete form, Dyce's programme presents a pantheon of heroes who serve monarchy. *Religion: The Vision of Sir Galahad and His Company* shows a physical rather than a spiritual Galahad; he appears as a corporeal manifestation of positive Christian endeavour. *Generosity: King Arthur Unhorsed Spared by Launcelot* personifies loyalty to the sovereign, show-ing Sir Launcelot preventing his cousin Sir Bors from slaying the fallen King. Two frescoes represent male deference to female honour. *Courtesy: Sir Tristram Harping to La Beale Isoud* represents the finer aspects of social graces that make a rugged warrior fit company for the 'fair sex'. In *Mercy: Sir Gawain Swearing to be Merciful and "Never be Against Ladies"*, Dyce placed Arthur's most rash knight on trial before Guenevere and her ladies. Both in sentiment and composition, this fresco echoes the message of Maclise's *Spirit of Chivalry* in the Lords Chamber.

Due to ill-health – and ultimately his waning interest – Dyce did not complete the Robing Room as planned. As early as 1852, he characterized his position as "a slave to my fresco labours in the Queen's Robing Room", and, throughout the remaining years, Dyce's procrastination proved a problem for the commissioners.[20] He did not begin the fresco *Hospitality: The Admission of Sir Tristram to the Fellowship of the Round Table* until 1859; it remained unfinished at his death in 1864. By this stage, work on *Hospitality* was well advanced, and was completed by Charles West Cope in 1866. But the final subjects proposed – *Courage: The Combat Between King Arthur, Sir Key, Sir Gawaine and Sir Griflet and Five Northern Kings* and *Fidelity: Sir Launcelot's Rescue of Queen Guenevere from King Meliagraunce* – were abandoned.[21] The iconographic programme was completed with eighteen bas-relief oak panels, carved by Henry Hugh Armstead. In addition, details such as the fabricated arms of the Knights of the Round Table painted on carved shields on the cornice extend the predominately masculine Arthurian themes in the room. However, the carved figures of medieval queens that line the upper part of the walls remind us once again that the Robing Room was created for a female monarch.

Taken together, the Lords Chamber and the Robing Room celebrate chivalry as an ideal that serves monarchy. But the connotations of this virtue, as expressed in the iconography within the Palace of Westminster, a setting for statecraft, not only redefined the medieval ideal for modern practice, but also advanced the significance of the chivalric knight beyond the romantic fascination of the Gothic Revival. As allegorized in these mutually supportive decorative schemes, chivalry was recognized as a part of the past that endured in the present: a symbol that informed – rather than constituted – reality.

Henry Hugh Armstead, *King Arthur Carried in a Barge to Avillon Attended by Queens*, oak relief, 1870. Robing Room, House of Lords, Palace of Westminster (WOA 5117).

# 16

## Sculpture and the New Palace of Westminster

Benedict Read

ABOVE: John Thomas, *Self-Portrait*, marble relief, *c.* 1850. Palace of Westminster (WOA S240).

LEFT: *Queen Victoria, Justice and Clemency* by John Gibson, seen from the Royal Gallery, Palace of Westminster. For the State Opening of Parliament the doors from the Royal Gallery to the Prince's Chamber are removed. Although it is often stated that Gibson's sculpture is too large for the relatively intimate proportions of the Prince's Chamber, the scale and position suggests that it was to be viewed from the Royal Gallery. The complementary pointed arches of the doorway and the sculpture's setting underline this.

We are told that the architect of the new Palace of Westminster, Charles Barry, had a very definite agenda for the decoration of the building: "His great idea was, by the aid of the sister arts, to make the New Palace a monumental history of England. Sculpture without, sculpture, painting and stained glass within, were to preserve the memorials of the past, and declare the date and object of the building. ... Not only did he desire to make his building a treasure-house of art and a sculptured memorial of our national history, but he also hoped to raise up in the course of its execution a school of decorative art, guided, but not servilely confined, by the examples of Gothic antiquity, and bringing to the evolution of Gothic principles all the resources of modern thought and science".[1]

This is obviously a post-dated account, and one that, written by the architect's son, might not be expected to be totally unbiased, so that ideas and ideologies may have become attached to it from other contemporary sources. There are nonetheless certain key elements to it: first, that the architect had his own ideas about decoration, which would obviously have a bearing on his dealings with any alternative authority that might be set up to take a role in this decoration, such as the Fine Arts Commission set up in 1841, of which Barry, though the architect of the building, was not a member; secondly, one should note the primary position in the quoted narrative given to sculpture, because in the succeeding histories of the building this is the one element that has been virtually forgotten and ignored.[2]

As far as the "sculpture without" is concerned, and to a certain extent some of that within, one should bear in mind certain practical conditions. Carved decorative stonework cannot be added superficially to a structure, like plaster or paint or wallpaper; it is integrally bedded in to the building process. Similarly with carved stone figures set in decorative niches: from an economic and logistical point of view, to have two distinct scaffolding operations running on separate schedules in such a vast building would cause serious delay and additional expenditure. Besides, the artisans responsible for both decorative carving and stone figurework, if they were not the same individuals, worked under a single section of the architect's office.

To superintend the ornamental and figurative stone carving at Westminster, Barry made an appointment soon after he had obtained the commission. Barry was still at work on the King Edward VI Grammar School at Birmingham, and there was a hold-up there in the supply of original models for workmen to use in executing ornamental bosses. One of these craftsmen, John Thomas, because of the delay had made one himself. Barry was so impressed with this he immediately took Thomas on for Westminster and sent him to Belgium to inspect original Late Gothic secular structures such as the town halls of Bruges, Ghent,

LEFT: View of Central Lobby showing
the sculptures of monarchs and consorts
*in situ.*

RIGHT: Exterior view of the south façade,
House of Lords, Palace of Westminster.

John Thomas, *Richard III*, stone, *c.* 1853.
Central Lobby, House of Commons,
Palace of Westminster (WOA S169).

Leuven (Louvain) and Ypres. Although Thomas was not formally appointed Superintendant of stone carving until 1846, Barry's arrangement with him had been sanctioned by the Office of Works from, at the latest, May 1841. By this time the building of the river, north and south fronts of the building was under way – in March 1843 Barry reported that a large quantity of "Masonry and Carving" was ready for setting in these areas.[3] Apart from the rich ornamental carving, there was sculpture on nearly all the main façades, consisting of figures of monarchs, other royalty, angels, saints, heraldic animals and coats of arms (an exception was made of Old Palace Yard, where figure work was excluded in sympathy with the treatment of the original Late Gothic Henry VII's Chapel opposite). There was also an extensive programme of such sculpture inside the building, particularly in the main circulation areas such as St Stephen's Hall and Central Lobby, which had a particular function as grand spaces.

Certain accounts of Thomas's work credit him not only with designing and modelling this sculpture but also with executing much of it himself. The figures of monarchs on the north front would have been among the first done as that was where the foundation stone had been laid in 1840. The plaster models of all the royal statues, from which the stone figures were executed, were valued so highly that when the programme was completed they were put on permanent display at the Crystal Palace, Sydenham, where they survived until the fire in 1936 that destroyed the building and its contents[4].

When the Fine Arts Commission was set up in 1841, its principal function was to see whether British art might be encouraged through the building of the new Palace of Westminster, and sculpture certainly featured within this brief. As mentioned before, though Barry was consulted by the commission, he was not a member of it, which led to some uncertainty of demarcation over areas of responsibility, sometimes (in relation to sculpture) with unfortunate results. Already in February 1843 Barry declared: "With respect to any further encouragement of the Fine Arts in the exterior of the building, I am not aware of any opportunities that offer, as arrangements have already been made for all the archetec-tonic or conventional sculpture that will be required to adorn the several elevations".[5] By this time, of course, Thomas was already at work.

Both parties, Barry and the commission, had ambitious plans for sculpture in the build-ing. In May 1843 the commission announced plans for "various statues in bronze and marble, of British Sovereigns and illustrious personages", and set out terms and conditions for an exhibition to be held in Westminster Hall in 1844 to which sculptors could submit their work.[6] In August 1843 Sir Robert Peel, the originator of the commission and an important member, reported that the House of Commons had proposed the commission should honour eminent civil, literary or scientific people with monuments in Parliament, and it should have full authority to consider any part of the building in which to incorporate these.[7]

In March 1844 Barry outlined his ideas to the commission. He had 220 niches available inside the building, but he also (he said) had room for 187 further non-architectural statues inside the building plus others outside, including his projected New Quadrangle in New Palace Yard, amounting to a total of 670 commemorative monuments, whether statues or sculptures fixed to the walls of the Quadrangle cloister. This number of sites could allow for the reincorporation of the monuments then seen by some as inappropriately filling the inte-riors of Westminster Abbey and St Paul's Cathedral in London.[8] At the same time the commissioners reported on their 1844 sculpture exhibition. They singled out the work of three sculptors who had exhibited, William Calder Marshall, John Bell and John Henry Foley,

John Thomas, models of monarchs and consorts for Central Lobby, Palace of Westminster, as exhibited at the Crystal Palace, Sydenham, destroyed in the fire of 1936. Parliamentary Works Directorate Archive.

Radclyffe after B. Sly, *Public exhibition of Frescoes and Sculpture* in Westminster Hall, engraving, 1844.

but as they did not yet know for certain when or where sculpture would feature in the building they were unable to proceed further.[9] They had nevertheless consulted the architect and were able to think in terms of statues for the Royal Gallery, either architectural or free-standing, 18 strictly architectural statues for the House of Lords Chamber, plus 68 niche statues and, if required, 24 free-standing ones for Central Lobby.[10]

In April 1845 the commissioners were able to give a more consolidated report on the sculptural programme. Two sub-committees had met to examine important topics. One of these studied the choice of subjects to be commemorated and included four historians – Sir Robert Harry Inglis MP, Antiquary to the Royal Academy between 1850 and 1855; Philip Henry Stanhope, sometime Viscount Mahon, again Antiquary to the Royal Academy between 1855 and 1875; and two major professional historians of different generations, Henry Hallam, author of, among other works, *The Constitutional History of England from the Accession of Henry VII to the Death of George II* of 1827, and last, but not least, Thomas Babington Macaulay, intermittent Member of Parliament between 1830 and 1857, whose *History of England from the Accession of James the Second* was to appear between 1848 and 1855. But he had already reviewed Hallam's *History* in 1828, including the significant observation for the programme of the commissioners: "History, at least in its state of ideal perfection, is a compound of poetry and philosophy. It impresses general truths on the mind by a vivid representation of particular characters [note] and incidents."[11]

With this sort of professional back-up, the sub-committee nominated 121 persons for commemoration, 63 unanimously, 58 by majority vote. The subjects came from a wide range of activities – political and parliamentary, legal, military, literary, artistic and architectural,

William Calder Marshall, *Edward Hyde, 1st Earl of Clarendon*, marble, 1847. St Stephen's Hall, House of Commons, Palace of Westminster (WOA S025).

View of St Stephen's Hall looking east towards Central Lobby, House of Commons, Palace of Westminster. Clockwise from left to right, William Murray, 1st Earl of Mansfield by Edward Hodges Baily, John, 1st Baron Somers by William Calder Marshall, Lucius Cary, 2nd Viscount Falkland by John Bell, Edward Hyde, 1st Earl of Clarendon (see above right) by William Calder Marshall, John Hampden (see illus., p. 60, top centre) and John Selden by John Henry Foley, Sir Robert Walpole, 1st Earl of Orford by John Bell, William Pitt, 1st Earl of Chatham and William Pitt the younger by Patrick MacDowell. The group is completed by Edmund Burke by William Theed and Henry Gratton by John Edward Carew. This photograph also shows The Building of Britain series described in chapter 14.

medical and general benefaction.[12] A separate sub-committee, though with the same members, came up with a programme for the Lords Chamber, consisting of selected Magna Carta signatories: the idea was first suggested by the sub-committee's chairman, who just happened to be Prince Albert. A detailed justification of the choice was provided by Hallam.[13]

In its main Report the commission confirmed the general outline of Barry's report the previous year. There were many placings for statues in niches, but because of their conformity with the Gothic architecture these were "uniformly narrow". There was scope for free-standing statuary but they could not be too definite about this as the architect had changed his design. They did, though, finalize the scheme for St Stephen's Porch and Hall — six military heroes in the Porch and sixteen statesmen for the Hall. Those commended in the 1844 Exhibition should get the first commissions: *Falkland* to be by Bell, *Clarendon* by Marshall and *Hampden* by Foley.[14] In a further memorandum they outlined a scheme for forty-four statues of royalty to run through from the Royal Entrance up to Peers Lobby. The Robing Room might have allegorical statues (though Barry had said no to this earlier), the Lower Waiting Hall should have eight scientists, the Upper Waiting Hall eight poets (with paintings to match) and others to go elsewhere as and when it became apparent what space was available.[15]

In the end, both Barry's and the commission's vision of hundreds of statues throughout the building proved seriously over-ambitious, but in certain areas they left a satisfactory account of what their dream might have been. Marlborough and Nelson never materialized in St Stephen's Porch, but in St Stephen's Hall a dozen Parliamentary heroes from *Clarendon*

and *Hampden* through to *Grattan* and *Burke* by various artists went up between 1848 and 1858.[16] The commissioners had perhaps been taking a certain risk. Nothing like it had been attempted in the country before, and potential sculptors had been asked, in the terms of the 1844 competition, not to send in, say, a likeness of Hampden, but instead the best they could do in a range of genres. Thus Foley submitted *Youth at the Stream*, an imaginative subject, and somehow from the supposed excellence of this, by an act of faith, the commissioners obtained his *Hampden* of 1850, in which, almost for the first time, the young sculptor revealed his capacity for sculpted naturalistic detail (for example floppy-topped boots) that was to add distinction to his subsequent career.

For the Lords Chamber the commission appointed nine sculptors in 1847 to execute eighteen statues of the Magna Carta signatories. These were installed by 1858; they were cast in zinc, coated with copper by electrolysis and chemically tinted as required. In addition to being a great saving on casting in bronze this also reflected Prince Albert's interest in new industrial techniques of sculpture production. The metallic appearance suited Barry's preference for bronze for niche figures (see above). The narrow Gothic angularity of the figures was also apparently to his prescription: when someone complained to one of the sculptors about this, the answer came, "Mr Barry will not allow us room for them".[17]

For the Royal series of figures, the commission started with the finale, the *Queen Victoria* in the Prince's Chamber. The artist selected was John Gibson, the leading British neo-classical sculptor, who lived in Rome and was a great favourite of Prince Albert. He appears to have been propositioned to prepare a design, then come over to England to prepare a model, with input from Barry and consultation with Prince Albert. When the

ABOVE LEFT: John Henry Foley, *Youth at the Stream*, plaster, 1844. Royal Dublin Society, Dublin; The Conway Library, Courtauld Institute of Art, London.

ABOVE CENTRE: John Henry Foley, *John Hampden*, marble, 1850. St Stephen's Hall, House of Commons, Palace of Westminster (WOA S045).

ABOVE RIGHT: Thomas Thornycroft, *Henry de Bohun, Earl of Hereford*, gilt metal, 1854. Lords Chamber, House of Lords, Palace of Westminster (WOA S049).

John Gibson, *Queen Victoria, Justice and Clemency*, marble, 1855. Prince's Chamber, House of Lords, Palace of Westminster (WOA S088).

commission met, a note was handed round the table from Prince Albert, expressing his entire approbation of Gibson's model. In Gibson's own words, "All then voted for the design and that it should be executed by me".[18] There was some debate about the overall format. Originally there was to be just the single figure of the queen. But Prince Albert pointed out the allocated recess was too wide for just this and suggested the addition of two allegorical figures. In the end *Justice* and *Clemency* were selected: "The expression of Justice is inflexible" (and Gibson told a friend that a woman who sold fruit in the market opposite the Pantheon in Rome was the model), while "Clemency is full of sympathy and sadness – sad for the constant sins that come to her knowledge, while with lenity she keeps the sword sheathed and offers the olive-branch, the sign of peace".[19] (One can perhaps understand Barry's reluctance to have allegorical sculpture after this, and no doubt the no-nonsense practicality of Peel would have agreed.) Gibson's group was unveiled in 1856, the same year a series of twelve bronze reliefs of scenes from Tudor history were completed in the same chamber; these were by William Theed, another Royal favourite, and incorporated with Richard Burchett's Tudor Royal portraits above (see chapter 14).[20]

Further statues in the Royal series were commissioned only after 1860, seven figures to go in the Royal Gallery. Royal favourites featured again: Theed and Thomas Thornycroft, as well as now-established figures – Henry Weekes (to be professor of sculpture at the Royal Academy from 1869) as well as Thomas Woolner, the Pre-Raphaelite sculptor who had actually participated in the 1844 exhibition, and another close Pre-Raphaelite associate, Alexander Munro. Unfortunately, when the first two figures were ready, Thornycroft's *James I* and *Charles I*, they were found to be too big for the designated niches, and the entire series was deposited in Westminster Hall before being incarcerated in the Old Bailey.[21] There had of course been ambiguity as far back as the 1844 Commission Report as to the nature of the Royal Gallery statues – architectural or free-standing. Besides, the cast of key players was being reduced. Prince Albert died in 1861, and much of the commission's momentum departed with him. In a fit of economy the Chancellor of the Exchequer, Gladstone, tried to curtail it in 1862. But Eastlake, by now Sir Charles and President of the Royal Academy as well as being Director of the National Gallery, had become involved as the Queen's artistic adviser to the London Albert Memorial. He wrote a "sad" letter to the Queen's Private Secretary saying how much he would love to see the Prince's scheme followed through, though he acknowledged the House of Commons had decided to limit the commission's function to finishing work in progress. He had thought, after all his service, he might have had a small retiring allowance … .[22] This seems to have worked, and the running down of the commission was postponed until after Eastlake's death in December 1865. Meanwhile, Barry had died in 1860, and responsibility for the building passed for a time to his son E.M. Barry, and it was he who resolved the Royal Gallery problem by commissioning replacement figures from John Birnie Philip. Philip accepted the commission in November 1867 and work was completed by November 1869.[23]

The sheer scale and nature of the sculptural programme at the new Palace of Westminster, both in aspiration and its ultimately incomplete state, were unique in Britain and the ideology behind it was very much of its time (these are qualities shared with the painting programme: the two are inseparable). The new Palace of Westminster is a Royal Palace, and Parliament is the monarch's parliament. This helps explain the series of monarchs from the Anglo-Saxon heptarchy to Queen Victoria that are the main features of the outside sculpture. Similarly, inside there was projected a series of monarchs from Egbert and Edgar through to Queen Victoria. The intended secular heroes inside – political, mili-

Thomas Woolner, *William III*, marble, 1867, commissioned for the Royal Gallery, House of Lords, re-sited to Westminster Hall in 1868 and transferred to the Central Criminal Court, Old Bailey in 1915. The Conway Library, Courtauld Institute of Art, London.

ABOVE: John Birnie Philip, *William III*, gilt Caen stone, 1869. Royal Gallery, House of Lords, Palace of Westminster (WOA S092).

RIGHT: John Birnie Philip, *Edward III*, gilt Caen stone, 1869. Royal Gallery, House of Lords, Palace of Westminster (WOA S0533).

tary, artistic — were symbols of a contemporary idea. A scheme for statues to the nation's benefactors had started in St Paul's Cathedral in the 1790s (*Dr Johnson* and *John Howard* by John Bacon, 1795), to be swiftly followed there by large numbers of military heroes who had saved the nation from the French in the wars against Napoleon (note Barry's willingness to incorporate these in his initial grand monumental plan).

But there was a particular political message to be read in those statues of political heroes that were among the relative minority actually put up. The Magna Carta signatories (House of Lords) represent an early manifesto of the nation guarding against monarchical dictatorship. And the Parliamentary heroes set up in St Stephen's Hall start with Civil War heroes such as Hampden and Falkland who resisted the attempted absolute monarchy of Charles I. This was part of an evolving notion of history at the time[24] (remember the pres-

ence of Hallam and Macaulay on the Fine Arts Commission), in which a continuing process of evolutionary democracy culminates in the Great Reform Act of 1832 in which the mercantile middle classes, particularly of the industrial North, finally obtain political standing. It was for this parliament that the new palace was built and decorated – Peel was the first Prime Minister to come from a rich industrial family, and incidentally Macaulay was elected to Parliament in 1832 as one of the two Members of Parliament for the newly enfranchised borough of Leeds.

There were, of course, models and prototypes. Thomas was sent by Barry to study the Late Medieval town halls of Belgium. Themselves ideological models of assembly/government buildings put up by a politically active mercantile bourgeoisie, it was in the first place their plethora of Late Gothic carved ornament that Thomas needed to observe. Few in fact had had any statuary in place at the time of the visit, but it was always implicit. The biblical kings and prophets, together with numerous counts and countesses of Flanders set up on the exterior of Bruges Town Hall from 1424 onwards had been pulled down and publicly smashed up in December 1792;[25] the Counts of Flanders and celebrated citizens set up in 1513 on the Cloth Hall of Ypres were destroyed in 1793 and replaced only between 1854 and 1875;[26] while at Ghent, although niches existed on the Town Hall of 1518–40, the provision of statues began only in 1887. Comparable situations existed elsewhere.[27] For Thomas's figures a possible source can be found on site: the six kings in niches on the interior south wall of Westminster Hall. Carved by Thomas Canon in 1385, the niches were reconditioned by Barry in the 1850s.[28]

Similarly with the interior free-standing statuary: the French state had set up a scheme for life-size statues of the Great Men ('*Grands Hommes*') of France in the 1770s, notionally for the Louvre as a great public building. Though the subjects were writers, astronomers, philosophers, artists, soldiers and statesmen, this was not a bourgeois scheme. Started under Louis XVI, it was continued by Napoleon and Louis-Philippe, who was still ruling in France in the 1840s at the time of the Westminster programme.[29] More politically in tune with

View of three of the kings commissioned by Richard II in the 1380s, on the south wall of Westminster Hall, repositioned by Charles Barry *c.* 1850, Palace of Westminster.

View of the marble sculpture of Sir Charles Barry by John Henry Foley, Committee Staircase, photograph, *c.* 1903. Farmer Collection, no number, House of Lords Record Office, London.

Baron Carlo Marochetti, *Richard Coeur de Lion*, bronze, 1856. This sculpture proved almost as contentious as the statue of Cromwell (see illus., p. 269), in the main because the sculptor was not British. F.T. Palgrave dismissed it as an overpriced piece of vacuous bravado, but John Ruskin considered that it was "the only really interesting piece of historical sculpture we have hitherto given to the City populace." Old Palace Yard, Palace of Westminster (WOA S074).

Westminster were the St Paul's heroes, who might have been transferred. There was also a relevant recent prototype for the interior Royal series in the statues by Ludwig Schwanthaler of the Wittelsbach royal line of the kings of Bavaria, set up in the Residenz in Munich between 1834 and 1842.[30] Cast in metal, and gilded (as Philip's figures are), there can be little doubt these would have been known to Prince Albert and Eastlake; Cornelius had come over from Munich to advise on the painting schemes.

The momentum for sculpture inside and outside the palace has continued. In 1860 Marochetti's *Richard Coeur de Lion* was installed in Old Palace Yard. This was certainly not part of the original scheme, having first been sited outside the Crystal Palace in Hyde Park housing the Great Exhibition of 1851. But Marochetti was *the* favourite sculptor of Prince

Albert and so negotiations began to find a place for it. Barry did not think it was in harmony with the building, various Fine Arts Commissioners gave their opinions and the decision to site the sculpture in Old Palace Yard was made in 1859.[31] Barry himself was commemorated inside the building with a statue by Foley of 1865. Between 1865 and 1869 E.M. Barry designed and built the arcade along New Palace Yard and provided niches for six statues of kings by Henry Hugh Armstead. Armstead also executed the eighteen carved wood panels of Arthurian scenes in the Robing Room of 1870; these filled spaces not utilized by Dyce's paintings on the same theme.[32] In the 1890s the question was raised as to why Oliver Cromwell was not commemorated by a statue in Parliament; eventually, in spite of vehement objections by Irish Members of Parliament, a bronze statue was commissioned and placed outside Westminster Hall in 1899.[33] Parliamentary figures continued to be commemorated inside the building: Pomeroy's statue of Gladstone of 1900 stands in Central Lobby, while since 1963 a series of busts of Prime Ministers from the elder Pitt to Lord Rosebery have come to occupy spaces in the Norman Porch originally designated for statues of medieval monarchs.[34]

One of the underlying motives for the decoration of the Houses of Parliament specified by both Barry and the Fine Arts Commissioners was to encourage the production of art in the country, and in the field of sculpture this was achieved to an extent they perhaps could not have hoped for. While ideas were still at the discussion stage at Westminster, the architect of St George's Hall, Liverpool (1841–56), H.L. Elmes, was planning in 1844 to decorate his neo-classical building with sculpture (and fresco painting). Eventually, under his successor, C.R. Cockerell, only sculpture featured, with a series of statues of nineteenth-century heroes of Liverpool in the Great Hall of this leisure temple for the 'Merchant Princes' of Liverpool.[35] Waterhouse's Manchester Town Hall (1868–74) has statues of local historic figures on the exterior, a Sculpture Hall inside with busts and statues of Manchester's great, with further statues and busts on the way up to the Great Hall, where sculpted Royalty and significant locals vie with murals by Ford Madox Brown.[36] Bradford Town Hall (1873) by Lockwood and Mawson has a series of thirty-five kings and queens of England set on its Gothic exterior. Like the external statues Manchester, these are by Farmer and Brindley.[37]

The bourgeois ideology and example of the St Stephen's Hall series also came at a crucial moment to support the developing notion of public statue commemoration in post-1832 urban Britain. It was appropriately the instigator of the Fine Arts Commission, Robert Peel, who, with his death in 1850, provided the opportunity for 'statuemania' to break out in Britain, with at least twenty-six public statues set up to him alone over the ensuing two decades, especially in the industrial towns first enfranchised in 1832. The climax to this movement came, again appropriately, with the death of the Commission's President, Prince Albert, in 1861 and the setting up of the National Memorial (the Albert Memorial) to him in London. The major element of the Memorial is its sculpture, which, under the careful guidance of Eastlake, was executed by nine sculptors, of whom seven had worked at the Palace of Westminster before going on to achieve senior positions in their profession. There could be no better tribute to the success of what was achieved at Westminster.

Sir William Hamo Thornycroft, *Oliver Cromwell*, bronze, 1899. John Thomas had produced a model of Cromwell for Central Lobby which was exhibited at Crystal Palace and destroyed in 1936. The debate over a sculpture of Cromwell at Westminster continued in both Parliament and the press from the 1840s onwards, until the issue was raised again in 1894, resulting in Thornycroft's commission. As an indication of the contentiousness of the sculpture, it was unveiled in 1899 by one of the masons, before a group of only five people, which included the policeman on duty. Westminster Hall Green, Palace of Westminster (WOA S029).

Chapter 1

I am most grateful to Dr D. Birch, Prof. L. Colley, Ms C. Pearson, Ms C. Riding, Sir John Sainty and Mr E.P. Silk for their help, advice and encouragement during the preparation of this essay.

1 Quinault 1992, p. 79.
2 For a fuller discussion of this contextual approach to the 'meaning' of buildings and ceremonial, see Cannadine 1983, pp. 101–08, and the further references cited there.
3 Boase 1954, p. 319; Solender 1984, pp. 27–30, 33.
4 Walker 1972–74, p. 100; Colley 1992, p. 325.
5 Authoritative accounts of the design and construction of the new Palace of Westminster are Port 1976; and Colvin, VI, 1973, pp. 573–626, on both of which I have freely and frequently drawn in subsequent paragraphs.
6 F.M.L. Thompson 1988, pp. 13–22; Rorabaugh 1973, p. 155.
7 Clark 1928, pp. 141–43; Girouard 1981, pp. 40–54; C.L. Eastlake 1970, pp. 50–57; Crook 1995, pp. 1, 4, 7–8, 11, 31–32; Frew 1982, pp. 315–19; Port 1976, pp. 6–7, 30–32.
8 Port 1976, pp. 24–28; Rorabaugh 1973, pp. 166–68. The fifth appointee, Samuel Rogers, declined to act.
9 Port 1976, p. 23.
10 Quinault 1992, p. 96; Pevsner 1957, p. 95; Rorabaugh 1973, pp. 164, 173; Port 1976, pp. 71, 232.
11 Port 1976, pp. 232–36.
12 Quinault 1992, pp. 81–86; Girouard 1981, pp. 116–24, 179–81; Bond 1980, pp. 44–59, 66–83.
13 Sawyer 1996, pp. 60–61, 68–72; Port 1976, pp. 203–05.
14 Stanton 1968, pp. 128–39; idem 1971, pp. 81–84, 91–92, 170–01; Meara 1995, pp. 45–61; Saint 1995, pp. 79–101; A. Wedgwood 1994a, pp. 43–61; O'Donnell, 1994, pp. 63–89; Belcher 1994, pp. 105–16; A. Wedgwood 1994b, pp. 219–36; Girouard 1981, pp. 30–38, 56–66; Port 1976,

pp. 256–57.
15 Quinault 1992, pp. 82, 86–91; Wainwright 1994a, pp. 127–42; Boase 1954, p. 332; Bond 1980, pp. 84–91; Port 1976, pp. 187, 245–53.
16 Wainwright 1995, pp. 63–71; Atterbury 1995, pp. 177–99; A. Wedgwood 1994c, pp. 26–30; Lambourne 1994, pp. 35–41. According to one contemporary, "the true bent of Pugin's mind was towards the theatre": Clark 1928, p. 174.
17 Quinault 1992, pp. 82–85; Arnstein 1990, pp. 184–85.
18 Quinault 1992, pp. 86–87, 103–04; Cannadine 1989, pp. 139–46; Le May 1979, pp. 22–96; Victoria 1926, II, pp. 165–66.
19 Plumb 1969, p. 116; Holmes 1976, pp. 9–24; Colley 1992, pp. 349–50; Beales 1992, pp. 139–50; O'Gorman 1993, pp. 171–83.
20 Boase 1954, p. 341; Hay and Riding 1996, pp. 104–06. Pugin himself designed many churches and chapels for Ireland: see O'Donnell 1995, pp. 137–59.
21 Martin, 1973, pp. 65–92; idem 1975, pp. 125–9; Bond 1980, pp. 11, 95. It was originally planned to commission a series of paintings referring to "the acquisition of the countries, colonies and important places constituting the British Empire"; but these were never proceeded with: Boase 1954, p. 342.
22 Gash 1965, pp. 1–59; Arnstein 1990, pp. 185–87.
23 Craig 1989, p. 67.
24 Port 1976, pp. 50–51, 73–80, 97–121; Rorabaugh 1973, pp. 155–75.
25 Port 1976, pp. 1, 53, 142–94, 298.
26 Port 1976, pp. 119, 232, 268–79; Boase 1954, pp. 343–58; Hay and Riding 1996, p. 10; Bond 1980, pp. 39–42.
27 Stanton 1971, p. 33; Meara 1995, p. 60; Saint 1995, p. 92.
28 Blake 1998, pp. 167–73, 190–202, 208–11, 270–78, 545–49, 562–69; Meara 1995, p. 55; O'Donnell 1994, p. 64; Girouard 1981,

pp. 80–86, 200. For a more nuanced account of Disraeli's attitude to the peerage and the upper House, see Slater 1981, pp. 66–76.
29 Port 1976, pp. 94–96.
30 Cannadine 1992a, pp. 19–24.
31 Cannadine 1983, pp. 133–34; Lant 1979.
32 Cannadine 1983, pp. 120–21, 139; Weston 1967, pp. 296–322; Bogdanor 1995, pp. 113–44.
33 Cannadine 1990, pp. 37–54, 195–206, 308–25, 458–72.
34 Butler 1963, pp. 7–57; Blewett 1965, pp. 27–56; Matthew et al. 1982, pp. 820–31; Tanner 1983, pp. 205–19.
35 Hunting 1981, p. 125; Cannadine 1990, pp. 184–95.
36 Pollard 1926, pp. 16–17; Wilding and Laundy 1968, p. 791.
37 Phillips 1979, pp. 82–110; Adonis 1993, pp. 210–39; Cannadine 1990, pp. 588–602.
38 Cannadine 1994, pp. 121–27.
39 Meath 1894, pp. 710–16; Marritt 1907, pp. 1003–17; Mitra 1910, pp. 1090–99; Cannadine 1994, pp. 109–10.
40 Pollard 1926, pp. 360, 369–73; Martin 1975, pp. 131–34.
41 Lowther 1925, I, pp. 306–07; Lee 1927, pp. 21–23; Brett 1934, I, pp. 284–85; Cannadine 1983, pp. 135–36.
42 For descriptions of State Openings in the reigns of George V and Edward VIII, see Channon 1967, pp. 74–75, 139; Rose 1983, pp. 101–05, 131; Donaldson 1976, pp. 233–34; Ziegler 1990, pp. 264–65.
43 Port 1976, p. 280; Hay and Riding 1996, pp. 26, 90–93, 98–101.
44 Pollard 1926, pp. vi, 3, 9, 11; Cannadine 1992b, pp. 110–26; Colley 1989, pp. 74–77. See also MacDonagh, 1921, p. 7: "Parliament ... is, perhaps, as fine and perfect an instrument of democratic government as can humanly be devised. ... It is the fabric of the life of the people. ... It is the country's chief political instrument of progressive civilisation."

45 London, House of Commons 1932, pp. 52–53; J.C. Wedgwood 1935, p. 173; idem 1936, pp. ii–iv.
46 Boardman 1960.
47 Surveys 1951, p. 70; Churchill 1974, VIII, pp. 8108–10.
48 Channon 1967, p. 75.
49 Cannadine 1994, p. 129; Thomson 1929, pp. 236–46; Martin 1986, pp. 182–88; idem 1975, p. 136.
50 Barker and Hyde 1982, pp. 150–53; Port 1976, p. 281.
51 Port 1995, pp. 233–51; Irving 1981, pp. 89–90, 166–70. The only British imperial legislature that the new palace seems to have influenced was that in Ottawa (1859–67): Port 1976, pp. 298–308.
52 Bowness 1973, pp. 24–25, 33–38; Tucker 1998, pp. 26–32; Shackleford and Stevens 1998, pp. 128–47.
53 Pevsner 1957, pp. 461–62; Boardman 1960, pp. 100–07. For two very well-disposed works, see K. Mackenzie 1950; James 1961.
54 Boardman 1960, p. 198; Hansard, The Official Report, ser. 5, DCCV, 1965, col. 668.
55 For a vivid account of her first State Opening, see Boardman 1960, pp. 109–13.
56 Dimbleby 1975, pp. 340–43.
57 Martin 1973, p. 66; idem 1975, p. 135.
58 Cannadine 1983, p. 157.
59 E. Taylor 1979, pp. 176–78; Young 1998, pp. 325–38, 422–34; Robbins 1994, pp. 376–86; Giddings and Drewery 1996.
60 Cannadine 1995, pp. 18–19; Young 1999, pp. 1–2.
61 Bogdanor 1999, p. 4.
62 Wilding and Laundy 1968, p. 434.
63 Cannadine 1990, pp. 663, 674–75, 680–83; Crick 1968, pp. 124–38.
64 Pevsner 1957, p. 95.
65 London, Parliamentary Works Directorate 1993; idem 1998. See also the following volumes of the History of Parliament: Roskell, Clark and Rawcliffe 1992; Bindoff 1982; Hasler 1983; Sedgwick 1970; Namier and Brooke 1964; Thorne 1986.
66 Dimbleby 1975, pp. 340–43; Day 1966, pp. 110–14. For a

recent re-articulation of this view, see Leonard 1998, pp. 1–2.
67 For recent re-affirmations of the Pugin-cum-Dimbleby view of the State Opening, see Brentnall 1975, pp. 132–34; Brooke-Little 1980, pp. 75–81.

Chapter 2

1 Sainty 1980, p. 1; Brooke-Little 1980, pp. 65–80; A. Napier 1953–54, pp. 49–59.
2 A.L. Brown 1981, p. 113.
3 Ibid., pp. 121–22.
4 Cooper 1938, pp. 97–138.
5 Wagner and Sainty 1967, pp. 128–29.
6 See Cobb 1999, pp. 303–15; Dean 1995, pp. 243–71.
7 Pronay and Taylor 1980, pp. 185–86; Rotuli Parliamentorum, 1783, VI, pp. 267–68.
8 London, British Library, Add. MS 5758, ff. 8–9, printed in Powell and Wallis 1968, pp. 543–44.
9 Cambridge, Trinity College, MS O.3.59, printed in Wagner and Sainty 1967, pp. 142–50, pls. xvii–xx; Powell and Wallis 1968, pp. 549–50.
10 Colvin 1982, IV/ii, pp. 286–87.
11 London, College of Arms, MS 2.H.13, ff. 396 & 403. A description of the 1529 opening is printed in Powell and Wallis 1968, pp. 563–64.
12 Windsor, Royal Library, Royal MS 1B, 2b, quire P f. 1, printed in Powell and Wallis 1968, pp. 555–57, pl. XX).
13 Colvin 1982, IV/ii, p. 286.
14 Cooper 1938, pp. 127–28.
15 London, College of Arms, MS 2.H.13, f. 404[a], printed in Dugdale 1685, pp. 502–03.
16 London, College of Arms, MS 2.H.13, ff. 410[v]–411[v].
17 Ibid., ff. 413[v]–414[v].
18 London, College of Arms, MS Le Neve W.A., f. 139; Tyler 1954, pp. 81–82; Machyn 1848, p. 74.
19 London, College of Arms, MS 2.H.13, f. 424; Brown and Bentinck 1890, pp. 22–23; 1892, p. 25; M.A.S. Hume 1892, p. 25; Machyn 1848, pp. 163–64.
20 Dublin, Trinity College, MS

535, ff. 1–3, printed in Hartley 1981–95, I, pp. 194–97; Duke of Northumberland (Alnwick Castle), Northumberland MSS, Alnwick MS no. 468, f. 121 (consulted in microfilm: London, British Library, Microfilm no. 342).

21  London, British Library, Add. MS 5758, ff. 73–74, printed in Hartley 1981–95, I, pp. 267–68; Alnwick MS no. 468, f. 122.

22  Milles 1610, pp. 64–68; von Wedel 1895, pp. 260–62; Neale 1949, pp. 349–52; Dean 1995, pp. 249, 254–62.

23  Alnwick MS no. 468, f. 123; London, College of Arms, MS Vincent 92, pp. 265–66; Neale 1949, pp. 352–53.

24  Foster 1983, pp. 3–5; idem 1979, pp. 129–46, 239–48; Bond 1981, pp. 21–26; Evelyn 1955, II, pp. 23–24.

25  Sainty 1980, pp. 1–2.

26  Cromwell's 'Other House' consisted entirely of men nominated by him, including a few hereditary peers and peers created by Cromwell himself, plus army officers and politicians. They seem generally to have been referred to as the 'Lords'. Schoenfeld 1967, pp. 50–63.

27  London, House of Lords 1908, IV, pp. 503–07; Burton 1828, II, pp. 322–23; Schoenfeld 1967 pp. 51–54; Hinds 1931, pp. 157–58.

28  London, House of Lords 1908, pp. 524–26; Burton 1828, III, pp. 1–2; Schoenfeld 1967, pp. 56–57.

29  Birkenhead 1661; Evelyn 1955, III, p. 286; Schoenfeld 1967, pp. 148, 219.

30  Daniell 1915, pp. xviii, 71; Jones 1983, pp. 56–57.

31  J.M. Robinson 1998, p. 90; A. Boyer 1712, X, p. 282.

32  Sainty 1980, pp. 1–2.

33  Hutchinson 1883–86, II, pp. 109, 108–10.

34  Brooke 1972, pp. 173, 573–74.

35  London, House of Lords 1977, XII, pp. 29–30; Grosley 1772, II, pp. 191–93.

36  Sainty 1980, pp. 5–7; E.A. Smith 1991, p. 13.

37  Discussed by Sean Sawyer in chapter 8 of this volume; Colvin 1973, VI, pp. 519–22; Quinault 1992, p. 84.

38  E.A. Smith 1991, pp. 13–14; Sainty 1980, p. 6.

39  E.A. Smith 1991, p. 15; idem 1992, pp. 19–21; Sainty 1980, p. 6.

40  W.J. Napier 1991, p. 103. (An account by Captain William John Napier RN, the 9th Lord Napier, a Lord-in-Waiting to William IV.)

41  Sainty 1980, pp. 6–8; E.A. Smith 1991, pp. 15–16; idem 1992, pp. 21–23; Arnstein 1990, pp. 184–87; Quinault 1992, pp. 82, 85.

42  E.A. Smith 1992, pp. 21–22; Arnstein 1990, pp. 184–85; The London Gazette, 21 November 1837, p. 3015.

43  London, House of Lords Record Office, Lord Great Chamberlain's Papers, IV, 2, pp. 22, 24, 52.

44  Colvin 1973, VI, p. 625; The Times, 4 February 1852, p. 2; The London Gazette, 6 February 1852, p. 323; Quinault 1992, p. 103.

45  Arnstein 1990, pp. 185–86; E.A. Smith 1992, pp. 23–24; Quinault 1992, p. 86.

46  Arnstein 1990, p. 184; E.A. Smith 1992, pp. 13, 19, 22; idem 1991, p. 16; The Times, 4 February 1852, p. 2; Chowdharay-Best 1972–73, pp. 19–23; Grosley 1772, II, p. 192n.; Quinault 1992, p. 98.

47  E.A. Smith 1992, pp. 24–25.

48  Neale 1949, pp. 352–53; Birkenhead 1661; MacDonagh 1921, I, p. 209; Arnstein 1990, p. 184.

49  London, House of Lords and House of Commons 1901, pp. 213–303.

50  E.A. Smith 1992, pp. 24–26; Sainty 1980, pp. 6–8.

51  Brooke-Little 1980, pp. 75–80; London, House of Lords 1982.

52  For example, Hall 1809, p. 675; Hartley 1981–95, I, pp. 72, 268–69, III, pp. 64–65; Dean 1995, pp. 266–67; Foster 1983, pp. 22, 29.

53  Sainty 1980, pp. 2, 5; Brooke-Little 1980, p. 80.

54  Sainty 1980, pp. 1, 3–6; Brooke-Little 1980, pp. 65–66.

55  Sainty 1980, pp. 2–4; Townshend 1934–35, pp. 23–26 (entry for 9 February 1598); Foster

1983, pp. 29–30; Pepys 1970–83, IV, 1971, pp. 249–51.

56  E.A. Smith 1992, pp. 8–9.

57  Ibid., pp. 20–3; idem 1991, pp. 14–16; Arnstein 1990, pp. 182–83; Sainty 1980, pp. 6–8; Lord Great Chamberlain's Papers, 2, IV, pp. 22, 24, 52; Quinault 1992, p. 82.

58  Arnstein 1990, pp. 183–84; Wright and Smith 1902–03, I, p. 316; Brooke-Little 1980, p. 80; Sainty 1980, p. 1.

Chapter 3

1  The Times, 17 October 1834, p. 2, col. 1; p. 3, cols. 3–5.

2  For an overview of the early development of Westminster see Rosser 1989.

3  Lethaby 1906, pp. 161–62; Swanton 1997, pp. 161–62.

4  Vita Edwardi Regis, extracts printed in R.A. Brown 1984, p. 89.

5  Gem 1980, pp. 33–60; Fernie 1987, p. 63–67.

6  Ordericus Vitalis 1968–80, II, pp. 184–85.

7  Evidence for William's work on the palace comes from a miracle story; this suggests construction was under way between 1070/75 and 1087. Gem 1987, p. 88.

8  For a discussion of the Romanesque hall see Smirke 1836, pp. 406–14, 415–21; idem 1838, pp. 135–39; Royal Commission on Historical Monuments in England, II, 1925, pp. 121–23; and Cooper 1936, pp. 168–228. Wilson 1997, pp. 33–59, offers many further insights and corrections to the conventional analysis of the hall.

9  Wilson 1997, p. 280.

10  For a discussion of royal government in this period see Warren 1987.

11  Colvin 1963, I, pp. 492–93 and 501.

12  An accessible and scholarly guide to the church proposes that it cost the equivalent of billions of pounds in modern terms. Wilson et al. 1986, p. 30.

13  The most detailed consideration of Henry III's work on the abbey is Binski 1995.

14  For the chamber and its paintings see Binski 1986.

15  Liversidge, Binski and Lynn 1995, pp. 491–501.

16  Colvin 1963, I, p. 545 and Wilson 1997, pp. 36 and 276.

17  Cooper 1938, pp. 109–22. For a bibliography and discussion of the thirteenth- and fourteenth-century development of Parliament see Prestwich 1980, pp. 115–36.

18  Cooper 1938, pp. 116–18.

19  Dixon-Smith 1999, p. 87.

20  Bony 1983, pp. 388–91.

21  For a discussion of St Stephen's Chapel and its influence see Topham 1795; F. Mackenzie 1844; Hastings 1995; Bony 1979; Wilson 1992; and idem 1980.

22  Martindale 1994, pp. 102–12; Howe 1999.

23  For a summary of the building history see Colvin 1963, I, pp. 510–22 and 525–6.

24  Ibid., I, pp. 535–36; A.J. Taylor 1965.

25  Wilson 1997, pp. 36–37; Colvin 1963, I, pp. 543–45.

26  Gordon 1993, p. 54.

27  Wilson 1997, p. 42.

28  The figures and their restoration are discussed in Hay and Kennedy 1993.

29  Wilson 1997, pp. 54–58. For the most recent discussion of the roof and its extensive bibliography see Waddell 1999, pp. 47–67.

30  Wilson 1997, p. 36.

31  Colvin 1963, I, pp. 536–37.

32  Wilson 1995, pp. 133–56; Colvin 1975, III, pp. 210–22.

33  Royal Commission on Historical Monuments in England, II, 1925, pp. 123–24.

34  Colvin 1982, IV, p. 286. For a recent discussion of Whitehall see Thurley 1999.

35  Colvin 1982, IV, p. 288; Jay 1921, pp. 226–28.

36  Colvin 1982, IV, pp. 289–94.

37  Ibid., pp. 296–98.

38  Colvin 1976, V, pp. 401–04 for the remodelling of St Stephen's Chapel, and pp. 385–87 for the changes to New Palace Yard.

39  Ibid., pp. 425–31.

40  Ibid., pp. 416–25.

41  Wyatt's career is considered in Robinson 1979, pp. 56–89. See also Colvin 1973, VI, pp. 512–15.

42  Carter 1800a, p. 736. This is one of about two hundred letters that Carter wrote to the magazine, criticizing various of Wyatt's schemes.

43  Cocke 1995, pp. 57–58; and Colvin 1973, VI, pp. 516–17.

44  Colvin 1973, VI, pp. 504–12.

45  Binski 1986, pp. 4–5.

Chapter 4

1  See Linda Colley's discussion of 'Britishness' in the late Georgian period in Colley 1992.

2  Cannon and Griffiths 1988, p. 530.

3  Colley 1992, p. 231.

4  Ibid., p. 232.

5  Cannadine 1983, p. 109 and passim.

6  George IV 1963–71, VII, p. 208.

7  Ribeiro 1995, p. 156.

8  Famously, when the forty-ton vase finally arrived at Windsor, it proved too heavy safely to be carried up the stairs, let alone stand on the chamber's raised floor. In 1836, it was donated to the new National Gallery by a relieved William IV, and after 1906 was cruelly exposed to the elements in the garden at Buckingham Palace.

9  See J.M. Robinson 1993, p. 93.

10  Millar 1969, I, p. xxxiii. Lawrence's portrait was, as Millar says, "a perfect image of the hero of the alliance to be sent overseas".

11  London, PRO, Work 21/14.

12  George's health was notoriously bad: immediately after his accession a severe relapse made many of his subjects wonder if his reign would be the shortest ever. Joseph Farington expressed the general worry that, even if George lived until his coronation, he would not be able to endure the long ceremony and would expire before its end. See Farington 1978–84, XVI, p. 5509.

13  As Valerie Cumming records, "The finest textiles were used in the Abbey: blue and gold brocade for the altar, garter-blue and gold Wilton carpet on the altar steps and sacrarium

floor, crimson velvet and sarsenet for the royal box and a good deal of crimson cloth for the boxes and benches inside the western aisle". Cumming 1992, pp. 43–44.

14 Mark Girouard remarks that "the most unique feature of the coronation was that almost everyone who took part in it wore clothes especially designed for the occasion". Girouard 1981, p. 26.

15 Cumming 1992, p. 46.

16 Girouard 1981, p. 26.

17 Ribeiro 1995, pp. 231–32.

18 Lockhart 1845, p. 455.

19 The vain prince had long been buying false hair to perpetuate the impression of youth, and by the time of the coronation "was ordering hair by the yard". Ribeiro 1995, p. 234.

20 In addition, the jewelled circlet designed to adorn his Cap of State was estimated at a further £8000. Memorandum from Rundell, Bridge and Rundell, dated 18 April 1820, in George IV 1938, II, p. 323. It is assumed that £1 in 1820 was worth the equivalent of about £50–£60 in 1999.

21 Scenes and portraits of the main participants from the coronation were published in two folios: Nayler 1825–27 and 1839; Whittaker 1821–41. Sir George Nayler was Clarenceux King of Arms at the coronation, but was acting for the Garter King of Arms (Girouard 1981, p. 294, n. 25.)

22 This post was a hereditary one, introduced at the coronation of Charles I in 1625, in order for the herbs to freshen the air and ward off disease. George IV's coronation was the last to employ the King's Herb Women, as, in 1831, William IV decided to dispense with the procession from hall to abbey. See Fox 1992, no. 37a, p. 250.

23 As quoted from the *Annual Register 1821* in Cumming 1992, p. 47.

24 London, PRO, Work 36/68.

25 *The Observer*, 22 July 1821.

26 Cobbett 1830, p. 456;

Farington 1978–84, XVI, p. 5703.

27 Cumming 1992, p. 44.

28 *Ibid.*, p. 43.

29 Lockhart 1845, pp. 495, 499.

30 For further information on caricature, see George 1978, p. 232.

31 As quoted in Cumming 1992, p. 47.

32 As quoted *ibid.*, p. 48.

33 For example, Lord Denbigh related that Prince Esterhazy was "said to have had jewels on his person estimated at *eighty thousand pounds*". As quoted in Hibbert 1976, pp. 192–93.

34 As quoted in Fulford 1935, p. 232.

35 T. Taylor 1853, I, p. 314.

36 W. Scott 1821.

37 *Idem* 1820, I, pp. 154.

38 Cumming 1992, p. 42. In her discussion, Cumming has recalculated the expense of the coronation to £211,428. 17s. 5d.

39 Finley 1982, p. 7.

40 Lockhart 1845, p. 454.

41 Cannadine 1983, p. 118. See also Ribeiro 1995; Cumming 1992; Girouard 1981; de Bellaigue 1993, pp. 174–83.

42 Ribeiro 1995, p. 234.

Chapter 5

1 *King Richard the Second*, II. i. 40–50. The quotation in the title is taken from *ibid.*, III. iii. 148.

2 These include: sculptures of Richard II on the exterior in New Palace Yard and in Central Lobby; sculptures of Richard's symbol of the white hart in Westminster Hall; stained glass in Commons Corridor and on the Committee Staircase; white harts and monogram tiles in Members Entrance; Pugin-designed wallpaper (one of the few heraldic papers associated with a particular monarch to be utilized within the building); the white hart, and Richard's other symbols of the broomcod and the rising sun (as seen on the tomb effigy), which appear on the Robing Room ceiling and within the stained glass.

3 For his reign see Saul 1997.

4 Goodman and Gillespie 1999, p. 1.

5 Lingard 1819–30, III, p. 274.

6 The portrait of Richard II enthroned and his tomb effigy, both in Westminster Abbey; the Wilton Diptych (National Gallery, London); and Westminster Hall (with the six statues of kings commissioned by Richard II). See Gordon 1993, and *ead.*, Monnas and Elam 1997.

7 Webb 1824; William 1846.

8 See J. Taylor 1999, pp. 15–35.

9 Knight 1862, VIII, p. 348.

10 John Carter (1748–1817), author of *The Antient Architecture of England*, 2 vols., London, 1795–1814. See Crook 1995.

11 Carter 1800c, p. 215.

12 Carter 1800b, p. 35.

13 Quoted in Colvin 1973, VI, p. 499.

14 *Ibid.*

15 For a summary of the restorations see *ibid.*, pp. 497–503.

16 Smirke 1834, p. 100.

17 *The Times*, 17 October 1834, p. 2, col. 1.

18 Carter 1800b, p. 35.

19 C.L. Eastlake 1872, p. 115.

20 Sir Samuel Rush Meyrick (1783–1848), author of *A Critical Inquiry into Ancient Armour*, 3 vols., London, 1824. Meyrick's armour can now be seen at the Wallace Collection in London. For further details on Meyrick see Wainwright 1989, pp. 168–241. For Scott's own collection see M.M.M. Scott 1893.

21 W. Scott 1820, I, pp. 1–2.

22 Nassau, n.d., p. 127.

23 C.L. Eastlake 1872, p. 113.

24 Incarnations of *Ivanhoe* included Thomas Dibdin's *Ivanhoe; or The Jew's Daughter* (Surrey Theatre, 20 January 1820), Alfred Bunn's *Ivanhoe; or, The Jew of York* (Coburg Playhouse, 24 January 1820) and Samuel Beazley's *Ivanhoe; or, The Knight Templar* (Covent Garden, 2 March 1820): see White 1927, pp. 103–08.

25 A reference in Pugin's incomplete and unpublished autobiography, dated 3 March 1831, states: "The ballet of Kennilworth [*sic*] composed by Mr. Desayes; for this ballet I painted 2

scenes: the interior of Cumnor Place and Greenwich Palace with the exception of the back cloth by Mr. Grieve. I likewise furnished documents for the costume and other scenes of the ballet." A. Wedgwood 1985, p. 28.

26 Lambourne 1994, p. 39.

27 E.W. Pugin 1867, p. 3.

28 C.L. Eastlake 1872, p. 105.

29 Knight 1864, II, p. 284.

30 Planché 1872, I, pp. 53–54.

31 Knight 1838, I, p. 85.

32 *Ibid.*, p. 85.

33 Nichols 1842, p. 33.

34 Hazlitt 1818, p. 179.

35 Wroughton 1815, p. 3.

36 Proctor 1835, II, p. 126.

37 Coleridge 1856, p. 3.

38 Smollett 1757–58, II, p. 210; Clarendon 1768, I, p. 375.

39 D. Hume 1762, II, p. 274.

40 Keightley 1839, I, p. 319.

41 Turner 1825, II, p. 328.

42 Webb 1824, p. 2.

43 *Ibid.*, pp. 1–2.

44 *Ibid.*, p. 6.

45 Quoted in Scharf 1867, pp. 26–27.

46 Knight 1838, I, p. 84.

47 *Ibid.*, p. 158.

48 Carter 1780–94, I, p. 56.

49 Scharf 1867, p. 24. The painting was exhibited at South Kensington in 1865 and afterwards restored under the supervision of George Richmond: see Alexander 1997, pp. 197–206.

50 Kean 1857, p. viii.

51 *Ibid.*

52 *Ibid.*, p. vii.

53 *Ibid.*, p. viii. For Meyrick see note 20 above. Frederick William Fairholt (1814–1866), author of *Costume in England*, London, 1846 and illustrator of Halliwell 1853–65. Joseph Strutt (1749–1802), generally considered the first serious costume historian, and author of *The Regal and Ecclesiastical Antiquities of England*, London, 1777; a revised edition of his *History of British Costume* was published in 1842 with additions by J.R. Planché.

54 Kean 1857, p. viii.

55 J.W. Cole 1859, II, p. 228.

56 *The Times*, 16 March 1857, p. 9, col. 6.

57 J.W. Cole 1859, II, p. 228.

58 Kean 1857, p. 64.

59 J.W. Cole 1859, II, p. 210.

60 Cited in Foulkes 1986, p. 52.

61 Based upon the portrait before restoration (see note 49).

62 Cole 1859, II, p. 213.

63 Kean 1857, p. vii.

64 Pater 1889, pp. 202–03.

Chapter 6

1 'Archilochus' 1837, pp. 19–20.

2 W.E.H. 1836, p. 412.

3 The phrase was made popular a century earlier by Alexander Pope in his 'Epistle to Burlington' (1731), advising the country gentleman to consult the 'genius of place' before designing his garden: Charlesworth 1993, pp. 43–48. Little work has been done on Pope's notion of genius loci; the best overview remains J.D. Hunt 1976, pp. 14–42.

4 M.C. Boyer 1996; Casey 1989, pp. 181–215; Hayden 1996, pp. 9–15; Forster, 1982, pp. 2–19.

5 Hobsbawm and Ranger 1983, pp. 1–14.

6 Port 1976, p. 20; Broughton 1911, pp. 22–23.

7 Port 1976, pp. 36–38.

8 As quoted in A. Wedgwood 1994b, p. 219.

9 London, House of Lords 1835, p. 96; Hansard, *Parliamentary Debates*, ser. 3, XXIX, 1835, pp. 3–5; Bassin 1984, pp. 1–35.

10 Port 1976, p. 45.

11 Cust 1835.

12 The most active of the resulting commissioners were Cust himself, Charles Hanbury Tracy MP (the chairman), the Hon. Thomas Liddell and George Vivian.

13 Anon. 1836a.

14 The commissioners awarded second place to John Chessell Buckler; third to David Hamilton; and fourth to William Railton. On the lack of time see Britton and Brayley 1835, pp. 504–06. For rejected plans see Barker and Hyde 1982, pp. 95–105. Much has been written on the so-called 'battle of the styles' – see Clark 1962,

15 Solender 1984, pp. 31–41.
16 As quoted in Redgrave and Redgrave 1947, p. 459.
17 For discussion of Turner's pictorial response to the fire see Solender 1984, pp. 42–65.
18 As quoted *ibid.*, p. 11.
19 Anon. 1834b, pp. 353, 355.
20 Anon. 1834c, p. 477.
21 *Ibid.*, p. 480.
22 For John Soane's earlier plans for a symbolic Westminster that would also have emphasized the Crown's historic legitimacy and current relevancy, see Sawyer 1996, pp. 54–76.
23 'Assimilation' and 'unity of expression' are phrases frequently used by architects in anon. 1836a. The same expressions are used for discussing Barry's first prize plan in anon. 1836b, pp. 264–70 and in Hansard, *Parliamentary Debates*, ser. 3, XXXVII, 1837, p. 1390.
24 Hopper 1842.
25 Archer 1983, pp. 241–64; Crook 1987; Hersey 1972.
26 See Pugin's letter to E.J. Wilson (6 November 1834) quoted in A. Wedgwood 1994b, p. 219. On Pugin's long-term participation in the project see *ibid.*, pp. 219–36 and Port 1976, pp. 53–96.
27 See Clark 1962; Brooks 1999, pp. 211–14. See also Germann 1972; Macaulay 1975.
28 Girouard 1968, pp. 20–24.
29 See Colley 1992.
30 Port 1976, pp. 35–40.
31 Jordan 1969, p. 291.
32 Tait 1993, pp. 39–70.
33 Hamilton 1836a; *idem* 1836b; *idem* 1837. For contemporary responses to Hamilton's letters, with long excerpts, see *Architectural Magazine*, IV, 1837, pp. 120–32; *Edinburgh Review*, LXV, 1837, pp. 174–79; and *Quarterly Review*, LXIII, 1837, pp. 61–82.
34 Ferrey 1835, p. 8.
35 A.W.N. Pugin 1836a, p. 2.
36 *Idem* 1836b.
37 Lubbock 1995, pp. 233–47.

38 Examples of such debates over place are recorded in Hansard, *Parliamentary Debates*, ser. 3, XXXI, 1836, pp. 234–45, and XLIII, 1838, pp. 695–710.
39 *Ibid.*, ser. 3, XLIII, 1838, pp. 698–705.
40 Huch and Ziegler 1985.
41 Port 1976, pp. 9–16; Weitzman 1961, pp. 99–107. For a brief history of earlier complaints and resulting changes see Cooke 1987, pp. 46–49.
42 Davison 1983, pp. 349–70; Sennett 1994, pp. 255–70.
43 Hansard, *Parliamentary Debates*, ser. 3, XVI, 1833, p. 373.
44 Hansard, *Parliamentary Debates*, ser. 3, XXXI, 1836, p. 234.
45 In 1836, Hume mentioned that the building could "occupy the position of Marlborough House", while in 1838 he situated it "opposite Marlborough House" or on the site of St James's Palace: Hansard, *Parliamentary Debates*, ser. 3, XXXI, 1836, pp. 234–45 and XLIII, 1838, pp. 706–09.
46 Anon. 1834a, pp. 319–34.
47 W.E.H. 1836, p. 415.
48 An earlier article also supported the spot behind the National Gallery or the Pall Mall location: *Westminster Review*, XXII, 1835, pp. 163–72; Smirke 1834.
49 Simo 1988.
50 Loudon 1836, pp. 100–03.
51 Loudon also proposed Lincoln's Inn Fields, open to Holborn and the Strand, in *ibid.*, pp. 102.
52 Rainy 1836, pp. 309–14. Rainy's plan may have resulted from the *Architectural Magazine*'s general call for new proposals in III, 1836, p. 109.
53 Crook 1992, pp. 77–96.
54 Fowler 1836.

Chapter 7
I am glad to acknowledge the exemplary primary research done by Professor M.H. Port in his book *The Houses of Parliament*, New Haven and London 1976, which I have used extensively in this account.
1 London, House of Lords and House of Commons 1836.
2 The competition drawings, the property of the Office of Woods and Forests, were lent back to Barry at his request. In 1845, he was requested to return them, and he replied that he would after he had copied them (London, PRO, Work 1/28, p. 281). Nothing further was ever heard of them.
3 Port 1976, p. 77.
4 London, PRO, Work 11/1/1, fols. 14, 16, 17.
5 Port 1976, p. 77.
6 E.W. Pugin 1867, pp. 23–24, 26, 28–29, 31.
7 See, for example, the Moulton-Barrett volume in the House of Lords Record Office.
8 E.W. Pugin 1867, pp. 28–29.
9 Port 1976, p. 75.
10 *Ibid.*, p. 98.
11 Barry 1867, p. 160.
12 London, House of Commons 1846.
13 London, PRO, Work 1/24, pp. 88–89, *loc. cit.*, Work 11/12, fols. 12, 15, 17, 19.
14 Port 1976, p. 103.
15 London, PRO, Work 1/25, p. 85.
16 Port 1976, p. 269.
17 London, House of Lords and House of Commons 1843, Appendix 1.
18 London, House of Lords 1844.
19 Barry 1868, p. 53.
20 *Ibid.*, p. 39.
21 *Ibid.*, pp.55–56.
22 *Ibid.*, p. 89.
23 Ferrey 1861, p. 248.
24 A. Wedgwood 1977, nos. 508–10, pp. 62–63.
25 London, PRO, Work 11/9/4, fol. 33.
26 Port 1976, p. 120.
27 London, Victoria and Albert Museum, MS L5158-1969: Pugin's diary for 1837, entries for 16 March, September, and 20 December.
28 *Illustrated London News*, X, no. 260, 24 April 1847, p. 260.
29 Port 1976, p. 262.
30 London, Victoria and Albert Museum, MS L5165-1969: Pugin's diary for 1845, entry for 2 October.
31 London, Victoria and Albert Museum, Mostyn Crace bequest, MS JGC-20; *Builder*, III, 1845, p. 426.

32 London, House of Lords and House of Commons 1846, pp. 9–10.
33 *Illustrated London News*, X, no. 259, 17 April 1847, pp. 245–47.
34 *Ibid.*, p. 247.
35 *Ibid.*, p. 247; Minton's name is given in the guidebook, anon. [1847a], p. 10.
36 London, House of Commons 1850.
37 Anon. 1860, p. 56. It seems likely that this glass was removed to Central Lobby during the 1860s and replaced by the simpler emblems of the United Kingdom that may be seen in photographs of 1897.
38 Anon. 1855, p. 55.
39 Hansard, *Parliamentary Debates*, ser. 3, CXVIII, 1851, pp 302–04.
40 *Builder*, X, 1852, p. 57.
41 London, PRO, Work 11/1/2, fols. 259–63 (Treasury Minute, 4 July 1856).
42 Port 1976, pp. 218–24.
43 *Ibid.*, p. 165.
44 Ryde 1849.
45 As demonstrated by Barry's drawings in the Royal Institute of British Architects.
46 Port 1976, p. 169.
47 Hansard, *Parliamentary Debates*, ser. 3, CLXXVI, 1864, p. 498; *idem*, ser. 3, CLXXIX, 1865, p. 247.
48 Port 1976, p. 178.
49 These figures were carved in the Dublin workshop of J.H. Hardman. Considerable research has failed to identify them.
50 London, House of Commons 1867–68.
51 Port 1976, p. 186.
52 *Ibid.*, p. 192.
53 See Miele 1998, pp. 220–44.

Chapter 8
1 Scharf documented some of the most significant architectural transformations in late Georgian and early Victorian London. See Jackson 1987.
2 Colvin 1973, VI, pp. 625–26.
3 Linda Colley has pursued the relationship between political and cultural identity, especially in Colley 1992. See also Port 1976, pp. 30–32.
4 The ceremonial splendour of the Tudor and Stuart courts is well known. However, the comparatively restrained character of the monarchy in the aftermath of the Glorious Revolution (1688) has stimulated little historical interest. As a result, in David Cannadine's words, "... English royal ritual has been almost entirely ignored for the period since the late seventeenth century ...". In his analysis of modern royal ritual, Cannadine identifies architecture and urban design as one of ten "aspects of ritual performance and context": Cannadine 1983, pp. 103, 107, 113.
5 In such fiscally constrained times, over £250,000 was expended on these projects. The commission resulted from the amalgamation of the Parliamentary committees to improve the approaches to the Houses of Parliament, first appointed in 1792, and the commissions established in 1777, 1799 and 1804 to supervise the development of the Westminster Sessions House. Its authority was consolidated by seven Acts of Parliament between 1800 and 1814, and any land it purchased became crown property. Colvin 1983, VI, pp. 515–16.
6 From the start of his Regency he had shown a strong interest in these ceremonies, and had first opened Parliament in person on 30 November 1812: *The Times*, 1 December 1812, p. 3. (George IV's coronation is discussed in chapter 4.) This accords with Walter Arnstein's findings for Victoria's reign, and, while Cannadine deems George IV's pageantry, particularly his coronation, farcical, he notes that "there is much about George IV's public style that anticipates subsequent developments ...": Arnstein 1990, pp. 182–83, 194; Cannadine 1983, pp. 118–18, n. 55. John Cannon and Ralph Griffiths deem George IV's accession as marking the inception of

the modern monarchy, or what they term the "popular monarchy": "... not in the sense that the monarchy has always been popular ... but that it compensated increasingly for the loss of formal political power by adopting a less remote attitude, by appealing to a wider range of its subjects, and by concerning itself greatly with its public image". Cannon and Griffiths 1988, p. 530. Colley locates this change in the latter part of George III's reign, but her analysis corresponds: "The revival of the monarchy in George III's reign would be very much a matter of a renovated and more assertively nationalistic royal image, not a resurgence of royal power in political terms." Colley 1992, p. 207.

7 This colonnade was probably added by John Vardy (1718–1765), contemporary with his construction of the adjacent structure for the Ordnance Office in 1753. This was commandeered by the House of Lords in 1762. Colvin 1976, V, p. 399.

8 Many drawings of Soane's designs survive at the Soane Museum, and the entire corpus is analysed, along with the archival evidence, in Sawyer 1999. The plan and perspective illustrated here are Sir John Soane's Museum Drawings 36/4/40 and 71/1/1.

9 Soane 1799, p. 15.

10 Every year for the next decade Soane included at least one drawing of his House of Lords project in the Academy exhibitions: Stroud 1984, pp. 286–87. The perspective of the revised design illustrated here is Sir John Soane's Museum Drawing F118.

11 This is labelled as such on Sir John Soane's Museum Drawing 16/3/18, which is the plan of the House of Lords project that Soane used as an illustration in his lectures as Professor of Architecture at the Royal Academy, beginning in 1809.

12 Crook 1995, passim; Frew 1982, pp. 315–19.

13 Colvin 1973, VI, pp. 518–19.

14 London, Sir John Soane's Museum Drawing 51/1/1AV.

15 Later survey drawings document that only the portal and vestibule were built: London, Sir John Soane's Museum Drawings 37/1/14; 37/1/22, 22A, 22AV; 89/3/49.

16 In this report he referred to the Royal Entrance being covered with "Oil Cloth", and stated that "when the Sovereign goes in State to the House a temporary platform is made to render the Royal Entrance practicable": London, Sir John Soane's Museum, private correspondence, XII.G.1.2.

17 The Times, 28 April 1820, p. 3.

18 London, Sir John Soane's Museum, private correspondence, Parcel 2, fol. 51. The State Opening just prior to Soane's commission had been conducted with particular panache, and the apartments leading to the throne had been lined with invited spectators: The Times, 6 February 1822, p. 4.

19 Sawyer 1996, pp. 66–72, examines the iconographic origins and interpretations of Soane's Royal Entrance, with particular reference to his project of July 1822 for constituting it as a 'National Monument', which would have preserved the fabric of the Prince's Chamber and old House of Lords.

20 The porte-cochère was only added, at the king's insistence, in September 1822, after construction of the extended arcade had begun: London, Sir John Soane's Museum, private correspondence, XI.H.1.

21 Soane had these watercolours bound into a volume: London, Sir John Soane Museum Drawings, LXI, fols. 28–37.

22 This is part of the important group of drawings that Charles James Richardson (1809–1872), Soane's pupil from 1824 to

1837, gleaned and copied during his years in the office and eventually sold to the Victoria and Albert Museum: London, Victoria and Albert Museum, Department of Prints, Drawings and Paintings, Richardson Collection 3306.105.

23 As Prince and Regent, his principal London residence of 1783–96, Carlton House, had been patterned after a neo-classical Parisian hotel and filled with smuggled French furniture. Many of these fittings and furnishings were then incorporated into the state apartments at Windsor Castle that he had Sir Jeffry Wyattville remodel in a chiefly neo-classical mode in 1824. Meanwhile, under his patronage, Nash's Buckingham Palace and Regent Street provided a neo-classical armature for the West End.

24 This reading challenges John Harris's assertion that "the effect of passing through must have been traumatic, for ... here was a recapitulation of the severe Peyrian neo-classicism of his House of Parliament design of 1794". Harris 1992, p. 289.

25 During the construction of this phase of the Royal Entrance, Soane notably demonstrated his familiarity with contemporary publications on the chapel in a note to John Britton of 28 December 1822: "I have the pleasure to send you Sir. H.W. [illegible] Architecture of Henry VII's Chapel I have – and the other I have looked over with satisfaction – it enlarges our sphere of knowledge on Gothic Arch: of which modern practitioners are in my opinion [illegible] defective in." Poughkeepsie, NY, Vassar College, Artist Autograph Collection. "The other" may be a reference to L.N. Cottingham's illustrated volume on the chapel, published that year.

26 Harris 1992, p. 290. The composition of the Ante-

Room portals is strikingly similar to the columned partitions flanked by antique torchères in Simonetti's Galleria dei Candelabri. This was probably in progress when Soane was in Rome, from 1778 to 1780.

27 These allegorical roundels are 80 cm in diameter, and another, half the size, depicted just The Rise of Rome and was probably located over the doorway at the top of the stair: London, Sir John Soane's Museum, private correspondence XI.H.6. The larger roundels were salvaged on the demolition of the Scala Regia and are now set into the walls of one of the subsidiary entrances to the new palace in Royal Court: Palace of Westminster, WOA S238, S239. All were fabricated from the casts of the roundels of Sol and Luna on the east and west sides of the Arch of Constantine, which Soane commissioned from Thomas Banks in 1801 and also used at the Bank of England and Pitzhanger Manor. See Richardson and Stevens 1999, p. 235, nos. 140–41.

28 The engraved section of the Scala Regia in Britton and Pugin's Illustrations of the Public Buildings of London shows the niches filled with neo-classical trophy groups, as Soane had suggested in an early design. Britton and Pugin 1828, II, third of three plates following p. 267, and London, Sir John Soane's Museum Drawing 71/2/44.

29 In 1831 Soane offered to commission these himself: Sawyer 1996, p. 75, n. 41.

30 Arnstein 1990, pp. 182–83, details Victoria's repeated participation in the State Opening and Closing early in her reign, beginning with the prorogation of 17 July 1837. The last State prorogation was in 1854. Soane's suite functioned as the principal entrance to the provisional House of Lords in the Painted Chamber, and remained functional in the interval between the

completion of the new Lords Chamber in April 1847 and the first use of Barry's Royal Entrance in February 1852: Port 1976, p. 316, n. 5.

31 Cannadine 1983, p. 118.

32 The degree of Pugin's contribution to the design of the palace is a complex and ultimately irresolvable question. Even Barry's supporters acknowledged that Pugin drew the most important interior perspectives for the competition, including those of the Royal Entrance. Colvin 1973, VI, pp. 578, 588–95.

33 This includes the Prince's Chamber, which Barry partitioned from it in response to complaints about the distance between the Robing Room and the House of Lords: ibid., p. 611.

34 Barry 1867, p. 246.

35 The Fine Arts Commission's report of 1847 defined the subject matter for the principal spaces of the new palace, including the Royal Gallery: Boase 1954, p. 342.

Chapter 9

1 Nicholson 1967, p. 166: entry for 16 May 1941.

2 Hansard, The Official Report, ser. 5, CCCLXXXXIII, 1943, cols. 408–09.

3 Ibid., col. 403.

4 Ibid., cols. 403–04.

5 Ibid., col. 437.

6 Ibid., col. 417.

7 Ibid., cols. 411–13.

8 Ibid., col. 421.

9 Ibid., col. 443.

10 Ibid., col. 436. The Lords Chamber was the same width as the old Commons Chamber, but twelve feet, nine inches longer.

11 Ibid., cols. 432 and 448.

12 Ibid., col. 437.

13 Ibid., col. 426.

14 Hansard, The Official Report, ser. 5, CCCCVII, 1945, col. 1006.

15 Anon. 1948, p. 5.

16 London, House of Commons 1944, p. 4.

17 Ibid., p. 5.

18 G.G. Scott 1933, pp. 5–14.

19 "The work, he said, had been of enormous complexity. It was the most complex building he had

ever had to deal with in his pretty long experience. The interior was rather like that of a battleship. To fit in all these arrangements was a most intricate business, and still more intricate to tuck them out of sight. The whole place was 'riddled with entrails' yet when the building was finished people would not realise that there was anything unusual there at all; everything would be plain, simple, and straightforward." *Architect and Building News*, 18 March 1949, p. 254, reporting the discussion after a lecture by Oscar Faber.

20 Hansard, *The Official Report*, ser. 5, CCCLXXXXIII, 1943, col. 408.

21 G.G. Scott 1944, p. 8.

22 *Ibid.*

23 *Ibid.*

24 *Architect and Building News*, CXCVIII, 1950, pp. 161–80 ("since any architect's freedom to design in a contemporary idiom would have been limited by the terms of reference, criticism would be invidious"); *Architects' Journal*, CXII, 1950, pp. 392–402; *Builder*, CLXXIX, 1950, pp. 450–68; *Surveys* 1951.

25 Driberg 1950, pp. 176, 178.

26 Lutyens 1950b, pp. 1272–75, pp. 1273, 1275.

27 G.G. Scott 1950, replying to Lutyens 1950a.

28 Brawne 1950, p. 7; the letter was signed by Michael Brawne, Alan Graham, Robert Maguire and Peter Matthews.

29 Pevsner 1962, pp. 483–84.

30 Pope-Hennessy and Wild 1953, p. 71.

Chapter 10
Acknowledgement is due to Amanda Girling-Budd, who undertook the transcription of relevant Gillows and Holland & Sons archival material. Her MA thesis, a study of the two major firms involved in the manufacture of this furniture, has also informed this essay. The quotation in the title, "New furniture ...", is taken from London, PRO, Work 11/8/9, p. 9.

1 Quoted in anon. 1847b,

p. 261.

2 Port 1976, p. 98; Colvin 1973, VI, p. 574.

3 Anon. 1845, p. 124.

4 Colvin 1973, VI, p. 574.

5 Girling-Budd 1998, pp. 89–91.

6 A small group of furniture in the style of the 1820s and 1830s, stamped with inventory marks associating them with the House of Commons and House of Lords during William IV's reign, has been catalogued within the Parliamentary estate.

7 Anon. 1861, p. 4.

8 *Ibid.*, p. 5.

9 Wright and Smith 1902–03, I, pp. 70–72.

10 Dixon and Muthesius 1978, p. 252.

11 Anon. 1841, p. 148.

12 Mandler 1997, pp. 7–17, 21–22.

13 Grier 1988.

14 Anon. 1852, p. 34.

15 Wright and Smith 1902–03, I, p. 67.

16 *Ibid.*, p. 67.

17 For previous descriptions of furniture made for the new Palace of Westminster, see Wainwright 1976, pp. 282–98; Wainwright 1992, pp. 303–06, and London, Victoria and Albert Museum 1974.

18 Ryde 1849. This was intended to be the first of a series describing and illustrating the progress of the new building.

19 A. Wedgwood 1985, pp. 207–12.

20 Wainwright 1976. Two chairs, stamped *Crace*, were catalogued in the Parliamentary Estate in 1994 (fig. 9.9).

21 Colvin 1973, VI, p. 622.

22 Port 1976, p. 149; Colvin 1973, VI, p. 621.

23 As Barry explained to the Board of Works: London, PRO, Work 11/8/7, p. 2.

24 London, RIBA, MSS Collection, PUG 7/66, letter from A.W.N. Pugin to Crace, postmarked 11 November 1850, postscript; quoted in A. Wedgwood 1977, p. 66.

25 London, PRO, Work 11/8/9, pp. 1–10. An enclosed list of summary estimates for the sixty-eight areas amounted

to £13,872: *ibid.*, pp. 14–20. The second inventory focused on furniture, including the Commons Chamber, and came to a total of £11,026.

26 *Ibid.*, pp. 12–13. Webb, a comparatively small business, did not tender. The other firms were Seddon and Dowbiggin, both struggling in the face of competition from firms supplying the new commercial markets. Crace submitted the most expensive estimate.

27 *Ibid.*, p. 21. Chairs, writing tables and desks and were to be covered with morocco leather, with embossed, gilt borders. The carcasses of furniture were to have three coats of staining and copal varnish, with French polishing for edges and certain surfaces, and were to be "Iron double tinned of various designs with matted screws as may be directed".

28 *Ibid.*, p. 22. On 25 June, the countersigned contract was put forward to the Treasury, with an estimate from Barry for £20,000, for furniture and upholstery for all areas that were to be ready for use at the beginning of the next session of Parliament.

29 London, PRO, Work 11/8/6, pp. 21–27.

30 London, Victoria and Albert Museum, Department of Prints and Drawings, E.1501-1912; A. Wedgwood 1985, pp. 218–20, 227–29.

31 London, Victoria and Albert Museum, Department of Prints and Drawings, E.137-1939 (1851–59).

32 Port 1976, p. 119.

33 London, PRO, Work 11/8/9, p. 21.

34 London, Westminster Archive Centre, Gillows Archive, Account Book 344/157 (1846–57), Estimate Sketchbooks 344/105 (1849–55) and 344/137 (1835–83). The business records of Gillow & Co. of London and Lancaster, the successful bidders for the new furniture contract, survive only for the Lancaster branch. By 1830, Gillow & Co. had been taken

over, and the two branches in London and Lancaster were run as separate businesses. About 88% of Lancaster's business, including orders for the Palace of Westminster, was for the London branch, which had its premises at 176 Oxford Street. There are, however, many furniture types with Gillows & Co. maker's stamps that survive in the Parliamentary Estate, which indicate the scale and additional variety of furniture supplied by the London branch of the business. Girling-Budd 1998, p. 83.

35 Drawings originally in the possession of J.G. Crace depict a bed of the type made for the Commons residences before 1855, and an elaborate chest of drawers and a towel horse showing the basic forms of examples made in great numbers by Gillow & Co. London, Victoria and Albert Museum, Department of Prints and Drawings, E.1580-1912, E.1652-1912; A. Wedgwood 1985, pp. 249–51.

36 See chapter 12 for a more detailed study of the evolution of this design by Pugin.

37 London, PRO, Work 11/8/9, fol. 61: letter from Gillow & Co. to Sir William Molesworth, the Chief Commissioner of Works, 6 March 1855.

38 Gillow & Co. walnut tables and some armchairs were also embellished with a new type of *VR* monogram, peculiar to Gillow & Co.-marked furniture of this type still surviving in the Parliamentary Estate.

39 The use of mahogany for the royal throne and two Chairs of State was probably influenced by the quality of carving that could be achieved.

40 For example, Blackie & Son London 1853, p. 23: "within the last few years another change has taken place, and walnut furniture has again become popular ... hence we find that in drawing-room

furniture especially, walnut is now very extensively employed".

41 London, PRO, Work 11/8/9, fols. 41–60.

42 *Ibid.*, fol. 61.

43 *Ibid.*, letter from Barry to the Office of Works, 4 November 1856. Mr Cox was the Clerk of the Office of Works, with whom Barry had most correspondence.

44 *Ibid.*, fol. 72. Fifteen more types of furniture were tendered for in addition to the twenty in 1851. The present location of the drawings is unknown.

45 *Ibid.*, fol. 72: Statement of the Tenders received, 15 November 1856. Only seven of the nine invited firms submitted.

46 *Ibid.*, fol. 72; London, Victoria and Albert Museum, Archive of Art and Design, Holland & Sons, 1857–60, Government Contracts Ledgers (AAD 13/220-1983), p. 225; London, Victoria and Albert Museum, Department of Prints and Drawings, E.137-1939 (1851–59).

47 The particular forms of monograms used for architectural and furniture embellishment in the new Palace of Westminster are based on illustrations in A.W.N. Pugin 1844.

48 London, House of Commons 1987.

49 As used throughout the House of Lords on floors and ceilings. Only one piece of red leather upholstery with a *VR* monogram is known to survive, reused to cover a non-palace chair in a private collection.

50 See chapter 5. One of Pugin and Barry's concepts for wallpapers during the 1840s appears to have been a range of heraldic papers, like that made for the Lords Refreshment Rooms. Although this was ultimately rejected, the Tudor rose, portcullis and royal lion were used in more simplified, stylized patterns.

51 London, PRO, Work 11/21/II, 1866–70, 28 June 1866.

52 London, House of Commons

1991.

53 London, PRO, Work 11/8/9 (1851–59), Work 11/30 (1867), Work 11/31 (n.d.), Work 11/32/P1-2 (1855). The illustration at the bottom of p. 171 shows residence furniture upholstered with Utrecht velvet and stamped wool velvet.

54 London, Victoria and Albert Museum, Department of Prints and Drawings, E.1501-1912; A. Wedgwood 1985, pp. 216–18.

55 See chapter 12.

56 London, PRO, Work 11/21/II, 24 June 1867.

57 A. Wedgwood 1977, X-frame drawing p. 68.

58 Grier 1988, pp. 6–8.

59 MacDonagh 1897, p. 95.

60 Gloag 1967, p. xviii.

Chapter 11
I should like to acknowledge the invaluable advice of the late Clive Wainwright, and Dorian Church.

1 2 Chronicles 9:17–19.

2 Eames 1977, pp. xix, 182.

3 H. Roberts 1989, p. 61.

4 Bagehot 1867, pp. 4–5.

5 Kuhn 1996, p. 20.

6 Bagehot 1867, p. 80.

7 Ibid., p. 81.

8 Kuhn 1996, p. 28.

9 Colley 1992, p. 235.

10 Eames 1977, p. 191; see also pp. 182, 192–98.

11 Ibid., pp. 197–98; idem 1971, pp. 45, 47.

12 Idem 1977, p. 198; Roberts 1989, p. 65.

13 Cited in Eames 1977, p. 188.

14 von Wedel 1895, pp. 260–62.

15 See Baillie 1967, pp. 169–99.

16 As quoted in Gregg 1980, pp. 71–72.

17 Colley 1992, p. 207.

18 H. Roberts 1989, pp. 64–66.

19 Mirror of Literature, Amusement, and Instruction, no. 691, 15 November 1834, p. 338.

20 Simond 1817, p. 363.

21 Hutchinson 1886, pp. 109, 110.

22 Cannon 1987, pp. 10, 11.

23 Colley 1992, pp. 210–17.

24 Mirror of Literature, Amusement, and Instruction, no. 691, 15 November 1834, p. 338; Roberts 1989, pp. 66–68.

25 A. Wedgwood 1984, pp. 62,

67–68, n. 24; H. Roberts 1989, p. 72 (see also pp. 65, 66).

26 Weitraub 1997, p. 87.

27 Lant 1979, p. 151.

28 Weitraub 1997, pp. 88, 337; Longford 1964, pp. 135–36; Woodham-Smith 1972, pp. 119, 199.

29 Greville 1840; Greville 1927, II, p. 119.

30 Arnstein 1990, p. 185; Gregg 1980, p. 72; D.B. Green 1970, p. 84.

31 As quoted in Arnstein 1990, p. 185.

32 As quoted in Weitraub 1997, p. 110.

33 As quoted in Woodham-Smith 1972, p. 375.

34 As quoted ibid., p. 238.

35 London, House of Lords Record Office, Lord Great Chamberlain, II/4, p. 194.

36 Ibid.

37 Prestwich 1997, p. 357.

38 Cannon and Griffiths 1988, pp. 183–86, 198.

39 London, House of Lords Record Office, Lord Great Chamberlain, II/4, p. 196.

40 H. Roberts 1989, pp. 72–73.

41 J.L. Wolfe, letter dated 26 September 1867, published in Barry 1868, pp. 66–67; for further discussion of the new palace's throne and canopy and for Barry and Pugin's working relation-ship, see A. Wedgwood 1984, pp. 59–68.

42 The design by Barry, which is a preliminary design for the throned end of the House of Lords Chamber, is dated c. 1843 (RIBA Drawings Collection, C. Barry sketches, I Quarto, p. 76) and is illustrated in A. Wedgwood 1984, p. 71, pl. 3a.

43 A. Wedgwood 1984, p. 62.

44 Quoted ibid., p. 63.

45 Ibid., p. 64.

46 Ibid., p. 65.

47 Anon. 1848, p. 20.

48 J.R. Herbert, letter dated 24 February 1868 to E.W. Pugin, published in E.W. Pugin 1868, p. 13.

49 Wainwright 1994b, pp. 131–32; Eames 1977, pp. 57, n. 12; see also pp. 182–87.

50 Anon. 1848, p. 20; Pugin's two rules of design were "that there should be no

features ... which are not necessary for convenience, construction, or propriety", and "that all ornament should consist of enrichment of the essential construction": A.W.N. Pugin 1841a, p. 1.

51 Eames 1977, pp. 171–72.

52 Ibid.; Eeles 1902, p. 107; H. Roberts 1989, p. 64; A. Wedgwood 1994b, p. 227.

53 Anon. 1848, pp. 19–20.

54 Burges 1863, p. 126; I am grateful to Clive Wainwright for bringing this article to my attention. See also Palmer 1953.

55 Burges 1863, p. 124.

56 Anon. 1848, p. 20.

57 Burges 1863, p. 124.

58 Mirror of Literature, Amusement, and Instruction, no. 691, 15 November 1834, p. 338.

59 Illustrated London News, XIV, no. 356, 3 February 1849, p. 73. I am grateful to Dorian Church for bringing this reference to my attention.

60 Clive Wainwright, verbal communication of April 1999.

61 Throne and canopy design, dated 8 November 1866, signed by E.M. Barry, London, PRO, Work 29/268.

62 Clive Wainwright, verbal communication of April 1999.

63 Percier and Fontaine 1801, pl. XLVIII. I am grateful to Clive Wainwright for bringing this design to my attention.

64 For example, François Gérard, Napoleon I, 1805 (Musée de Versailles); Dominique Ingres, Napoleon on the Imperial Throne, 1806 (Musée de l'Armée); Robert Lefèvres, Emperor Napoleon I, 1809 (Musée Carnavalet).

65 Pugin wrote, "I have perpetuated many of these enormities in the furniture I designed some years ago for Windsor Castle": A.W.N. Pugin 1841a, p. 41.

66 See Lant 1979, pp. 150–76; and Heffer 1998, pp. 24–25.

67 As quoted in Cannon and Griffiths 1988, p. 563.

68 Victoria 1985, pp. 192–93: letter dated 22 January 1866 (my emphasis).

69 Longford 1964, p. 348; see

also MacDonagh 1921, p. 211.

70 Victoria 1985, p. 193.

71 Anon. 1867, p. 55.

72 Heffer 1998, p. 6.

73 Ibid., pp. 6–7; Longford 1964, pp. 365–66, 391–92.

74 As quoted in Heffer 1998, p. 107.

75 Anon. [c. 1902], p. 39.

76 Mirror of Literature, Amusement, and Instruction, no. 690, 8 November 1834, p. 324.

77 Anon. 1739, p. 636; Thomas 1975, pp. 168–93.

78 Anon. 1739, p. 636.

79 For example, P. Tillemans, The House of Commons in Session, c. 1710 (Palace of Westminster); J. Thornhill and W. Hogarth, The House of Commons During the Administration of Sir Robert Walpole, 1730 (Clandon Park); K.A. Hinkel, William Pitt Addressing the House of Commons on the French Declaration of War, 1793 (National Portrait Gallery); G. Hayter, The House of Commons, 1833 (National Portrait Gallery). For the position of Speaker, see Wilding and Laundy 1968, pp. 688–94.

80 A. Wedgwood 1985, p. 213; A.W.N. Pugin 1835, pl. 20.

81 Port 1976, p. 146; A. Wedgwood 1994b, p. 234.

82 Bagehot 1867, p. 163 (my emphasis).

83 Ibid., p. 80.

84 Brooks 1999, p. 212.

Chapter 12
The Origins and Function of the Speaker's House
(Christine Riding)

1 Lummis 1900, as quoted in Laundy 1964, p. 12.

2 Russell 1978, p. 381; Wright and Smith 1902–03 II, p. 340; Wilding and Laundy 1968, p. 691.

3 Porrit 1903, p. 473; the title of 'First Commoner' held true until 1919; see Wilding and Laundy 1968, pp. 688–89.

4 Wilding and Laundy 1968, p. 688.

5 MacDonagh 1897, p. 119.

6 Colvin 1976, V, 1976, p. 408.

7 Tinniswood 1992, p. 20.

8 Colvin 1976, V, p. 408–09.

9 A. Wedgwood 1994d, p. 1.

10 Colvin 1973, VI, p. 533

11 Colvin 1973, VI, p. 532.

12 Colvin 1973, VI, p. 533.

13 A. Wedgwood 1994d, p. 8.

14 J. Thompson 1980, pp. 6–8.

15 Wright and Smith 1902–03, I, p. 57.

16 MacKay 1986, pp. 29–30.

17 Wright and Smith 1902–03, I, p. 59.

18 As quoted in Belfield 1959, p. 37.

19 Wright and Smith 1902–03, I, pp. 58–59.

20 Illustrated London News, XXXIV, no. 959, 12 February 1859, p. 164.

21 MacDonagh 1897, pp. 131–32.

22 Illustrated London News, LX, no. 1702, 20 April 1872, p. 374.

23 Maxwell-Hyslop 1998, p. 20, n. 4.

24 Ibid., p. 19.

The Origins of the Speaker's State Bed
(Christine Riding)

25 Eames 1977, p. 76.

26 Ibid., p. 76

27 Ibid., p. 74

28 Eames 1986, p. 2044.

29 Binski 1986, pp. 35–36; Eames 1977, p. 15.

30 Baillie 1967, pp. 176–78.

31 Ibid., p. 176; Eames 1971

32 Baillie 1967, p. 186.

33 Ibid., p. 186; Binski 1986, p. 36. The Woolsack is a square couch that, according to tradition, has been in the Lords Chamber from the reign of Edward III, representing the commercial wealth of England, which at that time was in the wool trade. When the House of Lords is sitting, the Woolsack is the seat of the Lord Chancellor, who is the Speaker of the House of Lords (Wilding and Laundy 1968, p. 791).

34 Thornton 1977, p. 137.

35 For example, A. Wedgwood 1994a, p. 22; Thornton, who describes the bed as "perhaps the last royal state bed to be made in this country" also opines "it has been the custom for the monarch to spend the night at the Speaker's residence before the annual Opening of parliament"! Thornton 1977, p. 143.

36 Banks 1820, p. 8.
37 Kempe 1831, p. 10.
38 Weir 1999, p. 38; Somerset 1991, pp. 71–72.
39 Banks 1820, p. 30.
40 J. Roberts 1727, p. 5.
41 Brooke 1972, p. 85.
42 Huish 1821, p. 188.
43 As quoted in H. Roberts 1989, p. 76, n. 82.

*The Speaker's House*
(Dorian Church)
44 Colvin 1973, VI, p. 580, p. 586, fig. 27.
45 *Ibid.*, VI, p. 596; London, House of Lords and House of Commons, *Appendix*, 1843, p. 11.
46 A. Wedgwood 1994a, p. 4.
47 London, PRO, Work 11/480.
48 Anon. 1859, p. 164.
49 London, House of Lords and House of Commons 1843, p. 11.
50 London, PRO, Work 6/262, Letter to the Treasury, November 1859.
51 In 1856, Braund printed such a pattern-book, a collection of mainly exhibition furniture that also contained two plates of Palace of Westminster desks from the House of Lords Library, and writing tables from the Lords Chamber. These had been designed by Pugin and first made before his death. The book was finally published as Braund 1858.
52 London, PRO, Work 29/2561-65, 2570-92.
53 Blackie & Son 1853, reprinted New York 1970, p. 36.
54 London, PRO, Work 6/259.
55 Forty-eight of these chairs were supplied by Holland & Sons to the Speaker's House in 1859, thirty-six for the state dining room, and twelve for the private dining room, London, PRO, Work 6/259, pp. 15, 20.
56 London, PRO, Work 6/259, p. 18.
57 London, PRO, Work 6/259, pp. 18, 20.
58 London PRO, Work 29/2579.
59 London, Victoria and Albert Museum, Archive of Art and Design, Holland & Sons, 1857–1860, Government Contracts Ledgers, AAD 13/220-1983, pp. 203, 215.
60 London, Victoria and Albert Museum, Department of Prints and Drawings, E.137-1939 (1851–59).
61 London, Victoria and Albert Museum, Department of Prints and Drawings, E.2588-2600-1910, L.1577-1969; A. Wedgwood 1985, pp. 153, 156.
62 London, PRO, Work 6/259, p. 11. The design for the State Bed is located in London, PRO, Work 29/2560.
63 A. Wedgwood 1994d, pp. 5, 22.

*Speaker's State Silver*
(Christopher Garibaldi)
At the time of publication the Speaker's State Silver is in the process of being researched and catalogued. This section is thus work in progress.
64 For a comprehensive survey of the history of Garrard see Clifford 1991.
65 Additions were made in 1897: soufflé-dishes and pepper pots (James Garrard); in 1901: sauce boats, teapots, and toast racks (James Garrard); in 1921: muffin dishes and two tea-kettles on stands (Sebastian Garrard).
66 Glanville 1987, pp. 323–24.
67 Jewel Office Records – London, PRO, Lord Chamberlain's Papers LC5 110: 1732–62.
68 Jewel Office Records – London, PRO, Lord Chamberlain's Papers LC5 111.
69 Illustrated in Newman 1987, pp. 294–95.
70 Jewel House Records – London, PRO, Lord Chamberlain's Papers LC5 110 & 111.
71 A. Wedgwood 1994d, p. 21.
72 Illustrated in *ibid.*, p. 18.
73 Belfield 1959, p. 36.
74 See Penzer 1971: p. 135, pl. xxviii (1809–10); p. 187, pl. liv (1815–16).
75 See the candelabrum centrepiece made by Storr in 1813 for Edward Bootle-Wilbraham MP (1st Baron Skelmesdale), illustrated in London, Christies, 1989, p. 177.

Chapter 13
1 Anon. 1843, p. 540.
2 Edwards 1840, p. 193.
3 *Ibid.*, p. 334.
4 In 1846 a sub-committee for sculpture was set up, and in 1847 another to determine the subject matter for the commissioned works of art. For a comprehensive list of the members of the Fine Arts Commission from 1841–65, see Robertson 1978, p. 325–27.
5 London, House of Lords and House of Commons 1842, p. 5.
6 The areas considered by the Fine Arts Commission were: 1844 – Lords Chamber; 1845 – St Stephen's Hall, Upper Waiting Hall; 1847 – St Stephen's Porch, Central Lobby, Committee Corridor, Lords Corridor, Central Corridor, Lords Robing Room, Prince's Chamber, Royal Gallery, Robing Room, guardroom, Lobby, North Porch, Lords and Commons Refreshment Rooms; 1850 – sculpture in Prince's Chamber; 1854 – Painted Chamber. The competition of 1844 was extended to include designs for sculpture and decorative arts, which thereafter were commissioned directly from known artists. For an account of the designs submitted to the Westminster competitions see F.K. Hunt 1846.
7 Ormond 1967, pp. 397–402.
8 See Yung 1981, p. 641, no. 343b: Prince Albert, *Sketch of the Fine Arts Commission, 1846.*
9 Anon. 1846b, pp. 812–13.
10 Jameson 1844. Introducing the volume, Mrs Jameson stated that "A volume, containing a similar analysis of the collections of the Duke of Devonshire, the Duke of Wellington, Lord Ashburton, Mr Hope, Mr Neeld, Mr Munroe, and some others would complete the work": p. xviii.
11 *Ibid.*, p. xxxix.
12 *Ibid.*, p. 387.
13 Anon. 1839b, p. 86.
14 Anon. 1839a, p. 17.
15 Hogarth 1833, p. 40. This extract was first published in a letter in the *London Magazine*, 1737.
16 H. Cole 1842, p. 176.
17 *Ibid.*, p. 180.
18 L.P. 1845, pp. 108–41, p. 125.
19 H. Cole 1842, p. 176.
20 Anon. 1840, p. 57.
21 Cunningham 1842, pp. 669–73, p. 670.
22 One of the first serious introductions to early nineteenth-century German art was Jameson 1834. The extent to which German art of the early nineteenth century influenced Victorian painting is examined in Vaughan 1979.
23 'Statements of Director Peter von Cornelius relating to the proposed decoration of the Houses of Parliament', in London, House of Lords and House of Commons 1842, Appendix 3, pp. 18–25.
24 Cunningham 1842, p. 669.
25 Haydon 1842, p. 22.
26 The journal published a series of engravings of work from the Royal Collection between 1835 and 1861, two-thirds of which were by British artists.
27 Cope 1891, p. 255.
28 Jameson 1845, p. 6. The garden pavilion was dismantled in 1928.
29 *Ibid.*, p. 11.
30 Anon. 1846a, pp. 889–91, p. 890.
31 Sir C.L. Eastlake 1870, pp. 171–72.
32 Cope 1891, p. 258.
33 *Ibid.*

Chapter 14
1 A full account of individual works is given in Walker 1988. Descriptions of the individual works can be found in Bond 1980, Hay and Riding 1996.
2 Haydon 1926, II, p. 573.
3 Bell 1963.
4 Trodd 1994.
5 The history of this project is given in Boase 1954, pp. 319–58.
6 Competitions were subsequently held in 1844 for decorative arts, sculpture and fresco-painting; in 1845 for designs and specimen frescoes for the arches in the Lords Chamber (discussed further in chapter 15); and in 1847 for oil paintings. The entries were exhibited in Westminster Hall, save for the 1844 decorative arts competition, which was exhibited at Crockford's Bazaar.
7 Bond 1980, p. 66.
8 For an account of this influence see Vaughan 1979, especially Chapter VI, 'The German Manner and English History Painting', pp. 177–226.
9 London, House of Lords and House of Commons 1843, Appendix I, p. 7.
10 *Ibid.*, Appendix VI, p. 65.
11 South wall: Charles West Cope, *Edward III Conferring the Order of the Garter on the Black Prince*; William Dyce, *The Baptism of King Ethelbert*; and Charles West Cope, *Prince Henry Acknowledging the Authority of Chief Justice Gascoyne*. North wall: Daniel Maclise, *The Spirit of Justice*; John Callcott Horsley, *The Spirit of Religion*; Daniel Maclise, *The Spirit of Chivalry*.
12 For a further discussion of this theme, and its relation to contemporary treatments of the Arthurian legends by Tennyson, see chapter 15.
13 London, House of Lords and House of Commons 1847, Appendix I, p. 13.
14 The subjects were listed as follows: i) *Boadicea Inciting Her Army*; ii) *Alfred in the Camp of the Danes*; iii) *Brian Boroimhe Overcoming the Danes at the Bridge of Clontarff*; iv) *Edith Finding the Dead Body of Harold*; v) *Richard Coeur de Lion Coming in Sight of the Holy City*; vi) *Eleanor Saving the Life of her Husband, afterwards Edward I, by Sucking the Poison from a Wound in his Arm*; vii) *Bruce, During a Retreat Before the English, Protecting a Woman Borne on a Litter, and Checking the Pursuers*; viii) *Philippa Interceding for the Lives of the Citizens of Calais*; ix) *Edward the Black Prince entering London by the side of King John of France*; x) *The Marriage of Henry V, at Troyes, with the Princess Katharine of France*; xi) *Elizabeth at Tilbury*; xii) *Blake at Tunis*; xiii) *Marlborough at Blenheim*; xiv) *The Death of Wolfe*; xv) *The Death of Abercrombie*; xvi) *Lord Cornwallis receiving the*

*Sons of Tippoo as hostages*; xvii) *The Death of Nelson at the Battle of Trafalgar*; xviii) *The Meeting of Wellington and Blücher after the Battle of Waterloo*. London, House of Lords and House of Commons 1847, Appendix I, p. 13.

15 Soane's projects for the processional route to the Lords Chamber are discussed in chapter 8.

16 For a full description of both the bronze reliefs and the portraits see Bond 1980, pp. 66–83.

17 For example, *Henry VIII* is based on various images by and after Hans Holbein. The image of Elizabeth I is after *Elizabeth I* by Hans Eworth (Royal Collection). See *ibid.*, pp. 75–83.

18 For a full description of the scenes see *ibid.*, pp. 92–101, and Hay and Riding 1996, pp. 86–89.

19 Bond 1980, p. 93.

20 London, House of Lords and House of Commons 1847, Appendix I, p. 10.

21 *Punch, or the London Charivari*, July–December 1847, p. 8.

22 London, House of Lords and House of Commons 1847, Appendix I, p. 10.

23 See Hay and Riding 1996, pp. 106–07.

24 The scenes were: *A Sitting of the Wittena-Gemot*; *The Feudal System*; *The Origin of the House of Commons*; *The Termination of the Baronial Wars*; *An Early Trial by Jury*; *The Signing of the Magna Charta*; *The Abolition of Villeinage*; *The Privileges of the Commons Asserted by Sir Thomas More Against Cardinal Wolsey*; *The Conversion of the Anglo-Saxons to Christianity*; and *The Reformation*. London, House of Lords and House of Commons 1847, Appendix I, p. 10.

25 The scenes were: *The Phoenicians in Cornwall*; *A Druidical Sacrifice*; and *Anglo-Saxon Captives Exposed for Sale in the Market-Place of Rome*. Opposite were: *Cook in Otaheite*; *English Authorities Stopping the Sacrifice of a Suttee*; and *The Emancipation of Negro Slaves*. *Ibid.*,

Appendix I, p. 11.

26 See Hay and Riding 1996, pp. 90–92.

27 See *ibid.*, p. 93.

28 Published in Newbolt 1897.

29 See *idem* 1927, and Hay and Riding 1996, pp. 98–101.

30 *The Times*, 29 June 1927, p. 9, col. 4.

31 Newbolt 1897, p. 4.

32 *Ibid.*, p. 2.

33 Walker 1988, III, part 5, p. 74.

34 Farr 1978, p. 335.

Chapter 15

1 See chapter 1 for a discussion of how this shift of power affected the balance in Parliament.

2 London, House of Lords and House of Commons 1844, p. 9.

3 See F.K. Hunt 1846. The commission selected: Thomas, *The Spirit of Justice* (later replaced by Maclise); Redgrave, *Prince Henry Acknowledging the Authority of Chief Justice Gascoyne* (later replaced by Cope); Horsley, *The Spirit of Religion*; Dyce, *The Baptism of Ethelbert*; Maclise, *The Spirit of Chivalry*; and Cope, *Edward III Conferring the Order of the Garter on the Black Prince*.

4 For a full discussion of popular medievalism and the chivalric revival, see Girouard 1981. See also chapter 4 in this volume for the ceremonial revival of Gothic traditions in the reign of George IV.

5 Lord Eglinton held this infamous tournament on his Ayrshire estate in August 1839 in lieu of the traditional summer races. The best-remembered incident is the torrential rainstorm that ended the pageantry before the knights even took the field. See Girouard 1981, pp. 87–110.

6 The costume ball reflected the enthusiastic interest in fancy dress that emerged in Britain in the 1820s and endured through to the end of the century. Those attending the ball were encouraged to wear extravagant costumes in the style of the late medieval

era, as a show of support for the Spitalfields silk industry. Staged entertainments included a procession, quadrilles and a re-enactment of the meeting of Anne of Brittany with Queen Philippa and King Edward III (the last two played by Victoria and Albert). For the vogue for fancy dress, see Stevenson and Bennett 1978, pp. 78ff.

7 Dickens 1845, pp. 124–25.

8 The competition cartoon and related fresco specimens relating to *The Knight* have been lost. Dafforn 1871, p. 30.

9 *Athenaeum*, no. 923, 1845, p. 663; *Art-Union*, VII, 1845, pp. 257, 349.

10 Dickens 1845, pp. 12–26.

11 London, House of Lords and House of Commons 1844 p. 36.

12 These were *The History of the Renowned Prince Arthur, King of Britain*, London, 1816; *La Mort d'Arthur*, London, 1816; and *The Byrth, Lyf and Actes of King Arthur*, ed. R. Southey, London, 1817. The last was regarded as authoritative. The next edition, in modernized language, did not appear for another forty years: *La Mort d'Arthure*, ed. T. Wright, London 1858. For a full account of the literary recovery, see Merriman 1973.

13 Tennyson 1974, pp. 63–64, ll. 344–47. *The Epic* first appeared in *idem* 1842.

14 W. Dyce, quoted in Aberdeen, Art Gallery, III, p. 992. Dyce was referring to works by Peter von Cornelius in the Glyptothek, and Julius Schnorr von Carolsfeld in the Residenz, both in Munich. See Vaughan 1979, pp. 44–53.

15 Aberdeen, Art Gallery, III, p. 992

16 Dyce to Sir Charles Eastlake, 20 July 1848, in Aberdeen, Art Gallery, III, p. 49. His reading included the two most respected historical studies of the day, Herbert 1836, and Davies 1809.

17 The designs possibly included the allegories of

Mercy, Generosity, Courtesy, Faith and Piety. Neither J.S. Dyce's memoir of his father's life nor the commissioners' response to the designs make this clear.

18 Dyce to Sir Charles Eastlake, 23 November 1848, in Aberdeen, Art Gallery, III, p. 58.

19 Dyce paraphrased the lines this way in a letter to J.T. Coleridge, 17 April 1849. In Aberdeen, Art Gallery, III, unpaginated.

20 Dyce to Henry Cole, 18 June 1852, in Aberdeen, Art Gallery, III, ch. 29, unpaginated insertion at end of chapter. For a summary of the commissioners' difficulties with Dyce, see Mancoff 1990, pp. 133–35.

21 The designs for these have not been located, so it is impossible to describe Dyce's interpretation for them.

Chapter 16

1 A. Barry 1867, pp. 258, 193.

2 The exception to this is Walker 1988, in which further information and referencing for all the sculpture can be found.

3 London, PRO, Work 11, 9/7, p. 3.

4 See Read 1976, pp. 232–45; for details about Thomas, see his obituary, anon. 1862, pp. 231–33.

5 For fuller details, see Robertson 1978, especially pp. 324–44. For a full contemporary account of its activities, including coverage of sculpture, see F.K. Hunt 1846.

6 London, House of Lords and House of Commons 1843, p. 11.

7 *Ibid.*, p. 68

8 *Idem* 1844, p. 12.

9 *Ibid.*, pp. 13–15.

10 *Ibid.*, p. 11.

11 *Ibid.*, pp. 16–18.

12 *Idem* 1845, pp. 9–10.

13 *Ibid.*, pp. 10–12.

14 *Ibid.*, pp. 7–8.

15 *Ibid.*, pp. 12–13.

16 See Read 1982, pp. 82–84, with further references.

17 See Read 1976, p. 233.

18 Matthews 1911, p. 176.

19 E. Eastlake 1870, p. 208.

20 See Bond 1980, pp. 66–83.

21 See Read 1982, p. 121.

22 Eastlake's letter of 20 November 1862 is in the Royal Archives at Windsor, RA VIC/ADD H2/321.

23 London, PRO, Work 22/2/49, 101.

24 For a detailed critical account of this, see Burrow 1981.

25 Tahon-Vanroose 1994, pp. 21–23.

26 Baedeker 1910, p. 44.

27 For Ghent, see van Tyghem 1978, pp. 254–58; for Leuven, see Vandekerchove 1998, pp. 83–92.

28 Cherry and Stratford 1995, pp. 68–73.

29 See Kalnein and Levey 1972, p. 155.

30 See Otten 1970, pp. 55–57, 115–16.

31 See Walker 1988, III, pp. 68–71.

32 See Bond 1980, pp. 44–59.

33 See Walker 1988, III, pp. 27–30; Manning 1982, pp. 129–31, 199.

34 See Bond 1980, pp. 102–06.

35 See Read 1989, pp. 33–36.

36 See Read 1982, pp. 109–13.

37 See A.H. Robinson n.d., unpaginated.

# BIBLIOGRAPHY

## Manuscripts

Aberdeen, Art Gallery
J.S. Dyce, 'Life,
Correspondence, and Writings
of William Dyce, RA
1806–1864, Painter, Musician,
and Scholar by his Son', 4 vols.
Cambridge, Trinity College
MS O.3.59
Dublin, Trinity College
MS 535
Duke of Northumberland
(Alnwick Castle)
Northumberland MSS, Alnwick
MS no. 468
London, British Library
Add. MS 5758
London, College of Arms
MS 2.H.13
MS Le Neve WA
MS Vincent 92
London, House of Lords Record
Office
Lord Great Chamberlain, II/4
Moulton-Barrett volume
London, Public Records Office
Lord Chamberlain's Papers LC5
110 (Jewel Office Records)
Lord Chamberlain's Papers LC5
111 (Jewel Office Records)
Work 1/24
Work 1/25
Work 1/28
Work 6/259
Work 6/262
Work 11/1/1
Work 11/1/2
Work 11/8/6
Work 11/8/7
Work 11/8/9
Work 11/9/4
Work 11/9/7
Work 11/12
Work 11/21/II
Work 11/30
Work 11/31
Work 11/32/P1–2
Work 11/480
Work 21/14
Work 22/2/49
Work 29/268
Work 29/2561
Work 29/2562
Work 29/2563
Work 29/2564
Work 29/2565
Work 29/2570
Work 29/2571
Work 29/2572
Work 29/2573
Work 29/2574
Work 29/2575
Work 29/2576
Work 29/2577
Work 29/2578

Work 29/2579
Work 29/2580
Work 29/2581
Work 29/2582
Work 29/2583
Work 29/2584
Work 29/2585
Work 29/2586
Work 29/2587
Work 29/2588
Work 29/2589
Work 29/2590
Work 29/2591
Work 29/2592
Work 36/68
London, Royal Institute of
British Architects
MSS Collection, PUG 7/66,
letter from A.W.N. Pugin to
Crace, postmarked 11
November 1850
London, Sir John Soane's Museum
Private correspondence, Parcel
2
Private correspondence, XI.H.1
Private correspondence,
XII.G.1.2
London, Victoria and Albert
Museum
MS L5158-1969: A.W.N. Pugin,
diary for 1837
MS L5165-1969: A.W.N. Pugin,
diary for 1845
Mostyn Crace bequest, MS
JGC-20
London, Victoria and Albert
Museum, Archive of Art and
Design
Holland & Sons, 1857–60,
government contracts ledgers
(AAD 13/220-1983)
London, Westminster Archive
Centre
Gillows Archive, 344/105:
estimate sketchbook (1849–55)
Gillows Archive, 344/137:
estimate Sketchbook (1835–83)
Gillows Archive, 344/157:
account book (1846–57)
Poughkeepsie, NY, Vassar College
Library
Artist Autograph Collection,
letter of John Soane to John
Britton, 28 December 1822
Windsor, Royal Archives
RA VIC/Add H 2/321, letter from
Sir Charles Eastlake to Gen.
Charles Grey, 20 November
1862
Windsor, Royal Library
Royal MS 1B, 2b

## Printed works

Anonymous works are listed
under "anon.". Works
produced by institutions or
organizations are listed by

place, then by the name of the
organization.
Adonis, A., *Making Aristocracy
Work: The Peerage and the
Political System in Britain,
1884–1914*, Oxford 1993
Alexander, J.J.G., and P. Binski,
*The Age of Chivalry: Art in
Plantagenet England, 1200–1400*,
exhib. cat., London, Royal
Academy, 1987
Alexander, J.J.G., 'The Portrait of
Richard II in Westminster
Abbey', in D. Gordon, L.
Monnas and C. Elam (eds.), *The
Regal Image of Richard II and the
Wilton Diptych*, London 1997,
pp. 197–206
Anon., 'A model for a New
Parliament-House', *Common
Sense*, 1 December 1739,
reprinted in *Gentleman's
Magazine*, IX, December 1739,
pp. 635–37
Anon., 'Parliament of our
Ancestors', *Westminster Review*,
XXI, 1834a, pp. 319–34
Anon., 'The Destruction of the
Houses of Parliament', *The New
Monthly Magazine*, XXXXII,
1834b, pp. 353–55
Anon., 'Conflagration of the Two
Houses of Parliament',
*Gentleman's Magazine*, [second]
new series, II, 1834c, p. 477
Anon., *Catalogue of the Designs
Offered for the New Houses of
Parliament, Now Exhibiting in the
National Gallery*, London 1836a
Anon., 'Minutes of Evidence
Taken before the Select
Committee of the House of
Lords, on Rebuilding the
Houses of Parliament, March 8,
1836', *Architectural Magazine*,
III, 1836b, pp. 264–70
Anon., 'Painting and Sculpture
Combined with the Decorative
Arts', *Art-Union*, no. 2, 15
March 1839a, p. 17
Anon., 'The British Institution,
The Ancient Masters', *Art-
Union*, no. 5, 15 June 1839b,
p. 86
Anon., 'Prince Albert and the
Fine Arts', *Art-Union*, no. 12,
15 April 1840, p. 57
Anon., *London Interiors*, London
1841
Anon., 'On the Decoration of the
New Houses of Parliament',
*Fraser's Magazine*, XXVII, 1843,
p. 540
Anon., 'New Parliamentary
Committee Rooms', *Illustrated
London News*, VI, no. 147, 22
February 1845, p. 124

Anon., 'Progress of English
Fresco Painting', *Athenaeum*,
no. 983, 29 August 1846a,
pp. 889–91
Anon., 'Third Report of the
Commissioners on the Fine
Arts, Presented to Both Houses
of Parliament by Command of
Her Majesty', *Athenaeum*,
no. 880, 7 September 1846b,
pp. 812–13
Anon., *The Palace of Westminster
with a Descriptive Account of the
House of Lords*, London (W.
Warrington & Co.) n.d. [1847a]
Anon., 'The new House of
Lords', *Illustrated London News*,
X, no. 260, 24 April 1847b,
p. 261
Anon., *The Palace of Westminster
with a Descriptive Account of the
House of Lords*, London 1848
Anon., *Descriptive Account of the
Palace of Westminster*, London
1852
Anon., *The New Palace of
Westminster*, London (W.
Warrington & Co.) 1855
Anon., 'The Houses of
Parliament', *Illustrated London
News*, XXIX, no. 959, 12
February 1859, p. 164,
supplement p. 161
Anon., *The Houses of Parliament*,
London (H.G. Clarke & Co.)
1860
Anon., *Descriptive Account of the
Palace of Westminster*, London
1861
Anon., 'The Late John Thomas,
Sculptor', *Illustrated London
News*, XXXI, no. 1160, 30 August
1862, pp. 231–33
Anon., 'Where is Britannia?', *The
Tomahawk: a Saturday Journal of
Satire*, no. 5, 8 June 1867,
London, pp. 49, 55
Anon., *The New Palace of
Westminster*, new edn., London
n.d. [c. 1902]
Anon., *The laying of the Foundation
Stone of the New Chamber of the
House of Commons by the Speaker
26th May 1948*, London 1948
Archer, J., 'The Beginning of
Association in British
Architectural Aesthetics',
*Eighteenth-Century Studies*, XVI,
no. 3, spring 1983, pp. 241–64
'Archilochus', *What Style? The
Royal or Baronial? The Priestly or
Monastic? or the Squirely? for the
New House of Parliament*, London
1837
Arnstein, W.L., 'Queen Victoria
Opens Parliament: the
Disinvention of Tradition',

*Historical Research*, LXIII, 1990,
pp. 178–94
Atterbury, P., 'Pugin and Interior
Design', in idem (ed.), *A.W.N.
Pugin: Master of Gothic Revival*,
London 1995, pp. 177–99
Baedeker, K., *Belgium and Holland*,
Leipzig 1910
Bagehot, W., *The English
Constitution*, London 1867
Baillie, H. Murray, 'Etiquette and
the Planning of the State
Apartments in Baroque
Palaces', *Archaeologia*, CI, 1967,
pp. 169–99
Banks, T.C., *Coronations of the
Kings of England*, London 1820
Barker, F., and R. Hyde, *London as
it Might Have Been*, London
1982
Barry, A., *The Life and Works of Sir
Charles Barry*, London 1867
Barry, A., *The Architect of the New
Palace of Westminster*, 2nd edn.,
London 1868
Bassin, J., *Architectural Competitions
in Nineteenth-Century England*,
Ann Arbor 1984
Beales, D.E.D., 'The Electorate
before and After 1832: the
Right to Vote, and the
Opportunity', *Parliamentary
History*, XI, 1992, pp. 139–50
Belcher, M., 'Pugin Writing', in P.
Atterbury and C. Wainwright
(eds.), *Pugin: A Gothic Passion*,
New Haven and London 1994,
pp. 105–16
Belfield, E.M.G., *The Annals of the
Addington Family*, Winchester
1959
Bell, Q., *The Schools of Design*,
London 1963
Bindoff, S.T. (ed.), *The House of
Commons, 1509–1558*, 3 vols.,
London 1982 (*The History of
Parliament*)
Binski, P., *The Painted Chamber at
Westminster*, London 1986
(*Society of Antiquaries Occasional
Papers*, n.s., IX)
Binski, P., *Westminster Abbey and
the Plantagenets: Kingship and the
Representation of Power,
1200–1400*, New Haven and
London 1995
Birkenhead, J. (ed.), *Kingdomes
Intelligencer*, no. 19, 6–13 May
1661
Blackie & Son, *The Cabinet-Maker's
Assistant*, London 1853
(reprinted New York 1970)
Blake, R., *Disraeli*, London 1998
Blewett, N., 'The Franchise in the
United Kingdom, 1885–1918',
*Past and Present*, no. 32, 1965,
pp. 27–56

Boardman, H., *The Glory of Parliament*, London 1960

Boase, T.S.R, 'The Decoration of the New Palace of Westminster 1841–1863', *Journal of the Warburg and Courtauld Institutes*, XVII, 1954, pp. 319–58

Bogdanor, V., *The Monarchy and the Constitution*, Oxford 1995

Bogdanor, V., 'Speaking Up for Stubborn England', *The Independent*, 4 February 1999, p. 4

Bond, M.H. (ed.), *Works of Art in the House of Lords*, London 1980

Bond ,M.H., *A Stuart Parliamentary Processional Roll*, London 1981 (House of Lords Record Office *Memorandum*, LXV)

Bony, J., *The English Decorated Style*, Oxford 1979

Bony, J., *French Gothic Architecture of the Twelth and Thirteenth Centuries*, London 1983

Borenius, T., 'The Cycles of Images in the Castles and Palaces of Henry III', *Journal of the Warburg and Courtauld Institutes*, VI, 1943, pp. 40–50

Bowness, A. (ed.), *The Impressionists in London*, London 1973

Boyer, A., *The History of the Reign of Queen Anne, Digested into Annals*, London 1712

Boyer, M.C., *The City of Collective Memory*, Cambridge, MA, 1996

Braund, J., *Illustrations of Furniture, Candelabra, Musical Instruments from the Great Exhibitions of London and Paris with Examples of Similar Articles from Royal Palaces and Noble Mansions*, London 1858

Brawne, A., *et al.*, Letter to the Editor, *The Times*, 13 October 1950, p. 7

Brayley, E.W., and J. Britton, *The History of the Ancient Palace and Late Houses of Parliament at Westminster*, London 1836

Brentnall, M., *Old Customs and Ceremonies of London*, London 1975

Brett, M.V. (ed.), *Journals and Letters of Reginald Viscount Esher*, I, *1870–1903*, London 1934

Britton, J., and A.C. Pugin, *Illustrations of the Public Buildings of London*, 2 vols., London 1825–28

Britton, J., and E.W. Brayley, 'An Address to the Commissioners, Appointed by His Majesty to Examine and Report on the Designs for the Proposed New Houses of Parliament; to Members of Parliament, to Architects', *Architectural Magazine*, II, 1835, pp. 504–06

Brooke, J., *George III*, London 1972

Brooke-Little, J., *Royal Ceremonies of State*, London 1980

Brooks, C., *Gothic Revival*, London 1999

Broughton, Lord, *Recollections of a Long Life*, ed. Lady Dorchester, V, London 1911

Brown, A.L., 'Parliament c. 1377–1422', in R.G. Davies and J.H. Denton (eds.), *The English Parliament in the Middle Ages*, Manchester, 1981

Brown, R., and G.C. Bentinck (eds.), *Calendar of State Papers (Venetian)*, VII, London 1890

Brown, R. Allen, *The Norman Conquest: Documents of Medieval History 5*, London 1984

Burges, W., 'The Coronation Chair', in G. Gilbert Scott, *Gleanings from Westminster Abbey*, Oxford and London 1863, pp. 121–26

Burrow, J.W., *A Liberal Descent: Victorian Historians and the English Past*, Cambridge 1981

Burton, T., *Thomas Burton's Diary*, ed. J.T. Rutt, 3 vols., London 1828

Butler, D., *The Electoral System in Britain Since 1918*, 2nd edn., Oxford 1963

Cannadine, D., 'The Context, Performance and Meaning of Ritual: The British Monarchy and the "Invention of Tradition", c. 1820–1977', in E. Hobsbawm and T. Ranger (eds.), *The Invention of Tradition*, Cambridge 1983, pp. 101–64

Cannadine, D., 'The Last Hanoverian Sovereign? The Victorian Monarchy in Historical Perspective, 1688–1988', in A.L. Beier, D. Cannadine and J. Rosenheim (eds.), *The First Modern Society: Essays in English History in Honour of Lawrence Stone*, Cambridge, 1989, pp. 127–66

Cannadine, D., *The Decline and Fall of the British Aristocracy*, London 1990

Cannadine, D., 'Gilbert and Sullivan: The Making and Un-Making of a British "Tradition"', in R. Porter (ed.), *Myths of the English*, London 1992a, pp. 12–32

Cannadine, D., *G.M. Trevelyan: A Life in History*, London 1992b

Cannadine, D., *Aspects of Aristocracy: Grandeur and Decline in Modern Britain*, London 1994

Cannadine, D., 'British History as a "New Subject": Politics, Perspectives and Prospects', in A. Grant and K.J. Stringer (eds.), *Uniting the Kingdom? The Making of British History*, London 1995, pp. 12–28

Cannon, J., *The Modern British Monarchy: A Study in Adaptation*, Reading 1987

Cannon, J., and R. Griffiths, *The Oxford Illustrated History of the British Monarchy*, Oxford 1988

Carter, J., *Specimens of Ancient sculpture and Painting*, 2 vols., London 1780–94

Carter, J., *The Ancient Architecture of England*, 2 vols., London 1795–1814

Carter, J., Statement addressed to Mr. Urban dated 20 August, in *Gentleman's Magazine*, LXX, no. 2, 1800a, pp. 736–37

[Carter, J.,] An Architect, 'The Pursuits of Architectural Innovation, No. XXI. The Antient [sic] Palace of the Kings of England at Westminster', *Gentleman's Magazine*, LXX/1, 1800b, pp. 33–36

[Carter, J.,] An Architect, 'The Pursuits of Architectural Innovation, No. XXI. The Antient [sic] Palace of the Kings of England at Westminster, continued. The Interior of the Great Hall', *Gentleman's Magazine*, LXX, no. 1, 1800c, pp. 214–17

Casey, E., *Remembering: A Phenomenological Study*, Bloomington 1989

Channon, H., 'Chips': The Diaries of Sir Henry Channon, ed. R. Rhodes James, London 1967

Charlesworth, M. (ed.), *The English Garden: Literary Sources and Documents*, Mountfield 1993

Cherry, J., and N. Stratford, *Westminster Kings and the Palace of Westminster*, London 1995 (*British Museum Occasional Papers*, CXV)

Chowdharay-Best, G., 'Peeresses at the Opening of Parliament', *The Table, Being the Journal of the Society of Clerks-at-the-Table in Commonwealth Parliaments*, eds. J.M. Davies and R.B. Sands, XXXXI, 1972–73, pp. 10–27

Churchill, W.L.S., *Winston S. Churchill: His Complete Speeches, 1897–1963*, ed. R. Rhodes James, 8 vols., London 1974

Clarendon, H., *A New and Authentic History of England*, 6 vols., London 1768

Clark, K., *The Gothic Revival: An Essay in the History of Taste*, London 1928

Clark, K., *The Gothic Revival: An Essay in the History of Taste*, 3rd ed., London 1962

Clifford, H., *Royal Goldsmiths, The Garrard Heritage*, exhib. cat., Garrard & Co., London 1991

Cobb, H.S., 'Descriptions of the State Opening of Parliament, 1485–1601: A Survey' in *Parliamentary History*, XXVIII, 1999, pp. 303–15

Cobbett, W., *History of the Regency and Reign of George IV*, London 1830

Cocke, T., *Nine Hundred Years: The Restorations of Westminster Abbey*, London 1995

C[okayne], G.E., *Complete Peerage*, revised edn., 13 vols., London 1910–59

C[ole], H., 'Prospects of the Fine Arts: Decoration of the Westminster Palace', *Westminster Review*, XXXVIII, 1842, pp. 168–93

Cole, J.W., *The Life and Theatrical Times of Charles Kean, FSA*, 2 vols., London 1859

Coleridge, S.T., *Seven Lectures on Shakespeare and Milton by the late S.T. Coleridge*, ed. J. Payne Collier, London 1856

Colle,. L., *Lewis Namier*, London 1989

Colley, L., *Britons: Forging the Nation, 1707–1837*, London 1992

Colvin, H.M. (ed.), *The History of the King's Works*, 6 vols., London 1963–82

Colvin, H.M., 'Views of the Old Palace of Westminster', *Architectural History*, IX, 1966, pp. 23–184

Cooke, R., *The Palace of Westminster: Houses of Parliament*, London 1987

Cooper, I.M., 'Westminster Hall', *Journal of the British Archaeological Association*, ser. 3, I, 1936, pp. 168–228

Cooper, I.M., 'The Meeting Places of Parliament in the Ancient Palace of Westminster', *Journal of the Architectural Association*, ser. 3, III, 1938, pp. 97–138

Cope, C.H., *Reminiscences of Charles West Cope, RA*, London 1891

Courtenay, L.T., 'The Westminster Hall Roof: a New Archaeological Source', *Journal of the British Archaeological Association*, ser. 3, CXLIII, 1990, pp. 95–111

Craig, F.W.S., *British Electoral Facts, 1832–1987*, 5th edn., Aldershot 1989

Crick, B., *The Reform of Parliament*, 2nd edn., London 1968

Crook, J. Mordaunt, *The Dilemma of Style: Architectural Ideas from the Picturesque to the Post-Modern*, Chicago, 1987

Crook, J. Mordaunt, 'Metropolitan Improvements: John Nash and the Picturesque,' in C. Fox (ed.), *London: World City, 1800–1840*, New Haven and London 1992, pp. 77–96

Crook, J. Mordaunt, *John Carter and the Mind of the Gothic Revival*, London 1995

Cumming, V., 'Pantomime and Pageantry: The Coronation of George IV', in C. Fox (ed.), *London: World City, 1800–1840*, New Haven and London 1992, pp. 39–50

[Cunningham, A.,?], 'Doings in Fresco', *Fraser's Magazine*, XXV, 1842, pp. 669–73

Cust, E., *A Letter to the Right Hon. Sir Robert Peel, Bart., M.P., on the expedience of a better system of control over buildings erected at the public expense; on the subject of rebuilding the Houses of Parliament (31 January 1835)*, London 1835

Dafforn, J., *Pictures by Daniel Maclise, RA*, London 1871

Daniell, F.H.B. (ed.), *Calendar of State Papers (Domestic)*, XXI, 1679–80, London 1915

Davies, E., *The Mythology and the Rites of the Druids*, London 1809

Davison, G., 'The City as a Natural System: Theories of Urban Society in Early Nineteenth-Century Britain', in D. Fraser and A. Sutcliffe (eds.), *The Pursuit of Urban History*, London 1983, pp. 349–70

Day, R., 'The State Opening of Parliament', in L. Miall (ed.), *Richard Dimbleby: Broadcaster*, London 1966, pp. 110–14

Dean, D., 'Image and Ritual in the Tudor Parliaments', in D.E. Hoak (ed.), *Tudor Political Culture*, Cambridge, 1995, pp. 243–71

de Bellaigue, G., 'A Royal Mis-en-Scene: George IV's Coronation Banquet', *Furniture History*, XXIX, 1993, pp. 174–83

[Dickens, C.], 'The Spirit of Chivalry in Westminster Hall', *Douglas Jerrold's Shilling Magazine*, II, July–Dec. 1845, pp. 124–25

Dimbleby, D., *Richard Dimbleby: A Biography*, London 1975

Dixon, R., and S. Muthesius, *Victorian Architecture*, London 1978

Dixon-Smith, S., 'The Image and Reality of Almsgiving in the Great Halls of Henry III', *Journal of the British Archaeological Association*, ser. 3, CLII, 1999, pp. 79–96

Donaldson, F., *Edward VIII*, London 1976

Driberg, T., 'The House of Commons: Client's Eye View', *Architectural Review*, CVIII, 1950, pp. 176–78

Dugdale, W., *A Perfect Copy of All Summons*, London 1685

Eames, P., 'Documentary Evidence Concerning the Character and Use of Domestic Furnishings in England in the Fourteenth and Fifteenth Centuries', *Furniture History*, VII, 1971, pp. 41–60

Eames, P., 'Medieval Furniture', *Furniture History*, XIII, 1977

Eames, P., 'Symbols of State: Medieval Beds and Cradles', *Country Life*, CLXXX, no. 4662, 25 December 1986, pp. 2044–46

Eastlake, C.L., *The History of the Gothic Revival*, London 1872

Eastlake, C.L., *A History of the Gothic Revival*, ed. J. Mordaunt Crook, Leicester, 1970

Eastlake, Sir C.L., *Contributions to the Literature of the Fine Arts with a Memoir Compiled by Lady Eastlake*, London 1870

Eastlake, E., Lady, (ed.), *Life of John Gibson, R.A., Sculptor*, London 1870

Edwards, E., *The Administrative Economy of the Fine Arts in England*, London 1840

Eeles, F.C., *The English Coronation Service: Its History and Teaching*, Oxford and London 1902

Evelyn. J., *The Diary of John Evelyn*, ed. E.S. de Beer, 6 vols., Oxford 1955

Fairholt, F.W., *Costume in England*, London 1846

Farington, J., *The Diary of Joseph Farington*, New Haven and London, eds. K. Garlick, A. Macintyre and K. Cave, 16 vols., 1978–84 (index pub. 1998)

Farr, D., *English Art, 1870–1940*, Oxford 1978 (*The Oxford History of English Art*, XI)

Fernie, E.C., 'Reconstructing Edward's Abbey at Westminster' in N. Stratford (ed.), *Romanesque and Gothic Essays for George Zarnecki*, I, Woodbridge, 1987, pp. 63–67

Ferrey, B., *Answer to 'Thoughts on Rebuilding the Houses of Parliament'*, London 1835

Ferrey, B., *Recollections of A.W.N. Pugin and his father, Augustus Pugin*, London 1861

Finley, G., *Turner and George the Fourth in Edinburgh 1822*, London 1982

Forster, K.W., 'Monument/Memory and the Mortality of Architecture', *Oppositions*, XXV, fall 1982, pp. 2–19

Foster, E.R., 'Staging a Parliament in Early Stuart England', in P. Clark, A.G.R. Smith and N. Tynacke (eds.), *The English Commonwealth*, Leicester 1979, pp. 129–46, 239–48

Foster, E.R., *The House of Lords 1603–1649*, Chapel Hill and London 1983

Foulkes, R., 'Charles Kean's King Richard II: A Pre-Raphaelite Drama', in *idem* (ed.), *Shakespeare and the Victorian Stage*, Cambridge 1986, pp. 39–55

Fowler, C., *On the Proposed Site of the New Houses of Parliament*, London 1836

Fox, C., (ed.), *London: World City, 1800–1840*, New Haven and London 1992

Frew, J.M., 'Gothic is English: John Carter and the Revival of Gothic as England's National Style', *Art Bulletin*, LXIV, 1982, pp. 315–19

Fulford, R., *George IV*, London 1935

Gash, N., *Reaction and Reconstruction in English Politics, 1832–1852*, Oxford 1965

Gem. R.D.H., 'The Romanesque Rebuilding of Westminster Abbey', *Anglo-Norman Studies*, III, 1980, pp. 33–60

Gem, R.D.H., 'Canterbury and the Cushion Capital: a Commentary on Pages from Goscelin's *De Miraculis Sancti Augustini*' in N. Stratford (ed.), *Romanesque and Gothic Essays for George Zarnecki*, I, Woodbridge 1987, pp. 83–101

George IV, *The Letters of George IV,* *1812–1830*, ed. A. Aspinall, 3 vols., Cambridge 1938

George IV, *The Correspondence of George, Prince of Wales 1770–1812*, ed. A. Aspinall, 8 vols., London 1963–1971

George, M.D., *Catalogue of Political and Personal Satires Preserved in the British Museum*, photolithe edition, 11 vols., London 1978

Germann, G., *Gothic Revival in Europe and Britain: Sources, Influences and Ideas*, trans. G. Onn, London 1972

Giddings, P., and G. Drewery (eds.), *Westminster and Europe: The Impact of the European Union on the Westminster Parliament*, London 1996

Girling-Budd, A., 'Holland and Sons of London and Gillows of London and Lancaster: A Comparison of Two Nineteenth-Century Furnishing Firms', unpublished MA thesis, London, Victoria and Albert Museum and Royal College of Art, 1998

Girouard, M., 'Attitudes to Elizabethan Architecture, 1600–1900', in J. Summerson (ed.), *Essays on Architectural Writers and Writing presented to Nikolaus Pevsner*, London 1968, pp. 13–27

Girouard, M., *The Return to Camelot: Chivalry and the English Gentleman*, New Haven and London 1981

Glanville, P., *Silver in England*, London 1987

Gloag, J., *Georgian Grace: A Social History of Design from 1660 to 1830*, 2nd edn., London 1967

Goodman, A., and J. Gillespie (eds.), *Richard II, The Art of Kingship*, New York and Oxford 1999

Gordon, D. (ed.), *Making and Meaning: The Wilton Diptych*, exhib. cat., National Gallery, London 1993

Gordon, D., L. Monnas and C. Elam (eds.), *The Regal Image of Richard II and the Wilton Diptych*, London 1997

Grant, L., 'Romanesque Sculptural Decoration at Westminster Hall', unpublished M.A. thesis, Courtauld Institute, University of London 1976

Green, D.B., *Queen Anne*, London 1970

Green, H.M., *et al.*, 'Excavations of the Palace of Westminster Defences and Abbey Precinct Wall at Abingdon Street, Westminster, 1963', *Journal of the British Archaeological Association*, ser. 3, CXXIX, 1976, pp. 59–76

Gregg, E., *Queen Anne*, London 1980

Greville, C., *The Precedence Question*, London 1840

Greville, C., *The Greville Diary*, ed. P.W. Wilson, 2 vols., London 1927

Grier, K.C., *Culture and Comfort: People, Parlors and Upholstery 1850–1930*, exhib. cat., Rochester, NY, The Strong Museum, 1988

Grosle,. P.J., *A Tour of London or New Observations on England and its Inhabitants*, trans. T. Nugent, London 1772

Hall, E., *Hall's Chronicle*, London 1809

Halliwell, J.O. (ed.), *The Works of Shakespeare*, 16 vols., London 1853–65

Hamilton, W.R., *Letter from W.R. Hamilton, Esq. to the Earl of Elgin, on the New Houses of Parliament*, London 1836a

Hamilton, W.R., *Second Letter from W.R. Hamilton, Esq. to the Earl of Elgin, on the propriety of adopting the Greek style of architecture in preference to the gothic, in the construction of the New Houses of Parliament*, London 1836b

Hamilton, W.R., *Third Letter from W.R. Hamilton, Esq. to the Earl of Elgin, on the propriety of adopting the Greek style of architecture in preference to the gothic, in the construction of the New Houses of Parliament*, London 1837

Hansard, *Hansard's Parliamentary Debates*, ser. 3, XVI, 1833

Hansard, *Hansard's Parliamentary Debates*, ser. 3, XXIX, 1835

Hansard, *Hansard's Parliamentary Debates*, ser. 3, XXXI, 1836

Hansard, *Hansard's Parliamentary Debates*, ser. 3, XXXVII, 1837

Hansard, *Hansard's Parliamentary Debates*, ser. 3, XLIII, 1838

Hansard, *Hansard's Parliamentary Debates*, ser. 3, CXVIII, 1851

Hansard, *Hansard's Parliamentary Debates*, ser. 3, CLXXVI, 1864

Hansard, *Hansard's Parliamentary Debates*, ser. 3, CLXXIX, 1865

Hansard, *The Official Report, House of Commons*, ser. 5, CCCXCIII, 1943

Hansard, *The Official Report, House of Commons*, ser. 5, CDVII, 1945

Hansard, *The Official Report, House of Commons*, ser. 5, DCCV, 1965

Harris, J., 'Soane's Classical Triumph: A Lost Westminster Masterpiece Revealed', *Apollo*, n.s., CXXV, no. 363, May 1992, pp. 288–90

Hartley. T.E. (ed.), *Proceedings in the Parliaments of Elizabeth I, 1558–1601*, 3 vols., Leicester, 1981–95

Harvey, J.H., *The Perpendicular Style*, London 1978

Harvey, J.H., *English Medieval Architects: A Biographical Dictionary down to 1540*, London 1987

Hasler, P.W. (ed.), *The House of Commons, 1558–1603*, 3 vols., London 1983 (*The History of Parliament*)

Hastings, M., *St Stephen's Chapel and its Place in the Development of the Perpendicular Style*, Cambridge 1995

Hay, M., and R. Kennedy, *The Medieval Kings c. 1388: An Exhibition of Three Statues from the South Wall, their History and Recent Conservation*, exhib. cat., London, Westminster Hall, 1993

Hay, M., and J. Riding, *Art in Parliament: The Permanent Collection of the House of Commons. A Descriptive Catalogue*, Norwich 1996

Hayden, D., *The Power of Place: Urban Landscapes as Public History*, Cambridge, MA, 1996

Haydon, B.R., *Thoughts on the Relative Value of Fresco and Oil Painting as Applied to the Architectural Decorations of the Houses of Parliament; Read at the Friday Evening Meeting at the Royal Institution, Albemarle Street, March 4, 1842*, London 1842

Haydon, B.R., *The Autobiography and Memoirs of Benjamin Robert Haydon, 1786–1846*, ed. T Taylor, new edn. with introduction by Aldous Huxley, 2 vols., London 1926

Hazlitt, W., *Characters of Shakespeare's Plays*, 2nd edn., London 1818

Heffer, S., *Power and Place: The Political Consequences of King Edward VII*, London 1998

Herbert, A., *Britannia After the Romans*, 2 vols., London 1836

Hersey, G., *High Victorian Gothic: A Study in Associationism*, Baltimore 1972

Hibbert, C., *George IV*, Harmondsworth 1976

Hinds, A.B. (ed.), *Calendar of State Papers (Venetian)*, XXXI, 1657–1659, London 1931

Hobsbawm, E., and T. Ranger (eds.), *The Invention of Tradition*, Cambridge 1983

Hogarth, W., *Anecdotes of William Hogarth, Written by Himself*, ed. J.B. Nichols, London 1833

Holmes, G., *The Electorate and the National Will in the First Age of Party*, Kendal 1976

Hopper, T., *Design for the Houses of Parliament*, London 1842

Horseman, V., and B. Davison, 'The New Palace Yard and its Fountains: Excavations in the Palace of Westminster', *Archaeological Journal*, LXIX, 1989, pp. 279–97

Howe, E., 'Divine Kingship and Dynastic Display: the Altar Murals of St Stephen's Chapel, Westminster', unpublished MA thesis, Courtauld Institute, London University, 1999

Huch, R.K., and P.R. Ziegler, *Joseph Hume: The People's MP*, Philadelphia 1985

Huish, R., *An Authentic History of the Coronation of His Majesty King George the 4th*, London 1821

Hume, D., The History of England, 2 vols., London 1762

Hume, M.AS. (ed.), *Calendar of State Papers (Spanish)*, I, *Elizabeth I*, London 1892

Hunt, F.K., *The Book of Art. Cartoons, Frescoes, Sculpture and Decorative Art, as Applied to the New Houses of Parliament and to Buildings in General: With an Historical Notice of the Exhibitions in Westminster Hall and Directions for Painting in Fresco*, London 1846

Hunt, J.D., 'Gardening, and Poetry, and Pope,' in *idem* (ed.), *The Figure in the Landscape: Poetry, Painting, and Gardening during the Eighteenth Century*, Baltimore 1976, pp. 14–42

Hunting, P., *Royal Westminster*, London 1981

Hutchinson, T., *Diary and Letters of His Excellency Thomas Hutchinson, Esq.*, ed. P.O. Hutchinson, 2 vols., London 1883–86

Irving, R.G., *Indian Summer: Lutyens, Baker and Imperial Delhi*, London 1981

J.B., 'The Shops in Westminster Hall', *Gentleman's Magazine*, n.s., XXXX, July–September 1853, pp. 602–04

Jackson, P., *George Scharf's London: Sketches and Watercolours of a Changing City, 1820–50*, London 1987

James, R. Rhodes, *An Introduction to the House of Commons*, London 1961

Jameson, Mrs [A.B.], *Visits and Sketches at Home and Abroad*, London 1834

Jameson, Mrs [A.B.], *Companion to the Most Celebrated Private Galleries of Art in London Containing Accurate Catalogues, Arranged Alphabetically, for Immediate Reference, each Preceded by an Historical and Critical Introduction with a Prefatory essay on Art, Artists, Collectors and Connoisseurs*, London 1844

Jameson, Mrs [A.B.], *The Decorations of the Garden-Pavilion in the Grounds of Buckingham Palace, Engraved under the Supervision of L. Gruner*, London 1845

Jay, W., 'The House of Commons and St Stephen's Chapel', *English Historical Review*, XXXVI, 1921, pp. 226–28

Jones, C., *The Great Palace*, London 1983

Jordan, R. Furneaux, *Western Architecture: A Concise History*, London 1969 (reprinted 1997)

Kalnein, W.G., and M. Levey, *Art and Architecture of the Eighteenth Century in France*, Harmondsworth 1972

Kean, C., *Shakespeare's play of King Richard II, Arranged for Presentation at the Princess's Theatre, with Historical and Explanatory Notes*, London 1857

Keightley, T., *The History of England*, 3 vols., London 1839

Kempe, A.J., *Some Account of the Coronation of King Richard the Second in the Year 1377*, London 1831

Kingsford, C.L., 'Our Lady of Pew: The King's Oratory or Closet in the Palace of Westminster', *Archaeologia*, LXVIII, 1917, pp. 1–20

Knight, C., *The Pictorial Edition of Shakspere* [sic], London 1838

Knight, C., *The Popular History of England*, 8 vols., London 1862

Knight, C., *Passages of a Working Life*, 3 vols., London 1864

Kuhn, W.M., *Democratic Royalism: The Transformation of the British Monarchy, 1861–1914*, London and New York 1996

L.P., 'Fresco Painting', *Westminster Review*, XXXXIV, 1845, pp. 108–41

Lambourne, L., 'Pugin and the Theatre', in P. Atterbury and C. Wainwright (eds.), *Pugin: A Gothic Passion*, New Haven and London 1994, pp. 34–41

Lant, J.L., *Insubstantial Pageant: Ceremony and Confusion at Queen Victoria's Court*, London 1979

Laundy, P., *The Office of Speaker*, London 1964

Le May, G.H.L., *The Victorian Constitution: Conventions, Usages and Contingencies*, London 1979

Lee, S., *King Edward VII: A Biography*, II, *The Reign*, London 1927

Leonard, M., 'The Empire's New Clothes', *The Guardian*, 21 November 1998, *Saturday Review*, pp. 1–2

Lethaby, W.R., 'The Palace of Westminster in the Eleventh and Twelfth centuries', *Archaeologia*, LX, 1906, pp. 131–48

Lindley, P., 'Absolutism and Regal Image in Richardian Sculpture' in D. Gordon, L. Monnas and C. Elam (eds.), *The Regal Image of Richard II and the Wilton Diptych*, London 1997, pp. 61–83.

Lingard, J., *A History of England*, 8 vols., London 1819–30

Liversidge, M., P. Binski and J. Lynn, 'Two Ceiling Fragments from the Painted Chamber at Westminster Palace', *Burlington Magazine*, CXXXVII, 1995, pp. 491–501

Lockhart, J.G., *Memoirs of the Life of Sir Walter Scott*, Edinburgh 1845

London, Christies, *The Glory of the Goldsmith, Magnificent Gold and Silver from the Al-Tajir Collection*, exhib. cat., Christie's, London 1989

London, House of Commons, *Second Report of the Select Committee Appointed to Consider the State of Westminster Bridge and the Palace of Westminster*, London 1846 (Parliamentary Papers, HC 1846 (349), XV, pp. 273ff.)

London, House of Commons, *First Report of the Select Committee on the New House of Commons*, London 1850 (Parliamentary Papers, HC 1850 (650-I), XV, pp. 125ff. and HC 1850 (650-II), XV, pp. 131ff.)

London, House of Commons, *Report of the Select Committee on Arrangements to Enable Members to Take Part in the Proceedings of the House of Commons*, London 1867–68 (Parliamentary Papers, HC 1867–68 (265), VIII, pp. 329ff.)

London, House of Commons, *Interim Report of the Committee on House of Commons Personnel and Politics, 1264–1832*, London 1932 (Parliamentary Papers, HC Cmd 4130)

London, House of Commons, *Report from the Select Committee on House of Commons (Rebuilding)*, London 1944 (Parliamentary Papers, HC 1943–44 (109), II, pp. 591ff.)

London, House of Commons, House of Commons Information Office, *The Portcullis*, London 1987 (Factsheet no. 12)

London, House of Commons, House of Commons Information Office, *House of Commons Green*, London 1991 (Factsheet no. 13)

London, House of Lords, *Report from the Select Committee to Consider Such Plans, as may be Submitted to Them for Providing a More Convenient Temporary Accommodation for the House of Lords, 2 July 1835*, London 1835 (Parliamentary Papers, HL 1835 (73), XVIII, pp. 609ff.)

London, House of Lords, Second Report of the Select Committee Appointed to Inquire into the Progress of the Building of the Houses of Parliament, London 1844 (Parliamentary Papers, HL 1844 (46), XIX, pp. 279ff. and HC 1844 (629), VI, pp. 601ff.)

London, House of Lords, *House of Lords Manuscripts (New Series)*, London 1908

London, House of Lords, *House of Lords Manuscripts (New Series)*, London 1977

London, House of Lords, House of Lords Information Office, *The State Opening of Parliament*, London 1982 (Information Sheet no. 10)

London, House of Lords and House of Commons, *Report of the Royal Commission to Consider Plans for the Building of the Houses of Parliament*, London 1836 (Parliamentary Papers, HL 1836 (10), IX, pp. 263 ff. and HC 1836 (66), XXXVI, pp. 487ff.)

London, House of Lords and House of Commons, *Report of the Commissioners on the Fine Arts, with Appendix*, London 1842 (Parliamentary Papers, HL 1842, XIX, pp. 521ff. and HC 1842 (412), XV, pp. 105ff.)

London, House of Lords and House of Commons, *Second Report of the Commissioners on the Fine Arts, with Appendix*, London 1843 (Parliamentary Papers, HL 1843, XXX, pp. 427ff. and HC 1843 (499), XXIX, pp. 197ff.)

London, House of Lords and House of Commons, *Third Report of the Commissioners on the Fine Arts, with Appendix*, London 1844 (Parliamentary Papers, HL 1844, XXIII, pp. 291ff. and HC 1844 (585), XXXI, pp. 169ff.)

London, House of Lords and House of Commons, *Fourth Report of the Commissioners on the Fine Arts, with Appendix*, London 1845 (Parliamentary Papers, HL 1845, XXV, pp. 517ff. and HC 1845 (671), XXVII, pp. 151ff.)

London, House of Lords and House of Commons, *Fifth Report of the Commissioners on the Fine Arts, with Appendix*, London 1846 (Parliamentary Papers, HL 1846, XXXIV, pp. 305ff. and HC 1846 (671), XXVII, pp. 151ff.)

London, House of Lords and House of Commons, *Seventh Report of the Commissioners on the Fine Arts, with Appendix*, London 1847 (Parliamentary Papers, HL 1847, XXXIV, pp. 83ff. and HC 1847 (862), XXXIII, pp. 267ff.)

London, House of Lords and House of Commons, *Report from the Joint Select Committee on the Presence of the Sovereign in Parliament*, London 1901 (Parliamentary Papers, HL 1901 (111), VIII, pp. 205ff. and HC 1901 (212), VII, pp. 213ff.)

London, Parliamentary Works Directorate, *The Victoria Tower Restored*, London 1993

London, Parliamentary Works Directorate, *Five Years of Restoration and Improved Facilities, 1992–1997*, London 1998

London, Victoria and Albert Museum, *A Report by the Victoria and Albert Museum Concerning the Furniture in The House of Lords Presented to the Sub-Committee of the Offices Committee on Works of Art in the*

House of Lords, London 1974

Longford, E., Victoria R.I., London 1964

[Loudon, J.C.], 'The Conductor', 'A New Site for the Houses of Parliament Suggested, and the Fundamental Principles on which they ought to be Designed Pointed out', Architectural Magazine, III, London 1836, pp. 100–03

Lowther, J.W., A Speaker's Commentaries, 2 vols., London 1925

Lubbock, J., 'Pugin: Preaching Design', in idem (ed.), The Tyranny of Taste: The Politics of Architecture and Design in Britain, 1550–1960, New Haven and London 1995, pp. 233–47

Lummis, E., The Speaker's Chair, London 1900

Lutyens, R., Letter to the Editor, The Times, 3 October 1950a, p. 7

Lutyens, R., 'The New House of Commons', Country Life, CVIII, no. 2805, 20 October 1950b, pp. 1272–75

Macaulay, J., The Gothic Revival, 1745–1845, London 1975

MacDonagh, M., The Book of Parliament, London 1897

MacDonagh, M., The Pageant of Parliament, 2 vols., London 1921

Machyn, H., The Diary of Henry Machyn, ed. J.G. Nichols, London 1848, (The Camden Society, XLII)

MacKay, W.R., Secretaries to the Speaker, London 1986 (House of Commons Library Documents, no. 14)

Mackenzie, F., The Architectural Antiquities of the Collegiate College of St Stephen, Westminster, London 1844

Mackenzie, K., The English Parliament, Harmondsworth 1950

Malory, T., The History of the Renowned Prince Arthur, King of Britain, London 1816

Malory, T., La Mort d'Arthur, London 1816

Malory, T., The Byrth, Lyf and Actes of King Arthur, ed. R. Southey, London 1817

Malory, T., La Mort d'Arthure, ed. T. Wright, London 1858

Mancoff, D.N., The Arthurian Revival in Victorian Art, New York and London 1990

Mandler, P., The Fall and Rise of the Stately Home, New Haven and London 1997

Manning, E., Marble and Bronze: The Art and Life of Hamo Thornycroft, London 1982

Marritt, J.A.R., 'The House of Lords as an Imperial Senate', Fortnightly Review, LXXXVII, 1907, pp. 1003–17

Martin, G.W., 'Empire Federalism and Imperial Parliamentary Union, 1820–1870', Historical Journal, XVI, 1973, pp. 65–92

Martin, G.W., 'The Idea of "Imperial Federation"', in R. Hyam and G. Martin (eds.), Reappraisals in British Imperial History, London 1975, pp. 121–37

Martin, G.W., Bunyip Aristocracy: The New South Wales Constitutional Debates and Hereditary Institutions in the British Colonies, London 1986

Martindale, A., 'Saint Stephen's Chapel, Westminster and the Italian experience' in D. Buckton and T.A. Heslop (eds.), Studies in Medieval Architecture Presented to Peter Lasko, Stroud and New Haven 1994, 102–12

Matthew, H.C.G., et al., 'The Franchise Factor and the Rise of the Labour Party', English Historical Review, LXXXXI, 1982, pp. 820–31

Matthews T., The Biography of John Gibson, R.A., Sculptor, Rome, London 1911

Maxwell-Hyslop, R. (ed.), Secretary to the Speaker: Ralph Verney's Correspondence, London 1998 (House of Commons Library Documents, no. 22)

Meara, D., 'The Catholic Context', in P. Atterbury (ed.), A.WN. Pugin: Master of Gothic Revival, London 1995, pp. 45–46

Meath, Lord, 'Shall Indian Princes Sit in the House of Lords?', Nineteenth Century, XXXV, 1894, pp. 710–16

Merriman, J.D., The Flower of Kings: A Study of the Arthurian Legend in England between 1485 and 1835, Wichita 1973

Meyrick, S.R., A Critical Inquiry into Ancient Armour, 3 vols., London 1824

Miele, C., 'The Battle for Westminster Hall', Architectural History, XXXXI, 1998, pp. 220–44

Millar, O., The Later Georgian Pictures in the Collection of Her Majesty the Queen, Oxford 1969

Milles, T., The Catalogue of Honor, London 1610

Mitra, S.M., 'The House of Lords and the Indian Princes', The Fortnightly Review, LXXXXIII, 1910, pp. 1090–99

Munich, A., Queen Victoria's Secrets, New York 1996

Namier, S.L., and J. Brooke (eds.), The House of Commons, 1754–1790, 3 vols., London 1964 (The History of Parliament)

Napier, A., 'The Queen in Parliament', Parliamentary Affairs, VII, 1953–54, pp. 49–59

Napier, W.J., 'State Opening of Parliament 1833', ed. Ettrick, The Guards Magazine: Journal of the Household Division, summer 1991, p. 203

Nassau, W., Reviews of the Waverley Novels, from Rob Roy to the Chronicles of the Canongate, London n.d

Nayler, G., The Coronation of his Most Sacred Majesty George IV, London editions of 1825–27 and 1839

Neale, J.E., The Elizabethan House of Commons, London 1949

Newbolt, H.J., Admirals All, and Other Verses, London 1897

Newbolt, H.J., The Building of Britain, London 1927

Newman, H., An Illustrated Dicitonary of Silver, London 1987

Nichols, J.G., 'Observations on the Heraldic Devices discovered on the Effigies of Richard the Second and his Queen in Westminster Abbey . . .', Archaeologia, XXIX, 1842, pp. 32–59

Nicholson, H., Diaries and Letters 1939–45, London 1967

O'Donnell, R., 'Pugin as a Church Architect', in P. Atterbury and C. Wainwright (eds.), Pugin: A Gothic Passion, New Haven and London 1994, pp. 63–89

O'Donnell, R., 'The Pugins in Ireland', in P. Atterbury (ed.), A.WN. Pugin: Master of Gothic Revival, London 1995, pp. 137–59

O'Gorman. F., 'The Electorate Before and After 1832', Parliamentary History, XII, 1993, pp. 171–83

Ordericus Vitalis, The Ecclesiastical History of Orderic Vitalis, ed. M. Chibnall, 6 vols., Oxford 1968–80

Ormond, R., 'John Partridge and the Fine Arts Commissioners', Burlington Magazine, CIX, 1967, pp. 397–402

Otten, F., Ludwig Michael Schwanthaler 1802–1848, Munich 1970

Palmer, W., The Coronation Chair, London 1953

Pater, W.H., 'Shakespeare's English Kings', in idem, Appreciations, with an Essay on Style, London 1889

Penzer, N.M., Paul Storr 1771–1844 Silversmith and Goldsmith, 2nd edn., London 1971

Pepys, S., The Diary of Samuel Pepys, ed. R. Latham and W. Matthews, 11 vols., London 1970–83

Percier, C., and P. Fontaine, Receuil des décorations intérieures, comprenant tout ce qui a rapport à l'ameublement . . . , Paris, 1801

Pevsner, N., The Buildings of England: London, I, The Cities of London and Westminster, Harmondsworth 1957

Pevsner, N., The Buildings of England: London, I, The Cities of London and Westminster, 2nd edn., Harmondsworth, 1962

Phillips, G.D., The Diehards: Aristocratic Society and Politics in Edwardian England, London 1979

Planché, J.R., The Recollections and Reflections of J.R. Planché: A Professional Autobiography, 2 vols., London 1872

Plumb, J.H., 'The Growth of the Electorate in England from 1600 to 1715', Past and Present, no. 45, 1969, pp. 91–116

Pollard, A.F., The Evolution of Parliament, 2nd edn., London 1926

Pope-Hennessy, J. and H. Wild, The Houses of Parliament, 2nd edn., London 1953

Porrit, E., The Unreformed House of Commons: Parliamentary Representation Before 1832, Cambridge 1903

Port, M.H. (ed.), The Houses of Parliament, New Haven and London 1976

Port, M.H., Imperial London: Civil Government Building in London 1851–1914, London 1995

Powell, J.E., and K. Wallis, The House of Lords in the Middle Ages, London 1968

Prestwich, M., The Three Edwards, London 1980, pp. 115–36

Prestwich, M., Edward I, 2nd edn., New Haven and London 1997

[Proctor, B.W.], The Life of E[dmund] K[ean], 2 vols., London 1835

Pronay, N., and J. Taylor, Parliamentary Texts of the Later Middle Ages, Oxford, 1980

Pugin, A.W.N., Gothic Furniture in the Style of the Fifteenth Century, London 1835

Pugin, A.W.N., A Letter to A. W. Hakewill, architect, in answer to his reflections on the style for rebuilding the Houses of Parliament, London 1836a

Pugin, A.W.N., Contrasts: or, a parallel between the noble edifices of the fourteenth and fifteenth centuries, and similar buildings of the present day; shewing the present decay of taste, London 1836b

Pugin, A.W.N., True Principles of Pointed or Christian Architecture, London 1841a

Pugin, A.W.N., Contrasts: or, a parallel between the noble edifices of the fourteenth and fifteenth centuries, and similar buildings of the present day; shewing the present decay of taste, London, 2nd edn., 1841b

Pugin, A.W.N., The Glossary of Ecclesiastical Ornament and Costume, London 1844

Pugin, E.W., Who was the Art Architect [sic] of the Houses of Parliament?, London 1867

Pugin, E.W., Notes on the Reply of the Rev. Alfred Barry, D.D. to the 'Infatuated Statements' made by E.W. Pugin, on the House of Parliament, 2nd edn., London 1868

Quinault, R., 'Westminster and the Victorian Constitution', Transactions of the Royal Historical Society, ser. 6, II, 1992, pp. 79–104

[Rainey, A.], 'Mr. Rainy's Plan for a "Metropolitan Improvement", Architectural Magazine, III, 1836, pp. 309–14

Read, B., 'Architectural Sculpture', in M.H. Port (ed.), The Houses of Parliament, New Haven and London 1976, pp. 232–45

Read, B., Victorian Sculpture, New Haven and London 1982

Read, B., 'From Basilica to Walhalla', in P. Curtis (ed.), Patronage and Practice: Sculpture on Merseyside, Liverpool 1989

Redgrave, R., and S. Redgrave, A Century of British Painters, ed. R. Todd, London 1947

Ribeiro, A., The Art of Dress: Fashion in England and France 1750–1820, New Haven and London 1995

Richardson, M., and M.A. Stevens (eds.), John Soane, Architect: Master of Space and Light, exhib. cat., London, Royal Academy, 1999

Ritvo, H., 'Gothic Revival in England and America: A Case Study in Public Symbolism', in M. Bloomfield (ed.), *Allegory, Myth, and Symbol*, Cambridge, MA, 1981, pp. 313–34

Robbins, K., *The Eclipse of a Great Power: Modern Britain, 1870–1992*, 2nd edn., London 1994

Roberts, H., 'Royal Thrones, 1760–1840', *Furniture History*, XXV, 1989, pp. 61–85

Roberts, J., *A Complete Account of the Ceremonies Observed in the Coronations of the Kings and Queens of England*, London 1727

Robertson, D., *Sir Charles Eastlake and the Victorian Art World*, Princeton and Guildford 1978

Robinson, A.H., *Bradford's Public Statues*, Bradford n.d.

Robinson, J. Martin, *The Wyatts, an Architectural Dynasty*, Oxford 1979

Robinson, J. Martin, 'The Nash State Rooms', *Apollo*, n.s., CXXXVIII, no. 378, August 1993, pp. 125–30.

Robinson, J. Martin, 'Why the Queen Comes with Crown, Cap and Sword', *Country Life*, CLXXXXII, no. 45, 5 November 1998, pp. 88–91

Rorabaugh, W.J., 'Politics and the Architectural Competition for the Houses of Parliament, 1834–1837', *Victorian Studies*, XVIII 1973, pp. 155–75

Rose, K., *King George V*, London 1983

Roskell, J.S., L. Clark and C. Rawcliffe (eds.), *The House of Commons, 1386–1421*, 4 vols., London 1992 (*The History of Parliament*)

Rosser, G., *Medieval Westminster 1200–1540*, Oxford 1989

*Rotuli Parliamentorum*, 6 vols., London 1783

Royal Commission on Historical Monuments in England, *An Inventory of the Historical Monuments in London*, II, London 1925

Russell, C., *The Crisis of Parliaments, 1509–1660*, Oxford 1978

Ryde, H.T., *Illustrations of the New Palace of Westminster*, London 1849

Saint, A., 'Pugin's Architecture in Context', in P. Atterbury (ed.), *A.W.N. Pugin: Master of Gothic Revival*, London 1995, pp. 79–101

Sainty, J.C., *The Parliamentary Functions of the Sovereign since 1509*, London 1980 (House of Lords Record Office Memorandum, LXIV)

Saul, N., *Richard II*, New Haven and London 1997

Sawyer, S., 'Sir John Soane's Symbolic Westminster: The Apotheosis of George IV', *Architectural History*, XXXIX, 1996, pp. 54–76

Sawyer, S., 'Soane at Westminster: Civic Architecture and National Identity, 1789–1834', unpublished Ph.D. dissertation, Columbia University 1999

Sayles, G.O., *The King's Parliament of England*, London 1975

Scharf, G., *Observations on the Westminster Abbey Portrait and Other Representations of King Richard the Second*, London 1867 (reprinted from the *Fine Arts Quarterly Review*)

Schoenfeld, M.P., *The Restored House of Lords*, The Hague and Paris 1967

Scott, G.G., 'The Inaugural Address', *Journal of the RIBA*, 11 November 1933, pp. 5–14

Scott, G.G., 'Report from the Architect', in *Report on House of Commons (Rebuilding)*, London 1944, p. 8

Scott, G.G., Letter to the Editor, *The Times*, 10 October 1950, p. 7

Scott, M.M.M., *Abbotsford: The Personal Relics and Antiquarian Treasures of Sir Walter Scott*, London 1893

Scott, W., *Ivanhoe; A Romance*, 2nd edn., 3 vols., Edinburgh 1820

Scott, W., 'Editorial', *The Edinburgh Weekly Journal*, 20 July 1821

Sedgwick, R., (ed.), *The House of Commons, 1715–1754*, 2 vols., London 1970 (*The History of Parliament*)

Sennett, R., *Flesh and Stone: The Body and the City in Western Civilization*, New York, 1994

Shackleford, G.T.M., and M.A. Stevens, 'Series of Views of the Thames in London, 1899–1904', in P.H. Tucker (ed.), *Monet in the Twentieth Century*, London 1998, pp. 128–47

Shakespeare, W., *King Richard II*, Harmondsworth 1989, (*The New Penguin Shakespeare*)

Simo, M.L., *Loudon and the Landscape: From Country Seat to Metropolis, 1783–1843*, New Haven and London 1988

Simond, L., *Journal of a Tour and Residence in Great Britain During the Years 1810 and 1811*, Edinburgh 1817

Slater, D., 'Beaconsfield: or Disraeli in the Elysian Fields', in H.S. Cobb (ed.), *Parliamentary History, Libraries and Records: Essays Presented to Maurice Bond*, London 1981, pp. 67–76

Smirke, S., *Suggestions for the Architectural Improvement of the Western Part of London*, London 1834

Smirke, S., 'Remarks on the Architectural History of Westminster Hall', *Archaeologia*, XXVI, 1836, pp. 406–14 and 415–21

Smirke, S., 'A Further Account of the Original Architectural History of Westminster Hall' *Archaeologia*, XXVII, 1838, pp. 135–39

Smith, E.A., 'The Pageant of Monarchy, Royal Ceremonial in the Early Nineteenth Century', *The Historian*, XXXI, 1991

Smith, E.A., *The House of Lords in British Politics and Society, 1815–1911*, London 1992

Smith, J.T., *Antiquities of Westminster*, London 1807

Smollett, T., *A Complete History of England*, 4 vols., London 1757–58

Soane, J., *A Statement of Facts Respecting the Design of a New House of Lords . . .*, London 1799

Solender, K., *Dreadful Fire! Burning of the Houses of Parliament*, exhib. cat., Cleveland Museum of Art, Cleveland 1984

Somerset, A., *Elizabeth I*, 3rd impression, London 1991

Spufforth, P., *The Origins of the English Parliament*, London 1967

Stanton, P., 'The Sources of Pugin's *Contrasts*', in J. Summerson (ed.), *Concerning Architecture: Essays on Architectural Writing presented to Nikolaus Pevsner*, London 1968, pp. 128–39

Stanton, P., *Pugin*, London 1971

Stevenson, S. and H. Bennett, *Van Dyck in Check Trousers: Fancy Dress in Art and Life 1700–1900*, exhib. cat., Scottish National Portrait Gallery, Edinburgh 1978

Stroud, D., *Sir John Soane Architect*, London 1984

Strutt, J., *The Regal and Ecclesiastical Antiquities of England*, London 1777

Strutt, J., *History of British Costume*, rev. J.R. Planché, London 1842

*Surveys. A Publication of the Ideal Press Technical Group*, I, no. 3, March 1951

Swanton, M. (trans. and ed.), *The Anglo-Saxon Chronicle*, London 1997

Tahon-Vanroose, M., 'Aspects of Late Gothic Sculpture', in J.W. Steyaert (ed.), *Late Gothic Sculpture: The Burgundian Netherlands*, exhib. cat., Ghent, Museum voor Schone Kunsten, 1994, pp. 21–23

Tait, A.A., *Robert Adam: Drawings and Imagination*, Cambridge 1993

Tanner, D.M., 'The Parliamentary Electoral System, the "Fourth" Reform Act and the Rise of Labour in England and Wales', *Bulletin of the Institute of Historical Research*, LVI, 1983, pp. 205–19

Taylor, A.J., *The Jewel Tower*, London 1965

Taylor, E., *The House of Commons at Work*, 9th edn., London 1979

Taylor, J., 'Richard II in the Chronicles', in A. Goodman and J. Gillespie (ed.), *Richard II, The Art of Kingship*, New York and Oxford 1999, pp. 15–35

Taylor, T. (ed.), *The Life of Benjamin Robert Haydon*, 2 vols., London 1853

Tennyson, A., *Poems*, London 1842

Tennyson, A., *The Poetical Works of Tennyson*, ed. G.R. Stange, Boston 1974

Thomas, P.W., 'Two Cultures? Court and Country under Charles I', in C. Russell (ed.), *The Origins of the English Civil War*, London and Basingstoke 1975

Thompson, F.M.L., *The Rise of Respectable Society: A Social History of Victorian Britain, 1830–1900*, London 1988

Thompson, J., *Carts, Carriages and Caravans*, Fleet 1980

Thomson, D.W., 'The Fate of Titles in Canada', *Canadian Historical Review*, X, 1929, pp. 236–46

Thorne, R.G. (ed.), *The House of Commons 1790–1820*, 5 vols., London 1986 (*The History of Parliament*)

Thornton, P., 'The Royal State Bed', *Connoisseur*, CLXXXXV, no. 784, 1977, p. 137–47

Thurley, S., *Whitehall Palace*, New Haven and London 1999.

Tillett, S., S. Turnbull and M. Walters, *"Iolanthe": A Commemorative Booklet for the Centenary of the First Production at the Savoy Theatre, Saturday 25 November 1882*, Sir Arthur Sullivan Society, 1982

Tinniswood, A., *Belton House, Lincolnshire*, The National Trust, 1992

Topham, J., *Some Account of the Collegiate Chapel of St Stephen's Westminster*, London 1795

Townshend, H., 'Hayward Townshend's Journal', eds. A.F. Pollard and M. Blatcher, *Bulletin of the Institute of Historical Research*, XII, 1934–35, pp. 1–31

Trodd, C., 'Culture, Class, City: The National Gallery, London and the Spaces of Education, 1822–57', in M. Pointon (ed.), *Art Apart: Art Institutions and Ideology across England and North America*, Manchester 1994, pp. 33–49

Tucker, P.H., 'The Revolution in the Garden: Monet in the Twentieth Century', in *idem* (ed.), *Monet in the Twentieth Century*, London 1998

Turner, S., *The History of England during the Middle Ages*, 2nd edition, 5 vols., London 1825

Tyler, R. (ed.), *Calendar of State Papers (Spanish)*, XIII, London 1954

van Tyghem, F., *Het Stadhuis van Gent*, Brussels 1978

Vandekerchove, V., 'Zes eeuwen van Leuven: Een overzicht van de restauraties en de opvulling van de nissen in de stadhuisgevels', in M. Smeyers (ed.), *Het Leuvense Stadhuis*, Louvain 1998, pp. 83–92

Vaughan, W., *German Romanticism and English Art*, New Haven and London 1979

Victoria, Queen of Great Britain, *The Letters of Queen Victoria*, ser. 2, 1862–85, ed. G.E. Buckle, 3 vols., London 1926

Victoria, Queen of Great Britain, *Queen Victoria in Her Letters and Journals: A Selection*, ed. C. Hibbert, Harmondsworth 1985

von Wedel, L., 'Journey through England and Scotland Made by Lupold von Wedel in the Years 1584 and 1585,' trans. G. von Bülow, *Transactions of the Royal Historical Society*, n.s., IV, 1895, pp. 223–70

W.E.H., 'Mr. Barry's Design for the New Houses of Parliament,' *Westminster Review*, XXV, 1836, pp. 409–24

Waddell. G., 'The Design of Westminster Roof', *Architectural History*, XXXXII, 1999, pp. 47–67

Wagner, A., and J.C. Sainty, 'The Origin of the Introduction of Peers in the House of Lords, *Archaeologia*, CI, 1967, pp. 119–50

Wainwright, C., 'Furniture' in M.H. Port (ed.), *The Houses of Parliament*, New Haven and London 1976, pp. 282–97

Wainwright, C., *The Romantic Interior*, New Haven and London 1989

Wainwright, C., 'Furnishing the New Palace: Pugin's Furniture and Fittings', *Apollo*, n.s., CXXXV, no. 363, May 1992, pp. 303–06

Wainwright, C., 'Ceramics', in P. Atterbury and C. Wainwright (eds.), *Pugin: A Gothic Passion*, New Haven and London 1994a, pp. 127–42

Wainwright, C., 'Furniture', in P. Atterbury and C. Wainwright (eds.), *Pugin: A Gothic Passion*, New Haven and London 1994b, pp. 127–42

Wainwright, C., 'A.W.N. Pugin and France', in P. Atterbury (ed.), *A.W.N. Pugin: Master of Gothic Revival*, London 1995, pp. 63–71

Walker, R,J,B,, 'The Palace of Westminster after the Fire of October 1834', *Walpole Society*, XXXXIV, 1972–74, pp. 94–122

Walker, R,J,B,, *Catalogue of Paintings, Drawings, Engravings and Sculpture in the Palace of Westminster Compiled during 1959–1977*, 7 parts in 4 vols., Croydon, 1988 (typescript; copies available in the House of Lords Record Office, the London Library, and the libraries of the National Portrait Gallery, London, and the Courtauld Institute, London)

Warren, W.L., *The Governance of Norman and Angevin England, 1086–1272*, London 1987

Webb, J., 'Translation of a French Metrical History of the Deposition of King Richard the Second', *Archaeologia*, XX, 1824, pp. 1–242

Wedgwood, A., *Catalogue of the Drawings Collection of the Royal Institute of British Architects: The Pugin Family*, Farnborough 1977

Wedgwood, A., 'The Throne of the House of Lords and its Setting', *Architectural History*, XXVII, 1984, pp. 59–73

Wedgwood, A., *Catalogue of Architectural Drawings in The Victoria and Albert Museum, A.W.N. Pugin and the Pugin Family*, London 1985

Wedgwood, A., 'Domestic Architecture', in P. Atterbury and C. Wainwright (eds.), *Pugin: A Gothic Passion*, New Haven and London 1994a, pp. 43–61

Wedgwood, A., 'The New Palace of Westminster', in P. Atterbury and C. Wainwright (eds.), *Pugin: A Gothic Passion*, New Haven and London 1994b, pp. 218–36

Wedgwood, A., 'The Early Years', in P. Atterbury and C. Wainwright (eds.), *Pugin: A Gothic Passion*, New Haven and London 1994c, pp. 26–30

Wedgwood, A., *Guide to the Speaker's House*, London 1994d

Wedgwood, J.C., 'The History of Parliament', *Fortnightly Review*, CXXXVIII, 1935, pp. 164–73

Wedgwood, J.C., *History of Parliament: Biographies of the Members of the Commons House, 1439–1509*, London 1936

Weir, A., *Elizabeth the Queen*, London 1999

Weitraub, S., *Uncrowned King: The Life of Prince Albert*, New York 1997

Weitzman, G.H., 'The Utilitarians and the Houses of Parliament', *Journal of the Society of Architectural Historians*, XX, 1961, pp. 99–107

Weston, C.C., 'The Royal Mediation in 1884', *English Historical Review*, LXXXII, 1967, pp. 296–322

White, H.A., *Sir Walter Scott's Novels on the Stage*, New Haven and London 1927

Whittaker, J., *The Coronation of His Most Sacred Majesty George IV*, 2 vols., London 1821–41

Wilding, N., and P. Laundy, *An Encyclopaedia of Parliament*, 3rd edition, London 1968

William, B. (trans.), *Chronique de la Traïson et Mort de Richart Deux Roy Dengleterre*, London 1846 (published in English and French)

Wilson, C., 'The Origins of the Perpendicular Style and its Development up to c. 1360', unpublished Ph.D. thesis, Courtauld Institute of Art, University of London 1980

Wilson, C., *et al.*, *Westminster Abbey*, London 1986

Wilson, C., *The Gothic Cathedral*, London 1992

Wilson, C., 'The Designer of Henry VII Chapel, Westminster Abbey', in B. Thompson (ed.), *Proceedings of the 1993 Harlaxton Symposium*, Stamford 1995, pp. 133–56

Wilson, C., 'Rulers, Artificers and Shoppers: Richard II's Remodelling of Westminster Hall, 1393–99' in D. Gordon, L. Monnas and C. Elam (eds.), *The Regal Image of Richard II and the Wilton Diptych*, London 1997, pp. 33–59

Woodham-Smith, C., *Queen Victoria: Her Life and Times 1819–1861*, London 1972

Wright, A., and P. Smith, *Parliament Past and Present*, 2 vols., London 1902–03

Wroughton, R., *Shakspeare's* [sic] *King Richard the Second: An Historical Play Adapted by Richard Wroughton Esq and Published as it is Performed at the Theatre Royal Drury Lane*, London 1815

Young, H., *This Blessed Plot: Britain and Europe from Churchill to Blair*, London 1998

Young, H., 'Why I'm so Glad to be European', *The Guardian*, 2 January 1999, *Saturday Review*, pp. 1–2

Yung, K.K., *National Portrait Gallery, Complete Illustrated Catalogue*, London 1981

Zarnecki, G., *English Romanesque Art, 1066–1200*, exhib. cat., Hayward Gallery, London 1984

Ziegler, P., *King Edward VIII: The Official Biography*, London 1990

Figures in italics refer to
   illustrations.